Perspectives on the Philosophy of William P. Alston

Studies in Epistemology and Cognitive Theory
Series Editor: *Paul K. Moser, Loyola University of Chicago*

Perspectives on the Philosophy of William P. Alston

Edited by
Heather D. Battaly and Michael P. Lynch

ROWMAN & LITTLEFIELD PUBLISHERS, INC.
Lanham • Boulder • New York • Toronto • Oxford

ROWMAN & LITTLEFIELD PUBLISHERS, INC.

Published in the United States of America
by Rowman & Littlefield Publishers, Inc.
A wholly owned subsidiary of The Rowman & Littlefield Publishing Group, Inc.
4501 Forbes Boulevard, Suite 200, Lanham, Maryland 20706
www.rowmanlittlefield.com

PO Box 317
Oxford
OX2 9RU, UK

British Library Cataloguing in Publication Information Available

Library of Congress Cataloging-in-Publication Data

Perspectives on the philosophy of William P. Alston / edited by Heather D. Battaly and
Michael P. Lynch.
    p. cm.—(Studies in epistemology and cognitive theory)
  "Publications of William P. Alston": p.
  Includes bibliographical references and index.
  ISBN 0-7425-1424-2 (hardcover : alk. paper)
    1. Alston, William P. 2. Knowledge, Theory of. 3. Religion—Philosophy. I.
Battaly, Heather D., 1969– II. Lynch, Michael P. (Michael Patrick), 1966– III. Series:
Studies in epistemology and cognitive theory (Unnumbered)

BD161.P46 2005
191—dc22   2005004313

Printed in the United States of America

♾™ The paper used in this publication meets the minimum requirements of American
National Standard for Information Sciences—Permanence of Paper for Printed Library
Materials, ANSI/NISO Z39.48–1992.

To Bill

With admiration, gratitude, and affection.

Contents

Acknowledgments

The editors are deeply grateful to the contributors. It is not easy to write a critical essay about a philosopher's work when one knows that he will be responding to it! Their papers, and Bill Alston's responses, have done exactly what we had hoped—they have made significant new contributions to epistemology, the philosophy of religion, and the philosophy of language; and have created a volume which evaluates Alston's overall impact on analytic philosophy. We would also like to thank Paul Moser and Eve DeVaro for their support of this project. Special thanks to Clifford Roth for his expertise in, and enthusiasm for, editing.

We regret that this volume was not finished in time for Phil Quinn to see it. Quinn, who was John A. O'Brien Professor of Philosophy at the University of Notre Dame, died on November 15, 2004. We are thankful for his contributions to the philosophy of religion and the philosophy of science and for his service to the profession.

Abbreviations for Alston's Works Frequently Referenced in This Volume

ATP   "Aquinas on Theological Predication: A Look Backward and a Look Forward." In *Reasoned Faith* (1993).

BTA   "Back to the Theory of Appearing." In *Philosophical Perspectives* 13 (1999).

CEJ   "Concepts of Epistemic Justification." In *Epistemic Justification* (1989).

DA   "Divine Action, Human Freedom, and the Laws of Nature." In *Quantum Cosmology and the Laws of Nature* (1993).

DCEJ   "The Deontological Conception of Epistemic Justification." In *Epistemic Justification* (1989).

DEE   *Beyond "Justification": Dimensions of Epistemic Evaluation* (2005).

DEWJ   "Doing Epistemology without Justification." In *Philosophical Topics* 29 (2001).

DNHL   *Divine Nature and Human Language: Essays in Philosophical Theology* (1989).

DPA   "A 'Doxastic Practice' Approach to Epistemology." In *Knowledge and Skepticism* (1989).

ED   "Epistemic Desiderata." In *Philosophy and Phenomenological Research* 53 (1993).

EJ   *Epistemic Justification: Essays in the Theory of Knowledge* (1989).

IE   "An Internalist Externalism." In *Epistemic Justification* (1989).

IASM   *Illocutionary Acts and Sentence Meaning* (2000).

JK   "Justification and Knowledge." In *Epistemic Justification* (1989).

PG   *Perceiving God: The Epistemology of Religious Experience* (1991).

RCT   *A Realist Conception of Truth* (1996).

RSP   *The Reliability of Sense Perception* (1993).

SDC   "Some Suggestions for Divine Command Theorists." In *Christian Theism and the Problems of Philosophy* (1990).

TCP   "Truth: Concept and Property." In *What Is Truth?* (2002).

Introductory Essay: Justification, God, and Truth

Heather D. Battaly

William Payne Alston was born in Shreveport, Louisiana (USA) in 1921. He graduated from Centenary College in 1942 with a degree in music, and, in the same year, was assigned to a U. S. army band in California, where he served for the duration of World War II. In 1951, he earned his Ph.D. in Philosophy from the University of Chicago, writing a dissertation on the metaphysics of Alfred North Whitehead under the supervision of Charles Hartshorne. His first appointment was at the University of Michigan, where he taught for twenty-two years (1949–1971). This was followed by teaching appointments at Rutgers University (1971–1976), the University of Illinois at Urbana-Champaign (1976–1980), and, finally, Syracuse University (1980–2000). Though Alston has officially been Professor Emeritus at Syracuse since 1992, he continued to teach and advise dissertations until 2000. He has also directed two National Endowment for the Humanities (NEH) Summer Seminars for College Teachers (1978, 1979), an NEH Summer Institute on the philosophy of religion (1986), and several seminars on religious experience and Christian scholarship. He is the founding editor of two journals—the *Journal of Philosophical Research* and *Faith and Philosophy*—and of *Cornell Studies in the Philosophy of Religion*, and has been a consulting editor for six additional journals. His leadership in the profession is further demonstrated by his service at home and abroad. He is a past President of the Central Division of the American Philosophical Association (1978–1979), of the Society of Christian Philosophers (1978–1981), and of the Society for Philosophy and Psychology (1976–1977). In 1987, he led a delegation of eight American epistemologists and philosophers of mind for a week of discussions with Soviet philosophers in Moscow and Leningrad. In 1991, he participated in a conference at Castel Gandolfo, Italy, on theology and physical cosmology, sponsored by the Vatican Observatory, and in 1994, he traveled to Peking University to participate in a Symposium of Chinese-American Philosophy and Religious Studies. He has been a Fellow at the Center for Advanced Study in the Behavioral Sciences at Stanford (1965–1966), a Distinguished Visiting Professor of Philosophy at the Center for Advanced Study in Theoretical Psychology at the University of Alberta (1975), and a Fellow of the American Academy of the Arts and Sciences (1990–present).

Over the course of his fifty-year career, Alston has had a deeply influential and wide-ranging impact on twentieth century analytic philosophy. He is a central figure both in epistemology and the philosophy of religion, and a leading proponent of realism about truth and the illocutionary act theory of sentence meaning. His incisive expositions, uncanny ability to see distinctions, and penetrating evaluations of competing views have helped set the standards for each of these fields. In the last fifteen years alone, Alston has authored or edited nine books: *Beyond "Justification": Dimensions of Epistemic Evaluation* (DEE) (2005); *Realism and Antirealism* (editor, 2003); *A Sensible Metaphysical Realism* (2001); *Illocutionary Acts and Sentence Meaning* (IASM) (2000); *A Realist Conception of Truth* (RCT) (1996); *The Reliability of Sense Perception* (RSP) (1993); *Perceiving God: The Epistemology of Religious Experience* (PG) (1991); *Divine Nature and Human Language: Essays in Philosophical Theology* (DNHL) (1989); and *Epistemic Justification: Essays in the Theory of Knowledge* (EJ) (1989).[1] In addition to several other books, including *Philosophy of Language* (1964), he has published a staggering total of more than one hundred and fifty articles on topics as wide-ranging as perception, ontological commitment, linguistic acts, epistemic circularity, the problem of evil, and feelings.[2] Indeed, Alston is so prolific that during the production of this volume it was difficult for the editors, each of whom is several decades his junior, to keep up with him. This volume focuses on the main areas in which Alston's work has had the greatest impact: epistemology, the philosophy of religion, the philosophy of language, and realism about truth. It is composed of ten new essays on Alston's philosophy, and his replies to each. It also contains a complete bibliography of Alston's publications up through and including works appearing in 2005. The first section of this introduction summarizes the main features of Alston's views in these areas, with an eye toward setting the stage for the contributed essays. The second section provides synopses of each of the chapters. I conclude with some personal remarks.

I. The Philosophy of William P. Alston

A. Epistemology

Alston has had a striking impact on epistemology. Though he describes himself as a "late bloomer"[3] in the field, his first articles on privileged access and foundationalism appeared in the early- and mid-1970's. His work in epistemology can be divided into three stages and one important corollary. In his earliest work, collected in *Epistemic Justification*, he advocates an account of justified belief that combines a core externalism with minimal accessibility to the grounds on which the belief is based. The second stage is his doxastic practice approach, which is the protagonist of *The Reliability of Sense Perception*, and of his account of the justification of religious belief in *Perceiving God*. In the third and most radical stage of his thought, Alston renounces justification and leads the charge to expunge it from epistemology. (See "Epistemic Desiderata" [ED], "Doing Epistemology without Justification" [DEWJ], and *Beyond "Justification": Dimensions of Epistemic Evaluation* [DEE].[4]) The corollary is his theory of appearing. While this is primarily a view about the ontology of perceptual experience, Alston argues that it has important repercussions for the epistemology of perceptual belief.

In *Epistemic Justification*, Alston defends fallibilist foundationalism, evaluates different concepts of justification, rejects "perspectival" internalism and higher-level requirements, and lays out his seminal account of justification, according to which a belief is justified if and only if it is based on a truth-conducive ground that is "fairly directly accessible." Alston contends that foundationalism is the only adequate solution to the epistemic regress argument. He thinks that we have some justified beliefs, and that this would be impossible if they were all "mediately" justified—that is, justified by their relations to one's other justified beliefs. Consequently, some of one's justified beliefs must be "immediately" justified—justified in some other way, for example, by experience or by self-evidence.[5] But, immediate justification does not require infallibility. According to Alston, perceptual beliefs, though fallible, will be immediately justified when their justification rests solely on perceptual experiences.[6] (Sometimes the justification of a perceptual belief will rest both on one's experience and on one's other justified beliefs, in which case its justification will be partly immediate and partly mediate.) All of the epistemologists in this volume are (now) foundationalists; but while Ginet, Greco, and Goldman also count perceptual beliefs amongst their foundations, BonJour clearly does not. Alston recognizes that foundationalism has yet to meet certain challenges, including explaining how the superstructure can be derived from the foundations.

Alston rejects what he calls "perspectival" internalism, a view that is exemplified in BonJour's work (past and, arguably, present).[7] BonJour argues that in order for a subject to be justified in believing that p, she must have a good reason for thinking that her belief is likely to be true. In Alston's words, she must *believe* that her belief that p is likely to be true, and this higher-level belief must itself be justified. (See Alston's remarks about "reasons" in his "Response to BonJour.") Alston raises several objections to this view. First, it fails to distinguish between the state of being justified, and the activity of showing that one is justified. Second, it leads to an infinite regress of higher-level beliefs.[8] And, finally, children have justified beliefs, but, presumably, lack higher-level beliefs about the epistemic status of their lower-level beliefs.

Alston delineates two main concepts of justification—one is deontological, the other invokes truth-conducive grounds. He rejects the former and defends the latter.[9] According to the deontological concept, S is justified in believing that p if and only if S does not violate any epistemic obligations in believing that p.[10] Alston argues that this concept is not viable because in order to be obliged to believe or refrain from believing, we must have direct voluntary control over belief. Clearly, we lack such control over perceptual beliefs—I cannot come to believe that it is snowing, when my experience is of a sunny summer day, simply by deciding to do so. But, Alston argues that *none* of our beliefs are under our direct voluntary control; not even beliefs that are radically underdetermined by evidence. In short, we have as little direct control over the formation of beliefs as we do over the secretion of gastric juices. Consequently, since 'ought' implies 'can,' the deontological concept collapses. Ginet defends deonticism against these criticisms in Chapter 1.

The concept of justification that Alston endorses centers on truth-conducivity. Of course, if we are to maintain a distinction between justification and truth, a belief's justification cannot simply consist in its being true. Rather, claims Alston, it consists in its being likely to be true given what the subject has to go on (her grounds). Accordingly, in "An Internalist Externalism" (IE), he argues that a belief's being prima facie justified consists in its being based on an adequate ground. Grounds are other beliefs or experiences of the subject. An adequate ground is one that is sufficiently indicative of the truth of the belief. Alston thinks that the ground *itself* must be fairly readily accessible to the subject. This is "accessibility," rather than "perspectival," internalism, though not the "whole-hog" accessibility internalism endorsed by Ginet. (See Chapter 1.) For the subject need not have access to the *adequacy* of her ground; her ground must simply *be* adequate. Hence, this view is primarily an externalist, reliable-indicator account of justification. In this volume, it is criticized both for being too strong (Greco), and for being too weak (Ginet). Greco argues that one need not have accessible grounds in order to be justified, while Ginet claims that one must have access to all of the factors that contribute to the justificatory status of one's belief.

In the second stage of his epistemological thought, Alston sets aside accessibility internalism, and argues that the prima facie justification of a belief consists in its being the product of a reliable doxastic practice.[11] A doxastic practice is a family of socially established belief-forming dispositions, or processes, that are bound together by similarities in their respective inputs and outputs. For example, the practice of sense perception (SP) is a family of entrenched dispositions, all of which have sensory experiences as their inputs, and beliefs about the physical environment as their outputs.[12] In *The Reliability of Sense Perception*

(RSP), Alston argues that any attempt to show that our basic doxastic practices (SP, memory, introspection, etc.) are reliable will be infected with epistemic circularity. An epistemically circular argument differs from a logically circular one in that it does not assume as a premise the proposition it is trying to prove. Nevertheless, its conclusion must be true in order for one to be justified in accepting its premises. To illustrate, one cannot mount an inductive track-record argument for the reliability of SP (1. At time t1, S formed perceptual belief PB1, *and PB1 was true*. 2. At time t2, S formed perceptual belief PB2, *and PB2 was true*. . . . Hence, SP is reliable) without relying on SP to generate the premises. Nor, Alston claims, will any other arguments for the reliability of SP—a priori or empirical—succeed in avoiding circularity.

One might think that we can circumvent circularity by beginning with sensory experience, and arguing that the best explanation of that experience is the existence of a stable physical world that causes it. After all, this argument seems to rely on introspection and inference to the best explanation, without relying on SP. But Alston rejects it on the grounds that: (1) the standard explanation of sensory experience is not clearly superior to skeptical alternatives; and (2) even if it were, the argument would fall short of establishing the reliability of SP.[13] BonJour and Alston have been defending opposite sides of this issue for some time. Their debate presses forward in Chapters 3 and 4.

Alston argues that what is true of SP is true of every basic doxastic practice: We can't show *any* of them to be reliable without epistemic circularity. And, even if we could construct a noncircular argument for the reliability of *one* practice, we would encounter circularity at the first or second remove, or somewhere farther down the line.[14] If all of this is correct, doesn't skepticism prevail? Alston thinks not. He argues that the beliefs that issue from our basic doxastic practices will still be prima facie justified, just as long as those practices are in fact reliable—showing that they are reliable is not necessary. Consequently, we will be justified in believing the conclusions of epistemically circular arguments as long as the practices they rely on *are* reliable. Alston recognizes that this offers cold comfort, but claims it is the best epistemic argument we can muster. Still, he thinks, all is not lost. For we can show that it is *practically rational* for us to continue to engage in our basic doxastic practices and to take them to be reliable. In his words, since "we cannot take a step in intellectual endeavors without engaging in some doxastic practice(s) or other," there is no practically rational alternative to "employing the practices we find to be firmly rooted in our lives."[15] In the "press of life," abstaining from practices like SP and memory is not a viable option. Hence, it is prima facie practically rational to engage in our firmly established doxastic practices. This prima facie practical rationality can be overriden by persistent inconsistencies within a practice, or between practices, and strengthened by "significant self-support." Alston argues that the prima facie practical rationality of SP (and our other basic doxastic practices) is not overriden. Despite Alston's claims to the contrary, several epistemologists have taken the argument of RSP to amount to an argument for skepticism, and relatively few have found solace in Alston's suggestion that it is practically rational to employ our basic doxastic practices. (See BonJour's remarks about Alston's "Reidian solution" in Chapter 3.)

Alston endorses direct realism about the *nature* of perceptual experience. According to his theory of appearing, in normal cases of sense perception, one's perceptual experience is a direct awareness of physical objects in the external environment. Thus, in "Perceptual Knowledge," he claims that "perceptual experience in itself involves, in normal cases, a cognitive relation with external objects that perceptual beliefs are about."[16] To illustrate, if all is going well, your current perceptual (visual) experience will consist in the page, an external object, appearing to you as rectangular, white and black, and so on. In contrast, the major ontological rivals of the theory of appearing—the adverbial theory and the (largely abandoned) sense-data theory—do not take sensory experience to consist in a relation between the subject and external objects; instead, they construe experience as entirely intramental. The sense-data theory claims that perceptual experience does consist in an awareness of objects, but maintains that those objects are mental particulars—sense-data. The adverbial theory claims that perceptual experience is not relational at all—it is not an *awareness of* mental or extra-mental objects, but "a *way* of being conscious."[17] According to the adverbial theory, if all goes well, your current visual experience would consist in your sensing rectangular-ly, white-and-black-ly, and so on. (In Chapter 3, BonJour endorses the adverbial theory.) It is also worth noting that Alston rejects the increasingly popular conceptualist view of perceptual experience. He argues that perception involves a *direct* awareness of external objects, unmediated by concepts. The primary objection to the theory of appearing as an ontological thesis is its difficulty in explaining hallucination.

Alston maintains that the theory of appearing has two significant repercussions for the epistemology of perceptual belief. First, the theory of appearing enables us to explain how perceptual experience can justify perceptual beliefs.[18] For, in normal cases of perception, the external object about which one forms a perceptual belief is already "within" the perceptual experience itself. In Alston's words:

> We are able to justifiably form beliefs about the external environment on the basis of our perceptual experience because objects in the external environment appear to us in that experience in such a way as to be constitutive of the character of the experience. And the beliefs so formed are prima facie justified just because they register what is presented there, they "read it off of" experience.[19]

Of course, Alston denies that our doxastic practice of sense perception is infallible—appearances are sometimes misleading, and belief-forming mechanisms can go awry.[20] But he thinks the theory of appearing can appeal to the "natural and plausible" principle that "whatever appears to one as so-and-so is thereby likely, . . . [absent] sufficient indications to the contrary, to be so-and-so."[21] Second, the theory of appearing is epistemically superior to the adverbial and sense-data theories, for which, Alston claims, corresponding principles are neither natural nor plausible. Because the adverbial and sense-data theories construe perceptual experience as entirely intramental (i.e., as involving no intrinsic connection to the external world), they must *actively show* that experience as they construe it is a reliable indicator of external facts. On Alston's view, their attempts to do so fail. Greco rejects both of the aforementioned epistemological theses in Chapter 5.

In his most recent work, Alston contends that epistemologists should abandon inquiry about justification, and instead devote their energy to investigating a plurality of epistemic desiderata. In *Beyond "Justification": Dimensions of Epistemic Evaluation*, he argues that there is no objective, epistemically crucial property of beliefs picked out by 'justified.' He arrives at this conclusion via an argument to the best explanation, taking the wide diversity of incompatible views about justification as his explanandum. He claims that there is no theoretically neutral way to uniquely identify the alleged target of the dispute. Reliability will be rejected by internalists, higher-level requirements by externalists. And descriptions like 'that which is valuable from an epistemic point of view' will not uniquely pick out justification. Nor, he claims, is there any way to zero in on the purported target by deploying shared paradigms. For paradigm cases of justified and unjustified beliefs differ from one party to the next. Consequently, the best explanation of the diversity is that there is no "common subject matter about the nature of which different 'theories of justification' are disagreeing."[22] Different parties are emphasizing different sets of epistemic desiderata, and hence, arguing past one another. Accordingly, "a large proportion of contemporary epistemologists . . . have been misguided in their researches, fighting under a false banner, engaged in a quixotic tilting at windmills."[23]

Though Alston repudiates justification and endorses pluralism, he continues to emphasize the superiority of truth-conducive desiderata, like reliability. He argues that the most basic goal of cognition is true belief, and that desiderata that are directly truth-conducive are best suited to attain that goal. In his words, "The desiderata . . . that are directly truth-conducive are the ones that are of the greatest interest and importance for the epistemology of belief, due to the overriding importance of true belief as a goal of our cognitive endeavors."[24] Consequently, the epistemology he develops preserves many of his earlier views (e.g., the epistemic importance of adequate grounds and reliability), but does so under a different rubric.

On its face, Alston's renunciation of justification is a radical departure from his previous work, and from the tradition. Though it is slowly gaining ground amongst analytic epistemologists, there are many who continue to vehemently defend the investigation of justification, including Alvin Goldman (see Chapter 7). But, as I have implied above, Alston's pluralism may be less plural, and less radical, than it first appears. For one might argue that Alston has simply replaced the central desideratum of justification with the central desideratum of true belief.

One will have noticed that Alston's epistemology focuses almost entirely on justification; he has relatively little to say about knowledge. In "Justification and Knowledge," he suggests that knowledge is information, and argues that as such it does not require grounds or justification. Ginet objects to this view in Chapter 1, and Alston invokes it in Chapter 6.

B. Philosophy of Religion

By all counts, Alston is one of our leading philosophers of religion. He began working in this area as early as the 1960's, publishing articles on the ontological argument and theistic belief. He returned to the philosophy of religion in the 1980's with an explosion of papers on the properties of God, divine action, and the literal application of predicates to God, many of which are collected in *Divine Nature and Human Language* (DNHL) (1989). His most pioneering work in this field is *Perceiving God* (PG) (1991), in which he develops a doxastic practice approach to the epistemology of religious experience.

In the papers in Part I of DNHL, Alston argues that it is possible to make true statements about God by using certain predicate terms *literally*. He notes that his thesis contradicts a view that is prominent in certain theological circles—that God can only be spoken of in irreducible *metaphors*. There are two central features of his arguments. First is his account of metaphor; second is his contention that personalistic predicates (e.g., 'commands,' 'loves') are literally true of God because God is a personal agent.

One group of theologians denies that predicates are literally true of God on the grounds that God, unlike us, is an ontologically simple being, an undifferentiated unity. In response to this group, Alston, and Wolterstorff in Chapter 15, argue that even Aquinas, a fervent advocate of the ontological simplicity of God, endorsed the literal application of "pure perfection terms" (e.g., 'good,' 'alive,' 'powerful') to God. In "Aquinas on Theological Predication" (ATP)[25], Alston claims that, according to Aquinas, pure perfection terms can be said literally of God because their meanings do not include "the imperfect mode in which a perfection [property] is realized in creatures."[26] In contrast, terms like 'rock' and 'lion,' whose meanings do include a "creaturely mode," can only apply to God metaphorically. All of these terms, pure perfection or otherwise, apply literally to human beings. Alston also interprets Aquinas to be arguing that pure perfection terms do not apply univocally to God and to human beings. At first, this combination of theses may appear inconsistent. But it isn't. The literal use of a term contrasts with its metaphorical use. In 'George knitted a hat,' the use of 'knit' is literal; whereas in Shakespeare's 'Sleep knits up the ravelled sleave of care,' it is metaphorical. 'Literal' and 'metaphorical' apply to individual uses of a term. In contrast, 'univocal' and 'equivocal' do not—it doesn't make sense to say that the use of 'bank' in 'I went to the bank on the 14th floor' is univocal or equivocal. Univocity requires that two different uses of a term have the same meaning; equivocity, that they have different meanings. To illustrate, we can say that the two uses of 'bank' in 'I went to the bank on the 14th floor' and 'I went to the bank of the Ganges' are equivocal. So, Aquinas is arguing that pure perfection predicates like 'alive' apply literally to God *and* to humans, but mean something slightly different when they do. The 'slightly' here is deliberate. Aquinas argues that 'alive' is not purely equivocal in its predication of God and of us; rather, the predications are related analogically.

Alston argues that matters get increasingly complicated when we try to incorporate Aquinas's theses about the *res significata* (RS) of a term (the thing it signifies) and the *modus significandi* (MS) of a term (its mode of signification). Roughly, the RS of a predicate term is the property it picks out. The MS of a predicate term is the way it presents that property. Aquinas maintains that a pure perfection term (e.g. 'alive') cannot apply to God in virtue of its MS, but does apply to God in virtue of its RS. But 'alive' also applies to humans in virtue of its RS; and the two applications appear to be univocal. Now, if all of *this* is true, then Aquinas *is* in trouble; for "the doctrine of . . . analogical meaning . . . has been frozen out," there is no room for it.[27] Alston and Wolterstorff (Chapter 15) disagree about how to rescue Aquinas from this morass.

In DNHL, Alston maintains that God is a personal agent, with intentions and plans, who performs actions in the world. He argues that some of the personalistic predicates that apply literally to God are *action* terms, and that some of the actions God performs are divine interventions: actions in which God brings about states of affairs that would not have occurred had only natural factors been operative. In "Divine Action, Human Freedom, and the Laws of Nature,"[28] he contends that, contrary to appearance, divine interventions are consistent with the laws of nature. He claims that we believe that divine interventions violate natural laws because we assume that natural laws specify sufficient conditions for their outcomes *without qualification*. But this assumption is false—natural laws do not make unqualified assertions. The law of hydrostatics, for instance, does not unqualifiedly claim that a sufficient condition for an object's sinking in water is its possessing a greater density than the water. If it did, then a scuba diver who was standing upright in a submerged shark cage that was not sinking would constitute a violation of the law. Alston maintains that the law of hydrostatics does not attempt to account for mitigating circumstances, like shark cages. It only attempts to specify sufficient conditions for an object's sinking "in the absence of any relevant factors other than those specified in the law."[29] Consequently, the laws of nature do not preclude interference from outside forces, and thus are not violated if a divine force intervenes. In Chapter 11, Mavrodes applies Alston's account of divine intervention to the conception and birth of Jesus Christ.

Divine commands are one type of (illocutionary) action that God performs in the world, and are themselves a species of divine interventions. Divine command (DC) theorists claim that the moral obligations of human beings are determined by God's commands. Alston's goal in "Some Suggestions for Divine Command Theorists"[30] is not to advocate DC theory, but to identify the most defensible version of it. DC theory is commonly thought to be impaled on the horns of the following "Euthyphro-like" dilemma: Ought we to do action A because God commands us to do A, or does God command us to do A because it is what we ought to do?[31] The DC theorist embraces the first horn. But, in so doing, she appears to make divine commands, and morality, arbitrary. For, if God's commands are not constrained by morality, then God can command anything at all, including torture and cruelty, which we would thereby be morally obligated to perform. This is the infamous "arbitrariness objection."

Alston argues that there is a way for the DC theorist to simultaneously embrace the first horn and escape the arbitrariness objection. To do so, she must claim that God's own moral goodness is constituted by something other than conformity to moral obligations or to divine commands—something that prevents God from commanding cruelty. Alston contends that moral obligations do not apply to God because God's nature is perfectly good. God's nature makes it metaphysically impossible for God to do, or command, anything that is less than "supremely good."[32] So, God's goodness is constituted by the divine nature, which is perfectly good, and God's commands, which are expressions of the divine nature, are not arbitrary. It is, thus, impossible for God to command gratuitous torture or cruelty. Alston argues that this move does not commit the DC theorist to claiming that there is an independent standard of morality, which God must consult and to which he is subject.[33] For God, himself, is the standard of goodness. In Chapter 13, Zagzebski agrees that God is the exemplar of goodness, but argues that Alston fails to fully answer the arbitrariness objection.

In *Perceiving God*, Alston applies his doxastic practice approach in epistemology to beliefs about God. He argues that the doxastic practice of mystical perception (MP) is analogous to the doxastic practice of sense perception (SP). Recall that SP is the practice of forming perceptual beliefs about the physical environment on the basis of sensory experiences (and justified beliefs). Likewise, in MP, beliefs about a religiously construed "ultimate reality" are based directly on putative experiences of that reality. Unlike SP, MP admits of different versions, which correspond to different religions: Christian Mystical Practice (CMP), Hindu Mystical Practice (HMP), Buddhist Mystical Practice (BMP), and so on. But, like SP, each of these MP's is a firmly entrenched, socially established doxastic practice. Hence, according to Alston, the beliefs that issue from these MP's will be prima facie justified just as long as those practices are in fact reliable.[34] We need not show that they are reliable in order for them to be reliable.

Alston argues here, and in RSP, that any attempt to show that a basic doxastic practice is reliable will be epistemically circular. This applies to all deeply entrenched doxastic practices, including mystical perception. But, taking CMP as his model, he argues that it is still *practically rational* to engage in CMP, and to take it to be reliable. This argument is analogous to the one he gives for the practical rationality of engaging in SP (see RSP). Since CMP, like SP, is a firmly established doxastic practice, it will be rational to engage in it unless its outputs are massively internally inconsistent, or persistently conflict with the outputs of other firmly established doxastic practices. He maintains that the beliefs generated by CMP do not suffer from large-scale internal inconsistencies. Nor are they massively inconsistent with the beliefs generated by SP, memory, or any other secular practice. Moreover, like SP, CMP enjoys significant self-support.

However, unlike SP, the beliefs in the overrider system of CMP are massively inconsistent with the beliefs in the overrider systems of other mystical practices, like HMP and BMP. The overrider system of a mystical practice includes beliefs about the central doctrines of its associated religion. These doctrines often conflict with one another; for example, the Buddhist conception of ultimate reality is inconsistent with the Christian conception. If each form of MP is incompatible with all of the others, then no more than one form of MP can be reliable. But, each form of MP is equally socially entrenched. Consequently, each form is confronted with "a plurality of uneliminated alternatives." And, thus, it appears that "in the absence of some sufficient independent reason, no one is justified in supposing her own practice to be superior in epistemic status to those with which it is in competition. And hence . . . no one is being rational in proceeding to employ that practice to form beliefs and to regard beliefs so formed as ipso facto justified."[35] In short, Alston's argument for the practical rationality of engaging in CMP runs up against the problem of religious diversity, which is the topic of Quinn's essay.

Alston responds by employing an argument by analogy. He asks us to imagine that there are multiple socially established practices of sense perception, whose outputs are internally consistent and serve their respective practitioners well but conflict with one another. He maintains that in a situation like this, the only rational course is to "sit tight" with one's own practice. Accordingly, he concludes that it is practically rational for the practitioners of any given mystical practice (CMP, HMP, BMP, etc.) to continue to engage in that practice and to take it to be reliable.

C. Meaning and Truth

Alston made his early reputation in the philosophy of language, publishing several articles on meaning and linguistic acts in the mid-1960's, and *Philosophy of Language* in 1964. There, he rejects the verifiability criterion of meaning, and referential theories, and contends that the meaning of a sentence consists in its illocutionary act potential. He returns to these issues in his recent *Illocutionary Acts and Sentence Meaning* (IASM) (2000), the thesis of which is twofold. First, he argues that to perform an illocutionary act of a particular type is to subject one's utterance to a particular illocutionary rule. Second, he defends the view that the meaning of a sentence consists in its being usable to perform illocutionary acts of a particular type.

Alston identifies five different categories of illocutionary acts: assertives (e.g., 'Some apples are green.'); directives (e.g., 'Clean up!'); commissives (e.g., 'I promise to meet you for lunch.'); exercitives (e.g., 'You're hired.'); and expressives (e.g., 'Yuck—mint jelly is disgusting.') To illustrate his account of the nature of illocutionary acts, let's use the utterance 'I will go to the grocery store.' Alston argues that the *normative stance* that the speaker takes toward her utterance is what makes it a performance of an illocutionary act of a given type. Thus, in uttering 'I will go to the grocery store,' the speaker performs the illocutionary act of promising the hearer that she will go to the grocery store if and only if she takes responsibility for the satisfaction of certain conditions, including: intending to go to the grocery store, and laying an obligation on herself to do so. In uttering, 'I will go to the grocery store,' the speaker performs the illocutionary act of predicting that she will go to the grocery store if and only if she takes responsibility for different conditions, the most salient of which is: its being the case that she will go to the grocery store. Alston enumerates different sets of conditions for each of the main types of illocutionary acts. In taking responsibility for the satisfaction of a particular set of conditions, the speaker renders herself liable to censure if they aren't satisfied. Alston argues that in so doing, the speaker subjects her utterance to a rule that implies that the utterance is permissible only if those conditions are satisfied. To illustrate, in uttering 'I promise to meet you for lunch,' I perform the illocutionary act of promising to meet you for lunch by subjecting my utterance to the following (abridged) illocutionary rule: 'I promise to meet you for lunch' may be uttered by the speaker if and only if (a) it is possible for the speaker to meet the hearer for lunch, (b) the speaker intends to meet the hearer for lunch, and (c) the speaker lays an obligation on herself to do so. Conditions (a)–(c) need not *be* satisfied for the speaker to perform the act of promising to meet the hearer for lunch; she need only *take responsibility* for their satisfaction. But they must *be* satisfied for her utterance of 'I promise to meet you for lunch' to be permissible. In sum, illocutionary acts have a normative character; they are rule-subjection acts. The difference between performing one type of illocutionary act and another lies in what the speaker does—which conditions she takes responsibility for, which illocutionary rule she subjects her utterance to.

Alston defends a use theory of meaning. That is, he argues that the meaning of an expression is a function of what it is used by speakers to do. Specifically, "an expression's having a certain meaning consists in its being usable to play a certain role (to do certain things) in communication."[36] Alston calls this the "Use Principle." What can sentences be used to do in communication? They can be used to perform illocutionary acts, of course! Alston reasons that, according to the Use Principle, the meaning of a sentence fits it to be used to carry a particular content. But an illocutionary act just is an act of performing an utterance with a particular content. Consequently, the meaning of a sentence consists in its being usable to perform illocutionary acts of a particular type; that is, in its illocutionary act potential.[37]

Use theories of meaning maintain that "apart from what members of a community do with [a] language there are no . . . semantic facts about it."[38] In short, they anchor semantic facts in facts about use. Alston claims that, in contrast, truth-conditional accounts of meaning—which claim that the meaning of a sentence consists in its truth conditions rather than its use—are guilty of leaving semantic facts "dangling in the air." He raises several additional objections to truth-conditional accounts, not the least of which is that many meaningful utterances fail to have truth-values. As Tanesini points out in Chapter 18, 'is true' only applies to assertives, not to any other categories of illocutionary acts. Tanesini also argues that Alston's theory of assertives ultimately undermines his Use Principle, and thereby commits *him* to leaving some semantic facts "dangling in the air."

Alston is a staunch advocate of realism about truth. In his most influential work in this area, *A Realist Conception of Truth* (RCT) (1996), he defends alethic realism, the view that: truth is important (good); and a proposition is true if and only if what it claims to be the case is the case. Accordingly, the proposition that grass is green is true if and only if grass *is* green. Nothing more is necessary for the truth of that proposition, and nothing less is sufficient. This is a *realist* conception of truth because the truth of a proposition is said to depend on a reality beyond itself (grass's *being* green), rather than on an internal or intrinsic feature of the proposition (e.g., its epistemic status).[39]

Alston argues that his concept of truth is captured by the generalization of the T-schema: for all p, the proposition that p is true iff p. In his words, "The T-schema suffices to uniquely locate the concept of propositional truth. If we realize that it is conceptually true that for any p, the proposition that p is true if and only if p, we thereby have grasped the realist conception of propositional truth."[40] Hence, his account is minimalist—it claims that our ordinary *concept* of truth is exhausted by the T-schema. But it is not deflationist. Deflationists deny that truth is a *property*, or, at least, deny that the property of truth has features that go beyond our concept of truth. Following Kripke and Putnam, Alston thinks that properties can have features that are not reflected in the concepts that pick them out. Water is a familiar example. Water is H_2O, but our ordinary concept of water as a clear, tasteless liquid does not reflect this. Alston argues that the same can be said of truth. The property (nature) of truth can have features that go beyond our ordinary concept, beyond the T-schema.

This brings us to the relation between Alston's minimalism and the correspondence theory of truth. Alston argues that his minimalism does not entail the correspondence theory because minimalism stops at the modest claim that a proposition is made true by a fact. It is silent about the nature of the relationship between that proposition and that fact. It does not, as the correspondence theory must, purport to give an account of the ontological status and nature of propositions, of facts, and of how they "correspond." But, the *property* of truth, which can have features that go beyond our ordinary concept, may well have the features embodied in the correspondence theory. Accordingly, Alston's minimalist concept of truth is consistent with the correspondence theory, even though it does not entail it.

It is also important to note that Alston's minimalism is not a redundancy theory. Redundancy theorists claim that 'grass is green' and 'it is true that grass is green' are synonymous, hence 'true' is redundant—it doesn't add anything. But Alston argues that these sentences are not synonymous, for one can understand the former without having any concept of truth at all.

In RCT, epistemic theories of truth are Alston's main opponents. Putnam's epistemic theory claims, roughly, that a proposition will be true if and only if it is justified in ideal epistemic circumstances. Alston's response is twofold. First, he argues that Putnam's epistemic theory is incompatible with the T-schema: the proposition that p is true iff p. After all, if p is both necessary and sufficient for the truth of the proposition that p, then there is no room for an epistemic condition. Second, even if epistemic theorists were successful in showing that every true proposition was in fact ideally justifiable (and vice versa), their epistemic condition still wouldn't be part of our ordinary *concept* of truth.[41] Like Alston, Lynch rejects epistemic, redundancy, and deflationary theories of truth (see Chapter 19). But he also rejects minimalism, arguing that the goodness of truth is part of our ordinary concept.

Alethic realism should not be confused with metaphysical realism. Alethic realism is a theory about what it is for a proposition to be true; whereas metaphysical realism claims that one or more categories of entities (physical objects, events, abstract objects, etc.) exist independently of our minds and conceptual schemes. Though Alston himself defends a version of metaphysical realism, he argues that his alethic realism is compatible with different types of metaphysical anti-realism, including idealism and Putnam's conceptual relativism. In his recent *A Sensible Metaphysical Realism* (2001), Alston argues that large and important stretches of reality do not depend on conceptual schemes for their existence.

For additional sources on Alston's life and work, I suggest Thomas D. Senor's anthology *The Rationality of Belief and the Plurality of Faith: Essays in Honor of William P. Alston*, and Daniel Howard-Snyder's website, which contains a regularly updated bibliography of Alston's publications, and an article on his work.[42]

II. Perspectives

A. Epistemology

This volume is divided into three main parts: Epistemology, Philosophy of Religion, and Meaning and Truth. Together, the essays on epistemology engage all three stages of Alston's work in this area, and his theory of appearing. In the opening chapter, **Carl Ginet** elucidates and challenges several of the most important features of Alston's earliest work on justification. He vehemently defends deonticism and "whole-hog internalism" against Alston's objections, maintains that the deontic account of justification escapes epistemic circularity, and argues, contra Alston, that justification is required for knowledge. Ginet explains that in "The Deontological Conception of Epistemic Justification" (DCEJ) Alston rejects deonticism because he denies that we have direct voluntary control over belief. Alston there argues that cases that seem to be ones of deciding to believe are really cases in which the subject has either been compelled to believe, or has adopted a working assumption. Ginet disagrees, insisting that often we do have direct voluntary control over belief. In the example he provides, in which the location of the family checkbook is in question, he argues that he can choose between: continuing to believe that he handed his wife the checkbook, believing that he did not, and suspending judgment. This choice is possible because he has significant reason to believe that he handed his wife the checkbook (he seems to remember doing so) and significant reason not to believe it (she denies that he did). Ginet claims that in cases like this where one has direct voluntary control, there is no problem with saying that one's belief is (un)justified because it is epistemically (im)permissible for one to adopt it. He goes on to argue that his deontological conception of justification can and should be extended to cases in which one's beliefs are not subject to direct voluntary control (e.g., perceptual beliefs).[43]

Having worked to clear the way for deonticism, Ginet tackles two of Alston's objections to "whole-hog" internalism—the view that "*all* facts constituting a subject's justification [for a belief] . . . must be directly accessible to that subject" in order for her belief to be justified.[44] The "less important" objection occurs in "Internalism and Externalism in Epistemology," where Alston argues that whether a subject would be justified in performing an action sometimes depends on factors that are *not* directly accessible to her. To illustrate, whether one would be legally justified in deducting the cost of a computer on one's tax return depends on the regulations of the IRS, which are not at that moment directly accessible to the subject. Ginet claims that this objection misses the mark because it fails to address whether the subject has justification for her action *at the moment* that the question is raised; that is, *before* she investigates the regulations.[45] He argues that she will have justification only after she has investigated the regulations, only when she is directly aware of (i.e., has active beliefs about or experiences of) all of the factors that contribute to the justificatory status of her action. Alston's second objection is that "whole-hog" internalism is not sufficient for justification—externalism is needed to establish a link between justification and truth. Specifically, the ground on which one's belief is based must be a reliable indicator of the truth of that belief. Ginet contends that adequacy of grounds is not required because our doppelgangers in the demon world are justified in their beliefs. But he argues that his internalism still respects the intuition that justification is connected to truth. For a set of justification principles will be acceptable only if "one who believes in accordance with them will have no reason to think they are not reliable."[46]

Finally, Ginet thinks that the main argument in *The Reliabilty of Sense Perception* is a success—we cannot show that our basic belief-forming practices are reliable without epistemic circularity. (Of course, on his view, this gives us all the more reason to reject reliabilism.) But he claims that we can show that those practices are *deontically* justified without circularity, because our basic principles of justification are self-evident.

In response, Alston argues that Ginet does not have direct voluntary control over believing that he handed his wife the checkbook. This is because believing that p, unlike accepting the proposition that p, involves spontaneously feeling confident that p. Accordingly, Ginet's example is best described as one in which he decides to accept a proposition. In reply to the demon world case, Alston maintains that even when we do epistemology sans justification, the victims of the demon world do not fare as well as their reliable counterparts who lack internalist desiderata. This supports his claim that reliable belief-forming mechanisms are "the most important epistemic desideratum from an epistemic point of view."[47]

Laurence BonJour and Carl Ginet are both internalists and foundationalists, but they disagree about the success of Alston's main argument in *The Reliability of Sense Perception* (RSP).[48] In Chapter 3, BonJour contends that we *can* show that our doxastic practice of sense perception is reliable without epistemic circularity.[49] Contra Alston, he argues that our beliefs about the material world (that are based on our sensory experiences) are likely to be true because the regularities in our patterns of sensory experience are best explained by the hypothesis that those experiences are caused by a stable world of physical objects. BonJour thinks that this argument avoids epistemic circularity because it depends on the reliability of our foundational practices of introspection and a priori insight, without assuming the reliability of sense perception. Clearly, he is relieved that Alston's argument fails. For he claims that if it were successful—if there were no non-circular reason for thinking that sense perception is reliable—

then our commitment to sense perception would be based on "nothing at all beyond familiarity and/or native instinct."[50] Moreover, Alston's "Reidian solution"—his claim that it would still be rational to use sense perception and take it to be reliable—would be inadequate because it takes the threat of skepticism "too lightly."

BonJour argues that the threat of skepticism is particularly urgent for beliefs about the material world that are based on sensory experience because "the experience . . . is ontologically quite distinct from the putative objects that the beliefs are about."[51] Trees are one kind of object; experiences of trees are a wholly distinct kind—inhabiting an entirely separate "ontological region." (Here, BonJour denies what Alston endorses—direct realism about the nature of sensory experience—opting instead for the adverbial theory.) Consequently, we would be in an alarming situation if we had no non-circular argument for the reliability of sense perception. BonJour claims that Alston's subsequent "Reidian commitment" to sense perception is too weak to offer much solace. But, thankfully, we need not go that route because Alston is mistaken in thinking that all of our basic doxastic practices are epistemically on a par.

According to BonJour, introspection and a priori insight are more epistemically secure than sense perception, and can thus be used to establish the latter's reliability. In the practice of introspection, one forms beliefs about one's conscious experiences on the basis of those experiences. So, there is no "ontological gap" between the experiences on which introspective beliefs are based and the objects those beliefs are about. In the practice of a priori insight, one forms beliefs about abstract entities on the basis of one's awareness (experience) of those entities. For example, one forms the belief that nothing can be simultaneously both red and blue all over on the basis of one's awareness of those properties and that relation. Unlike introspective beliefs, a priori beliefs are not about the "experiences" on which they are based. But a priori insight is still more secure than sense perception because a priori beliefs are based on an awareness of the very entities that those beliefs are about. (Whereas, according to the adverbial theory, sensory experience is *not* an awareness of material objects.) Though a priori insight has more skeptical challenges to answer than introspection, BonJour argues that both practices enjoy "epistemological priority" and are reliable (though fallible).

BonJour then reasons that since a priori insight is reliable, our beliefs about which explanations are best are likely to be true. And, since introspection is reliable, our beliefs about the character of our conscious experiences are likely to be true. These are the starting points for his argument that the "common-sense hypothesis" is the best explanation of the regularities in our patterns of sensory experience. BonJour defends his explanatory argument against two of Alston's objections. First, Alston maintains that the explanandum must be limited to one's *own* sensory experience, else the argument will be epistemically circular. But then, the regular patterns in one's own experience might just be a matter of luck—one might be the only human being in existence whose experience has that character. In response, BonJour argues that "even the experiences I have in one eight-hour day are enough to make the improbability that all this is due to chance large enough to satisfy any reasonable standard short of complete certainty."[52] In other words, even the regularities in the patterns of a single person's experience demand an explanation. Alston's second objection is that the common-sense hypothesis is not clearly superior to alternative physicalist explanations and "non-digital" demon hypotheses.[53] BonJour and Alston agree that alternative "digital" hypotheses (e.g., the demon consults a model of the common-sense physical world in deciding which experiences to generate) are not as simple as the common-sense hypothesis. But, contra Alston, BonJour rejects alternative "analog" explanations (e.g., alternative physicalist hypotheses) on the grounds that they are either implausible or not significantly different from the common-sense hypothesis. He also argues that alternative "non-digital" hypotheses (e.g., the demon does not consult a model of the world but nonetheless generates experiences which exactly fit that model) are less probable than the common-sense hypothesis.

For his part, Alston agrees with large segments of BonJour's arguments for the reliability of introspection and a priori insight, but maintains that his argument for the reliability of sense perception is still epistemically circular. According to Alston, BonJour's argument for the reliability of a priori insight is itself circular because it presupposes the reliability of our grasp of the principles of deduction. His argument for the reliability of introspection may itself escape circularity, but his use of introspection to show that sense perception is reliable will not. Alston claims that a complete argument for the reliability of introspection must assume the reliability of sense perception because reliably attributing conscious states to *oneself* requires perceptual knowledge of oneself. Moreover, he asserts that in appealing to one's own experience over an eight-hour day, BonJour assumes the reliability of memory. And arguments for the reliability of memory will either be circular themselves, or presuppose the reliability of sense perception. Finally, Alston contends that even if BonJour's argument had escaped circularity, it would not show that sense perception is a reliable doxastic practice. This is because arguments for the existence of the external world are insufficient for establishing the reliability of the way in which we form beliefs about that world on the basis of our experiences.

John Greco and Laurence BonJour address different aspects of Alston's epistemology of sense perception. While BonJour is engaged in the activity of showing that sense perception is reliable, Greco is concerned with the conditions under which a perceptual belief is justified. In Chapter 5, Greco argues that Alston's account of the justification of perceptual belief combines three major elements: the theory of appearing, doxastic practices, and grounds reliabilism. So, for Alston, S's perceptual belief that X is P is justified if and only if: "(a) X appears P to S; (b) forming the belief that X is P on the basis of X's so appearing is a socially entrenched and reliable doxastic practice; and (c) X's appearing P to S is a reliable indication that X is P."[54] Greco contends that none of these elements are necessary for the justification of perceptual belief, nor are any of them what makes it the case that perceptual beliefs are justified. Instead, the key element is the agent's reliable cognitive power of perception.

Greco begins by rejecting one of the theses of "Back to the Theory of Appearing." He argues that the theory of appearing (TA) does not explain how perceptual experience justifies perceptual beliefs; at best, it explains why perceptual beliefs are likely to be true. Greco reasons as follows. First, if TA is true, then in normal cases of perception, subject S forms the perceptual belief that X is P on the basis of X's appearing P to S (where appearing is an irreducible relation between S and an object in the physical environment, X). Second, if Alston is correct, then on the assumption of TA, it is "natural and plausible" to assume that whatever appears P to S is thereby objectively likely (absent sufficient indications to the contrary) to be P. So, according to TA, perceptual beliefs are prima facie likely to be true. But Greco insists that an additional, reliabilist premise is needed to link objective probability with justification. Hence, it is reliabilism, not the theory of appearing, that is doing the real epistemic work. Moreover, since the adverbial and sense-data theories could "just as well wed their accounts of . . . perceptual consciousness to reliabilism, and . . . get the same result,"[55] the theory of appearing has no epistemic advantage over its ontological rivals. In response, one might (as Alston does) defend the epistemic superiority of the theory of appearing on the grounds that its rivals do not have comparable access to the principle that: whatever appears P to S is thereby objectively likely to be P. After all, unlike its rivals, the theory of appearing makes the object of perception "intrinsic to" perceptual experience, and thus seems to establish "a more immediate connection between X's appearing P to S and X's being P."[56] Greco's rejoinder is twofold. He argues that the principle is ambiguous, admitting of "comparative" and "non-comparative" readings. On the comparative reading (if X appears P to S—appears in the way that objects having P normally appear—then it is objectively likely that X is P), the principle will not be true unless we build reliability into it. But, then sense-data and adverbial theorists would be free to build reliability into analogous principles.[57] And, on the "non-comparative" reading (if X appears P to S—X's appearing has phenomenal property F—then it is objectively likely that X is P) the principle could only be contingently true, again leveling the playing field. In short, if Greco's argument succeeds, the theory of appearing is not necessary for the justification of perceptual belief.

Save reliability, nor are any of the other features involved in Alston's two remaining conditions—(b) and (c) above—necessary for justification. To that end, Greco argues that an agent's perceptual beliefs can be justified even if her sense perceptual practice is not *socially entrenched*. After all, a lone agent whose doxastic practices are reliable, but not shared, will still have justified beliefs. Nor must justified perceptual beliefs be based on *accessible* grounds. According to Greco, we can imagine blindsight cases in which subjects lack *conscious* visual experience (i.e., accessible grounds), but are highly reliable in detecting the location of objects, and hence justified in their resulting perceptual beliefs. He also points out that normal perception depends on a great deal of "*non-conscious* information uptake." (My emphasis.)

In order to reply, Alston reluctantly assumes his former justification-friendly persona. First, he contends that the theory of appearing *is* epistemically superior to the sense-data and adverbial theories. He argues that Greco's objections to the comparative and non-comparative readings of the aforementioned principle fail. Consequently, sense-data and adverbial theorists cannot appeal to it, and must *argue* that "being aware of a certain sense datum or being 'appeared to' in a certain way renders a perceptual belief based on that . . . likely to be true." [58] It is worth noting that Alston could garner support from BonJour on this point. Assuming the adverbial theory, BonJour states:

> In the case of sense perception, the experiential state is entirely distinct from the realm of objects that the resulting belief is about, leaving it completely uncertain, *in the absence of a connecting argument* of some sort, why facts in the former realm should be regarded as good reasons for beliefs about the latter realm. [59]

Of course, Alston's view is that no such arguments (not even BonJour's) succeed. Second, Alston maintains that he does not think a doxastic practice must be socially entrenched in order to be reliable. Finally, he concedes that *accessible* grounds are not required for justification. In this chapter, Alston also makes several remarks about knowledge, reiterating his claim that justification is not necessary for knowledge, and suggesting that belief isn't necessary either.

In "Disagreement in Philosophy," **Alvin I. Goldman** engages Alston's most recent, and most radical, work on epistemic justification—his "crusade" for doing epistemology without it. [60] Fighting to save epistemological inquiry about justification, Goldman argues that Alston's nihilism is unwarranted. He recounts Alston's eliminativist argument in ED, DEWJ, and DEE as follows: Because there is persistent disagreement about justification and no theoretically neutral way to uniquely identify the alleged property about which epistemologists are disagreeing, there is no unique objective property of epistemic justification. Consequently, the debate over justification should be dropped, and the topic should be excised from epistemology. In his initial reply, Goldman enumerates some neutral, albeit partial, descriptions of justification, and casts doubt on Alston's claim that the absence of a theory-neutral description is sufficient for concluding that justification does not exist. [61] But his primary argument against deleting the topic of justification is twofold. First, he claims that as philosophers we should not simply drop the subject, but explain why the dispute over justification is so persistent. Second, he argues that Alston's approach to ending disagreement in epistemology threatens to end disagreement in other areas of philosophy. It commits us to jettisoning other philosophical topics "near and dear to [our] hearts"—like consciousness and identity—that are also fraught with persistent disagreement.

Pursuing the first line of argument, Goldman explores the possibility that the dispute is persistent because 'justification' is polysemous—disputants are employing different concepts, senses, or meanings of 'justification.' He contends that Alston formulates his eliminativist argument this way in "Epistemic Desiderata." But Goldman insists that even if 'justification' is polysemous, "understanding why and how that can be so is important to epistemology."[62] Accordingly, he argues that rather than abandon inquiry about justification, epistemologists should explain how the different senses of 'justification' developed and how they are related. Goldman shows how lexical and frame semantics can make a start on that project. Using lexical semantics, he suggests that 'justified' instantiates complementary polysemy, and may also instantiate "lexical narrowing" or "broadening." If frame semantics is correct, the meaning of 'justified' depends on social norms of epistemic evaluation, and different accounts of justification appeal to different social norms.

In his second line of argument, Goldman maintains that since the topics of consciousness and identity also suffer from persistent disagreement, Alston must claim that they too should be eliminated. In defense of these topics, Goldman argues that lexical semantics can be used to show that 'consciousness' is not ambiguous but subject to modulation, and as such has a unique type of referent. He also claims that there are facts about our concepts or conceptions of identity which can be revealed by developmental psychology. In short, Goldman argues that since there is an objective subject-matter to be discussed in each case, consciousness and identity have been "rescue[d] from Alstonian deletion" and disagreement in philosophy has been preserved.

In response, Alston agrees that it is worthwhile to explore the relations between different senses of 'justification,' but denies that he abandons justification *because* of polysemy. He argues that a multiplicity of concepts or senses of 'justification' is not sufficient for denying the existence of the property of justification, because epistemologists could use "a more generic device to locate a common subject matter"—like shared paradigms.[63] He also maintains that the absence of *any* theoretically neutral way to locate a common target of competing uses of 'justification' is sufficient for denying the existence of the property of justification, even if it is not the best explanation of the dispute. Alston agrees that consciousness and identity should not be eliminated because he thinks that, in each case, we can use shared paradigms to locate a common target of the dispute.

B. Philosophy of Religion

The essays in this part of the volume reflect Alston's wide-ranging impact on the philosophy of religion. In Chapter 9, **Philip L. Quinn** defends Alston's response to the problem of religious diversity against the objections of Robert McKim, who claims that Alston's response is too strong. Quinn's argument has three parts. First, he contends that McKim has misinterpreted Alston. Contra McKim, Alston does not claim to have *shown* Christian mystical practice (CMP) to be reliable, or *shown* that Christians are prima facie justified in beliefs that result from CMP. Second, he defends Alston against McKim's contention that some of the outputs of reliable doxastic practices are not prima facie justified. And, finally, he responds to McKim's objection that given religious diversity, it is not practically rational to "sit tight" with a mystical practice.

Quinn explains that in *Perceiving God* Alston claims to have shown that it is practically rational for the practitioners of any given mystical practice, be it CMP or any other socially established form of MP, to continue to engage in that practice—to "sit tight." He also claims to have shown that it is practically rational for practitioners of CMP to suppose that CMP is reliable and that the beliefs it generates are prima facie justified. (He thinks the same can be said of the other forms of MP.) But, Quinn argues, he does not claim to have shown that CMP is reliable or that the beliefs it generates are prima facie justified. In fact, contends Quinn, Alston "carefully avoids claiming that he has shown any such thing."[64] After all, Alston insists that any attempt to show that CMP is reliable will be infected with epistemic circularity. Circularity forces him to abandon *epistemic* attempts to demonstrate the reliability of our doxastic practices and fall back on *pragmatic* arguments for the rationality of taking them to be reliable. Quinn thinks that McKim has been led astray by Alston's assertions that CMP is reliable and that the beliefs it generates are in fact prima facie justified. But Alston can claim that CMP issues in justified beliefs while simultaneously denying that he has *shown* this to be the case because he holds that one need not *show* justification in order to *be* justified. In sum, if Quinn's analysis is correct, McKim's "stronger reading" of Alston's project is untenable.

According to Quinn, McKim rejects Alston's thesis that all beliefs generated by a reliable doxastic practice are thereby prima facie justified. McKim asks us to suppose that three agents, lost in a desert, examine an object on the horizon through a telescope. The first believes that it is a tent, the second that it is an oasis, and the third that it is a camel. McKim thinks that each of these beliefs can fall short of being prima facie justified, even though they are all products of SP (which is reliable). If McKim is correct, then the practical rationality of taking a practice to be reliable does not entail the practical rationality of taking its output beliefs to be prima facie justified—Alston's response is overstated. In reply, Quinn argues that Alston can "hang tough," that is, continue to claim that all output beliefs of a reliable doxastic practice are prima facie justified, while providing an alternative explanation of McKim's example. Specifically, Alston can claim that the belief that the object is a tent (oasis, etc.), though prima facie justified, is not justified all things considered because of the presence of sufficient overriders.

Lastly, Quinn attacks McKim's suggestion that the appropriate response to religious diversity is not to "sit tight" with an MP, but to "sit loosely" with it. McKim argues that given the disagreement amongst the different MP's, it is not practically rational to "carry on with business as usual." At best, it is practically rational to engage in one's MP in a tentative mode. Quinn maintains that this "sitting loose" is not a genuine alternative to "sitting tight," for in both cases one continues to engage in one's mystical practice. The only genuine alternative to sitting tight with a practice is ceasing to engage in it. But that is not what McKim recommends.

Welcoming Quinn's exposition and defense of his views, Alston focuses on the notion of prima facie (PF) justification in his response. He argues that the difference between PF justification and justification all things considered (ATC) only makes sense from within the perspective of a given individual or group. He thinks that PF justification is an early status of a belief, which is lost when the individual or group searches for sufficient overriders. If such overriders are found, the belief is unjustified ATC; if they are not found, it is justified ATC so far as the group can tell. From outside the group's perspective, from an objective point of view, the belief in question is either justified ATC or it isn't; there is no point in introducing the notion of prima facie justification.

In "Born of the Virgin Mary," **George I. Mavrodes** argues that the biblical account of the conception and birth of Jesus Christ—the virgin birth—can be made consistent with Alston's views about divine intervention. Mavrodes maintains that the virgin birth is commonly thought to be a miracle; and that (following Hume) miracles are often understood to be violations of the laws of nature. But this account of the virgin birth conflicts with Alston's claim that divine interventions are not violations of the laws of nature. According to Mavrodes, Alston denies that divine interventions violate the laws of nature on the grounds that those laws are utterly silent about supernatural beings.

Mavrodes lays out two different ways of thinking about divine interventions—one which construes them as violations of natural law, and another which does not—and shows how the latter can be applied to the virgin birth. He explains the distinction with a thought experiment: What could God do in order to keep a feather from falling to the ground? He argues that God could either tamper with the laws of gravity, thus violating those laws; or, working within the laws of physics, supply the requisite force needed to keep the feather afloat. What could God do to bring about the virgin birth of Jesus Christ, who was fully human and thus possessed a full complement of human chromosomes? Mavrodes argues that, working within the laws of genetics, God could have created half of Jesus's chromosomes (the other half of which were contributed by

Mary). He also suggests that God could have created a set of chromosomes that exactly matched the genetic information that would have been supplied by Joseph.

In reply, Alston clarifies his reason for thinking that divine interventions do not violate natural laws. His reason is not their silence about matters supernatural. For he claims that even if the laws were silent about God, as long as they "assert[ed] unqualifiedly that certain natural conditions must yield a certain result," God could not bring about a different result without violating them.[65] Rather, he thinks divine interventions fail to violate natural laws because those laws do not make unqualified assertions. They contain riders, which indicate that they only hold in closed systems where there is no interference from "outside" forces—be they natural or supernatural.

In Chapter 13, **Linda Zagzebski** criticizes some of Alston's suggestions for divine command (DC) theorists and expands on others, arguing that her developments enable DC theory to avoid the traditional objections. Neither Alston nor Zagzebski endorses DC theory, but both are interested in making it more viable. Zagzebski enumerates two "Euthyphro-like" dilemmas for DC theory. First, "Ought we to do X because God commands us to do X, or does God command us to do X because we ought to do X?"; and second, "Is moral goodness what it is because of God's commands, or are God's commands what they are because of moral goodness?"[66] Zagzebski agrees with and expands on Alston's way of embracing the second horn of the second dilemma, but argues that his way of embracing the first horn of the first dilemma fails to answer the arbitrariness objection.

According to Zagzebski, the most virulent form of the arbitrariness objection claims that God does not have sufficient reasons for the particular commands he makes. Even if the divine nature prevents God from commanding certain things, like cruelty, it might still fall short of determining the commands he actually issues. If this were the case, then (assuming we embrace the first horn of the first dilemma) our obligations would be arbitrary because they could have been other than what they are—God could have commanded something else that was equally compatible with his nature. As she explains: "If the divine nature is compatible with alternative commands, arbitrariness creeps in. Why command X rather than Y if both X and Y are compatible with the divine nature?"[67] Zagzebski considers and rejects two ways of responding to this objection. Alston responds to it by arguing that God's commands are "an expression of his perfect goodness."[68] But Zagzebski thinks this fails to fully answer the objection. After all, if God's commands are not entailed by his goodness—if there is more than one command that is equally expressive of the divine nature—then the commands God issues will still lack sufficient reasons. And, if God's commands are entailed by the divine nature, then the commands themselves will be superfluous; we will be left with a divine nature theory of moral obligation, rather than a divine command theory. The second response Zagzebski considers (developed by Robert Adams) argues that obligations arise within loving relationships; specifically, that A's loving relationship with B gives A the right to make demands on B. She rejects this on the grounds that it fails to make commands the source of our obligations, arguing that it does not take a "command/demand to give me a reason to do what [a loving] person wants or prefers, even when that person is God. A *request* will do just as well."[69] In sum, Zagzebski thinks that in order to keep DC theory from collapsing into either a divine nature theory or a divine request/preference theory, DC theorists must find a way to "fill the gap" between the divine nature and divine commands.

Her solution is to fill the gap with God's personality. This view builds on the exemplarism that she and Alston employ in defending the second horn of the second dilemma. Exemplarism claims that God is the standard, the exemplar, of goodness. Zagzebski argues that as an exemplar, God is not simply the instantiation of the divine nature, but a person, who has a "personality." She thinks that God's personality is not entailed by the divine nature because personalities cannot be reduced to natures or to individual essences. One's personality is what gives rise to the motives, emotions, and perceptions that make one unique. These motives can cause one to issue commands. Accordingly, Zagzebski concludes that the DC theorist should claim that "the motives and the [commands] they cause which are such that alternative motives/[commands] are compatible with the divine nature" arise from the personality of God.[70] She thinks this solution answers the arbitrariness objection—it enables the DC theorist to explain why God commands one thing rather than another when both are compatible with the divine nature—without making commands superfluous.

In response, Alston agrees that the divine nature does not determine divine commands, and applauds Zagzebski's notion of divine personality. However, he argues that she fails to develop a viable version of DC theory. As he explains her view: God's commands are caused by motives which arise from the divine personality and are constrained (but not determined) by the divine nature. He contends that this is a combined divine nature and divine personality theory of obligation, rather than a divine command theory. As such, it *does* make divine commands metaphysically superfluous. (He employs against Zagzebski's solution the objection that she used against his.)

In "Alston on Aquinas on Theological Predication," **Nicholas Wolterstorff** agrees with Alston's claim that it is possible to make true statements about God by using predicate terms literally. He and Alston also concur that Aquinas held this view with regard to predicate terms like 'good' and 'alive'—pure perfection terms. But, contra Alston, Wolterstorff argues that Aquinas thinks these predicates apply univocally to God and to us. He thinks they have the same meaning because the property predicated of God in 'God is alive' is identical to the property predicated of Joe in 'Joe is alive.' He maintains that he can nevertheless preserve Aquinas's view that the predications of these terms to God and to us are related analogically by locating the analogy in the predication relation, rather than in the meanings of the predicate terms themselves.

Wolterstorff interprets Aquinas to be claiming that a predicate term can only apply literally to God in virtue of its *res significata* (RS). Recall that the *res significata* of a predicate term is the property it signifies (e.g., 'alive' signifies the property of being alive). A predicate term will never apply literally to God in virtue of its *modus significandi* (MS)—roughly, our way of apprehending the property it signifies—because its MS arises from our experiences of bodily creatures. According to Wolterstorff's Aquinas, the difference between terms that are said literally of God (e.g., 'alive') and terms that are said metaphorically of God (e.g., 'stone') is that the former do not "include bodily conditions" in their RS, whereas the latter do. In short, the RS of a pure perfection term is "stripped entirely clean of all creaturely modes of signification, including the fact that we participate in perfections [properties] as complex beings."[71] Wolterstorff also recognizes that Aquinas is usually interpreted to deny the univocal application of pure perfection terms to God and to us.

Wolterstorff, like Alston, observes that this combination of views lands Aquinas in the following predicament. The RS of a pure perfection term like 'alive' is just the property of being alive, not any particular mode of participating in that property. In other words, the RS of 'alive' is unadulterated—it is not affected by its MS or by the different ways in which complex and simple beings participate in it. This is precisely what enables terms like 'alive' to be applied literally to God. But, since the RS of 'alive' stands unaffected, it appears that 'alive' will have the very same RS when predicated of human beings. And if, as seems reasonable, 'alive' also applies literally to us, then the predications 'God is alive' and 'Joe is alive' will be univocal after all.

Wolterstorff and Alston disagree about how to extricate Aquinas from this dilemma. Alston denies univocity by arguing that 'God is alive' and 'Joe is alive', do not predicate the same RS of God and of Joe. Rather, the RS in the second case is analogous to the RS in the first. Wolterstorff rejects this because he thinks it commits Alston's Aquinas to claiming that pure perfection terms are only metaphorically true of us. Instead, he claims that the RS is exactly the same. It is "our *predicating* of the predicate term to God that is analogous to our predicating it of Joe; the analogy is to be located, not in the sense (meaning) of the predicate term itself but in the copula."[72] (The meaning of a term is comprised of its RS and MS.) Wolterstorff argues that because Aquinas endorses God's ontological simplicity, the 'is' in 'God is wise' will have a different force from the 'is' in 'Joe is wise.' The force of the copula in the second case will be analogous to the force of the copula in the first. He marshals textual evidence in support of this thesis.

In reply, Alston rejects Wolterstorff's claim that the analogy should be located in the force of the copula. Alston argues that Aquinas does not think the copula is a name, and that 'is' serves too humble a purpose—binding subject and predicate together—to be the source of the equivocation. Alston also defends his view that pure perfection terms do not apply univocally to God and to us by countering Wolterstorff's textual evidence with some of his own. He interprets Aquinas to be denying univocity both with respect to the RS of terms and with respect to the MS of terms. Thus, unlike Wolterstorff, he locates the analogy in the meanings of the predicate terms. Finally, he argues that denying univocity does not commit Aquinas to claiming that pure perfection terms apply metaphorically to us.

C. Meaning and Truth

The final part, Meaning and Truth, contains two essays. The first engages Alston's views on illocutionary acts and sentence meaning; the second, his realism about truth. In Chapter 18, **Alessandra Tanesini** raises several problems for Alston's theory of assertives, and offers an alternative (albeit sympathetic) account of her own. Assertives (e.g., the assertion that some apples are green) are one of five categories of illocutionary acts that Alston identifies in IASM. Tanesini explains that according to Alston (IASM, Chapter 3), the normative stance that a speaker takes toward his or her utterance is what makes that utterance a performance of an illocutionary act of a particular type. To illustrate, the utterance 'You are not going to buy cigarettes today' will be a command if the speaker takes responsibility for (among other things) being in a position of authority over the hearer. However, it will be a prediction (a type of assertive) if the speaker takes responsibility for its being the case that the hearer is not going to buy cigarettes today. As Tanesini points out, Alston recognizes that assertions pose a problem for this account of illocutionary act types (IASM, Chapter 5). That account claims, roughly, that an utterance of 'Some apples are green' is an assertion if (and only if) the speaker takes responsibility for its being the case that some apples are green. But if this were correct, then every illocutionary act (promise, command, etc.) would also be an assertion. For in promising that, say, I will meet you for lunch, I take responsibility for its being the case that I intend to meet you for lunch, that it is possible for me to meet you for lunch, and so on.

Alston's solution is to impose an independent condition on assertions—one that is not related to the speaker's normative stance. Accordingly, he thinks that for an utterance to be an assertion, not only must the speaker take responsibility for the correctness of what is asserted, but the sentence uttered must "explicitly present the proposition which is being asserted."[73] Tanesini contends that this proposal either lands Alston's account of assertion in circularity, or undermines his theory of sentence meaning. She argues that propositions are either ontologically dependent on assertions, or have a mode of existence that is independent of assertions. If the former is true, Alston's account of assertions will be circular—the nature of assertions will depend on the nature of propositions, which will depend on the nature of assertions. And, if Alston tries to avoid circularity by claiming that propositions exist independently, he will undermine his use theory of meaning, according to which a sentence's having a particular meaning consists in its being usable to play a particular role in communication. Tanesini claims that the use theory will be undermined because the fact that a sentence stands in a particular relation to an independently existing proposition is not a fact about use.

Tanesini proposes an alternative theory of assertives that, she argues, avoids these problems. On her view, assertives are distinct from all other illocutionary acts because the conditions one takes responsibility for in performing an assertive act do not vary from speaker to speaker. When speaker X and speaker Y assert that some apples are green, they take responsibility for the very same conditions; namely, its being the case that some apples are green. In contrast, when X and Y issue the command to clean up, they take responsibility for different conditions: X takes responsibility for X's authority over the hearer; Y, for Y's authority over the hearer. Unlike assertives, all other types of illocutionary acts will have at least one condition that is speaker-relative. Tanesini argues that her account is superior to Alston's because it explains why truth-talk is applicable to assertives, but not to any other illocutionary acts. She thinks this is so because in using the utterance 'that is true,' one can simultaneously agree that another speaker's illocutionary act was in order and perform the same illocutionary act oneself. But, one cannot simultaneously do these things unless the act in question is an assertive.

Alston praises Tanesini's alternative account of assertives, but rejects her criticisms of his view. He argues that his theory of assertives does not undermine his use theory of meaning. Following Tanesini, suppose that the fact that an utterance is an assertion depends on facts about independently existing propositions, which are not facts about use. Still, claims Alston, there would be no violation of the Use Principle, because facts about whether an utterance is an assertion are *not* facts about the meaning of linguistic items. He also maintains that Tanesini does not establish a connection between her account of assertives and the minimalist concept of truth that is featured in RCT. At best, she establishes a connection to a deflationary concept of truth.

The minimalist concept of truth is exactly what is at issue in **Michael P. Lynch**'s "Truisms about Truth." Lynch argues that minimalism is false because it leaves out a basic truism about our concept of truth; namely, that it is good to believe what is true. Minimalism, Lynch explains, is the view that the content of our ordinary concept of truth is exhausted by the T-schema and what it entails. Like Alston, Lynch thinks that the T-schema is a vital constituent of our concept of truth; but, unlike Alston, he argues that it is not its sole constituent.[74] He maintains that our concept of truth is also partly constituted by the idea that truth is good, in more formal terms, by:

TN: Other things being equal, it is good that I believe a proposition if and only if it is true.

Thus, truth is a thick value concept—one that has both descriptive and evaluative elements.

Lynch argues that the T-schema is the conceptual root of the truism that truth is minimally objective; that is, that true beliefs are those that "tell it like it is." It is also the source of the truism that truth is distinct from justification. But, Lynch warns, the T-schema does not entail the correspondence theory of truth. For one can claim that [p] is true iff p, while remaining silent about the ontological status of p.[75] On all of these points, Lynch and Alston resoundingly agree.

What they disagree about is whether the goodness of truth is also constitutive of our concept of truth. Lynch argues that one of the primary roles of our concept of truth is to evaluate our beliefs about the world—to commend beliefs that are true. Accordingly, our concept of truth has a normative dimension such that anyone who denies TN fails to fully grasp our concept of truth. In defending the view that TN is a truism about truth, Lynch notes that he is not committed to claiming that truth is always valuable all things considered. Though truth is both instrumentally and intrinsically valuable, its value will sometimes be overridden by other things of value (e.g., one's health).

If Lynch is correct, TN is a crucial constituent of our concept of truth. Moreover, since TN, which is normative, cannot be derived from the nonnormative T-schema, minimalism is false. Lynch considers several objections to this argument, including an anticipated objection from Alston. Alston might deny that TN is part of our *concept* of truth (thus preserving minimalism) while maintaining that TN is a constituent of the *property* of truth. Specifically, Alston might try to show that TN is not a *conceptual* truth by arguing that it is not obviously incoherent to deny that it is good to believe what is true. Since Lynch agrees that the property of truth can have features that go beyond our ordinary concept of truth, it is important for him to address this objection. To that end, Lynch argues that "while . . . it is not . . . obviously incoherent to deny that it is good to believe what is true . . . this only shows that 'it is good to believe that p' and 'it is true that p' are not synonymous."[76] Since TN need not be synonymous with 'it is true that p' in order to be a constituent of the concept of truth, the objection fails. Still, Lynch thinks that we won't really settle this issue until we develop a systematic way of distinguishing between beliefs that constitute a concept and beliefs that go beyond it.

In his final response of the volume, Alston agrees that TN is true, and that truth is both instrumentally and intrinsically valuable; but, as expected, argues that TN is not a constituent of our concept of truth. He maintains that one can deny TN without misunderstanding our ordinary concept of truth, and that Stephen Stich does exactly that.[77] Alston admits that it is possible that there are two concepts of truth—one that is exhausted by the T-schema, and another thick concept that also includes TN. But he doubts that people actually use a thick evaluative concept of truth, claiming instead that they combine the T-schema concept with a "firm belief" that TN is true. I note that, here, a theory of which beliefs are concept-constituting would, as Lynch suggests, help settle the matter. Alston declines to make the precise objection that Lynch anticipates, arguing instead that TN is not constitutive of the property of truth. He claims that since the goodness of true beliefs does not explain their conformity to the T-schema, TN is not part of the property of truth.[78]

I was a student of Bill Alston's at Syracuse University in the 1990's. I spent the summer of 1992 ingesting *Epistemic Justification* in preparation for my first course with Bill the following fall. His seminar in epistemology was both ex-hilarating and challenging—we wrote weekly papers on a host of theories of justification, and on Bill's pluralism (which would later be published as "Epis-temic Desiderata"). I quickly realized that I wanted to be like Bill—inquisitive, compassionate, honest, and rigorous. He treated his students with great respect, and took our views and our development as philosophers seriously. (He has probably read thousands of weekly papers over the years.) He also showed us how analytic philosophy should be done, which is no small feat. The skills and values I learned in that seminar have had the single greatest impact on the way I practice and teach philosophy today.

It took a semester-long independent study on theories of knowledge (1993) for me to summon enough courage to ask Bill to be my dissertation advisor. After we had left a *fourth* view in ruins, I finally made my request. Bill know-ingly replied, "I was wondering when you were going to get around to that." As a supervisor, he exhibited a near saintly combination of patience and prodding. He was open-minded, encouraging me to write on a topic that best served my interests rather than his. He pushed when appropriate, and even managed some-how to absolve me of guilt when writing was slow. I count on Bill to be both challenging, and supportive. I rely on him to tell it like it is, and know that in so doing he is asking me to figure things out with him. Better exemplars are not to be had, and I am proud to be a member of Bill's philosophical family. How does one thank another for helping to develop her philosophical identity? (A book is certainly a start!) But, perhaps, the best way is to demonstrate this identity in her philosophical activities.

Notes

1. All of these monographs were published by Cornell University Press, save *A Sensible Metaphysical Realism*, which was the 2001 Aquinas lecture delivered at Marquette

University, and published by Marquette University Press.

2. *Philosophy of Language* was published by Prentice Hall.

3. EJ, ix.

4. William P. Alston, "Epistemic Desiderata" (ED), *Philosophy and Phenomenological Research* 53, no. 3 (1993), 527–551; "Doing Epistemology without Justification" (DEWJ), *Philosophical Topics* 29 (2001), 1–18.

5. See William P. Alston, "Two Types of Foundationalism" in EJ, 19–38.

6. Alston distinguishes between two different types of perceptual beliefs—those that result from sense perception, and those that result from mystical perception. For more on the justification of sense perceptual belief, see the summary of the theory of appearing below. For an explanation of the doxastic practice of mystical perception, see the summary of PG. Alston counts immediately justified sense perceptual beliefs and immediately justified mystical perceptual beliefs amongst his foundations. When I use 'perceptual belief' without a qualifier, I intend it to mean 'sense perceptual belief.'

7. William P. Alston, "Internalism and Externalism in Epistemology," in EJ, 185–226; Laurence BonJour, *The Structure of Empirical Knowledge* (Cambridge, MA: Harvard University Press, 1985). BonJour may be endorsing "accessibility," rather than "perspectival," internalism in Laurence BonJour and Ernest Sosa, *Epistemic Justification* (Malden, MA: Blackwell, 2003).

8. William P. Alston, "An Internalist Externalism" (IE), in EJ, 239.

9. See William P. Alston, "Concepts of Epistemic Justification" (CEJ), in EJ, 81–114; and "The Deontological Conception of Epistemic Justification" (DCEJ), in EJ, 115–152.

10. CEJ, 86.

11. PG, 76. Doxastic practices are introduced on page 100.

12. The inputs are the subject's grounds. Sometimes the justification of a perceptual belief will rest both on the subject's experiences *and* on her other justified beliefs. So, justified beliefs are also inputs of SP.

13. See RSP, Chapter 4.

14. We would eventually encounter circularity when we tried to prove, for each successive argument, the reliability of the practices that generated the argument's premises.

15. RSP, 125–126.

16. William P. Alston, "Perceptual Knowledge," in *The Blackwell Guide to Epistemology*, ed. John Greco and Ernest Sosa (Malden, MA: Blackwell, 1999), 233.

17. William P. Alston, "Back to the Theory of Appearing" (BTA), in *Philosophical Perspectives 13: Epistemology*, ed. James Tomberlin (Cambridge: Blackwell, 1990), 182. His emphasis.

18. We have shifted gears. In RSP, Alston criticizes attempts to *show* that SP is reliable. Here, he is explaining the conditions under which perceptual beliefs *are* justified.

19. BTA, 198.

20. As Alston claims in his "Response to BonJour," our perceptual belief-forming mechanisms may not be "appropriately sensitive" to their experiential inputs.

21. BTA, 198.

22. DEE, 23. All page references to DEE are to manuscript pages. Page numbers may differ in the published version.

23. ED, 541.

24. See DEE, Chapter 8, section v.

25. William P. Alston, "Aquinas on Theological Predication: A Look Backward and a Look Forward" (ATP), in *Reasoned Faith*, ed. Eleonore Stump (Ithaca, NY: Cornell University Press, 1993), 145–178.

26. ATP, 147.

27. ATP, 165.

28. William P. Alston, "Divine Action, Human Freedom, and the Laws of Nature" (DA), in *Quantum Cosmology and the Laws of Nature*, ed. R. J. Russell, N. Murphy, and C. J. Isham (Vatican City State: Vatican Observatory Publications, 1993), 185–207.

29. DA, 190.

30. William P. Alston, "Some Suggestions for Divine Command Theorists," in DNHL, 253–273. My page references are to DNHL. In Chapter 13, Zagzebski's page references refer to *Christian Theism and the Problems of Philosophy*. The abbreviation SDC applies to her references, but not mine.

31. "Some Suggestions for Divine Command Theorists," in DNHL, 255.

32. "Some Suggestions for Divine Command Theorists," in DNHL, 259.

33. Because Alston uses 'he' to refer to God, I preserve that usage here.

34. Because Alston has since renounced justification, we can assume that he would reconstrue this thesis in terms of his epistemic desiderata approach.

35. PG, 270.

36. IASM, 154.

37. IASM, 160–161.

38. IASM, 276–277.

39. RCT, 7.

40. RCT, 53. He responds to objections to this claim on 53-55.

41. See RCT, 209, 213.

42. Thomas D. Senor, ed., *The Rationality of Belief and the Plurality of Faith: Essays in Honor of William P. Alston* (Ithaca, NY: Cornell University Press, 1995). Daniel Howard-Snyder, "William P. Alston," <http://www.ac.wwu.edu/~howardd/alston/alston.html> (1 Sept. 2004).

43. Suppose that my perceptual belief that there is a truck coming toward me is justified. Ginet argues that this is so because the following counterfactual is true: If I could have avoided coming to have that belief, given what I was aware of, I still should have adopted it.

44. Ginet, Chapter 1, my emphasis. Ginet thinks that in rejecting deonticism, Alston is also rejecting the deontic argument for "whole-hog" internalism.

45. According to Ginet, this example only addresses whether the subject *would be* justified if she *were* aware of the regulations; and is thus not a counterexample to whole-hog internalism.

46. Ginet, Chapter 1.

47. William P. Alston, Chapter 2.

48. BonJour no longer defends the coherentism of his *The Structure of Empirical Knowledge*. For a recent version of his defense of foundationalism, see Part I of BonJour's and Sosa's *Epistemic Justification*.

49. In the doxastic practice of sense perception, beliefs about the material world (e.g., the belief that the table is round) are based on, or formed on the basis of, sensory experiences (e.g., the experience that the table looks round). As BonJour points out, this is consistent with different views about the nature of sensory experience (i.e., direct realism, sense-data, and the adverbial theory). Hereafter, I use "sense perception" to stand for "the doxastic practice of sense perception."

50. BonJour, Chapter 3.

51. BonJour, Chapter 3.

52. BonJour, Chapter 3.

53. "Non-digital," "digital," and "analog" are BonJour's terms. An analog hypothesis is one in which the features of experience are correlated with features of the entities that cause it. In digital hypotheses, the features of experience are not correlated with features of the entity—the demon—that causes it. But, the demon does use a model of the world to determine which experiences it should cause. In non-digital hypotheses, the demon generates the very same experiences it would if it were consulting a model of the world, but it does so because of "a plan of its own" that in no way refers to such a model.

54. Greco, Chapter 5.

55. Greco, Chapter 5.

56. Greco, Chapter 5.

57. They could build reliability into the following principles: If S has a sense datum that represents X to be P (the sort of sense datum that objects having P normally produce), then it is objectively likely that X is P. If S is appeared to (X is P)-ly (the way of appearing that objects having P normally produce) then it is objectively likely that X is P.

58. Alston, Chapter 6.

59. BonJour, Chapter 3, my emphasis.

60. Goldman, Chapter 7.

61. He does this by arguing that: It is likewise difficult to provide theory-neutral descriptions of color and of morality, but we do not deny the existence of colors and of morality on those grounds.

62. Goldman, Chapter 7.

63. Alston, Chapter 8.

64. Quinn, Chapter 9.

65. Alston, Chapter 12.

66. Zagzebski, Chapter 13.

67. Zagzebski, Chapter 13.

68. In other words, Alston responds by endorsing the second horn of the second dilemma.

69. Zagzebski, Chapter 13, my emphasis.

70. Zagzebski, Chapter 13.

71. Wolterstorff, Chapter 15.

72. Wolterstorff, Chapter 15.

73. Tanesini, Chapter 17.

74. Lynch represents the T-schema as TS: [p] is true iff p.

75. In the final section of the chapter, Lynch argues for a stronger claim—that the normative element in our ordinary concept of truth prevents the property of truth from being reduced to correspondence.

76. Lynch, Chapter 19.

77. Of course, Alston thinks that Stich's view is false. Here, his point is that even though Stich has a "wild" view about truth, it doesn't follow that he is confused about the concept.

78. I would like to thank Bill Alston and Michael Lynch for commenting on an earlier draft. Thanks to Amy Coplan for her encouragement, and to Clifford Roth for his constant support and feedback.

Part I: Epistemology

1

Alston on Epistemic Justification

Carl Ginet

The bulk of Alston's work in nonreligious epistemology has been devoted to explicating the concept of epistemic justification. (In two recent papers,[1] however, he argues that there is no viable concept of epistemic justification and epistemology should devote itself to explicating various other epistemic desiderata.) I shall first give a short sketch of Alston's account of epistemic justification, after which I will elaborate and critically examine some of the points in the sketch.

At the most general level Alston's account is simply stated: A belief is justified if and only if it is based on adequate grounds. The following are features of his account that are not revealed by this simple statement:

His account is staunchly anti-deonticist. He opposes the idea that epistemic justification is a normative concept, one that invokes principles that should guide us in forming or maintaining beliefs, principles that tell us under what sorts of circumstances adopting or continuing a belief with this or that content would be epistemically permissible. His reason is that he thinks belief is never subject to voluntary control and, since 'ought' implies 'can,' adopting or withholding or continuing a belief cannot be subject to any 'ought': it makes no sense to say that I ought not to have a certain belief if I could not avoid having it.

Alston rejects whole-hog internalism about justification. He rejects the thesis that all facts constituting a subject's justification—that is, all facts on which the subject's being justified supervenes—must be directly accessible to that subject. He does so partly because, as he rightly observes, this thesis is motivated entirely by the idea that justification is a deontic concept and that the norms—the "oughts"—of justification must be such that a subject who has knowledge of them and enough will could at all times be correctly guided by them in adopting or continuing or abandoning her beliefs. His account is, however, partly internalist, as well as partly externalist. He holds that the grounds on which a belief is based must be more or less directly accessible to the subject, but he thinks that the facts that make the grounds adequate need not be so accessible. For example, the basis of my belief that there is a tree in front of me is the directly accessible fact that it looks to me as if there is. But the adequacy of this basis (according to Alston) consists in the fact that basing beliefs on perceptual experience in this way is a reliable way of forming beliefs—that is, a way that produces mostly true beliefs, and in general the adequacy of any sort of grounds consists in the fact that basing beliefs on such grounds is a reliable way of forming beliefs. And this fact is not directly accessible.

His account is foundationalist in the sense that it supposes that there must be noninferential justification (which Alston calls direct or immediate justification) if there is to be any justification at all. The only sorts of noninferential justification Alston discusses at any length are the sort we have for beliefs as to the nature of our current conscious states and the sort we have for some perceptual beliefs. (I find little discussion in his writings of memory justification or a priori justification.) The adequate basis for my perceptual belief that there is a tree in front of me is not another belief from which I infer this, but my visual experience of its looking to me as if there is a tree there plus my having no "overriding" beliefs (ones that constitute reason to think that this visual experience may be misleading). The adequate basis for my belief that I now have a headache is the experience of the headache itself.

The account rejects higher-order requirements on justification. A belief's being based on adequate grounds is always sufficient for its being justified. One does not need also to believe that one's belief is justified.

Alston has pondered at length the problem of epistemic circularity, which, in neutral terms, is the problem of how we can show that we are justified in engaging in our basic belief-forming practices without relying on the assumption that we are so justified. His answer in the end, after astute criticism of a number of different attempts to show otherwise, is that we can't.

On the relation between justification and knowledge, Alston holds that a belief's being justified is not necessary for its being knowledge.

Let me now discuss some of these points.

I. Alston's Anti-deonticism

I have long been inclined to suppose that the concept of epistemic justification *is* a deontic concept. Indeed, "nondeontic notion of justification" sounds to me like a contradiction in terms. And it appears that Alston shares this semantic intuition. He says in "Justification and Knowledge" (JK):

> I myself find it quite infelicitous to use 'justified' for anything other than some kind of absence of blameworthiness, some way of being within what the rules allow. That is, I find any nonnormative use of 'justified' to be misguided.[2]

And in "Epistemic Desiderata" he says:

> [I]f we abandon that [deontic] conception, terms in the justification family are
> left without any natural interpretation, or at least without their most natural in-
> terpretation. Perhaps the most honest course would be to abandon the term al-
> together in epistemology.[3]

And that is what he recommends doing.[4] If it were true that no deontic notion of
justification is applicable to belief, then that certainly would be good reason for
epistemology to eschew talk of justification of belief. But in his earlier work
Alston was led to try to define a nondeontic concept of epistemic justification by
his conviction that direct voluntary control of belief is impossible. I find myself
unpersuaded by the case he has made for this conviction.

It must be admitted, of course, that a very great many of our beliefs have
not been arrived at by our simply deciding to adopt them—are such that it was
not subject to our direct voluntary control whether we adopted them or not; and
a very great many are such that it is not subject to our direct voluntary control
whether we continue to hold them or not, such that we cannot simply decide to
give them up and forthwith do so; and a very great many propositions are such
that we cannot simply decide to believe them and forthwith do so.

But all this is compatible with its being the case that *sometimes* we do come
to believe a proposition by simply deciding to believe it, and with its being the
case that *sometimes* we do cease believing a proposition simply by deciding to
stop believing it. No doubt Alston would admit this much, but he insists (in "The
Deontological Conception of Epistemic Justification" [DCEJ]) that in fact there
are no such cases.[5] He is convinced that any case one might be tempted to describe as someone's coming to believe that p just by deciding to do so must actually be either: a case where its seeming highly likely to the subject that p compelled the subject's belief, or a case where the subject did not come to believe
that p but just decided to proceed on the assumption that p.

He takes this, as do I, to be an empirical claim.[6] It is therefore susceptible of
refutation by experience, and it seems to me that in my own experience there are
frequent cases of my coming to believe something by simply deciding to do so,
cases that do not satisfy either of Alston's alternative descriptions. For example,
my wife had need to find the checkbook and asked me where it was. I sincerely
asserted, on the basis of my memory, that I handed the checkbook to her when I
came into the house a few hours earlier. She confidently asserted that I had not
done so. I was then confronted with a situation in which, as it seemed to me, it
was open to me to choose either of three alternatives: to continue to believe that
I did recently hand her the checkbook (and it is therefore incumbent on her to try
to recall what she did with it), to believe instead that my memory is deceiving
me (as it sometimes has done) and I did not hand her the checkbook that morning (and it was therefore incumbent on me to try to recall what I did with it), or
to suspend judgment on the matter pending further investigation.

Moreover, it seems to me that a plausible understanding of what believing is makes it unsurprising that there should be such cases.[7] Such an understanding also, I think, makes it unsurprising that cases of deciding to believe (stop believing) that p are psychologically possible only where the subject has significant reason to believe that p and also significant reason not to believe that p.

I might, of course, be under some sort of illusion when it seems to me that I come to believe by simply deciding to do so: I would not claim infallibility for these impressions. But it seems reasonable for me to take them at face value until I've been offered a good reason (either in a specific case or in general) not to do so, and so far I haven't been. (I don't consider anyone's mere assertion, or conviction, that such a thing is psychologically impossible to be a good enough reason.)

Clearly, if there are cases of coming to believe by simply deciding to do so, then there is no voluntariness problem with saying of such a case that the subject ought not to have adopted the belief, or, alternatively, saying that his adopting it was justified (i.e., epistemically permissible). But what about the very great many beliefs that their subjects have *not* come to have in that directly voluntary way? What could it mean to say of one of them that the subject ought not to have come to have it, given that the subject could not have helped doing so? In such a case we have to say, I think, that it means that, if the subject *could* have avoided adopting the belief, she ought not to have adopted it. In cases where we make the judgment that a subject ought not to have adopted a certain belief and we don't know whether she could have helped doing so, our judgment will have the tacit proviso 'if she could have helped doing so.'

Alston has commented on such a move to "extend a deontological concept of justification to irresistible beliefs by invoking a counterfactual" as follows:

> (1) This renders epistemic justification quite different from the justification of action, where 'justified' and other deontological terms are withheld from actions the subject couldn't help performing. (2) Insofar as we can make a judgment as to what would be permitted or forbidden were a certain range of involuntary states within our voluntary control, it will turn out that the deontological evaluation is simply a misleading way of making evaluations that could be stated more straightforwardly and more candidly in other terms. Suppose that we judge that if we had voluntary control over the secretion of gastric juices, then we ought to secrete them in such a way as to be maximally conducive to health and a feeling of well being. . . . But since gastric juices are not within our voluntary control, this would seem to be just a misleading way of saying that a certain pattern of secretion is desirable or worthwhile. (DCEJ, 125n18)

Regarding Alston's point (1): It seems to me not true that we always withhold deontic terms from actions the subject could not help performing. We make sense, and at least sometimes convey a truth, when we judge that compulsive behaviors of addicts, or irresistible acts compelled by intense pain, fear, or depression, are unjustified from the point of view of rational prudence, or from the point of view of morality. Clearly what we intend in such a judgment is that the action was such that, *if* the agent *had* been able to help it, she ought not to have done it (because it would not have accorded with norms of rational self-interest, or norms of morality).

Regarding Alston's point (2): It must of course be conceded that for a kind of state or change or process like the secretion of gastric juices, where we never have, and have no idea what it would be like to have, direct voluntary control over an instance of that kind, we have no idea what sort of thing a counterfactual supposition of having direct voluntary control over it could be talking about. But it is quite different for the state of belief, where we often, but by no means always, do have direct voluntary control over coming to have or ceasing to have such a state and, so, can have an idea of what such control is like. In this respect the state of believing is like the state of intending. Intending is a kind of commitment to acting in a certain way in a certain eventuality, or to a policy of acting in a certain way in certain sorts of circumstances. Clearly we often come to have this sort of commitment, or give up having it, by simply deciding to do so: Intention is, I hope no one will want to dispute, a sort of mental state that is often under our direct voluntary control. But by no means always. When I'm driving my car and see a stop sign at the cross street ahead and a stream of traffic moving across the intersection, I can no more avoid coming to have the intention to stop and wait for a clearing in the stream of traffic before proceeding than I can avoid coming to have the belief that I see a stop sign and a stream of traffic. It is nevertheless perfectly intelligible and accurate to say that, if I had been able to avoid coming to have that intention, if it had been subject to my direct voluntary control, I ought nevertheless to have come to have it. This is intelligible because we know what it is like for it to be open to one at a particular time either to forthwith adopt a certain intention or not to do so. Similarly, it is perfectly intelligible and accurate to say that, if I had been able to avoid coming to have that belief (that the intersection ahead has a stop sign and traffic moving through it), I should, given what I was actually aware of, nevertheless have adopted it. This is intelligible because we know what it is like for it to be open to one at a particular time either to forthwith adopt a certain belief or not to do so.

II. Alston's Anti-internalism

Alston takes it that he has removed whatever appeal (whole-hog) internalism about justification might have by having argued for the falsity of the crucial premise in the case for internalism, namely, that the concept of justification is a deontic concept. But, as I've tried to show, Alston's argument is not successful. So, if I'm right, one who has embraced that crucial premise need have no qualms about continuing to do so and continuing to endorse the deontic argument for internalism. However, the internalist is not out of the woods just yet. Alston puts forward two other considerations against internalism.

Let me take up the less important one of these first. Alston asserts that often when one asks whether or not one would be justified in acting in a certain way (where one is unquestionably using a deontic notion of justification), one is not asking about only things that are then immediately accessible to one.

> Often I have to engage in considerable research to determine whether a pro-
> posed action is justified. If it is a question of whether I would be justified in
> making a certain decision as department chairman without consulting the ex-
> ecutive committee or the department as a whole, I cannot ascertain this just by
> reflection, unless I have thoroughly internalized the relevant rules, regulations,
> bylaws, and so on. Most likely I will have to do some research. Would I be le-
> gally justified in deducting the cost of a computer on my income tax returns? I
> had better look up the IRS regulations and not just engage in careful reflection.
> The situation is similar with respect to more strictly moral justification. Would
> I be morally justified in resigning my professorship as late as April 12 in order
> to accept a position elsewhere for the following fall? This depends, *inter alia*,
> on how much inconvenience this would cause my present department, which
> faculty resources there are already on hand for taking up the slack, how likely it
> is that a suitable temporary replacement could be secured for the coming fall;
> and so on. There is no guarantee that all these matters are available to me just
> on simple reflection.[8]

This objection entirely misses the mark. The examples Alston gives do not counter what the internalist wants to require. When one takes the question "Would I be justified in acting in such-and-such a way?" to depend on facts one is not now aware of and needs to undertake investigation to become aware of— as the protagonist of Alston's examples clearly does—then, obviously, the question one has in mind is not the question "Do I *at this moment* have justification for *now* undertaking such an action?" But it is only this question that the inter-nalist claims must be answered by facts that one is *then* directly aware of. And the answer to this question in Alston's examples is clearly "No." Clearly we are to suppose that the facts that the agent is aware of at the time of raising the ques-tion do not justify him in then going ahead with the action. That is why he is obliged to get more information, in order to find out whether, when he has it, he would *then* be justified in going ahead with it. The question Alston's protagonist is asking is, rather, "Would I be justified in this action if I knew as much about the relevant facts as I should know before deciding whether to undertake it?" No clearheaded internalist would think that the facts that determine the answer to this question must be among the facts the asker is directly aware of at the time of asking it.

I have been characterizing the internalist requirement on justifiers as a re-quirement that they be facts of which the subject is directly aware at the time of the decision (to act or to believe) that they purport to justify. I mean such facts to exclude, not only facts about which the subject has no belief at that time, but also facts about the subject's merely dispositional beliefs or memories that would take effort of recollection to bring to active memory. In some previous writings where I maintained that the facts that justify must be directly recognizable or accessible, I thought of such facts as including inactive beliefs and memories that the subject could bring to active memory merely by reflection on the appropriate question. I now think that was wrong. In deciding at a given time whether to act in a certain way, or whether to believe a certain proposition, a subject cannot be obliged to take account at that moment of facts that she is not then directly aware of and that would require some time and effort (whether of recall or investigation) for her to become aware of. (She can, however, be obliged, by relevant normative principles, prudential, moral, or epistemic, to put off deciding on the action or the belief until she has recalled or gathered more relevant information.) Of course, it should not be thought that the facts in the field of a subject's direct awareness at a given time are limited to active beliefs or active propositional attitudes of other sorts. They may also include, for example, facts as to the subject's current perceptual experiences and their subtle features that enable recognition of persons and objects. A mother of identical twins who can by looking at them distinguish one from the other may not be able to tell you precisely what features of their appearances she goes on, but she is directly aware of them.

An objector might grant that it is plausible to require direct accessibility for justifiers of conscious decisions to adopt or give up a belief (or for involuntary conscious events of acquiring or losing a belief), but ask: What about stored dispositional beliefs? Can't they be justified even when inactive? Surely they are not then justified by anything then in the believer's field of direct awareness. True. The internalist must say that, insofar as a belief has a justification at a time when the belief is merely dispositional, that justification must also be dispositional. The dispositional justification, like the dispositional belief, is constituted by counterfactual facts about the subject: If a belief existing as a disposition at a given time is justified at that time, it is justified by the fact that had the belief become active at that time, it would have been accompanied by direct awareness of something justifying it.

But, the objector is likely to ask, what about a belief that was originally adopted on a justifying basis and that has later become active on a particular occasion when the subject does not then actively recall the basis on which she originally adopted the belief? Can't the belief nevertheless be justified at the time of its current activation? If not, probably most of our justifiedly formed beliefs are unjustified at the later times we actively deploy them to justify doxastic and other decisions—a surely unacceptable result. To be sure, when a subject justifiedly actively deploys a belief that p, which she came to have earlier, in support of a further judgment or decision, she does not often actively recall the original basis on which she came to believe that p. But it will typically seem to her that p is something she has come to know; it will be her confident memory impression that she has acquired the right to take it to be a fact that p. And if it does not seem to the subject that she has come to know that p, then she has no business taking p to be evidence for what she currently decides to believe (or as a reason for deciding to do what she currently decides to do). This confident memory impression, besides being necessary, is also sufficient to make the activated belief justified even when the impression is false and the belief is not knowledge—whether its failure to be knowledge is because, though its original adoption was justified, other conditions of knowledge were not then satisfied, or because the original adoption was not justified.[9]

The other, more important consideration that Alston supposes goes against internalism is the idea that epistemic justification must be linked to truth-conducivity. Alston identifies epistemic justification with "goodness from the epistemic point of view," which is "defined by the aim of maximizing truth and minimizing falsity." He remarks:

> If goodness from an epistemic point of view is what we are interested in, why shouldn't we identify justification with truth, at least extensionally? . . . The logical independence of truth and justification is a staple of the epistemological literature. . . . [But] what reason is there for taking [justification in the good-from-the-epistemic-point-of-view sense] to be independent of truth? I think the answer to this has to be in terms of the "internalist" character of justification.[10]

A belief's being epistemically justified—good from the epistemic point of view—he says,

> consists not in the belief's fitting the way the facts actually are, but something more like the belief's being true 'so far as the subject can tell from what is available to the subject.' In asking whether S is [epistemically justified] in believing that p, we are asking whether the truth of p is strongly indicated by what S has to go on; whether, given what S has to go on, it is at least quite likely that p is true. ("Concepts of Epistemic Justification" [CEJ], 99)

Alston refers to "what the subject has to go on" which prompts her belief as the *ground* on which she bases the belief.

Alston's externalism comes in with his claim that a belief is justified only if that ground is *adequate* and his explication of what makes a ground adequate. About the latter he says:

> [L]et's note that a belief's being *justified* is a favorable status vis-a-vis the basic aim of believing or, more generally, of cognition, viz., to believe truly rather than falsely. For a ground to be favorable relative to this aim it must be "truth-conducive"; it must be sufficiently indicative of the truth of the belief it grounds. In other terms, the ground must be such that the *probability* of the belief's being true, given that ground, is very high.[11]

Only this, he takes it, can "render it intelligible that justification is something we should prize from the epistemic point of view" (CEJ, 111). He explains further:

> It is an objective probability that is in question here. The world is such that, at least in the kinds of situations in which we typically find ourselves, the ground is a reliable indication of the fact believed. . . . I am thinking in terms of some kind of "tendency" conception of probability, where the lawful structure of the world is such that one state of affairs renders another more or less probable. ("An Internalist Externalism" [IE], 232)

So the ground on which S bases a belief must be something S is directly aware of (part of "what S has to go on") at the time of acquiring the belief. But the further fact that the ground is adequate—which he takes to be the fact that a belief based on such a ground is likely to be true—is not something S can be directly aware of, because it is a general fact about how the world works. So not all of the facts that constitutes S's being justified in acquiring the belief can be ones of which S is directly aware at the time of acquiring it.

The proponent of a deontic and internalist account of epistemic justification needs to meet this challenge, needs to show how such an account can respect the intuition that there is a connection between epistemic justification and the epistemic goal of "maximizing truth and minimizing falsity" in our beliefs (or "the basic aim of believing . . . viz., to believe truly rather than falsely").

I will explain how I think this should be done, but first it is important to point out that the strong connection claimed by Alston does not square with intuitions about all possible cases. It seems intuitively clear to me that there are possible cases of fully justified belief where the ground on which the belief is based is not a reliable indicator of its truth in the kinds of situations the believer typically finds herself in. I have in mind, of course, a believer who exists in a world run by a Cartesian demon, or who is embodied as a brain in a vat, all of whose perceptual experience has, through a fairly long life, been contrived by his handlers to be (a) qualitatively the same as mine during my life so far but (b) totally hallucinatory, never in the least representative of his actual environment. Suppose this person had all the same perceptual and memory impressions that I have had and was prompted to have all the same beliefs about the external world that I have. Most of these would be justified in the same way that the corresponding beliefs of mine are, but nearly all of them would be false and (the crucial point here) the grounds on which they were based would not be reliable indicators of their truth, given the way *that subject's* world works.

It will not help to avoid this counterexample to suggest that the reliability of a belief's grounds should be gauged in the actual world, to say that if the sorts of perceptual and memory impressions that ground basic empirical beliefs in the demon world are reliable indicators of the truth of similar beliefs in our world then that fact makes those demon-world beliefs justified, even though those sorts of grounds are not reliable indicators of truth in the demon-world. This would be to say that our concept of justification is indexed to reliability of grounds in the actual world and that is why it is right for us to regard the demon-world beliefs as justified. This suggestion misses the point of the counterexample. The point is that the demon-world believers would, if they were to apply the same concept of justification we use, be right to regard their beliefs as justified. If there is an indexical element in the concept of justification, in their application of the concept it could not refer to how things are in *our* world but would have to refer to how things are in *their* world. But since their grounds for their justified beliefs are not reliable in their world, the concept of justification, used by them and us, cannot be indexed to reliability of grounds in the user's world.

So the connection between truth-conduciveness and justification cannot be the simple, straightforward one that Alston claims it is. He says (in "Epistemic Circularity") that a principle of justification of the form

> If a belief of type B is based on a ground of type G, then the belief is justified

is acceptable only if forming a B on the basis of a G is a reliable mode of belief formation.[12] This is right, of course, if justification is conceived in Alston's way. But if we conceive justification in a deontic and internalist way, a way that endorses the intuition that demon-world believers are justified in their false beliefs, what should we say instead is the link between the acceptability of such a justification principle and truth? I think we should say this: A total set of justification-principles that includes such a principle is acceptable only if that set of justification principles supports its own reliability; that is, one who believes in accordance with them will have no reason to think they are not reliable. The totality of correct principles of belief justification must be such that in any possible world the beliefs that would be justified by the application of those principles by the believers in that world are (not, as Alston would have it, mostly true but) such as to support the thesis that forming beliefs in accordance with those principles generally leads to having true beliefs. They must do this even in possible worlds (like the demon-world) where that thesis is false.

This constraint on the principles of epistemic justification makes it the case that they respect the epistemic goal that one's beliefs be true rather than false. This is an aim or desire that any believer has as such and that is independent of the believer's desires or evaluative attitudes with respect to the truth-values of propositions that are candidates for belief.[13] The principles will satisfy the aforementioned constraint and properly respect this desire if it is the only desire that the principles give any weight to in determining what counts, from the point of view of epistemic justification, as a reason for believing a particular proposition; and they give no weight at all to any desire a believer might have that the proposition be true (or false) or to any evaluation she might have of its being true (or false).

On the deontic and internalist conception of justifying grounds, there is a sense of "probable" in which justifying grounds make the belief they justify probable. It is not the subjective sense in which the probability of a proposition is relative to the believer and determined by her degree of confidence in it. It is an objective kind of probability, but not Alston's objective kind, which is causal and determined by "the lawful structure of the world." Nor is it the statistical kind, determined by actual-world track-records, nor the gambler's kind, determined by the ratio to an exhaustive set of alternative possibilities or a subset of them. It is, rather, a peculiarly epistemic or evidential kind. It is measured by the degree of confidence in the truth of a proposition that a given kind of evidence for its truth, or basis for believing it, would make it reasonable for a subject to have. This is determined by objectively true normative principles of belief justification.

III. Epistemic Circularity

Alston takes the problem of epistemic circularity—the problem of how to show that we are justified in our basic belief-forming practices without relying on the assumption that we are so justified—to be the problem of how to show that our basic belief-forming practices are reliable without assuming that they are reliable. This is because he understands "justified" in his nondeontic sense in which to say that a belief is justified is to say just that it is based on a ground that is a reliable indicator of its truth.

He defines a basic belief-forming practice as one "for the reliability of which any otherwise effective track-record argument would be circular"; that is, it would, in taking its premises to be justified, presuppose the reliability of that practice.[14] Since a belief's being justified is, for Alston, its being formed in a reliable way, a way that generally leads to true beliefs, he construes the question of how, if at all, we can show that we are justified in relying on our basic belief-forming practices as the question of how we can show that those practices are reliable. Taking the practice of forming beliefs on the basis of sense perception (e.g., being prompted to believe that there is snow on the ground by its looking to me as if there is snow on the ground and my lacking any reason to think that in this instance my eyes might be deceiving me) as his central example of a basic belief-forming practice, Alston argues most persuasively, in *The Reliability of Sense Perception*, that no a priori argument for the reliability of this practice will work. And he points out that any a posteriori argument, from the practice's good track record, in assuming its premises (which are products of that practice) to be justified, must assume the reliability of that practice—that is, the argument must be epistemically circular. (The argument is not logically circular because none of the many premises of the track-record argument is or entails the conclusion, and those premises are all justified if sense-perception is reliable. But if a reflective subject presses the question of why she should regard those premises as justified, the reliability conception of justification has no satisfactory answer: Another track-record argument cannot satisfy if the first one didn't, and appealing to the general proposition that sense-perception is reliable would be logically circular.)

From the standpoint of a deontic, internalist conception of justification—on which it is not required that a justified belief be formed in a reliable way—the prospects of explaining satisfactorily why we are entitled to rely on our basic belief-forming practices do not look so bleak. For, from this point of view, the question "Are we justified in our basic belief-forming practices?" is *not* equivalent to the question "Are those practices reliable?" It is, rather, "Are we justified in accepting the justification principles that determine those practices?" And our justification for accepting those normative principles will have to be ultimately a priori, since the justification for accepting any basic normative principle will have to be a priori. A priori principles can be used in combination with contingent beliefs they justify to derive a posteriori principles, ones that depend on contingent general facts about the world.

I haven't the space here to elaborate this picture and try to make it convincing, but let me briefly indicate a kind of principle of justification for which I think we have a priori justification because such principles are self-evident. (In saying a proposition is self-evident, I mean that accepting it is a necessary condition of fully understanding it. The proposition that five is the next integer after four is self-evident in this sense: If someone is uncertain whether to accept that proposition, then that is knockdown evidence that she does not [fully] understand it.) Consider principles of the form:

> If S's visual experience is as if she sees X in normal viewing conditions and S has no reason to think that in this instance viewing conditions are not normal or her visual experience is deceptive, then S is justified in believing that she sees X

where 'X' is replaced with some description of basic visible properties.[15] It seems to me that anyone who showed resistance to accepting the dictates of such a principle in a particular case—who, for example, while seeming to allow that S had a visual experience as of seeing in normal light a blue smear on a white surface and had no reason to think that viewing conditions or her sight might in this instance be deceptive, nevertheless seemed to deny or question that S was justified in believing that she saw a blue smear on a white surface—would therein show that she does not fully understand the principle: Either she fails to understand some of the nonnormative terms, or she fails to grasp the normative concept of what it is to be rationally justified in such a belief.

If basic principles of justification are self-evident (or deducible from self-evident principles), then it is clear how we are justified in accepting them. We are justified in the same way we are justified in accepting that five is the next integer after four, or (to give a normative example) in accepting that it is (morally) wrong to run over a child with your car merely in order to avoid the inconvenience of applying the brakes, or (to give an epistemic normative example) in accepting that anyone who understands the proposition that 5 is the next integer after 4 is justified in believing it. And there is no circularity in such an explanation.

IV. Justification and Knowledge

Let me discuss one more claim for which Alston argues and which I am inclined to dispute: namely, that a belief's being justified is not necessary for that belief to be knowledge. He argues that neither justification on the deontic conception I favor nor justification on the nonnormative, reliabilist conception he favors is necessary for knowledge.

Concerning the deontic or normative conception, Alston says that it:

> will apply only to beings that can be subject to . . . obligations to conduct their cognitive operations so as to attain truth and avoid falsity. But obligations, and the associated praise, blame, reproach, and so on, attach only to beings that are sufficiently self-conscious and sufficiently sophisticated to be capable of governing their behavior in light of norms, principles, rules, and the like. And this condition is by no means satisfied by all knowing subjects. Lower animals, very small children, and idiots acquire and utilize much perceptual knowledge. . . . But they are not capable of acting in light of rules. So J_n [i.e., justification normatively conceived or, as we might say, justification properly so called] is at best a necessary condition for the knowledge possessed by the likes of normal mature human beings. (JK, 173)

I think that the advocate of the normative conception must agree with this point. The normativist's claim must be that a belief's being justified is necessary for its being knowledge only in believers to whom a normative concept of belief justification is applicable.

But Alston doubts even this restricted claim. He says:

> Much of the perceptual knowledge you and I utilize in reacting to our surroundings is acquired and utilized unconsciously. . . . And whatever may be the case with respect to our conscious belief acquisitions, it is highly doubtful that we are subject to any intellectual obligations vis-a-vis these inevitably unconscious perceptual beliefs. (JK, 173)

This is indeed a point that normativists need to take account of. They can do so, I think, by treating unconscious perceptual beliefs in a way parallel to the way I suggested they treat involuntary beliefs. Such a belief is unjustified if and only if the subject ought not to have adopted the belief if she had been aware of adopting it and could have helped doing so; and the belief is justified if and only if it is not the case that the subject ought not to have adopted the belief if she had been aware of adopting it and could have helped doing so.

Alston argues that being justified (in the normative sense) in believing that

p on the basis of the (truthful) testimony of (what is in fact) a reliable and con-
scientious person is not necessary for knowing that p on the basis of such testimony. His argument assumes that "I have an intellectual obligation . . . to investigate the credibility of a person before accepting that person's reports of the
doings or conditions of others" (JK, 175), and also that I may very well know
something on the basis of a reliable person's testimony even though I have not
investigated the credentials of that person. The latter assumption is, I think, in-
disputable, but not the former. It is implausible to suggest that I am never justified in believing that p on the basis of a particular person's testimony that p until
I have checked out that person's reliability. When an agitated stranger sat down
beside me on the train and told me that she had just heard on her portable radio
that the space shuttle had disintegrated on reentry, surely I was justified (not
violating any normative principle of belief justification) in believing her.

Concerning his nonnormative concept of justification, Alston argues that it
too is not necessary for knowledge. S's belief that p is justified in Alston's non-
normative sense if and only if the belief "is based on . . . grounds that provide a
sufficiently strong [i.e., reliable] indication of the truth of the belief" and "S
lacks overriding reasons to the contrary [i.e., for believing that not-p]" (JK, 178-
179). Alston gives an example that he claims shows the possibility of knowledge
without justification in this sense. S has "friends" who:

> convince him that for about half the time his sense experience is a radically un-
> reliable guide to his current situation, and that he cannot tell when this is the
> case. They provide very impressive evidence. The totality of the evidence
> available to S strongly supports their story. S . . . justifiably believes that his
> senses are not to be trusted. (JK, 178)

But there comes an occasion when S:

> is about to cross a street and seems to see a truck coming down the street. In
> fact his perceptual belief-forming apparatus is working normally and a truck is
> coming down the street. Forgetting his skepticism for a moment he waits for
> the truck to pass before venturing into the street. He acquired a momentary per-
> ceptual belief that a truck was coming down the street. . . . [I]t seems clear that
> he did acquire knowledge. . . . [G]iven the fact that his senses were functioning
> in a perfectly reliable and normal fashion, and given the fact that he thereby felt
> certain that a truck was coming down the street . . . is it not clear that S *learned*
> (*ascertained, found out*) that a truck was coming, that he was *cognizant* of the
> truck, that he received *information* about the state of affairs in the street? (JK,
> 178-179, his emphasis)

There may be a sense in which S "received the information" that a truck
was coming down the street (roughly the same sense in which the tape in a video
camera might receive that information), and it may be that S was justified in not
taking any chances by stepping out into the street. But my intuition is that, be-

cause S was aware of strong reason to doubt what his senses were telling him, S did not, on their basis, learn, ascertain, find out, or come to know that truth. Consider an analogous case (or so it seems to me) concerning the testimony of a person. I am a spectator at a trial and witness A comes to the stand. My friend sitting next to me, whom I have no reason to doubt, whispers to me, "I've read about A. You can't trust a thing he says in the witness box. He's perjured himself in previous trials." Despite having this good reason to doubt A's testimony I am won over by A's very sincere manner and believe his statement that the accused was with him at the time of the crime. Suppose that in fact A is an extremely reliable and honest person who would never dream of asserting under oath what he did not know, and my friend sincerely told me otherwise because he had mistaken who A is: A's name closely resembles the name of the person my friend remembered reading about. Despite the fact that my ground for believing what A says—namely, that A said it in a serious and sincere manner and under oath—is in fact a very reliable indicator of its truth, given A's character, it seems clear that I do not know that what A says is true, and I fail to know it just because, given the reasons for doubt I have, I am not justified in believing what A says.

V. Conclusion

I've been occupied here in criticizing Alston's views and defending mine on some issues about which we disagree: whether a deontic concept of epistemic justification is the right concept, whether justifiers of a belief must be directly accessible to the subject, how bleak the prospects are for explaining in a noncircular way why we are justified in relying on our basic sources of belief such as sense-perception, and whether justification in any sense is necessary for knowledge. But I am very much in Alston's debt for his strong challenges on these issues, which have forced me to refine my views and to get clearer about my reasons for holding them. There are other topics—such as foundationalism, the nature of privileged access to one's conscious states, and of noninferential justification of basic empirical beliefs—that I've not discussed here and on which I largely agree with Alston and can only admire the helpful analyses and arguments he's given. Epistemologists generally, whatever the extent of their agreement with him, are in his debt for highly illuminating discussions of every epistemological topic on which he has touched. All of his work has a characteristic astuteness, penetration, and clarity. Reading it always leaves me feeling that you're in good hands with Alston.

References

Alston, William P. "Doing Epistemology without Justification" (DEWJ). *Philosophical Topics* 29 (2001): 1–18.

———. "Epistemic Desiderata" (ED). *Philosophy and Phenomenological Research* 53, no. 3 (September 1993): 527–551.

———. *The Reliability of Sense Perception* (RSP). Ithaca, NY: Cornell University Press, 1993.

———. *Epistemic Justification: Essays in the Theory of Knowledge* (EJ). Ithaca, NY: Cornell University Press, 1989.

———. "The Deontological Conception of Epistemic Justification." Pp. 257–299 in *Philosophical Perspectives 2: Epistemology*, edited by J. E. Tomberlin. Atascadero, CA: Ridgeview Publishing Co., 1988.

———. "Justification and Knowledge." In *Proceedings of the XVIIth World Congress of Philosophy, Volume 5*. Montreal: Editions Montmorency, 1988.

———. "An Internalist Externalism." *Synthese* 74 (March 1988): 265–283.

———. "Epistemic Circularity." *Philosophy and Phenomenological Research* 47, no. 1 (September 1986): 1–30.

———. "Internalism and Externalism in Epistemology." *Philosophical Topics* 14, no. 1 (1986): 179–221.

———. "Concepts of Epistemic Justification." *The Monist* 68, no. 1 (January 1985): 57–89.

Ginet, Carl. "Deciding to Believe." Pp. 63–76 in *Knowledge, Truth, and Duty*, edited by M. Steup. New York: Oxford University Press, 2001.

Goldman, Alvin I. "Internalism Exposed." *Journal of Philosophy* 96, no. 6 (1999): 739–758.

Velleman, J. D. "The Aim of Belief." Pp. 244–281 in *The Possibility of Practical Reason*. Oxford: Oxford University Press, 2000.

Williams, Bernard. "Deciding to Believe." Pp. 95–111 in *Language, Belief, and Metaphysics*, edited by H. M. Kiefer and M. Albany. New York: State University of New York Press, 1970.

Notes

1. See William P. Alston, "Epistemic Desiderata" (ED), *Philosophy and Phenomenological Research* 53, no. 3 (September 1993): 527–551; and "Doing Epistemology without Justification" (DEWJ), *Philosophical Topics* 29 (2001): 1–18.

2. William P. Alston, "Justification and Knowledge" (JK), reprinted in Alston, *Epistemic Justification: Essays in the Theory of Knowledge* (EJ) (Ithaca, NY: Cornell University Press, 1989), 175n7.

3. ED, 532.

4. He elaborates on this recommendation in DEWJ.

5. William P. Alston, "The Deontological Conception of Epistemic Justification" (DCEJ), reprinted in EJ, 115–152.

6. Unlike Bernard Williams ("Deciding to Believe," in *Language, Belief, and Metaphysics*, ed. H. M. Kiefer and M. Albany [New York: State University of New York Press, 1970], 95–111), Alston does not deny that it is conceptually possible for there to be cases of a person's coming to believe something just by deciding to do so; he denies only that it is psychologically possible. For criticism of Williams's arguments that deciding to believe is conceptually impossible, see Carl Ginet, "Deciding to Believe," in *Knowledge, Truth, and Duty*, ed. M. Steup (New York: Oxford University Press, 2001), 63–76.

7. For my attempt to explicate what believing is, see Ginet, "Deciding to Believe." Roughly, my account says that to believe that p is to be disposed to count on p's being true, where counting on p's being true entails not only staking something on the truth of p, but also not preparing oneself for the possibility of p's being not true.

8. William P. Alston, "Internalism and Externalism in Epistemology," reprinted in EJ, 217–218.

9. It may seem strange that a belief originally acquired in an unjustified way could in a later activation be justified just in virtue of a false memory impression of having come to know the proposition in question. But I don't find this an unacceptable result. What would be unacceptable, of course, would be the claim that a true belief adopted in an unjustified way could later become knowledge just in virtue of the subject's false memory impression that she came to know the proposition in question. The objections to internalism discussed in the preceding two paragraphs in the text have not, as far as I know, been made in print by Alston; but they are current and have been well expounded in Alvin I. Goldman, "Internalism Exposed," *Journal of Philosophy* 96, no. 6 (1999): 739–758.

10. William P. Alston, "Concepts of Epistemic Justification" (CEJ), reprinted in EJ, 98.

11. William P. Alston, "An Internalist Externalism" (IE), reprinted in EJ, 231–232. His emphasis.

12. William P. Alston, "Epistemic Circularity," reprinted in EJ, 322.

13. Something like this construal of the idea that belief, by its very nature, aims at truth is suggested by David Velleman in "The Aim of Belief," in *The Possibility of Practical Reason* (Oxford: Oxford University Press, 2000), 244–281. Note that it will not be satisfactory to take the idea to be merely that behind any belief there must be a desire that it be true (or, equivalently, that one cannot come to believe something while lacking any desire that one's belief be true). For this requirement would be satisfied in a case where a subject's reason for believing that p in the teeth of counter-evidence, and thus without epistemic justification, was the subject's very strong desire that p be true.

14. See William P. Alston, *The Reliability of Sense Perception* (RSP) (Ithaca, NY: Cornell University Press, 1993), 14.

15. By a basic visible property P, I mean one such that if S's visual experience is as if she were seeing in normal viewing conditions something having P but S is not seeing in normal viewing conditions something having P, then it follows that either viewing conditions are not normal or S's visual experience misrepresents. If S's visual experience is as if she were seeing a blue smear on a white surface in good light a short distance in front of her when she is not seeing a blue smear, etc., then it follows that either viewing conditions are abnormal or her visual experience represents inaccurately, her visual perception is not working properly. On the other hand, if S's visual experience is as if she were see-

ing a computer when she is not seeing a computer, it does not follow that either viewing conditions are abnormal or her visual experience misrepresents, since things that are not computers can in normal viewing conditions look objectively as would a computer.

2

Response to Ginet

William P. Alston

Most of Ginet's trenchant and interesting paper is devoted to arguing with me about the epistemic justification of belief. Since, as he points out in his second sentence, I have in these latter days held that 'justified' in application to beliefs fails to pick out any objective feature of beliefs about which different "theories of justification" can be correctly said to be disagreeing, I am not concerned to defend my previous theories of this supposed topic. Does that mean that I have nothing to say about Ginet's paper? If it did, I would not be maintaining my credentials as a philosopher. And, fortunately for my professional standing, much of what Ginet has to say under the rubric of 'justification' raises issues which I can discuss in other terms.

One clear case is the question as to whether beliefs are subject to voluntary control. As Ginet points out, I have more than once opined that the only apt use of 'justified' in application to beliefs is the same as the indubitably apt one in application to actions, and that this presupposes that beliefs are under voluntary control. Hence if I thought that beliefs do satisfy that condition, that it is the sort of thing that can be permitted, required, or forbidden, I would recognize that 'justified' picks out an objective feature of beliefs. The issue of voluntary control is, so to say, on the threshold of Ginet's "deontic" account of epistemic justification, rather than being something that can only be discussed within a justificationist orientation.

Ginet and I have been arguing this question for many years. But rather than replaying some of those arguments, I will add something new. In "Belief, Acceptance, and Religious Faith," loosely following Cohen's *An Essay on Belief and Acceptance*, I distinguish between *belief*, which is a complex dispositional state that one simply "finds oneself with"—not something which one adopts, deliberately or otherwise—and *acceptance*, which is a mostly similar dispositional state that one deliberately takes on by an act of mental assent, an act that is, unlike belief, under voluntary control. The dispositional state that one takes on in acceptance differs from the one that constitutes belief precisely in lacking the disposition to feel (more or less) confident that p when the question is raised. It is the lack of this confidence, of being *struck* by p's being the case, that requires the voluntary assent, the *taking* the proposition that p on board as one of one's commitments, letting it guide one's actions and reasoning. When I wrote "The Deontological Conception of Epistemic Justification," which Ginet quite properly takes as my major published statement on the voluntary control issue, I had not yet spelled out the belief-acceptance distinction as I did in "Belief, Acceptance, and Religious Faith." Having done so, this gives me an additional option for situations in which Ginet and his allies claim that one voluntarily takes on a belief. Thus in "The Deontological Conception" I considered situations like those stressed by Ginet in which "the subject has significant reason to believe that p and also significant reason not to believe that p." My main examples were a philosopher's trying to reach a conclusion on free will (between a libertarian and a compatibilist conception) and a general trying to decide how enemy forces are disposed. In neither case is it clear to them just what is the case, though they are cognizant of reasons that support each alternative. But the philosopher through frustration with continued indecision, and the general through the practical necessity of disposing his forces in some way, makes a decision anyway. In that earlier essay, I suggested that both cases are better construed as voluntarily adopting a working assumption rather than a belief. But now I prefer to suggest that they are best construed as accepting a proposition. That goes beyond an assumption in that it involves a definite commitment to the truth of the proposition, albeit one that needs more or less constant reinforcement to be maintained.

I would say the same about Ginet's example of trying to choose between continuing to believe, as he seems to remember, that he handed his wife the checkbook or to form the belief that he didn't, as she asserted, or to suspend judgment for the moment. He claims that he can make any of these choices at will, for example, to believe that he did not hand her the checkbook. But in terms of the belief-acceptance distinction, I find it impossible to believe that Ginet, or anyone else, could voluntarily bring it about that he is so disposed as to spontaneously *feel confident* that p whenever he considers the question. A much more plausible supposition is that all he can do at will is to accept the proposition that he didn't hand her the checkbook, as 'accept' was explained above. (And for what it's worth, having known both Carl and his wife Sally for forty years, my money is on Sally!)

In a recent article, "Deciding to Believe," Ginet distinguishes between belief and acceptance differently. There he holds that belief differs from acceptance by its involving "counting on the truth of p," and he dissents from Cohen's view that the differentia is that belief involves a disposition to "feel it true that p" when the question arises. This is a shift from his earlier view in *Knowledge, Perception, and Memory*, where his favored locution for believing that p is "feeling confident that p." It is clear to me that feeling confident that p is not under direct voluntary control. As for counting on the truth of p, I am inclined to make the same judgment, but, at the moment, am feeling less confident of it.

In the remainder of this response I will discuss issues raised by Ginet but do so in a way that avoids applying 'justified' to beliefs. First, consider what he calls the "less important" of my objections to his form of internalism about epistemic justification. Ginet's version of internalism holds that any fact that contributes to the justificatory status of S's belief that p is directly recognizable by S. His argument for this depends on his "deontic" conception of epistemic justification.

> Assuming that S has the concept of justification for being confident that p, S *ought* always to possess or lack confidence that p according to whether or not he has such justification. . . . But if this is what S ought to do . . . then it is what S can do. That is, assuming that he has the relevant concepts, S can always tell whether or not he has justification for being confident that p. But this would not be so unless the difference between having such justification and not having it were always directly recognizable to S. And that would not be so if any fact contributing to a set that minimally constitutes S's having such justification were not either directly recognizable to S or entailed by something directly recognizable to S.[1]

A fact is directly recognizable to S, in Ginet's sense, if and only if provided S has the concept of that sort of fact, S needs only to reflect on the question of whether that fact obtains in order to know that it does.[2]

Since I have forsworn 'justified' in application to beliefs, it is fortunate, for our discussion, that the same issues arise for actions, at least those that are under voluntary control. Ginet cites me as objecting to an exactly parallel argument for actions as follows:

> It is not only what is directly recognizable by S that affects whether a given action is or is not justified. If the question is whether I as department chair would be justified in deciding a certain matter without consulting my colleagues I might have to do some research to determine this. Just asking myself the question wouldn't do the trick unless I had thoroughly internalized the relevant rules and regulations.[3]

In response, Ginet says that the "objection entirely misses the mark." The requirement of direct recognizability applies, he says, to the question "Do I at this moment have justification for taking such an action?" rather than "Would I be justified if I were aware of certain facts I am not presently aware of?" Well, perhaps Ginet is right with respect to just the way he frames the questions. But, unless his requirement is to have very limited application, it would also need to apply to "Would I be justified in doing this?" And, it seems clear to me that as we ordinarily speak of the justification of actions, if I discover only after having done the deed that it was something that is permitted by the relevant rules, regulations, by-laws, or whatever, we would say that I *was* justified in doing it (when

I did it), not that I became justified after I had completed my post facto research. Of course, like most normative and evaluative statuses, general regulations would render my action only prima facie justified, subject to being overridden by contrary considerations (not including, for this point, Ginet's severe restrictions on what can count for justification!). But in the absence of such overriders, my inability to directly recognize the crucial determining factors at the time of action does not prevent it from being the case that I *was* justified in doing it.

The final point of Ginet's on which I will touch has to do with whether we should say that a subject, Mo, in a world controlled by a Cartesian deceiving demon has (generally) justified beliefs, provided he forms them on the same kind of directly accessible bases as those on which we commonly form ours. This is one of the points at which philosophers' intuitions diverge sharply. Again, since I don't think that the question is well conceived, I feel no obligation to answer it. But I can explore how to understand intuitions on both sides from my pluralistic epistemic desiderata approach. Ginet is right that there is some epistemic value in Mo's belief formation. He is forming beliefs on what, so far as he can tell, are excellent grounds, and such grounds are indeed objectively excellent grounds in the actual world. But the more externalist intuition also has something right, viz., that the grounds are not objectively excellent (since not truth conducive) in the demon world. They are not such as to be objectively likely to produce mostly true beliefs, and hence they are not conducive to the attainment of the basic cognitive aim of believing what is true rather than what is false about matters of interest or importance. So both groups of epistemologists emphasize what are epistemic desiderata.

But without lapsing into an attempt to determine which one constitutes "justification," we can ask about their relative value, worth, or importance from an epistemic point of view. And to avoid begging the question by construing that point of view in an internalist or an externalist way, let's consider how subjects would rank them if they were fully apprised of the situation. To sharpen the issue, let's make Mo's counterpart in the actual world, Curley, conform to typically externalist desiderata—objectively truth-conducive grounds of belief—but not generally conform to internalist desiderata as construed by Ginet—support of beliefs from directly accessible grounds the conformity of which to self-evident epistemic principles is itself directly accessible. In particular, let's say that though Curley generally conforms to the first of Ginet's requirements, he generally fails to conform to the second. On the other hand, Mo fails to satisfy externalist desiderata but scores highly on Ginet's internalist criteria. Now we bring our two subjects out from their veil of ignorance and apprise them fully of their situation. Which of them would be more satisfied with it? Which would feel that he is further along in the cognitive endeavor? I have to assume here that Mo is being kept alive somehow despite the fact that most of his beliefs are false. And, of course, the demon would have to manage this by suitable manipulations in order to preserve the deceit.

Trying as hard as I can to be unbiased, I cannot help but think that Curley would feel better about his situation than Mo. Mo may well feel that receiving the internalist prize is not adequate compensation for being successfully duped by the demon and miserably failing in the quest for truth. While Curley would most likely feel that being downgraded by Ginet for not having directly accessible grounds (the conformity of which to directly accessible epistemic principles for taking his grounds to be adequate) is not so important, in comparison with reliably reaching the truth for the most part in what he believes. He may well think, "So long as the activation of my belief-forming tendencies results in true beliefs for the most part, why is it so important whether I have directly accessible sufficient reasons for supposing my beliefs to be justified?" Such, in broad outline, is the case for taking truth-conducively adequate grounds for belief—alternatively, generally reliable belief-forming mechanisms (habits)—to be the most important epistemic desideratum from an epistemic point of view.

In conclusion I want to thank Ginet for engaging in extensive email discussion of the issues raised by a draft of this response. I hope he learned something from it, and I certainly learned a great deal that is reflected in this version. As the saying goes, I take full responsibility for any remaining errors.

References

Alston, William P. "Belief, Acceptance, and Religious Faith." Pp. 10–27 in *Faith, Freedom, and Rationality*, edited by Jeff Jordan and Daniel Howard-Snyder. Lanham, MD: Rowman & Littlefield, 1996.

Cohen, Jonathan L. *An Essay on Belief and Acceptance*. Oxford: Clarendon Press, 1992.

Ginet, Carl. "Deciding to Believe." Pp. 63–76 in *Knowledge, Truth, and Duty*, edited by M. Steup. New York: Oxford University Press, 2001.

———. *Knowledge, Perception, and Memory*. Dordrecht, Holland: D. Reidel, 1975.

Notes

1. Carl Ginet, *Knowledge, Perception, and Memory* (Dordrecht, Holland: D. Reidel, 1975), 36. His emphasis.

2. *Knowledge, Perception, and Memory*, 34.

3 . This is a paraphrase of part of Ginet's quotation of my "Internalism and Externalism in Epistemology."

3

Sense Perception, Epistemic Practices, and Skepticism

Laurence BonJour

In his book *The Reliability of Sense Perception* (RSP),[1] Alston argues that it is impossible to establish in a non-circular way that our standard way of arriving at beliefs about the material world on the basis of sense perception ("sense perceptual practice") is reliable. The argument proceeds via detailed criticisms of the various ways in which philosophers have attempted to establish an opposing conclusion, and with one exception (to be considered further below), Alston's objections to these various attempts seem to me to be utterly decisive.

Supposing for the moment that Alston's main conclusion is correct, what exactly should we make of this result? Alston's own view is that such a conclusion is not as alarming as it might at first seem, because: (a) it is only to be expected that our most basic "belief-forming practices" could not be shown to be reliable in non-circular ways, since we have nothing beyond those practices themselves to appeal to; and (b) because it is satisfactory enough to regard our acceptance of such practices in a broadly Reidian way as "rock-bottom commitments" that are rational both because there are no viable alternatives and because they are not impugned by the sort of internal criticism that would result from their leading to contradictory beliefs. This is of a piece with Alston's more general attitude that worries about skepticism have been greatly over-emphasized in epistemological circles.

I find myself unable, however, to rest content with this Reidian solution, and in this paper I will try to explain why and invite Alston's response. In the first place, such a view seems to me to take the threat of skepticism too lightly and also to fail to appreciate fully the specific way in which the issue arises in relation to sense-perception, which I will try to elucidate. Second, a somewhat related point, Alston's view, also derived from Reid, that all "basic belief-forming practices" are essentially on a par in relation to this sort of skeptical worry seems to me to be mistaken; I think, as I will explain, that a case can still be made for the epistemological priority of introspection and a priori reason. Third, while most of Alston's criticisms of the various ways of trying to argue for the reliability of "sense perceptual practice" seem completely decisive and quite devastating, this does not seem to me to be as clearly so in the case of the one that is arguably the most historically important of all—namely the attempt to defend the resulting claims about the material world via an explanatory inference from the character of our sense experience. I will discuss these three points in the three main sections of the present paper, though limited availability of space and no doubt also of insight will make the discussion merely tentative and suggestive for the most part. My main hope is to evoke from Alston some further help with these specific points, to go along with all that I have already learned from his excellent book (and, of course, from many, many of his other writings).

I. Why There Is a Problem about Sense Perception

In my own view, the most fundamental epistemological question about sense perception is whether and why sensory experiences of various ordinary sorts constitute good reasons for thinking that the various beliefs that we arrive at as a result of them are *true* (or at least quite likely to be at least approximately true— qualifications that I will sometimes omit). By a good reason, I mean here one whose cogency is, as it might be put, intellectually transparent, capable of being grasped simply by reflection on the situation or via arguments whose individual steps have this status.

In posing this question, I have deliberately eschewed the term "justification" (or "epistemic justification"). I continue to think that there is a clear and important sense in which the beliefs that result from sense perception are justified just in case I have a good reason of the sort indicated for thinking that they are true. But I have also come to think, here to a substantial extent following Alston,[2] that the focus on justification has been relatively unhelpful in epistemological discussion, mainly because it is not clear that there are not at the very least a number of quite different concepts, answering to rather different standards, that these terms can reasonably be used to express.[3] I also think that the most important epistemological issues can be formulated clearly enough without using this disputed terminology.

The question about sense perception that I am claiming to be most fundamental is obviously related to, but still distinct from, the one on which Alston's book focuses. To have a good reason in general for thinking that the beliefs that result from sense perception are true would be to have a good, though not conclusive reason for thinking that forming beliefs in this way is a reliable "epistemic practice." But of course this practice might in fact be reliable even if no such reason could be found.

It is obvious that a question of this general sort can be raised about *any* way of arriving at beliefs on the basis of any sort of "experience," taking this latter notion broadly enough to include any conscious undergoing. But it does not follow, as Alston (and many others) seem to assume, that all such questions are on a par with each other or can only be answered in the same ways. In what follows, I want to try to spell out more fully than is usually done the deepest intellectual motivation for the specific question about beliefs arrived at on the basis of sensory experience—a motivation that seems to me to make the Reidian response that Alston favors quite unsatisfying. The following section will then try to argue that the analogous issues about introspection and a priori reason are not entirely parallel in this respect, thereby opening the door in those cases to more satisfactory responses (and setting the stage for the explanatory argument to be considered in the final section). My own view, however, is that the utter unsatisfactoriness of the Reidian answer to the question concerning sense perception does not depend on whether or not more satisfactory answers are available in other areas.

What then is it that gives the question about beliefs arrived at on the basis of sense experience its distinctive force and urgency? Here, there are two closely related facts about the situation that are relevant, both of them basically quite obvious, but each still worthy of specific discussion. In considering them, it will be helpful to have a moderately specific example in front of us.

As I sit in my study and look out my window, I form a variety of beliefs about the rather tangled portion of my yard that is (as I believe) within my view: that there is a row of evergreen trees extending diagonally into the distance, that there are bare branches and twigs projecting in complicated specific patterns from the left (from a deciduous tree that is mostly out of view), that there is a portion of roof below (over the front door) and another extending from above and downward to the right, that the lower roof is littered with soggy, partially decomposed leaves, that there are vines extending up one of the trees, and so on. I have not tried to describe directly the specific features of sense experience, specifically visual experience, that give rise to these beliefs, but at least their approximate contours seem likely to be familiar to anyone who enjoys experiences of this general sort.

The first fact that needs to be noticed about this situation is what Lovejoy long ago referred to as *epistemological dualism*[4]: The experience on the basis of which I form the beliefs in question is ontologically quite distinct from the putative objects that the beliefs are about. My experience of the (apparent) roof is one thing and the roof itself quite another. To be sure, philosophers operating under the banner of "direct realism" have sometimes denied or at least seemed to deny this basic fact. I have no room here for any real discussion of views of this kind, but can only say that no version of direct realism that has even minimal plausibility seems to me to genuinely support such a denial.[5]

A second, related fact about the perceptual situation is that the features of experience on the basis of which I arrive at my various perceptual beliefs are in general quite distinct from the features that those beliefs ascribe to various material objects. Thus, for example, the experience on the basis of which I come to believe in the existence and characteristics of the deciduous branches and twigs involves what might be described as colored lines of various colors, shapes, and thicknesses in my visual field. Perhaps a few of the features of the lines are the very same features that are ascribed to the branches and twigs, but this is not at all clearly so, and in any case many of the correlative features are clearly distinct: The lines apparently intersect even where the twigs I believe in do not; a bright patch on one of the lines (due, as I believe, to sunlight) does not lead to a corresponding belief in a different color at that point on the branch; and of course many of the features ascribed to the branches and twigs (solidity, roughness, dampness, etc.) are not even correlated in any very close way with features of my experience.

Claims of this sort may seem to be reminiscent of the classical sense-datum theory, a view that many will regard as having been decisively refuted. I also have no room in this paper for an extensive discussion of the ontology of sense experience. But perhaps it will help if I say that while I myself am inclined to favor an "adverbial" account of sense experience, this has in my view no bearing at all on the point presently at issue. Adverbially characterized experiential states are still ontologically quite distinct from external material objects, and the adverbial features of those states are, if anything, even more clearly distinct from the properties of material objects than would be the properties of sense-data. And this would be so even if it were the case (as seems to me clearly not to be the case) that those adverbial properties could only be described obliquely in terms of the sorts of material objects that a normal perceiver will take to be present when they occur.

The general picture which all of this seems to lead to is this. In arriving at beliefs about the material world on the basis of perceptual experience in the way that we standardly do, we are accepting claims about what is true in one ontological region, about the existence and properties of one general kind of object, on the basis of facts that pertain to a quite separate ontological region, to quite distinct sorts of objects or states and largely or entirely distinct features of these latter entities. And this is why the question of whether the experiential starting point on the basis of which we in fact accept those beliefs is a good reason for thinking that they are true arises so urgently. Why is accepting beliefs about *that* on the basis of facts about *this* likely to lead us to the truth? Clearly not just any "belief-forming practice" of this general form would be likely to lead to true beliefs or would be even marginally reasonable. So what is different about this one, beyond its being familiar and normally taken for granted? It is this seemingly fundamental question that underlies the long history of philosophical attempts to grapple with "the problem of the external world."[6]

Seen from this perspective, Alston's conclusion—which amounts in my terms to saying that there simply is no non-circular reason for thinking that the experiences make it likely that the beliefs they lead to are true—seems very alarming indeed, in effect a confession that at this very fundamental point our cognitive practice is based on nothing at all beyond familiarity and/or native instinct.

Moreover, when seen in this light, the idea of a Reidian commitment offers very little solace. Such a commitment is in Alston's view based upon or at least motivated by two main facts: (a) that there is no real alternative, and (b) that accepting beliefs in this way leads (at least for the most part) to consistent results. Here point (a) seems entirely unhelpful. For there are of course, in principle at least, many other possible ways of forming beliefs about the material world, if having some reason to think that the resulting beliefs are likely to be true is not required. We could accept beliefs on the basis of anything from wishful thinking to astrological prediction. To be sure, many of these alternatives are in fact not equally practical because we do not have the same unproblematic access to the relevant "evidence" that we do to the character of our experiences—a point to be illuminated in the following section. But the Reidian cannot appeal to our special access to the content of experience without undermining his claim that all "belief-forming practices" are on a par.

Part (b) of the Reidian rationale is at least a little better, since being internally free of contradiction in this way seems plausibly to be a necessary condition for a way of accepting beliefs that is likely to lead to the truth—though this claim relies on another "belief-forming practice," a priori insight, for whose reliability there is, in Alston's view, also no non-circular argument possible. But this condition is in any case plainly not sufficient, and it is far from clear that there are not other ways of arriving at such beliefs that would meet it equally well if not better (accepting beliefs about the material world on the basis of sufficiently consistent wishful thinking is an initially plausible example).

The result here seems to me to be that the Reidian commitment to our standard sense perceptual practice is rational only in the *very* weak sense that: (a) we need to have some way of arriving at beliefs about the material world (though the status of even this claim is uncertain at this point); (b) this way of arriving at beliefs is at least natural and familiar, supported by "animal faith" if nothing else; and (c) this way of arriving at beliefs satisfies the minimal necessary condition of not landing us in contradictions and other sorts of conflicts. But is there really nothing better than this to be said in favor of the epistemic relevance of sense perception? In the balance of this paper, I will explore a broadly traditional alternative, one that Alston's arguments do not seem to me to have ruled out in any decisive way.

II. Two Starting Points for an Epistemological Account of Sense Perception

I have argued that Alston's idea of a "Reidian commitment" fails to constitute a satisfactory response to the basic issue about sense perception. One of Alston's central claims, however—though this is suggested more than argued for in detail in the book that I am primarily dealing with—is that nothing better is to be had, that all of our "belief-forming practices" are fundamentally in the same boat, leaving us with no place to start in the attempt to find a reason for thinking that our perceptual beliefs are likely to be true that is not equally insecure. The traditional view, of course, is that there are two main bases for belief whose epistemological status is more secure and which might therefore provide a more secure starting point: (i) introspective awareness of one's own states of mind and (ii) a priori reason or insight. In the present section, I will try to give an account of each of these, aiming mainly in each case at showing why, contrary to Reid, Alston, Plantinga, and others, the "belief-forming practices" in question, while not immune to any sort of skeptical worry, do not raise the same sort of urgent issue that I have argued to pertain to sense perception. (As will be seen, neither account is simply identical to the most traditional views in these areas, which seem to me to be suggestive but in the end inadequate.)

A. Introspection

Return to the example considered above of my perceptual experience as I look out my window. In any ordinary frame of mind, that experience would lead me to accept various beliefs of the sort earlier indicated about the material world. But I can, of course, also come to have beliefs about the content of the conscious experience itself, beliefs of the general sort briefly indicated earlier: that it involves a complicated pattern of lines of various colors and thicknesses intersecting with each other (and more detailed descriptions of that pattern); that it involves large patches of green (and more specific descriptions of the relative sizes and shapes and more specific colors of those patches); and so on. I form these beliefs on the basis of my awareness of the conscious sensory experience itself.

Here we have a situation that might initially seem parallel to the case of perceptual beliefs about the material world considered earlier: There is a certain sort of experience on the basis of which I come to form and accept various beliefs about a certain ontological region. Thus, a question may be asked that is at least superficially parallel to the one raised earlier: What reason is there for thinking that the experiences on the basis of which I form these beliefs provide good reasons for thinking that they are true? But a little reflection reveals that the two cases are in fact not at all closely parallel. For whereas in the earlier case of perceptual beliefs about the material world, the experiences upon which they are based and the subject matter of the beliefs themselves (that in virtue of which they are true or false) are ontologically quite distinct, in the case with which we are presently concerned, this ontological gap simply does not exist: The beliefs are about the *very* experience on the basis of which they are accepted, so that whether or not they are true depends on only the character of that experience itself. This is the basic answer to Reid's question, cited by Alston (RSP, 126–127), as to why those who raise skeptical questions with regard to beliefs about the material world do not raise parallel skeptical questions pertaining to beliefs about their own experiences: When the situation is properly understood there is simply no dialectical room for such a parallel question. And this is also, of course, the most fundamental insight that underlies the broad tradition of Cartesian epistemology.[7]

Consider again the case we are focusing on. I have a complicated passage of sensory experience, of whose content I am aware in the most basic way simply by having it—it is after all *conscious* experience. I also have various concepts for describing that experiential content available to me, concepts whose content I presumably understand, where this means that I understand what a passage of experience has to be like to be properly describable by such a concept. If all this is so, then I am seemingly in an excellent position to judge whether a given conceptual description fits a particular passage of experience. I can directly compare the conceptual content of the conceptual description with the experiential content of the experience it purports to describe and see whether or not they are in accord (where this will normally mean that the more specific content of the experience falls under the more abstract content of the conceptual description).

If this characterization of the basic situation is correct, then it seems overwhelmingly plausible to say that my awareness of the experiential content, an awareness that is intrinsic to the conscious experience itself rather than a reflective awareness of it from the outside, can offer a good reason to think that a particular conceptual description of that experience is correct. And this is a situation that, as far as I can see, can only obtain where it is conscious experience that is the subject matter of the beliefs in question—which is why, according to this view, conscious experience possesses a fundamental kind of epistemological primacy.

Contrary to what those in the Cartesian tradition have standardly claimed, however, nothing about the situation as described supports the claim that the resulting beliefs are infallible or incorrigible or completely certain. Though the character of my conscious experience is directly accessible to me in a way that no other contingent state of affairs possibly could be, I might still make mistakes about it—through carelessness or distraction or some other similar sort of inadvertence. Such mistakes are most obviously possible either where the experience is complicated or where the conceptual description is complicated or extremely precise. Indeed, extreme situations of these kinds can pretty obviously make some degree of error more likely than not.

This point does not, however, alter the fact that the specific and extremely urgent skeptical problem that we have seen arise for beliefs about the material world derived from sense perception simply *does not arise at all* for introspective beliefs about the character of one's own experience—nor, I submit, for other sorts of introspection pertaining to the contents of other conscious states, for basically parallel reasons. For these cases, there is a straightforward account of why the experiences in question constitute good reasons for the resulting beliefs, even if not one that precludes all possibility of error. And this in turn is enough to make introspection a more secure starting point for further epistemological inquiry.

B. A Priori Insight

But of course it is abundantly clear that good reasons for thinking that perceptual beliefs are likely to be true cannot be based solely on introspective beliefs about the character of that sense experience, nor even about the whole range of conscious experience, no matter how secure these introspective beliefs may themselves be. To arrive at such reasons, something like a cogent argument from the character of such experience to the likely truth of the claims about the material world that are based on it will be needed. And, any such argument will obviously require premises or principles of reasoning whose justification can in the end only be a priori in character. It is thus no accident that a priori insight was the second main foundational element in the classical Cartesian picture.

Philosophers in that tradition have sometimes tried to give an account of a priori insight that is superficially parallel to that offered for introspection. But if the foregoing account of the special status of introspection is right, it is clear that this will not work, that the two cases are not at all closely parallel. For while the subject matter of beliefs about conscious experience is the very experiential content on the basis of which they are accepted, this is obviously not so for the standard sorts of a priori beliefs. Such beliefs are arrived at on the basis of a kind of experience, in the broadest sense of something that one consciously undergoes, even though not the sort of experience that would make them a posteriori or empirical.[8] But this experience, roughly that of subjectively finding a proposition or argumentative transition to be (apparently) necessary, is obviously quite distinct from the things that the resulting beliefs are about—which I will assume here, with no real argument, to be abstract entities, mainly properties of various sorts. Thus, the sort of account that was offered for why the experiences upon which introspective beliefs are based constitute good reasons for thinking that they are true is simply not applicable to the case of a priori beliefs.

But while the case of the a priori is not parallel to that of introspection, it is, I want to suggest, still not parallel to that of sense perception either. In the case of sense perception, the experiential state is entirely distinct from the realm of objects that the resulting belief is about, leaving it completely uncertain, in the absence of a connecting argument of some sort, why facts in the former realm should be regarded as good reasons for beliefs about the latter realm. But with regard to a priori beliefs, there is a subtle but crucial way in which this is not so.

This point can be approached by asking what makes it the case that an a priori insight, say the insight that nothing can be both red and blue all over at the same time, is genuinely about those properties and that relation in a way that is intelligible to the person in question—which is, of course, essential for it to be that specific insight at all. On the currently most popular theory of mental content, mental states have the content that they do by involving symbols in what is described metaphorically as "the language of thought"—where what makes a symbol merely a symbol is that it is not intrinsically about whatever it stands for, but plays this role only in virtue of some external relation in which it stands. But despite the popularity of this view, it is, I believe, easy to see that it cannot be correct. For if all that is in a person's mind when he or she thinks of redness and greenness is two symbols, analogous to the words "red" and "green," then such a person does not really understand what it is that he or she is thinking about—and so does not genuinely have any intelligible thought at all. And to say that what is in such a person's mind is not merely the symbol, but also an independent understanding of its meaning, is to abandon the symbolic view and raise anew the issue of what this further understanding amounts to.

My suggestion is that any account of thought content that makes it possible for a person to genuinely grasp the content of his or her thoughts in an intelligible way will have to say in the end that anything that genuinely qualifies as a thought (in general) or apparent insight (in particular) that nothing can be red and blue all over at the same time must essentially involve in some way the very properties that this thought is about, and involve them in a way that shapes the conscious content of the thought itself. Thus, for a person to entertain in an intelligible way the proposition that nothing can be both red and blue all over at the same time essentially involves that person having a kind of non-symbolic awareness of the properties in question and of the relation of incompatibility that the proposition holds to exist between them. And it is, of course, this awareness of its various ingredients that seemingly makes the resulting a priori insight or apparent insight possible: Being aware of the two properties in question, such a person finds it immediately apparent that they necessarily exclude each other and thus that the proposition in question must be true.

It is obvious that skeptical questions can still be raised about this sort of picture. Even if a person who has an apparent a priori insight has a kind of awareness of the relevant properties, it can still be questioned whether the resulting apparent insights into the character and relations of these properties constitute genuinely good reasons to think that the claims in question are true. Perhaps the seeming grasp of necessity that is involved is a kind of illusion. Certainly there is no clear way to guarantee that a mind that has access to properties in this way will also be able to accurately discern necessary connections among them.

Thus, we have a second way in which the case of the a priori is not strictly parallel to the case of introspection: In addition to the fact that the "experience" on which a priori beliefs are based is not what those beliefs are about, it must · also be admitted that it is a good deal less obvious that the sort of judgment that is being made is one that is reliably within our powers. While being able to correctly judge the application of a conceptual description to the conscious content of our experience is something that it is hard to see how we could be generally unable to do, it is easier to question whether the sort of awareness of properties that we must have in order to understand propositions that are about them really enables us to discern their necessary features and relations in an accurate way.

But there are at least three reasons why this sort of skepticism is still very different from that which pertains to the case of perceptual beliefs. The first is that the two situations are once again not at all closely parallel. In the sense perception case, we have found so far *no reason at all* for thinking that the experience in question has any bearing on the subject matter of the resulting beliefs—beyond the fact that we naturally or instinctively assume this. Whereas, in the a priori case, the alleged insights in question are, as we have seen, based on an awareness of the very entities which the resulting beliefs are about, the issue being only whether the awareness we have of those entities is adequate to enable us to arrive at beliefs of this sort in an accurate way. This is still obviously a serious question. But it is not at all parallel to the question about sense perception because the very relevance of the "experience" in question to the truth of the resulting beliefs is not in doubt in the same radical way.

Second, while I can see no way to provide a guarantee that the sort of access we have to the properties which a priori beliefs are about is sufficient for us to arrive at such beliefs in a generally accurate way, it seems broadly reasonable to suppose that this is so, given that we seem to find ourselves able to do it in a pervasive and systematic way. What, after all, does intelligence amount to if not the ability to grasp connections or relations between one thing and another, given an appropriate awareness of them? Thus, while a certain sort of skepticism is admittedly possible in the case of the a priori, there seems to be no compelling reason to take it seriously. Whereas in the case of sense perception, as argued above, the very structure of the situation makes the skeptical worry extremely urgent indeed.

Third, not only is there no very compelling reason to take the skeptical concern about the a priori seriously, it is clearly intellectually catastrophic to do so. For if we really do not have the capacity to accurately discern necessary features of the properties that we understand, then any sort of reasoning or intellectual inquiry is inherently futile, including of course any attempt to answer or even formulate this skeptical worry itself. Thus, if we are not to commit what is at least attempted intellectual suicide, we have no alternative but to accept a priori insight as generally accurate and hence as a basis for justification. Perhaps this amounts to a Reidian commitment of sorts, but one that is substantially less avoidable than in the case of sense perception.

III. Can an Inference from Sense Experience to the Material World Be Justified?

I turn finally to the issue of whether it is possible to argue on the basis of the starting points just defended that our sensory experiences do in fact constitute good reasons for thinking that the beliefs about the material world that we arrive at on the basis of them are at least approximately true—and hence, in Alston's formulation, that sense perceptual practice is indeed reliable. A full discussion of this issue is obviously impossible within the confines of this paper. My more limited aim is to present the main outlines of what I regard as the best version of such a justificatory argument, clarify Alston's main objections in relation to that version, and explain why those objections seem to me far less decisive than he claims.[9]

A. The Explanatory Argument

As indicated at the beginning of the paper, the central idea of the argument to be considered is that the hypothesis that there is a physical world corresponding at least approximately to our perceptual beliefs is the best explanation of the sensory experiences upon the basis of which we arrive at those beliefs—where "best" here must be understood in a way that yields the result that the best explanation is thereby more likely to be true than competing explanations and sufficiently more likely to make it likely to be true (or approximately true) simpliciter.

The first point to be made about this argument concerns the precise nature of the explanandum. It is tempting to appeal here to characterizations of sensory experience in physical object terms: in relation to the example given earlier, to the fact that it looks as though there are trees and branches and rooflines; or to the corresponding "adverbial" characterizations of such experiences: being appeared to such-and-such treely, and the like. But while such characterizations of sensory experience are very natural, they obviously depend on the very correlation between experiences and physical objects that we rely on in forming our perceptual beliefs, the reliability of which is precisely the central point at issue. It is hard to say whether this correlation (which I will refer to as the standard correlation) is learned or innate or some combination of the two, but to rely on a characterization of experience that depends on it, and in particular to take for granted that the very different experiences that it lumps together under one physical-object-related characterization really have something importantly in common that demands a common explanation, seems to me to incur too great a risk of begging the main question at issue.

Thus, to find an adequate basis for the sort of argument we are looking for, we must, I think, try to think of sensory experiences in their own right, independently of any physical-object-based characterization. This is admittedly hard to do and raises serious problems about the availability of the resulting argument to ordinary perceivers, but I think that the difficulties in this area have also been exaggerated to some extent. In fact, I would suggest, the physical-object characterizations already rejected as providing the main description of sensory experience can still be helpful, if used with care, in pointing toward the various features of experience considered in itself that the argument should rely on. Instead of merely saying that there seems to be a certain sort of object before me, one must say instead that I am having the sort of experience one would have (according to the standard correlation) when perceiving a certain sort of object from a certain perspective at a certain approximate distance, etc., relying on the reader's familiarity with the standard correlation to allow him to fix on at least approximately the sort of experience, envisioned in its own right, that is in question. (See the earlier example for a very modest and approximate effort in this direction.)

The fundamental idea is then that the intrinsic features of our sensory experience, and especially the extended patterns into which that experience falls, are best explained by the hypothesis that those experiences reflect and are systematically caused by a world of physical objects and processes, arranged in three-dimensional space, existing through time, and obeying various causal laws, all in ways that correspond in close approximation to our common-sense conception. Call this the *common-sense hypothesis*. My suggestion would be that the rationale for this hypothesis is best understood in several distinct stages, starting with the broad outlines and gradually filling in more specific details. The first stage, to which most of my attention will be devoted here, appeals primarily to spatial patterns of experience and invokes a corresponding explanation in terms of the spatial characteristics and arrangement of material objects.[10]

Think then, as a kind of schematic example, of the sorts of experiences one might have, according to the standard correlation, while observing and moving through and around a moderately large array of physical objects of relatively regular shapes, some of them large enough to block the view of others from some perspectives, which occupy a space the size of perhaps a city block or so, in relatively good, uniform lighting, and with normally functioning sense organs. (Remember that the point of these descriptions is merely to focus attention on some relatively specific sorts and patterns of experience, not to assume that this is the way that those experiences must be explained.) Consider the experiences correlated, as we think, with moving around, for example, a cube with a three-foot edge, while looking at its various sides and top, from closer and farther distances, thereby experiencing patches of color that are variously square, trapezoidal, and irregularly quadrilateral and that shade gradually into each other in ways that can be reversed or repeated by changing the apparent direction of motion (where this involves both kinaesthetic experiences of various sorts and experiences that according to the standard correlation are experiences of a human body, namely one's own). Consider now the experiences correlated, as we think (I will henceforth assume this qualification) with moving through the collection of objects, arriving back at the same apparent point from different directions, and observing the ways in which some objects are temporarily occluded by others. Consider also the experiences associated with touching the various objects in various ways, feeling their surfaces and corners and curves, perhaps climbing onto some of them, while observing visually at the same time.

It seems obvious that we often have sets of experiences of this general sort that are highly regular in the sense that they can be repeated and varied in orderly and predictable ways. Such regularities, as Alston points out (RSP, 71–72), are not complete enough to constitute even approximate natural laws. From the standpoint of the standard correlation, this is due mainly to events that take place outside of experience (objects moved, altered, etc.), to large-scale changes of location of the observer (perhaps while asleep), and to the existence of multiple objects that are effectively indiscernible from each other. But they are still far too regular and pervasive not to demand an explanation. And one obvious explanation is the one that appeals to the common-sense hypothesis: There are approximate regularities of this sort in experience because that experience is produced in regular ways by a fairly stable world of objects in three-dimensional space, having approximately the shapes that common-sense attributes to them, through which observers move in the ways that they common-sensically seem to do. This explanation also needs to say something about the causal mechanisms via which the resulting experiences are produced, but nothing, I think, that is nearly as specific as the full modern scientific account. It is enough, I would suggest, to say roughly that the various sorts of experience depend on sensory receptors located in specific parts of the body, that the experiences result from signals of some sort that travel in approximately straight lines, that many of these signals are substantially weakened in proportion to the distance traversed, and that touch requires actual contact with the object by some part of the body, with the detail and character of the resulting experience depending on which part is involved.[11]

Obviously this is only the roughest characterization of an explanation and an explanatory argument about which much more would have to be said in even an approximately complete account. But for present purposes I will limit myself to a series of supplementary comments, each of them only a quick approximation to a longer story, before turning to a consideration of Alston's objections.

First, in a situation of the sort described, it seems clear that the common-sense hypothesis would enable me to predict future experiences as well as explain past ones: to predict, for example, the various experiences I would have while moving closer to or farther away from or in some other direction in relation to a given apparent object. Alston (RSP, 97–101) takes this to be an important addition to the explanatory argument, but I would suggest that it was always assumed by proponents of such arguments, even if not mentioned as explicitly as it might have been. This is just to say that the sort of explanatory inference in question is an instance of the fairly standard "hypothetico-deductive method," in which the reason for thinking that an explanatory hypothesis is true depends on both its capacity to explain previous data of the relevant sort and its capacity to predict new data of the same kind.

Second, even if entirely successful, the argument suggested so far would yield only what might be thought of as the spatio-temporal framework of the external world, involving objects of various sizes and shapes, arranged in space, and varying over time. In other words, it would account mainly for primary qualities. Already included, however, would be that highly questionable member of Locke's list of primary qualities, namely solidity in the sense of at least relative impenetrability and rigidity, since this is needed to explain the patterns involving contact between such objects when they move—including, of course, the contact involved in touching them with a part of the observer's body. Other broadly causal properties could, I submit, be added on the basis of correlations between apparent changes in these initial qualities, as reflected in the experiential pattern, together with other correlated sensory qualities: such things as the effects of an object that is a source of heat on surrounding objects that are subject to melting or burning, together with the sensations of heat themselves, all varying in strength in proportion to the distance between the objects in question (including the observer) and also reflecting the way in which one object may be shielded by another. To fill out this account to include all of the relevant causal properties, some arrived at on the basis of others and eventually extending to those whose causes and effects are not directly observable, is a formidable task, but I can see no reason to think it cannot be successfully accomplished.

Third, secondary qualities require a quite different story. At best the explanatory argument will justify attributing to physical objects only those features that are clearly required to explain the character of our experience. It thus seems clear that it will not extend to secondary qualities like color, as commonsensically conceived, but only to the causal powers required to systematically produce experiences of such qualities in us, thus leading to the familiar Lockean view of such qualities as existing only in the mind and not genuinely in the external object. For this reason, the hypothesis in question might more properly be labeled only as "quasi-commonsensical." (Alston [RSP, 65–66] deals with secondary qualities by adopting the view, also reflected somewhat inconsistently in some of Locke's discussion, that judgments about them attribute only such causal powers.)

What then are Alston's objections to an explanatory argument of this sort, one that also appeals to successful prediction of experience? Though the issue is complicated by the fact that the argument I am suggesting is not quite the version of an explanatory argument that Alston seems to have foremost in mind, it seems to me that he would offer two main objections, one that he presents very briefly and that seems to me to require only an equally brief response, and one—historically the main one—that will require more extended discussion.

B. The Limitation to One's Own Experience

The briefer argument is in effect a reminder that one dimension of the problem of the external world is the problem of other minds. I have spoken so far as though the patterns of experience that provide the explanandum for the explanatory argument are shared by all human perceivers. But of course, as Alston points out (RSP, 101), to base the argument on such an assumption would be utterly question-begging, since it is clear that my reasons for thinking that there are any other experiencing subjects at all, let alone that they have experience similar to mine, themselves depend on beliefs about mind-external objects arrived at via sense perception. Thus the explanandum for the sort of argument that I am suggesting must be initially limited to the sensory experience of the single person who is putting it forward.

How serious a problem does this create? Alston's claim is that it is very serious indeed. His discussion of the point focuses on the dimension of prediction mentioned in the previous comment, but the general suggestion seems to be that the order in my experience, including that involved in successful predictions of future experience on the basis of the common-sense hypothesis, might simply be a matter of luck—by which, I take it, he means that this order might result entirely from chance, rather than being truly explained by the common-sense hypothesis or any of its (yet to be discussed) competitors. I might, he in effect suggests, be the only one out of the billions of human beings who have existed whose experience has reflected the orderly patterns in question—though of course any view about the size of the relevant population is equally something that cannot be assumed at the outset of the argument, and the main issue in any case is simply how improbable it really is that mere chance would produce orderly experiences of the sorts in question.

My own view, though I do not know how to argue for it briefly on other than sheerly intuitive grounds, is that this improbability in relation to even a few minutes' worth of experience in a simple environment of the sort described earlier is astronomically great, far greater than the several billion to one that Alston seems to propose. Think again of the experiences I have as I walk through and around my simple group of objects, anticipating my experiences as I go. Think of the indefinitely large number of other experiences, even limiting myself to visual experiences of the same general sort, that are abstractly possible and that would fail to even approximately satisfy my expectations. And now expand the cases to include more complicated apparent environments and longer stretches of experience. My suggestion would be that even the experiences I have in one eight-hour day are enough to make the improbability that all this is due to chance large enough to satisfy any reasonable standard short of complete certainty—even though chance remains a bare possibility, however increasingly remote that possibility may become.

Thus, I submit, one person's experience is more than enough to create an overwhelming demand for a non-chance explanation and thereby to make a compelling case for the truth of the best such explanation, assuming that one can be determined. In order to arrive at a justified belief in the portions of the external world that are beyond that person's immediate purview, however, the experience of other people will have to eventually be brought in. The details of this would be very complicated, involving among other things something like the argument from analogy and an account of the justification of testimony, but I again see no reason to think that all of the details could not be successfully worked out and elaborated.

C. Alternative Explanations

Alston's other main objection, and the one to which he devotes by far the larger share of his discussion, is the claim that the common-sense hypothesis cannot be shown to be superior to a variety of alternative explanations—or at least not clearly enough superior to warrant concluding on the basis of this argument that it is likely to be true. He lists the following main kinds of alternatives:

(1) Cartesian demon explanation
(2) Berkeleyan God explanation
(3) Alternative physical explanations
(4) Panpsychist explanation
(5) Self-generation explanation (RSP, 77)

This listing seems to me, however, less than fully perspicuous, because it includes explanations of very different kinds to which very different sorts of responses are appropriate. Thus I will begin by attempting to distinguish three broad categories into which such alternative explanations might fall.[12]

The first category consists of explanations in which many of the features of experience are explained by systematically correlated features of the entity or entities appealed to in the explanation so that a particular feature of experience is caused by a correlated feature of the explanatory entities in such a way that it can reasonably be said, from an intuitive standpoint, to be a perception, albeit perhaps a highly perspectival or distorted one, of that correlated feature. As Alston himself puts it at one point, such explanations appeal to "the causal impact on the subject of a variegated environing world of finite substances on roughly the same scale as physical substances" (RSP, 75). The common-sense hypothesis obviously falls into this category. For example, the size and shape of a particular patch of color in my visual field might be explained by appeal to correlated features of the surface of an external object, together with my distance from it, the angle from which I am looking, etc. Appealing to a rough but suggestive comparison, I will refer to an explanation of this sort as an analog explanation.

The alternative to an analog explanation is one in which the features of experience are not systematically correlated with and caused by features of the entity or entities that produce it. Consider, for example, the explanation that appeals to the familiar idea of a Cartesian demon. When I experience a patch of color of a certain specific shape, I am not, according to this explanation, in anything like a perceptual relation to a feature of the entity appealed to in the explanation, namely the demon. The demon has no features that could play this role, and I am not perceiving any of the features that it actually has.

How then are the experiences that the demon produces in me determined? One answer, which seems to me (though Alston disagrees) to be the only tenable one, is that the demon is relying on some sort of representation or model of the common-sense physical world in order to determine which experiences it should cause me to have. But my experiences are not directly caused by its representation, nor am I experiencing the features of that representation in any meaningful sense. Instead, the demon is producing experiences in me which are of the sort that I would have if the world that fits that representation really existed and I was located in it in a specific way, experiences that emulate the experience that I would have if the common-sense hypothesis were true—in at least approximately the way that a computer game might emulate the experience one would have in a certain situation. Exploiting the same analogy referred to earlier, I will refer to an explanation that has this character as a digital explanation.

Most of the alternatives to the common-sense hypothesis offered in the literature on this topic fall into one of these first two categories, with the overwhelming majority falling into the second. But there is also, as Alston points out, a third initially possible alternative: an explanation that appeals to the same sort of entity or entities as what I am calling a digital explanation, for example a Cartesian demon, but that does not invoke anything like a representation of the world depicted by the common-sense hypothesis to account for the details of experience. Obviously those details will have to somehow be accounted for by any plausible version of such an explanation, but I will leave for later discussion the issue of how this might be accomplished. I will refer to explanations of this third sort as non-digital skeptical explanations.

Returning now to Alston's list of alternatives to the common-sense hypothesis, it is clear that alternatives (1) and (2), which Alston admits not to be importantly different, will include both digital and non-digital skeptical versions. So also will alternative (5). Alternative (3), on the other hand, apparently consists of alternative analog explanations, ones that appeal to physical entities and processes:

> Another large class of explanations that is rarely given so much as a nod comprises those that invoke physical causes with quite different properties from

those we believe ourselves to perceive; there will, of course, have to be suitably
different laws to make it possible for these bodies and forces to produce our
sense experience. (RSP, 74)

He adds that "The range of such explanations is limited only by our ingenuity"
(RSP, 74).

Just what is included in category (4), on the other hand, seems to me to be
harder to sort out, and I have no space here for an adequate exploration. Alston
mentions Leibniz and Whitehead in particular, and the general idea seems to be
that the entities invoked by such explanations are not physical in character, but
rather have perceptions or feelings of some sort, albeit not in a way that involves
full consciousness of the human sort. To the extent that I can figure out what
Alston has in mind here, there seem to me to be two rather different general possibilities. One is that the psychical entities in question are in fact arranged in
space and have, at least as groups, genuinely spatial features, with their non-
physical character consisting merely in their also having psychical qualities at
some level. This would be the view, suggested by Alston, that matter is not
"(completely) dead" (RSP, 75). Assuming that features of my experiences are
correlated with and caused by real features of complexes of such entities, such
an explanation would fall into the general category of analog explanations. A
view like Leibniz's own, on the other hand, according to which there is no real
space but only perceptions that seem to reflect space and spatial entities, would
be either a digital explanation (if those perceptions are generated in accordance
with a representation or model of the common-sense world) or a non-digital
skeptical explanation (if they are generated in some other way). Leibniz's own
view, since the monads are "windowless," seems to be a version of a "self-
generation explanation," but I suppose it would be possible to have a telepathic
version in which one monad's perceptions are partially caused by those of other
monads. Since none of the monads really have spatial features or anything like
them, this would still be either a digital explanation or a non-digital skeptical
explanation under my classification.

The main reason for distinguishing these various categories of explanations
is that they require, in my judgment, very different sorts of responses. My view
concerning alternative analog explanations can be put very simply: I can see no
reason to think that there are any that (i) differ from the common-sense hypothesis enough to make it no longer at least approximately correct and that (ii) are at
least minimally plausible. I have no space here for a full discussion of the issues
surrounding this claim, but the main points are the following (in which I focus
mainly on the issue of the spatial character of the entities invoked by the alternative explanations). First, it is very hard to see how the spatial features of experience could be explained in analog fashion by anything other than a spatial
world: Certainly a multi-dimensional world seems needed to account for the
various sorts of experiential paths that return to the same experiential starting

point, and it is hard to see how such a world could be anything but spatial. Second, for essentially the same reason, a world that is spatially two-dimensional does not seem to have enough internal structure to account for all of the possible experiential sequences and variations. Thus an alternative analog hypothesis would apparently have to involve at least a three-dimensional spatial world containing objects whose shapes and spatial relations differ systematically from those that are actually reflected in our experience, with the experiences in question thus involving what amounts to a systematic distortion of what is really to be found in the world. But if the differences in question are supposed to be large enough to be interesting, then the very features that make the common-sense hypothesis work so well also seem to me to make it hard to see how such an alternative hypothesis could work at all. Here the crucial point is that while it is easy to imagine a systematic distortion of secondary qualities like color, whose relations to other qualities (of the same and other sorts) are sufficiently unstructured that they can be varied more or less independently, it is difficult or impossible to imagine a similar distortion of systematically interconnected primary qualities like shape, size, and spatial orientation, where distortions in one respect demand compensating distortions in other respects, and those in still other respects, etc., with no prospect of ever achieving a stable and coherent view.[13] Think here of the multifarious ways in which objects can be stacked on top of each other, fitted together, placed inside of each other, and so on. At least it seems fair to say that no one has ever actually even begun to describe in even an approximate way an alternative hypothesis involving such systematic primary quality distortion, making it reasonable, I submit, to place the burden of proof on those who seriously believe that such alternatives genuinely exist (contrary to what Alston suggests at one point [RSP, 106–107]).

The foregoing points seem to me enough to suggest, though obviously without making anything like a complete case, that any analog explanation of the details of our experience will involve a realm of three-dimensional objects in space and time that closely approximates the common-sense hypothesis. This does not so far rule out differences of other sorts, such as the attributions of psychical qualities that would be made by a "panpsychist explanation" or perhaps other sorts of differences pertaining to causal properties. My suggestion, however, would be that once the basic framework of objects in space and time is in place, further such issues would become broadly empirical issues to be settled by scientific investigation, and here it seems quite plausible to suppose that the common-sense hypothesis would largely or entirely prevail, for basically the same sorts of reasons that have led to its adoption in the first place. This is to say that arriving at this initial framework of objects in space and time is really the main event, so that if I am right that there are no interestingly different alternatives at that level, the prospect of analog explanations that are significantly different becomes quite dim. Alston may want to respond here that I believe this only because of the limits of my own ingenuity, but it again seems to me that the burden of proof is on those who want to claim that interestingly different analog alternatives genuinely exist.

Even if I am right about this, however, there are still of course at least the digital alternatives. Indeed, it seems obvious that given any adequate analog explanation, there are always guaranteed to be indefinitely many possible digital explanations, since anything that can be explained by appeal to the features of a given world can also be explained by appeal to a representation of that world (perhaps in conceptual terms or perhaps in a form analogous to a map) together with a translating mechanism of some appropriate sort. In the present case, such explanations will involve some kind of representation of the world depicted by the common-sense hypothesis, together with some agent or mechanism (a Cartesian demon, my own unconscious mind, or whatever) that generates experiences of the sort that we would have if the represented commonsensical world were actual.

Is there then any basis for regarding the analog explanation offered by the common-sense hypothesis as more likely to be true than the various digital alternatives that make use of it in this indirect way?[14] Perhaps somewhat surprisingly, Alston seems to grant that explanations of this sort do not provide explanations that are as good as the one provided by the common-sense hypothesis:

> These alternatives are riding piggyback on the standard theory. They haven't been developed independently. . . . This means, first of all, that these alternatives are less simple, for they contain, if fully spelled out, all of the complexity of the standard account, plus something extra. And, worse, the alternatives suffer from being ad hoc. There is no serious theoretical motivation or justification for tacking the demon or self-generation or pan-psychist hypothesis onto the detailed [common-sense hypothesis]. (RSP, 103)

I agree that digital explanations have these problems, which arise of course from their basic *modus operandi*. It seems clear that there is something rather arbitrary or even perverse about adopting such a view, as partially reflected in the fact that there is and apparently could be no basis at all for preferring one such digital mechanism to another. But is this enough to show that they are less likely to be true, and if so, why? Some further argument is needed on this point, and it does not seem to me that obvious how it should go.[15] Since the main purpose of this paper is to explore Alston's views, however, I will tentatively follow him in setting such digital explanations aside.

What then is left, other than the supposed alternative analog explanations, about whose existence I have already expressed skepticism? As already briefly noticed above, Alston's view is that there is a third category of possible explanations: variants of his alternatives (1), (2), (4), and (5) that are neither analog nor digital in character, as I have drawn this distinction. Such explanations would appeal to the distinctive sort of cause invoked by each of these general sorts of explanation, but would be filled out in such a way as to account for the details of experience and especially for our ability to predict future experience, not by an ad hoc reliance on the common-sense hypothesis, bur rather by an appropriately developed account of the underlying causal entity or entities themselves: a psychology of the Cartesian demon, an account of the nature and operations of my unconscious mind, etc. And the suggestion is that it is an open possibility that a developed account of this sort might explain the details of experience just as well or even better than the common-sense hypothesis. Alston grants that this sort of elaboration of one or more of these alternative sorts of explanations has not yet taken place, but argues that this is no reason to exclude such developments as relevant possibilities.

Here I must confess to being at least somewhat unsure whether I fully understand the sort of explanation that Alston has in mind. Concentrating on the demon possibility for expository convenience, the idea seems to be that a suitably elaborated demon psychology and general demonology might make it possible to explain the relevant details of my experience with no reliance at all on the common-sense picture (and thus, I take it, no reliance on the idea that the demon is out to deceive me into thinking that a material world of a certain specific sort actually exists). When, for example, I am, as it seems to me, walking around the cubical object described earlier, predicting and then realizing various experiences involving various shapes, the demon is producing those experiences in me according to some purpose or plan of his own, one that in no way refers or alludes to such a cubical object. Thus, as I understand the view, it is supposed to be simply a coincidence, according to this explanation, that the experiences that fit his purpose or plan also exactly fit what would be expected under the common-sense hypothesis, a coincidence that continues and becomes more and more complicated and seemingly surprising as further aspects of my experience are brought into the picture. And the obvious problem is that this increasingly massive coincidence seems to a parallel degree increasingly unlikely to occur, crying out for some explanation of why the results of the demon's purpose or plan agree so amazingly well with what would be expected from an entirely different situation. This in turn seems to me to be an entirely sufficient reason, one whose strength grows greater as more experience is added, for thinking that the non-digital demon hypothesis and other non-digital skeptical hypotheses of the same general sort are vastly less likely to be true than the common-sense hypothesis.

The upshot seems to me to be that the only alternatives to the common-sense hypothesis that remain standing are the digital explanations. I agree with Alston that these seem very unappealing, basically for the reasons that he offers. But I also think, to repeat, that no completely clear and adequately worked out reason has yet been given for thinking that it follows from their objectionable features that such explanations are less likely to be true than the common-sense hypothesis upon which they are parasitic. My own conviction, however, is that such a reason can be given, and I would surmise that Alston agrees.

An adequate defense of the common-sense hypothesis would require spell-

ing out a reason of this sort. In addition to this, it is obvious that more elaboration is also needed of the reasons briefly sketched above for rejecting the possibility of other analog hypotheses. But even with these threads still left hanging,
my own conclusion is that the prospects for showing that our sense experiences
do offer good reasons for our perceptual beliefs seem surprisingly good—a result that would also have as a corollary that our ordinary "sense perceptual practice" is indeed (probably) reliable.

Notes

1. William P. Alston, *The Reliability of Sense Perception* (RSP) (Ithaca, NY: Cornell University Press, 1993). Though Alston has written many other things that are relevant to this general topic, I will, for reasons of space, confine myself in the present paper
almost entirely to this book. Page references to it will be placed in parentheses in the text.
2. See, for example, William P. Alston, "Epistemic Desiderata" (ED), *Philosophy
and Phenomenological Research* 53, no. 3 (September 1993): 527–551.
3. For my own views on this issue, see Laurence BonJour, "The Indispensability of
Internalism," *Philosophical Topics* 29 (2001): 47–65.
4. In Arthur O. Lovejoy, *The Revolt Against Dualism* (La Salle, IL: Open Court,
1930).
5. For more discussion, see Laurence BonJour, "In Search of Direct Realism," *Philosophy and Phenomenological Research*, forthcoming.
6. Many but not all other epistemological issues are fundamentally parallel in this
respect and thus raise an analogous issue. One that seems to me clearly parallel in this
way is the issue of whether religious experiences provide good reasons for beliefs in the
existence and nature of God, an issue that looms large in Alston's work on the epistemology of religion.
7. I have elaborated this view more extensively than is possible here in a number of
places. See, for example, my contribution to Laurence BonJour and Ernest Sosa, *Epistemic Justification: Internalism vs. Externalism, Foundations vs. Virtues* (Oxford: Blackwell, 2003), Chapter 4.
8. For some discussion of this point, see Laurence BonJour, *In Defense of Pure Reason* (Cambridge: Cambridge University Press, 1998), 7–8.
9. In the following discussion, I have made use of some material from my paper
"Foundationalism and the External World," in *Philosophical Perspectives 13: Epistemology*, ed. James Tomberlin (Cambridge: Blackwell, 1999), 222–249.
10. For very useful discussion of these issues, see D. L. C. Maclachlan, *Philosophy
of Perception* (Englewood Cliffs, NJ: Prentice Hall, 1989).
11. Alston himself takes note of at least approximately this line of argument and
seems to concede its explanatory force in RSP, 72–74.
12. The present three-way distinction is related to two-way distinctions that I have
drawn in other places, though I am not satisfied that I have ever gotten even the two-way
version quite right. See Laurence BonJour, *The Structure of Empirical Knowledge* (Cam-

bridge, MA: Harvard University Press, 1985), Chapter 8; and the paper referred to in note 9.

13. I have been greatly influenced here by Jonathan Bennett's discussion of "size blindness" in his "Substance, Reality, and Primary Qualities," *American Philosophical Quarterly* 2 (1965): 1–17.

14. It is fairly common to offer reasons for preferring the common-sense hypothesis that have no clear bearing on likelihood of truth, such as the claim that it is less fruitful for further investigation, and Alston discusses some moves of this sort. Here I will simply stipulate that such reasons are irrelevant to the main issue.

15. For a very tentative attempt, see my contribution to Laurence BonJour and Ernest Sosa, *Epistemic Justification: Internalism vs. Externalism, Foundations vs. Virtues* (Oxford: Blackwell, 2003), 94–96.

4

Response to BonJour

William P. Alston

Before beginning the response to BonJour's penetrating and challenging paper, it will be useful to bring out a way in which the title of my book on which Bon-Jour is concentrating, *The Reliability of Sense Perception* (RSP), is misleading. To speak of sense perception (SP) as a reliable source of belief is to say that it is a reliable indication or reflection of the subject matter of beliefs to which it gives rise. But that is not enough for the reliability of the doxastic (belief-forming) practice of forming perceptual beliefs on its basis, or better on the basis of the sensory experience involved.[1] For that, it is also required that the belief-forming mechanisms (habits, tendencies) are properly responsive to the indications provided by sensory experience.[2] Both BonJour in his essay and I in RSP are well aware of that. At the end of this response these additional requirements will turn out to be of great importance. But, for now, it needs to be made explicit that it is what we may call the practice of forming perceptual beliefs on the basis of sense experience in the way we typically do (PBP, short for 'perceptual belief practice'), the reliability of which is at issue.

My contention in RSP was that any otherwise impressive argument for the reliability of PBP is infected with epistemic circularity. Though BonJour finds my criticisms to be in general "utterly decisive," he identifies a type of argument he claims to be a counterexample. Moreover, he expresses dissatisfaction with my "Reidian" position that it is reasonable to use well-entrenched doxastic practices, and to take them to be reliable, without any adequate, non-circular argument for their reliability, and he indicates that he would still consider the position to be unsatisfactory even if no adequate argument for the reliability of PBP could be found. The bulk of BonJour's essay is devoted to the elaboration and defense of his chosen way of arguing for the reliability of PBP. This response will observe that same proportion.

But, first, I will make a preliminary comment on his dissatisfaction with the "Reidian" position. One reason he gives is that it "takes the threat of skepticism too lightly." I suppose that the allegation of light treatment stems from the fact that the Reidian position denies that what the skeptic requires for rationality is possible, and that it rests content with our usual doxastic practices despite that. BonJour seems to hold that if no adequate argument for the reliability of a given doxastic practice can be given, the only rational stance is a skeptical one. It is not clear just what he takes that stance to involve. If the only skeptical feature of it is the lack of confidence that the practice is a reliable one, while continuing to use it in a way that presupposes that it is generally reliable, then this differs from the Reidian position only in the "frosting" of an absence of felt certainty. For all practical purposes the two positions are the same. But, if it involves deed as well as feeling, by abstaining from using any such practices, then it clearly is not a possibility for human beings. We form beliefs willy-nilly on the basis of sense perception, memory, various forms of reasoning, etc., however we feel about what is going on, and we proceed to trust them and use them as a guide to behavior and thought in a way that evinces a trust in their general reliability. If my claim about the absence of adequate arguments is warranted, then there really is no alternative to something like the Reidian position.

The argument for the reliability of PBP that BonJour takes to escape my criticisms is that the best explanation for certain kinds of patterns in sense experience is that the beliefs about the physical world at which we arrive on that basis are at least approximately true. The premises for the argument are arrived at by introspection and a priori insight, two doxastic practices that BonJour takes not to be subject to so urgent a skeptical challenge as PBP, though he confesses them not to be wholly immune to skeptical doubts. I find his account of how introspective experience gives rise to introspective beliefs in a relatively unquestionable way to be convincing, and I make the same judgment for his treatment of how a priori insight gives rise to beliefs in necessary truths. But postponing deeper problems with the argument for the reliability of PBP, there is one obvious hole and a less damaging hitch. The hole is found in the attempt to use the account of a priori belief formation to validate claims as to what explanations are better than others. What wrecks that attempt is that he has shown a priori belief formation to be generally reliable only for necessary truths, and judgments as to the relative worth of explanations certainly don't qualify as necessary truths that one can ascertain just by understanding them. BonJour also criticizes in considerable detail my criticism of the claim that (something like) his explanatory hypothesis is superior to all other explanations of the same explanandum. I find his discussion impressive and illuminating, and I don't want to use any of my space here to contest it. Indeed, I find it difficult to reach a settled conclusion on the issue.

The minor hitch concerns the ontological gulf that he alleges to loom between sensory experience and the subject matter of the beliefs to which it gives rise. First, this depends on taking sensory experience to be purely internal to the mind. (BonJour specifically endorses an adverbial account, but any other purely internal account would raise this issue.) He acknowledges that direct realists about perceptual experience would deny any such gulf, but he dismisses them without a hearing. But this undefended preference is not crucially important to the argument, for the alleged gulf does not have the significance he attributes to it. Though it is supposed to mark a crucial epistemological difference between sense experience and introspection (the latter lacking the gulf), when these modes of experience are contrasted it is not the absence of a gulf between ontological *kinds* that is crucial for the epistemological status of belief formed on introspection, but the absence of any difference between a *particular* introspective experience and what it is thought to be an experience of. That is not an irremediable defect of the argument, for BonJour could just as well, or rather better, have stressed that kind of gulf for sense experience. But it is worth pointing out that the ontological gulf he specifies is at least not a necessary condition of a special problematicity of PBP. Consider the practice of forming beliefs about other minds, particularly about the sense experiences of other minds, on the basis of one's own sense experience. Here there is no such ontological gulf, and yet this is, if anything, more vulnerable to skeptical doubts than sense experience of physical objects.

Before getting into deeper problems about the argument, it will help to clean it up a bit. Just what is it that BonJour claims to be directly ascertainable about particular introspective beliefs and for which he claims that an argument is needed where sense perceptual beliefs are concerned? There are two different answers to this question in his essay, answers that are not properly distinguished and interrelated. First, there are frequent references to having a good *reason* for thinking that beliefs resulting from sense experience (introspection) are true. These passages are naturally understood as using 'reason for a belief' to refer to some fact, or alternatively to knowledge or well-supported belief that such a fact obtains, in any event something with a propositional structure. This interpretation is reinforced by such a passage as this:

> In arriving at beliefs about the material world on the basis of perceptual experience in the way that we standardly do, we are accepting claims about what is true in one ontological region . . . on the basis of *facts* that pertain to a quite separate ontological region. (Emphasis added.)

But the trouble is that in other passages he speaks of an experience as being a good reason for beliefs. And that is certainly not the ordinary use of 'a reason' specified above. Indeed, it strikes me as a misuse of language. An experience is not something one can appeal to or cite as a reason, though, unlike the fact that one has had such an experience. And, so, though I agree with BonJour that perceptual and introspective experience can and do provide adequate support for the beliefs that arise from them, his case for this is clouded by an unfortunate and unnecessary inflation of 'a reason.'

To be sure, if experience were construed, as not a few philosophers do, as propositionally structured and even including beliefs, then it would at least not be clear that it couldn't function as a reason. But I'm sure that BonJour would not welcome this way out. In his present, foundationalist mode he needs experiential support to function as a way of stopping the regress of reasons which it would not do if propositionally structured, as BonJour's earlier coherentist self argued.

So what is going on here? My suggestion is that two different types of epistemological support are being conflated under 'a reason': support by having a reason for the belief (or basing it on a reason), and support by the experience from which it issues. This diagnosis is supported by the fact that sometimes but not always BonJour speaks of experience as that "*on the basis of which* I arrive at my various perceptual beliefs," that which "*leads [me] to accept various beliefs* . . . about the material world." (My emphases.) Shortly thereafter, he oscillates back and forth between "experience on the basis of which I come to form and accept certain beliefs" and "what reason is there for thinking that the experience on the basis of which I form these beliefs provide good reasons for thinking that they are true?" In this last sentence the conflation of experience *on the basis of which* one forms beliefs and *good reason* for thinking those beliefs are true is in full swing.

But this conflation between modes of support reflects a deeper conflation between different contexts with respect to which we can speak of support. These are the contexts of the ordinary naive subject of perceptual beliefs and the philosopher's reflective epistemological assessment of these beliefs. The two agents in their respective contexts are engaged in different activities. The former is unselfconsciously undergoing the process of beliefs about physical objects arising from sensory experience. The latter is engaged in determining whether that process is a reliable one, fitted to produce mostly true beliefs. The former is innocent of the aims and concerns of the latter. S/he is no more engaged in the philosopher's assessment than the birds are in ornithologists' classifications and theories. The latter takes the former as her subject matter and, like all humans, frequently occupies that lower-level position herself. But when functioning as an epistemologist she is engaged in quite a different activity. It is the philosopher who searches for reasons and constructs arguments; the naive subject of perceptual beliefs simply lets the beliefs arise from sense experience. Moreover, this difference of role involves a difference in what is claimed and hence subject to epistemic assessment. For the naive perceiver the "claim" is embodied in a particular perceptual or introspective belief and doesn't extend beyond that. This lower-level "claim" sets the problem for the philosopher's assessment, and what he is aiming at is a true or well-supported higher-level claim about the general truth, reliability, or epistemic status of those lower-level claims. It is for this latter that good reasons in the proper sense are needed, not for the former.

BonJour might react to the above by claiming that it doesn't show that forming perceptual beliefs on an adequate experiential basis isn't at least connected with epistemological assessment in this way. If it is impossible for someone to construct a cogent argument from the character of the experience to the likely truth of the belief formed on the basis of it, then the experience does not adequately support the belief. But even if that is accepted, as I do not, it doesn't show that the experience that gives rise to a perceptual belief is a reason for taking it to be true.

None of this "cleaning up" is intended to show that there is anything wrong with BonJour's argument for the reliability of PBP; it is only designed to put it in a proper perspective. But I shall now proceed to argue that not all is well with the argument.

Since that argument depends for its premises on claims for the reliability of introspection and rational insight, I will have to program my computer to run a virus check on the arguments for those claims as well. (Would that I possessed that philosophically adept a computer!)

BonJour's case for the general reliability of introspection is this. Since there is no distinction between the experience on which an introspective belief is based and what is believed in that belief, there is no gap between the experience and what it gives rise to a belief about, such as we find in PBP. And hence the belief can go astray only by inattention, conceptual confusion, misspeaking, or the like. I have already agreed with this position. But BonJour also seems to think that this implies that no argument is needed for taking introspection as reliable. But that would be to think that the argument for the reliability of introspection just indicated implies that it itself is not needed! If it was not needed, why was it given? I'm afraid that this dilemma results from failing to distinguish properly the first-level formation of introspective beliefs and the higher-level attempt to answer questions about the reliability of that formation, the same kind of conflation exposed earlier. Once we appreciate the difference, we see that the mere fact that when I form the belief that I feel drowsy, the identity of the experience on which it is based and the experience in the existence of which I come to believe is not itself an adequate argument for the reliability of that way of forming beliefs, just because it is not an argument at all.

So what about the above argument? Can it be claimed that just by being aware of the introspective experience and the experience thereby believed in, we can ascertain that they are the same and hence that this doxastic practice is such as to be (at least very probably) reliable? I find the argument convincing.[3] This would be an experiential analogue to BonJour's claim that just by being aware of a pair of properties and having the necessary concepts we can tell whether they are necessarily connected in a certain way. So once we distinguish between the introspective experience and the above argument, we can appreciate the force of the latter.

I turn now to whether BonJour's argument for the reliability of PBP is free of circularity. As just pointed out, since his argument depends on the reliability of introspection, if the argument for that assumes the reliability of PBP, that will infect the argument for PBP, though not the argument for the reliability of introspection itself. Here is a reason for attributing such a dependence. When one believes that one feels relieved, the belief is not just that there is a feeling of relief somewhere in ontological space, but that "*I* feel relieved." And what is required to show that the practice is reliable not only for the conscious state attributed but also for the one to whom it is attributed, for the subject as well as for the predicate? How are we to construe the subject of such beliefs? This is a notoriously thorny issue, bringing in all the puzzles about the self, its relation to the body, how, if at all, one can become aware of the self, and so on. I can't get into all that without making this response longer than the respondee. I will confine myself to the following. It seems clear that when I attribute conscious states or anything else to myself, I mean to be attributing them to the same being who is sitting in a certain chair at a certain time, is of a certain weight and height, once frequently played squash, as well as has certain capacities and incapacities, a certain social and professional position, and so on. It is equally clear that I could not come to know all these things (and many more) about myself without relying on sense perception. Hence a complete argument for the reliability of introspection assumes the general reliability of PBP. This would not entail a threat of circularity if we were only interested in introspection, but where it is being used as a source of premises for an argument for the reliability of PBP, that argument is thereby infected with circularity, assuming as required for the argument what it is designed to establish.

Does circularity rear its unlovely head elsewhere in the argument? Consider BonJour's response to a criticism I make in RSP of an argument similar to his. I point out that if my explanandum is certain pervasive patterns in the sense experiences of human beings *generally*, I assume that I have ascertained such patterns in the experience of people other than myself. But there is no way I can find out about those experiences without relying on PBP, that is, taking it to be reliable, as well as on certain forms of reasoning. But then in order to avoid epistemic circularity I am forced to restrict myself to my own experience. And although it would be a remarkable coincidence if everyone's sense experience were just as it would be if produced by a physical environment in the ways we generally suppose it to be without being so produced, it would not be such a remarkable coincidence for that to hold for a single individual. And to avoid epistemic circularity, that is what we are confined to. BonJour responds that if we take into account my sensory experiences over as small a period as one eight-hour day, that would still be a remarkable coincidence, too remarkable to have any significant probability of rational acceptance.

I don't agree with BonJour's last judgment, but rather than contesting that, I will point out that any appeal to my experience beyond the present moment assumes the reliability of memory. Why does that matter? As I pointed out in RSP, if we could establish the reliability of PBP without assuming the reliability of that practice, we would still have to assume the reliability of whatever practices were providing the premises of the argument. Memory is among those practices in the present case. What basis do we have for taking it to be reliable? It seems very plausible to suppose that any otherwise cogent argument for the reliability of memory would involve appealing to past uses of memory, thereby assuming memory itself to be reliable. And so we find the taint of epistemic circularity at the first remove. But suppose this was not the case and the argument for the reliability of memory relies only on PBP (to check the accuracy of some memories) and deductive and inductive reasoning. In that case the reliability of PBP, the conclusion of the whole argument, is being assumed, so that we run into epistemic circularity at this remove. Even this brief exploration illustrates the general point that since the number of distinct basic doxastic practices available to human beings is severely limited, we will sooner or later find ourselves assuming the reliability of some practice the reliability of which had already been assumed at an earlier stage of the argument. And if so, whether or not epistemic circularity can be postponed for a while, it will eventually pop up to infect the argument for the conclusion of the whole line of reasoning. (A more rigorous presentation of this regress is found in my "Epistemic Circularity," reprinted in my *Epistemic Justification*.)

Perhaps that is enough to indicate a distinct threat of epistemic circularity for BonJour's argument. But suppose we set aside these criticisms and accept his claim that certain pervasive patterns in our sense experience are best explained by what he calls the "common-sense hypothesis." Does it follow from that, as BonJour claims, that PBP is indeed reliable? I think not.

In RSP I warn the reader not to suppose that an "argument for the existence of the external world" amounts to, or can be easily transformed into, an argument for the reliability of PBP. BonJour's argument is of the former sort, with an addition concerning how sense experience is caused. One might think that this addition guarantees that the argument entails the reliability of PBP. But it doesn't, for it is more than logically possible that sense experience is caused in the way he specifies, but the way in which perceptual beliefs are formed on the basis of that experience is not one that has a sufficient tendency to be reliable. In RSP I concede that something like BonJour's common-sense hypothesis implies that so long as we are in normal environments differences in our experience will consistently reflect differences in causes concerning which perceptual beliefs are normally formed. But I go on to say that this implies that PBP is generally reliable only in conjunction with two other premises: (1) Our perceptual belief-forming mechanisms are themselves appropriately sensitive to differences in their experiential inputs. (2) We are usually in normal environments. For if either of these assumptions is false, PBP cannot be counted on to be generally reliable even if what BonJour puts into his hypothesis holds.

Well, why couldn't BonJour add those premises to the argument? He could, but what he couldn't do is include them in his hypothesis and still claim that *it* (as a whole) is the best explanation of patterns in sensory experience. So far as I can see, they play no role at all in that explanation. And so unless the explanation is to be fatally weakened by containing explanatorily redundant components, the hypothesis by itself will still not entail the general truth of ordinary perceptual beliefs.

There is another reason why the derivation of reliability with the additional premises would not satisfy BonJour. What it gives us is reliability that satisfies an externalist standard for a strong positive epistemic status. But BonJour, to the best of my knowledge, has remained a staunch internalist in epistemology, in a sense in which it requires that to enjoy positive epistemic status a belief must be likely to be true so far as the subject can tell, so far as what the subject has to go on, from the subject's own perspective. This undoubtedly plays a major role in his insistence that sense experience must provide a *reason* for perceptual beliefs, a position I criticized earlier. But the earlier criticism was that experience itself, as something not propositionally structured, could *be* a reason. Perhaps there is something in the neighborhood that could give BonJour positive epistemic status on internalist terms.

Of course there is, but it would require a still further premise to be added to the hypothesis. What would do the trick would be the stipulation that perceptual belief formation involves an inference from the *fact* that the subject has the sensory experience to the perceptual belief in question. (Note that BonJour took pains to point out that people can and do form beliefs about their experience.) The only drawback to this is that it is generally false of ordinary perceptual belief formation. If anything is clear in this area, it is that no such inference occurs. At least no such conscious inference occurs. And sufficient reason would have to be given for the claim that there are such unconscious inferences in typical perceptual belief formation. I won't lengthen this response by discussing the moves that might be made with "implicit" inferences, or weakened senses of 'inference' in which the mere fact that one unhesitatingly forms a certain belief on having a certain experience is a kind of inference from the latter to the former.

Thus the upshot is that BonJour's explanatory hypothesis will not by itself guarantee that PBP is generally reliable, and that even if it is supplemented by premises that fill that gap, this will give the sought for epistemological result only on an externalist reading. While to make the result satisfy internalist constraints, an assumption is needed that seems patently false.

In this response I have acknowledged that BonJour has succeeded in shooting down some of the positions I took in RSP. But I have also claimed to find some fatal difficulties in his attempt to display a counterexample to my main thesis in RSP. But much more important than counting up the points to see who won is the fact that I have learned much and received much stimulation from his excellent essay, for which I extend to him my hearty thanks.

Notes

1. By 'perceptual belief' I understand not a belief that one is perceiving something, but a belief about what one takes oneself to be perceiving.

2. And a condition of general normality of context is also required, but more of that later.

3. One may think that my endorsement of BonJour's claim about the epistemic status of introspection and its resultant difference from PBP contradicts the "Reidian" thesis that all basic doxastic practices are on a par epistemically, a thesis he attributes to me. But neither Reid nor I hold any such unqualified thesis. We both recognize epistemic differences between doxastic practices. Indeed, Reid in *Essays on the Intellectual Powers of Man* and I in RSP mention just the ones singled out by BonJour as (at least possibly) having a different status from PBP, though BonJour's reasons for regarding them as different are superior to any that either of us adduce. But does BonJour's discussion of introspection refute my view that any otherwise cogent argument for the reliability of a basic doxastic practice suffers from epistemic circularity? It is clear that, on his own showing, a priori insight is not a counterexample to this generalization. Any argument for the reliability of that will, like any argument, presuppose the reliability of our grasp of principles of deduction. The case of introspection is not so clear. Does an argument for its reliability make use of introspection to identify the content of beliefs? Does it presuppose the reliability of memory in calling up prior examples of introspection, or the reliability of PBP in cataloging the ways in which introspection could go wrong, thus giving rise to the sort of situation discussed later in the text concerning the dependence on memory in an argument for the reliability of PBP? I won't try to answer these questions here. At least, BonJour has done a superb job of bringing out the way in which introspection is at least much closer to being shown to be reliable without falling into epistemic circularity than other basic doxastic practices.

5

Alston's Epistemology of Perception

John Greco

I am so much indebted to William Alston for my thinking on perception, epistemology, and the epistemology of perception, that it seems somehow inappropriate to write an essay disagreeing with him on these issues. At the very least, it seems dangerous! Nevertheless, an essay expressing only praise and admiration would not be acceptable to the editors, and probably not to Bill either. In the essay that follows, then, I will try to explicate some of the most important features of Alston's epistemology of perception. I will then raise some criticisms of it.

Alston's thinking on the epistemology of perception combines three major elements. First, Alston defends a position about the nature of perceptual consciousness, or perceptual experience, that he calls "The Theory of Appearing" (hereafter, TA). Strictly speaking, TA is a thesis about the ontology of perceptual consciousness (perceptual experience). However, Alston thinks that some aspects of the theory are epistemically relevant. Second, Alston defends a "doxastic practice approach" to epistemology. In general, a belief is justified if it results from a socially entrenched and reliable doxastic practice, that is, a practice of forming and maintaining beliefs. In particular, a perceptual belief is justified if it results from a socially entrenched and reliable sensory practice, that is, a practice of forming and maintaining perceptual beliefs on the basis of sensory experience. Third, Alston defends a kind of "reliable grounds" view that has a special application to the epistemology of perception. In general, Alston thinks, a belief is justified only if it is believed on the basis of reliable grounds. In particular, a perceptual belief is justified only if it is believed on the basis of reliable perceptual grounds.[1]

We therefore get the following general picture regarding the justification of perceptual beliefs. Consider some perceptual belief that X is P, where X is an external object and P is a perceptual property. In cases where a person S is perceptually justified in believing that X is P, we find the following features: a) X appears P to S, b) forming the belief that X is P on the basis of X's so appearing

is a socially entrenched and reliable doxastic practice, and c) X's appearing P to
S is a reliable indication that X is P. A question that now arises is this: Which
features of this general picture are fundamental, epistemically speaking? Put
another way: Which features *make it the case* that S's belief is justified? Which
features are doing the epistemic work?

Passages from Alston suggest that each of the three features is essential.

> At bottom, the reason for the epistemological superiority of the Theory of Ap-
> pearing is that for it, but not its rivals, the external object about which, in nor-
> mal perception, the perceptual belief is formed is *within* the sensory experience
> itself, appearing to be so-and-so. . . . Since the link with that object is already
> embodied in the constitution of the experience itself, one can readily under-
> stand that, and how, the experience provides justification for beliefs about that
> object.[2]

> Thus we can translate our basic issue concerning the reliability of belief
> sources, or modes of belief-formation, into an issue concerning the reliability of
> doxastic practices. A practice is reliable *iff* its distinctive belief forming mecha-
> nisms (modes of belief-formation) are reliable. And we can similarly restate the
> "reliability constraint" on principles of justification in these terms. A (general
> enough) principle of justification . . . will be true (valid, acceptable . . .) only if
> the doxastic practice in which we form beliefs in the way specified in that prin-
> ciple is reliable.[3]

> In a word, my view is that to be justified in believing *p* is for that belief *to be
> based on an adequate ground.* . . . To get the appropriate criterion of adequacy,
> let's note that a belief's *being justified* is a favorable status vis-à-vis the basic
> aim of believing or, more generally, of cognition, viz., to believe truly rather
> than falsely. For a ground to be favorable relative to this aim it must be "truth
> conducive"; it must be sufficiently indicative of the truth of the belief it
> grounds.[4]

In the essay that follows, I will argue that none of these features, alone or in
combination, are fundamental to the justification of perceptual beliefs: None get
at *what makes it the case* that perceptual beliefs are justified. In fact, I will argue, no one of these features is even a necessary condition on the justification of
perceptual beliefs. In the following three sections, I will consider each feature of
Alston's account in turn. In the final section, I will offer an alternative account
of perceptual justification.

I. The Theory of Appearing

As noted above, the theory of appearing is primarily a theory about the ontology
of perceptual consciousness. Alston describes the position as follows.

> The theory of appearing . . . takes perceptual consciousness to consist, most ba-
> sically, in the fact that one or more objects *appear* to the subject *as so-and-so*,
> as round, bulgy, blue, jagged, etc. . . . . Thus TA takes perceptual consciousness
> to be ineluctably *relational* in character. And, where one is genuinely perceiv-
> ing objects, situations, and events in the external environment, it takes this to
> involve relations to external objects. ("Back to the Theory of Appearing"
> [BTA], 182, his emphasis)

Alston thinks that TA has epistemological consequences. It is also an answer to
the question, "How, if at all, is perception a source of justification of beliefs
about (or a source of knowledge of) the physical environment?"[5] Here is what
Alston says on this matter.

> My visual experience justifies me in supposing that the large object I see in
> front of me is a beech tree just because what appears to me, as being in front of
> me, looks like a beech tree. We have no need either to construct elaborate in-
> ferences from purely subjective experiences to an external reality, or to lay
> down obiter dicta concerning intrinsic prima facie justification. We can simply
> appeal to the natural and plausible principle that whatever appears to one as so-
> and-so is thereby likely, in the absence of sufficient indications to the contrary,
> to be so-and-so. (BTA, 198)

According to Alston, then, TA explains how perceptual consciousness justifies
perceptual belief via the following "natural and plausible" general principle:

> G.   Whatever appears to one as so-and-so is thereby likely, in the ab-
>   sence of sufficient indications to the contrary, to be so-and-so.

Alston endorses a similar principle elsewhere. Here again, he is discussing how
TA accounts for the justification of perceptual beliefs.

> The basic point is this: If something looks like a computer, that provides prima
> facie credibility for supposing that it is a computer. Not an infallible basis, of
> course. That's the point of the 'prima facie' qualification. . . . But the principle
> that things are generally what they look to be, and hence that if X looks P it can
> be presumed to be P until it is shown otherwise is one that commends itself to
> reason.[6]

I take it that the principle that "commends itself to reason" here is supposed to
be analogous to, or perhaps just a different way of stating, principle G above.
Thus we have:

> G'.   If X appears P it can be presumed to be P until it is shown other-
>   wise.

Alston's reasoning seems to be as follows. First, according to TA, perceptual consciousness *just is* some external object X appearing P to S. Moreover,
according to TA, in normal cases of perception, S forms the perceptual belief

that X is P on the basis of X's appearing to be P. But then, via G or G', we have an explanation of how S's episode of perceptual consciousness manages to justify S's perceptual belief. That is: If X appears P to S, then it is likely, absent sufficient indications to the contrary, that X is P. Alternatively: If X appears P to S then, until it is shown otherwise, S's believing that X is P is prima facie credible. In sum, the theory of appearing, when combined with "natural and plausible" principles, or principles that "commend themselves to reason," entails the desired result that perceptual beliefs based on perceptual consciousness are prima facie likely or prima facie credible. Here is the argument a bit more formally.

Argument A
1. According to TA, in normal cases of perception, S forms the perceptual belief that X is P on the basis of X's appearing to be P.
2. G. Whatever appears to one as so-and-so is thereby likely, in the absence of sufficient indications to the contrary, to be so-and-so. Alternatively, G'. If X appears P it can be presumed to be P until it is shown otherwise.
Therefore,
3. According to TA, in normal cases of perception, perceptual beliefs are prima facie likely to be true. Alternatively, according to TA, in normal cases of perception, perceptual beliefs are prima facie credible. (1, 2)

That seems to be Alston's reasoning. I want to argue, however, that the reasoning does not hold up. Specifically, I want to argue that principles G and G' are multiply ambiguous. And once these ambiguities are cleared up, problems with Alston's reasoning become apparent.

The first way that the principles are ambiguous regards how we are to understand "likely" and "credible." Are these to be understood in a non-epistemic way, to mean something like "objectively probable"? Or are they to be understood epistemically, to mean something like "justified" or "reasonable"? In the former case, the principles are making a factual claim as follows:

O. If X appears P to S, then (absent sufficient indications to the contrary) it is objectively likely that X is P.

In the latter case, the principles are making a claim about conditions for prima facie justification.

J. If X appears P to S, and S forms the belief that X is P on this basis, then S is prima facie justified in believing that X is P.

Suppose that Alston intends the former reading. If so, then Alston's premises do not yield the desired conclusion. He was supposed to be showing why, on TA, beliefs based on perceptual experience are *justified*. But on the present reading, he has shown only that such beliefs are objectively probable. What we need to get the desired conclusion is some further premise stating that beliefs that are objectively probable are justified. For example, we need a premise endorsing some kind of reliabilism about justification. The new line of reasoning will look like this:

Argument A1
1. According to TA, in normal cases of perception, S forms the perceptual belief that X is P on the basis of X's appearing P to S.
2. Reliabilism: Beliefs that are formed on the basis of reliable grounds are prima facie justified.
O. If X appears P to S, then (absent sufficient indications to the contrary) it is objectively likely that X is P. In other words, X's appearing P to S is a reliable indication that X is P.
Therefore,
3. If X appears P to S, and S forms the belief that X is P on this basis, then S is prima facie justified in believing that X is P. (2, O)
Therefore,
4. According to TA, in normal cases of perception, perceptual beliefs are prima facie justified. (1, 3)

Fair enough. I think that some such premise as 2 is true. But then TA is not doing any epistemic work here. Consider that a sense-data theorist or an adverbial theorist could just as well wed their accounts of perception and perceptual consciousness to reliabilism, and those theories would get the same result. Thus a sense-data theorist could endorse reliabilism together with the following premise:

SD. If S has a sense-datum that represents X to be P, then (absent sufficient indications to the contrary) it is objectively likely that X is P.

And an adverbial theorist could endorse reliabilism together with the following premise:

ADV. If S is appeared to (X is P)-ly, then (absent sufficient indications to the contrary) it is objectively likely that X is P.

By doing so, each theory would get the result that, in normal cases of perception, perceptual beliefs are justified. TA has no advantage here, epistemically speaking.

Suppose Alston does not intend the "objectively probable" reading of "likely" and "credible." Suppose he intends these terms to mean something like "justified" or "reasonable." In that case a similar dialect ensues. Alston is able to reach his desired conclusion, but only by adding the premise that X's appearing P to S is a reliable indication (absent indications to the contrary) that X is P. The new line of reasoning will look like this:

Argument A2
1. According to TA, in normal cases of perception, S forms the perceptual belief that X is P on the basis of X's appearing P to S.
2. Reliabilism: Beliefs that are formed on the basis of reliable grounds are prima facie justified.
3. X's appearing P to S is a reliable indication that X is P.
Therefore,
J. If X appears P to S, and S forms the belief that X is P on this basis, then S is prima facie justified in believing that X is P. (2, 3)
Therefore,
4. According to TA, in normal cases of perception, perceptual beliefs are prima facie justified. (1, J)

But then, again, TA has no advantage over its rivals. For again, the sense-datum theorist and the adverbial theorist can add analogous premises. The sense-data theorist can add that the relevant sense-data are a reliable indication that X is P, the adverbialist can add that being appeared to in the relevant way is a reliable indication that X is P, and both can endorse reliabilism.

One might think that this move is less plausible for the sense-data theorist and the adverbial theorist than it is for the proponent of TA. In other words, one might think that TA builds reliability right into its account of perceptual consciousness, whereas other theories of perceptual consciousness have to *establish* reliability, and will have problems doing so. The following passage suggests that this is in fact Alston's view.

> Our question, then, is this: just how is it, if at all, that having a sensory experience of a certain sort renders me justified in a certain perceptual belief about a perceived object? The sense datum and adverbial theories are not in a good position to answer this question. . . . These attempts have ranged over various forms of phenomenalism and, on the realist side, attempts to show that sensory awareness of a certain sort is a reliable sign of certain external facts. Confining ourselves to the realist versions, note that these attempts are unable to make use of anything we have learned about the physical world from perception. For by doing so they would be assuming that, somehow, sensory experience is a source of justification for perceptual beliefs, just what they are trying to establish. (BTA, 198)

The passage is dense. But in light of Alston's work on epistemic circularity, I take it that the point is this: Whereas other theories of perceptual consciousness face an insurmountable task of showing or establishing the reliability of perceptual experience in a non-circular way, TA faces no such problem. On the contrary, TA makes the object of perception intrinsic to perceptual consciousness, and thereby establishes a more immediate connection between X's appearing P to S and X's being P. The passage above continues as follows.

> In contrast to this less than satisfactory situation, the theory of appearing has a natural and plausible account of the justification of perceptual beliefs. My visual experience justified me in supposing that the large object I see in front of me is a beech tree just because what appears to me, as being in front of me, looks like a beech tree. We have no need either to construct elaborate inferences from purely subjective experiences to an external reality, or to lay down obiter dicta concerning intrinsic prima facie justification. We can simply appeal to the natural and plausible principle that whatever appears to one as so-and-so is thereby likely, in the absence of sufficient indications to the contrary, to be so-and-so. (BTA, 198)

Here Alston seems to be arguing that, on the assumption of TA, it is natural and plausible to assume the reliability of sensory experiences: "We can simply appeal to the natural and plausible principle that whatever appears to one as so-and-so is thereby likely . . . to be so-and-so." And, so, TA does have this advantage over its rivals after all.

However, the appearance that Alston's principle is "natural and plausible" is an illusion. We can see this by considering a second way in which G and G' are ambiguous. This second way concerns the locutions "appears P" and "appears to one as so-and-so." For ease of exposition, I will focus on "appears P" and similar formulations, such as "looks P," "feels P," and "sounds P."

As Alston notes, the relevant locutions are ambiguous. Two important senses of the locutions are the "comparative" sense and the "noncomparative" sense.[7] In the comparative sense, "X looks P to S" means "X looks to S the way that things having property P normally look." Notice that one could not grasp this meaning without grasping the relevant concepts involved therein. So, for example, one could not grasp the meaning of "X looks like a mango" if one lacked the concept of a mango. In the noncomparative sense, "X looks P to S" reports the qualitative distinctness of the look that X gives. Put another way, it reports the phenomenal character of the look. It reports, for example, a distinctive color and shape. Notice that one could grasp this meaning even if one did not have the concept of a mango. So long as one could understand what it is to experience that sort of look, that sort of color and shape, one could understand what it is to "look like a mango" in this sense.

As Alston points out, we are not considering two different looks here, but rather two different look concepts: We are considering two different ways to pick out, or refer to, the same look. One concept (the comparative) refers to the look indirectly, by describing it in relational terms. The other concept (the noncomparative) refers to the look more directly, by describing its (intrinsic) phenomenal qualities. As Alston puts it, "Only one of the concepts, the phenomenal one, can be used to specify the intrinsic character of that look; the others identify it by its relations to other things. But it is the same look that is identified, now intrinsically and now relationally."[8]

We may now apply this distinction to TA and the principles that Alston associates with it. In particular, we may apply it to premise O of argument A1.[9]

> O. If X appears P to S, then (absent sufficient indications to the contrary) it is objectively likely that X is P.

How are we to understand "X appears P" here? In the comparative sense, the claim in O reads as follows:

> OC. If X appears P to S (appears in the way that objects having P normally appear), then (absent sufficient indications to the contrary) it is objectively likely that X is P.

In the noncomparative sense the claim reads as follows:

> ONC. If X appears P to S (X's appearing has phenomenal property F), then (absent sufficient indications to the contrary) it is objectively likely that X is P.

Once the principle is disambiguated in this way, however, the apparent advantage of TA over its rivals vanishes. Consider the first reading. One problem with OC is that it is false, absent certain assumptions. Thus suppose that many things that do not have P normally look the same way as things that do have P, and suppose that there are many more not-P things than P things. Then OC is false.

Even so, one might think that OC is nevertheless "natural and plausible" in the following sense: Under certain assumptions about the distribution of perceptual properties, assumptions that we reasonably assume to be true in the actual world, OC is true. However, there is a second problem for TA on the present reading of O. Namely, there are analogous principles available to the sense-data theorist and the adverbial theorist. Thus we have:

> SDC. If S has a sense-datum that represents X to be P (the sort of sense-datum that objects having P normally produce), then (absent sufficient indications to the contrary) it is objectively likely that X is P.

> AC. If S is appeared to (X is P)-ly (the way of appearing that objects having P normally produce) then (absent sufficient indications to the contrary) it is objectively likely that X is P.

In effect, OC has reliability built right into it: Under certain assumptions about the distribution of perceptual properties, if objects having P normally appear a certain way, then it is objectively likely that X has P if X appears that way. But SDC and AC build in reliability in exactly the same way. Again, there is no advantage for TA here, epistemically speaking.

Now consider the noncomparative reading of O, or ONC. I have used the variable 'F' in ONC to represent whatever phenomenal property is normal for an appearance of an X that is P. Stating the principle this way underscores the point that there will be no necessary relation between P and F in the typical case. For example, there is no necessary relation between the property of being a mango and the qualitative character of a mango's look: There are possible worlds where mangos appear blue to normal perceivers. Likewise, there are possible worlds where skunks smell like roses and birds sound like cats. In general, then, properties substituted for P and F in ONC will have no logical or conceptual relation. Rather, they will be related only by the laws of nature that are actually in place.

Notice that, thus understood, ONC lacks the superficial plausibility of OC. Once we are clear about what ONC says, it becomes clear that whether ONC is true, for a particular substitution of P and F, is an entirely contingent matter. It is a matter that depends on the actual laws of nature governing how external objects appear phenomenally. In fact, it is questionable whether ONC should be considered a general principle at all. When we write, "If X looks P then probably X is P," that looks like a general principle. We think we can substitute various properties for P to generate specific instances. But this is an illusion if we give a noncomparative meaning to "looks P." As Alston puts it, "looks P" must be treated here as a single semantic unit.[10] P is not operating as a variable for which we can substitute properties. On the contrary, "looks P" and "is P" are operating as distinct variables, and we have no recipe for filling in their values a priori. The most we could have, I assume, is an a posteriori list of propositions with the form of ONC: propositions that state that some phenomenal property of X's appearance is a reliable indication of some external property of X itself. But similar lists would be available to the sense-data and adverbial theorists. Again, TA has no advantage here.

In sum, Alston claims that TA has an advantage over other theories about the nature of perceptual experience, in that it explains how perceptual experiences can justify perceptual beliefs. Since TA makes the perceptual object intrinsic to the experience itself, Alston argues, one can readily understand how the experience provides justification for beliefs about that object. I have argued that the apparent advantage is an illusion, however. Whatever advantages the theory of appearing has over its rivals as an ontological or metaphysical theory about the nature of perceptual experience, it has no advantages as a theory about the epistemology of perception. Put another way, the theory of appearing does not explain how or why perceptual experiences can justify perceptual beliefs.

This suggests that it is the other elements of Alston's thinking about perception that do the explanatory work in this regard. In other words, it is his doxastic practice approach and/or his grounds reliabilism that works to explain the epistemology of perception. On this interpretation, the fact that X appears P to S is relevant for the justification of S's perceptual belief that X is P, but only because forming the belief that X is P on the basis of X's appearing P is a socially entrenched and reliable doxastic practice. Alternatively, X's appearing P to S is as a matter of fact a reliable ground for believing that X is P. In the next two sections, I will consider each of these possibilities.

II. Doxastic Practices

Recall two of Alston's principles about sensory appearings.

G'.   If X appears P it can be presumed to be P until it is shown otherwise.

J.   If X appears P to S, and S forms the belief that X is P on this basis, then S is prima facie justified in believing that X is P.

Also recall that, according to Alston, "A (general enough) principle of justification . . . will be true (valid, acceptable . . .) only if the doxastic practice in which we form beliefs in the way specified in that principle is reliable" ("A 'Doxastic Practice' Approach to Epistemology" [DPA], 7). This suggests that, on Alston's view, G' and J are true and valid epistemic principles just *because* they specify socially entrenched, reliable doxastic practices. It is this fact that *makes it the case* that perceptual beliefs are justified, in cases where they are.

It is important to note that, on Alston view, doxastic practices are both socially entrenched and reliable. The passage just quoted emphasizes the reliability requirement. But Alston also says the following:

> These practices are thoroughly *social*: socially established by socially monitored learning, and socially shared. We learn to form perceptual beliefs about the environment in terms of the conceptual scheme we acquire from our society. This is not to deny that innate mechanisms and tendencies play a role here. We still have much to learn about the relative contributions of innate structures and social learning in the development of doxastic practices. . . . But whatever the details, both have a role to play; and the final outcome is socially organized, reinforced, monitored, and shared. (DPA, 8, his emphasis)

Alston's emphasis on the social raises the following question, however. Why should we deny justified belief to cognitive agents that are not part of a social group, and who therefore do not engage in social doxastic practices? If a lone agent's doxastic practices are nevertheless reliable, what motivation is there for denying that beliefs so grounded are justified? At one point Alston considers this kind of objection. He writes:

Why not take *all* practices to be prima facie acceptable, not just socially established ones? Why this prejudice against the idiosyncratic? . . . It is a reasonable
supposition that a practice would not have persisted over large segments of the
population unless it was putting people into effective touch with some aspect(s)
of reality and proving itself as such by its fruits. But there are no such grounds
for presumption in the case of idiosyncratic practices.[11]

But even if this point is relevant to considerations about *practical* rationality, it
is irrelevant to considerations about *epistemic* justification. Concerning the latter, Alston's view is that our doxastic practices give rise to justification so long
as they are in fact reliable. He explicitly rejects, and quite rightly, any requirement that we have reasons for believing that our practices are reliable.

Finally, consider the possibility that there are no socially entrenched sensory practices. This would be the case if persons in our social groups are sufficiently dissimilar in the ways things appear phenomenally. Suppose, for example, that minute differences in eye structure radically affect the phenomenal
qualities of visual appearances. Then there will be no shared practices of basing
certain sorts of perceptual belief on certain sorts of appearings, and so there will
be no social practices of doing so. But that hardly seems to rule out the possibility of justified perceptual beliefs. For example, even if the way mangos appear
visually to you is very different phenomenally from the way mangos appear to
me, it seems that we could both be justified in believing that there is a mango on
the table, and be so on the basis of our respective visual experience. Suppose
that the way the mango appears to you is a reliable indication for you that there
is a mango on the table, and that the (different) way the mango appears to me is
a reliable indication for me that there is a mango on the table. Why should the
fact that we do not share a doxastic practice, with each other or with anyone
else, be relevant to the justification of our shared belief about the mango?

These considerations suggest that the reliability of one's sensory experience
is more important to justification than the social nature of one's practices, even
if those practices are in fact social. If so, then it is Alston's grounds reliabilism
that is fundamental in his epistemology of perception, rather than his theory of
appearing or his social practices approach. The picture we have arrived at is the
following: According to Alston, whenever some person S is perceptually justified in believing that X is P, we find that: a) X appears P to S; b) forming the
belief that X is P on the basis of X's so appearing is a socially entrenched, reliable doxastic practice; and c) X's appearing P to S is a reliable indication that X
is P. However, it is the third element of this picture that is most fundamental.
Even if, as a matter of fact, the first and second elements of the picture correctly
describe normal cases of human perception, it is not plausible that either explains what makes it the case that perceptual beliefs are justified. If anything in
Alston's picture adequately does this, it is his grounds reliabilism.

III. Grounds Reliabilism

Recall that for Alston, "to be justified in believing *p* is for that belief *to be based on an adequate ground*" ("An Internalist Externalism" [IE], 227, his emphasis). Moreover, for a ground to be adequate it "must be 'truth conducive'; it must be sufficiently indicative of the truth of the belief it grounds."[12] In particular, perceptual justification involves perceptual grounds:

> A doxastic practice can be thought of as a system or constellation of *dispositions* or habits, or, to use a currently fashionable term, *mechanisms*, each of which yields a belief as output that is related in a certain way to an 'input.' The sense perceptual practice (hereinafter SPP) is a constellation of habits of forming beliefs in a certain way on the basis of inputs that consist of sensory experiences. (DPA, 5, his emphasis)

Alston calls his view an "internalist externalism." The view is externalist because the criterion for adequate grounds is externalist: In particular, the grounds must be truth-conducive. The view is internalist because Alston thinks that justifying grounds must be "a psychological state of the subject and hence 'internal' to the subject in an important sense" (IE, 233). Moreover, a justifying ground "must be the sort of thing whose instances are fairly directly accessible to their subject on reflection" (IE, 238).

I want to raise two objections to the epistemology of perceptual beliefs that is put forward here. The first objection challenges the claim that justified perceptual beliefs must be based on perceptual experience. The second challenges the claim that the accessible grounds of justified perceptual beliefs must be reliable.

First, Alston's grounds reliabilism requires that justified beliefs be based on accessible grounds. Moreover, in the case of perceptual beliefs these grounds must be phenomenal appearings. But it seems possible that one could have a justified perceptual belief that some object X is P even if X does not appear phenomenally to one at all. Thomas Reid thought that this was at least in principle possible, because God could have made our perceptual faculties function differently from the way they do. In particular, God could have made us so that physical impressions on our sense organs (for example, light on the retina) carried information about objects in the environment directly to our cognitive faculties, without first causing phenomenal sensations.[13] For example, God could have made us, or could have made other perceivers, who detect the locations of physical objects in the environment, even without the benefit of the object's phenomenally appearing to be located in the relevant space.

In fact, just this sort of thing actually occurs in "blindsight" cases, and occurs in just the way that Reid speculated that it could. Blindsight is now a widely documented phenomenon, occurring in subjects with damage to the primary visual cortex. Subjects who are blind in some part of their visual field can nevertheless discriminate size, shape, location, and/or orientation of objects in the blind part, despite the absence of any conscious visual experience. Presumably, this is because information from the undamaged eye still reaches the brain, although bypassing parts of the visual cortex that are normally responsible for conscious visual experience.[14] In actuality, blindsight is not as reliable as normal human vision. But suppose that it were. Why should we deny that blindsighters perceive objects in their environment, or that their beliefs about those objects are justified?

Perhaps one would rather not call this "perception." Perhaps there is reason to restrict that term only to information uptake about the environment that involves phenomenal appearings. Nevertheless, it has been argued that non-conscious information uptake is a part of normal human perception.[15] The idea is that visual and other phenomenal appearings carry information in perception, but that non-conscious mechanisms for the acquisition of information operate simultaneously with these. This can sound like science fiction at first, but given the way that normal perception is assumed to work, it is a small step to think that some information about the environment is carried to the brain without sensory awareness. All we need suppose is that the path from physical stimulus to conscious belief does not go through sensory experience. Moreover, so long as reliable perception is *partially* a function of non-conscious inputs, it will be false that the conscious inputs alone are a reliable indication of the truth of perceptual beliefs. Suppose that reliable perception is a function of a) initial phenomenal appearings, b) existing beliefs in the system with relevant content, and c) initial non-conscious inputs. If this is the case, then (by hypothesis) perception will be reliable, but it will be false that phenomenal appearings are a reliable indication of, or a reliable grounds for, perceptual beliefs.

Notice that the present objection to grounds reliabilism does not depend on the actual workings of human perception. Whether reliable perception is partially a function of non-conscious inputs is a matter of contingent fact, to be decided by empirical investigation into the actual workings of human cognition. In other words, whether or not perception does work that way, it is possible that perception works that way. But that is all that is needed to mount the objection against Alston's requirement of accessible reliable grounds. For suppose that in some possible world (and perhaps the actual world) reliable perception does not involve accessible reliable grounds. We should hardly conclude that, in such a world, perceptual beliefs are not justified in the typical case. Rather, we should conclude that perceptual knowledge and perceptual justification work differently than might be supposed. But if it is possible that S has justified perceptual belief without having accessible reliable grounds, then it is not a necessary condition on the justification of perceptual beliefs that S does have accessible reliable grounds. The form of the argument is as follows (where GR = grounds reliabilism, J = S has a justified perceptual belief, and G = S has reliable grounds):

1. If GR, then it is necessary that (J only if G).
2. It is possible that (J and not-G).
Therefore,
3. It is not the case that GR. (1, 2)

IV. Agent Reliabilism

In Section 1, I argued that the epistemology of perception need not be wedded to a particular account of the ontology of perceptual consciousness. In Section 2, I argued that grounding in socially entrenched practices is not a necessary condition of justified belief, and in Section 3, I argued that accessible reliable grounds are not a necessary condition. None of this suggests, however, that perception *itself* need not be reliable for perceptual beliefs to be justified. In fact, the considerations above suggest quite the contrary: viz., that it is the reliability of perception that is *fundamental* to the justification of perceptual beliefs, whether or not perception reflects a socially entrenched practice, and whether or not perceptual grounds are reliable by themselves. This is the alternative epistemology of perception that I would like to defend: S is perceptually justified in believing that X is P, just in case S's believing that X is P is the result of S's reliable perception. On this account, the seat of reliability is S herself, or more exactly, S's faculty of perception. Moreover, the account leaves open questions about the ontology of perceptual experience, the reliability of perceptual grounds, and the social nature of associated doxastic practices. It is possible that each of these questions is to be answered exactly as Alston answers them, but that is not what *makes it the case* that perceptual beliefs are justified. That is not what explains why or how perceptual beliefs are justified, when they are.

The present epistemology of perception fits naturally into a general epistemology that we can label "agent reliabilism." On this view, what is fundamental to epistemic justification is that S's beliefs result from reliable cognitive dispositions—what we might call cognitive powers or virtues. The justification of perceptual beliefs is simply an instance of this, since reliable perception is one kind of cognitive power.[16]

I will end by noting that the seeds for this view are to be found in Alston's work. Recall that, according to Alston, an epistemic principle is true just in case it captures a reliable doxastic practice. "A (general enough) principle of justification . . . will be true (valid, acceptable . . .) only if the doxastic practice in which we form beliefs in the way specified in that principle is reliable" (DPA, 7). Recall also that Alston defines a doxastic practice as follows: "A doxastic practice can be thought of as a system or constellation of *dispositions* or habits, or, to use a currently fashionable term, *mechanisms*, each of which yields a belief as output that is related in a certain way to an 'input'" (DPA, 5, his emphasis). If we put these two claims together, we get a position that is more or less equivalent to agent reliabilism. For a reliable "constellation of *dispositions* or habits, or . . . *mechanisms*" just is a cognitive power or virtue. What I have been arguing is that the remaining elements of Alston's view are superfluous to the epistemology of perception, and that this is so even if those elements describe perception correctly.[17]

Notes

1. In early essays Alston tells us that his target of analysis is "epistemic justification," where this is understood as justification having to do "with a specifically *epistemic* dimension of evaluation," or evaluation "defined by the aim at maximizing truth and minimizing falsity in a large body of beliefs." For example, see William P. Alston, "Concepts of Epistemic Justification" (CEJ), in Alston, *Epistemic Justification: Essays in the Theory of Knowledge* (Ithaca, NY: Cornell University Press, 1989), 83. In a later essay, however, Alston argues that the term "justification" fails to pick out any unique property of central importance to epistemology. Rather, the proper task of epistemology is, among other things, to explicate various important epistemic desiderata. See William P. Alston, "Epistemic Desiderata" (ED), *Philosophy and Phenomenological Research* 53, no. 3 (September 1993): especially 542ff. Below I will use the terms "justification" and "epistemic justification" to designate the kind of evaluative property that is required for knowledge. In other words, I will use the terms to designate that particular epistemic desideratum, rather than some unique or "master" concept of epistemic justification, the likes of which Alston rejects in later work. Here I am assuming that Alston countenances such a desideratum. Thus in "Epistemic Desiderata," he writes that "provided the concept of a Gettier problem is sufficiently determinate . . . the question 'What is such that when added to true belief, in the absence of Gettier problems, it gives us knowledge?' is an intelligible and significant question. I am by no means disposed to deny that this formulation does identify a common target concerning which different theorists hold different views" (ED, 535–536). I am also assuming that the views of his I discuss below pertain to this very target. In other words, I am assuming that Alston's earlier views about the justification of perceptual belief are relevant to his current views about perceptual knowledge.

2. William P. Alston, "Back to the Theory of Appearing" (BTA), in *Philosophical Perspectives* 13: *Epistemology*, ed. James Tomberlin (Cambridge: Blackwell, 1999), 200–201. His emphasis.

3. William P. Alston, "A 'Doxastic Practice' Approach to Epistemology" (DPA), in *Knowledge and Skepticism*, eds. Marjorie Clay and Keith Lehrer (Boulder, CO: Westview Press, 1989), 7.

4. William P. Alston, "An Internalist Externalism" (IE), in Alston, *Epistemic Justification: Essays in the Theory of Knowledge* (Ithaca, NY: Cornell University Press, 1989), 227, 231–232. His emphasis.

5. BTA, 181.

6. William P. Alston, "Sellars and the 'Myth of the Given'," *Philosophy and Phenomenological Research* LXV, no. 1 (2002): 82.

7. See "Sellars and the 'Myth of the Given'," 74; and BTA, 188–189. As Alston notes, the distinction is due to Chisholm.

8. "Sellars and the 'Myth of the Given'," 76.

9. Similar considerations apply to premise 3 of argument A2.

10. "Sellars and the 'Myth of the Given'," 81.

11. William P. Alston, *Perceiving God: The Epistemology of Religious Experience* (PG), (Ithaca, NY: Cornell University Press, 1991), 169–170. His emphasis.

12. IE, 231–232.

13. See Thomas Reid, *Philosophical Works*, ed. H. M. Bracken (Hildesheim, Germany: Georg Olms, 1983), 186ff.

14. See L. Weiskrants, *Blindsight: A Case Study and Implications* (Oxford: Clarendon Press, 1986).

15. For an informative review of relevant literature, see Paul Lewicki, Thomas Hill and Maria Czyzewska, "Non-conscious Acquisition of Information," *American Psychologist* 47, no. 6 (1992): 796–801.

16. "Agent reliabilism" is to be distinguished from other forms of reliabilism in just this respect; that is, it grounds justification and knowledge in the reliability of the knower, as opposed to the reliability of the knower's evidence, or methods, or cognitive processes, etc. For further discussion of agent reliabilism and its advantages over other kinds of reliabilism, see my "Agent Reliabilism," in *Philosophical Perspectives 13: Epistemology*, ed. James Tomberlin (Cambridge: Blackwell, 1999), 273-296.

17. I would like to thank William Alston and Heather Battaly for helpful comments on early drafts of this paper.

6

Response to Greco

William P. Alston

John Greco and Larry BonJour both focus on my epistemology of perceptual belief but manage the remarkable feat of avoiding virtually any overlap. Perhaps this is not so surprising, given that I have written too much on the subject. To put it concisely, BonJour is primarily concerned with my treatment of what he (though not I) calls skeptical doubts about perceptual knowledge, while Greco focuses on my (former) substantive views on the conditions for the justification of perceptual beliefs. More specifically, BonJour criticizes both my claim, in *The Reliability of Sense Perception* (RSP), that any otherwise cogent argument for the reliability of our customary way of forming perceptual beliefs is infected with epistemic circularity (criticizing it by producing an alleged counterexample) and my "Reidian" way of resting content with the absence of any wholly satisfactory argument for that reliability. Whereas Greco deals critically with a three-part condition for the justification of perceptual beliefs that he puts together from various writings of mine. There are other significant differences between the two papers. Whereas BonJour takes seriously my turning my back on epistemic justification and even agrees with me on that, Greco is still battling the Alston who was concerned with the justification of perceptual beliefs. Again, Greco, unlike BonJour, fully recognizes my conviction that the account one gives of perception is strongly relevant to the epistemology of perceptual belief. A reader might be pardoned from doubting that the two critics are dealing with the same philosopher.

I

It is time to switch from comparative BonJour-Greco exegesis to a critical examination of Greco's interesting and valuable paper. Right at the outset, before getting to the details, I am faced with the same dilemma I faced in deciding how to respond to Ginet's paper. In both cases the author, though recognizing that I

had turned my back on "epistemic justification" for what I took and still take to
be sufficient reasons, proceeds to criticize my former views on that, as I now
think, fictitious subject matter. This is fair enough, since I did publish those
views in more than one venue. Indeed, even after my conversion I, no doubt
misguidedly, continued to speak in those terms when dealing with various epistemological problems so as to avoid intruding my anti-justificationist orientation
into a consideration of those problems. (This includes the 1999 essay, "Back to
the Theory of Appearing" [BTA], cited more than once by Greco.) But it does
make difficulties in deciding how to respond. In my response to Ginet I managed to find plenty to say, from my present pluralistic epistemic desiderata approach, about issues he raises. But I haven't found a good way to do this with
Greco. The issues he raises are tied too closely to concerns with the conditions
of epistemic justification to make that possible. Hence I have no choice but to
meet him on his own ground and respond to his objections to (what he takes to
be) my former views.

But the relation between my former views and Greco's objections to them,
along with his own views from which those objections stem, is complicated by
the fact that he announces in footnote 1 that he "will use the terms 'justification'
and 'epistemic justification' to denote the kind of evaluative property that is
required for knowledge." That is certainly his right. He even seeks to enlist my
support for this by quoting a passage in "Epistemic Desiderata" (ED) in which I
say that something like Greco's chosen sense of 'epistemic justification' "does
identify a common target concerning which different theorists hold different
views." But it does not follow, as Greco thinks, that this implies that this is the
sense in which I was using 'justified' in application to beliefs in the formulations that Greco is criticizing. Where I have tried to explain what it is for a belief
to be justified, nothing is said about the evaluative property required for knowledge. Indeed, I said nothing about knowledge in this connection. That was deliberate. A sufficient reason for the omission was, I blush to state, that I was and
still am quite uncertain as to what the best account of propositional knowledge
is. Insofar as I have any definite leanings they are counter to the view that there
is some evaluative property that is required for knowledge; they are in the direction of regarding knowledge as a purely factual matter. Moreover, since the
evaluative property in question would be a property of beliefs, Greco's way of
identifying justification presupposes that to know that p is to have a *belief* that p
that has certain properties. And I am not at all sure that knowledge is related to
belief in that way. I find myself favorably disposed toward the kind of account
given by Timothy Williamson's recent book, *Knowledge and Its Limits* (Oxford
University Press, 2002). Moreover, in my "Justification and Knowledge" (JK) I
argue that on any halfway plausible account of justification it is not necessary
for knowledge. All that being the case, Greco is wrong to assume, as he seems to
be doing at the end of footnote 1, that the views of mine he discusses use 'justi-

fied belief' in the way he indicates that he does. And so the gulf between what he is talking about under this heading and even my former justificationist self cannot be spanned. Hence in discussing Greco's objections to my views on the justification of perceptual beliefs I not only have to take a former and abandoned persona, but I have to assume that what he says about those views makes sufficient contact with them in spite of the differences in our conceptions of justification. Consider it done.

II

Enough of prolegomena. Turning to the substance of Greco's paper, I must first point out some organizational and exegetical difficulties. As noted above, the critical part of the paper (everything except the short last section) is organized in terms of what Greco variously calls "three major elements" or "three features" of my views as to the conditions for the justification of perceptual beliefs. Here is his concisest formulation of these: "(a) X appears P to S, (b) forming the belief that X is P on the basis of X's so appearing is a socially entrenched and reliable doxastic practice, and (c) X's appearing P to S is a reliable indication that X is P." This sets the stage for what Greco says are the central questions of his discussion—whether each of these features is necessary for the justification of a perceptual belief, and whether individually or all together they are sufficient for this. But a moment's scrutiny will reveal that although (b) and (c) make sense as possible conditions for the justification of perceptual beliefs, (a) does not. What perceptual belief would (a) be a justification for, and how would it have to be related to that belief to provide justification for it? In fact, Greco's discussion that is allegedly about (a) is really directed to a much richer cousin that could be put this way: S's belief that X is P is based on X's appearing P to S. In the ensuing I will be understanding (a) in this richer form.

Greco leads up to his statement of the central issues of his criticism as follows: "A question that now arises is this: Which features of this general picture are fundamental, epistemically speaking? Put another way: Which features *make it the case* that S's belief is justified? Which features are doing the epistemic work?" (His emphasis.) He then asserts that "Passages from Alston suggest that each of the three features is essential," and he exhibits three passages that he takes to support this. We need to examine the passages to make sure that they do.

As for the second and third, only minor adjustments are called for. But the first passage is considerably further from being as advertised. It would be best to reproduce it in full.

> At bottom, the reason for the epistemological superiority of the Theory of Appearing is that for it, but not its rivals, the external object about which, in normal perception, the perceptual belief is formed is *within* the sensory experience itself, appearing to be so-and-so. . . . Since the link with that object is al-

ready embodied in the constitution of the experience itself, one can readily understand that, and how, the experience provides justification for beliefs about that object. (BTA, 200-201)

This passage is closer to Greco's target than the others by being explicitly concerned with perceptual beliefs, and it suggests that what provides justification for them is a perceptual experience. But its focus is not on that, but rather on the different claim that the Theory of Appearing (TA) enables us to "understand that, and how, the experience provides justification for beliefs about that [the perceived] object." This is in fact the primary concern of the section devoted to the "first feature." Since that section occupies at least four-fifths of the paper, I will have much more to say about this and other points below.

Before turning to the examination of each of these sections, some further exegetical work is called for. Here is Greco's canonical statement of his program for the critical portion of the essay: "I will argue that none of these features, alone or in combination, are fundamental to the justification of perceptual beliefs: None get at *what makes it the case* that perceptual beliefs are justified. In fact, I will argue, no one of these features is even a necessary condition on the justification of perceptual beliefs." (His emphasis.)

Restricting ourselves to the above quotations from Greco, we find problems about aligning some crucial terms. The notions of "necessary" and "sufficient" conditions (for the justification of perceptual beliefs) are obviously crucial. But how are they expressed and by what terms? In the last quotation Greco explicitly speaks of "necessary condition." But he seems to shy away from the term 'sufficient.' What he often uses that would seem to express that concept is 'what makes it the case that.' For the sake of a standard treatment, I will replace this by 'sufficient for.' But what about 'fundamental to'? In the last quoted passage it is clearly being equated with 'what makes it the case that'; that is, sufficient. However, in the last few sentences of the section on (b), 'fundamental' is used as a degree term. But sufficiency cannot be a matter of degree, though there can be degrees of approximation to sufficiency. Elsewhere he uses 'fundamental' to mean something like 'central' or 'important.' I think we will have to cope with the ambiguity of 'fundamental' and decide how to interpret it by attending to its context. In the light of all this, I will reformulate the canonical statement of Greco's main critical aim as follows: I will argue that none of these features, alone or in combination, are sufficient for the justification of perceptual beliefs. In fact, I will argue, no one of these features is even a necessary condition on the justification of perceptual beliefs.

In announcing this as what he will argue, Greco obviously assumes that this is contrary in some way to positions of mine. But just how? He says, "Passages from Alston suggest that each of the three features is essential" (for the justification of perceptual beliefs). If that were the case, his arguing that none of them are necessary would be directed against me. He also says that none of them, alone or in combination, "get at what makes it the case that perceptual beliefs are justified," thus assuming that I think that either some of them, or all of them together, are sufficient for the justification of perceptual beliefs. Let me say, as a kind of Ariadne's thread through the labyrinth, that I think, or did think when I was dealing in epistemic justification, that there are some ways of construing the sorts of things Greco is getting at with his "features" in which they are individually necessary and together sufficient for epistemic justification. But I most emphatically do not think that in the way he formulates them, they have that status.

Although his programmatic announcement naturally leads the reader to expect that Greco's criticism of my epistemology of perception will be dominated by arguments for the conclusions specified there, the reader will be disappointed by what she finds. (From now on, I will refer to the three sections of the paper that are allegedly devoted to discussing his (a), (b), and (c), respectively, as sections (a), (b), and (c).) It is only in sections (b) and (c) that one finds any of this. Section (a), which is far and away the largest, is wholly taken up with contesting my claims: (1) that TA enables us to "understand that, and how, the experience [perceptual experience] provides justification for beliefs about that [the perceived] object"; and (2) that it does a better job of this than other accounts of perceptual experience. We hear nothing about whether the TA version of perceptual experience is either necessary or sufficient for the justification of perceptual beliefs to which it gives rise. At least nothing is explicitly said to this effect. For anything like an explicit argument that enriched (a) is not necessary for the justification of perceptual beliefs we must wait for section (c).

III

I now turn to an examination of Greco's argumentation in criticism of the above claims of mine and in support of their denial. He constructs a number of arguments that he presents as a reconstruction of the way I "seem" to be arguing for the claims and contends that none of them adequately support them. For the sake of concision I will focus on alternative versions of a single line of argument.

1. According to TA, in normal cases of perception, S forms the perceptual belief that S is P on the basis of X's appearing P to S. [I have changed the appearing locution to be in line with my way of construing it.]
2. There are two versions of premise 2:
    2A. Whatever appears P to one is thereby likely, in the absence of sufficient indications to the contrary, to be P.
    2B. If X appears P, it can be presumed to be P until it is shown otherwise.
Therefore,
3A. According to TA, in normal cases of perception, perceptual beliefs

are prima facie likely to be true.
3B. According to TA, in normal cases of perception, perceptual beliefs
    are prima facie credible.

Greco distinguishes two versions of premise 2 because he takes them to
embody two different principles (one of which I term "natural and plausible")
that I appeal to in my argumentation. But note that the conclusions of the two
arguments employing these two different principles are not themselves either of
my claims in question, but rather have to do with what TA takes to be perceptual
beliefs with positive epistemic status of one kind or another. Presumably Greco
takes me to be supposing that the argumentation he is attributing to me *exhibits*
the way in which TA provides understanding of that and how a perceptual experience provides justification (or other positive epistemic status) for perceptual
beliefs that arise from it (taken by TA to be "normal perception"). But, of
course, it would have been better had Greco made all this explicit and presented
the arguments as terminating in the conclusions that are the focus of the discussion. But leaving aside these quibbles, let's get into the substantive issues.

Note that the alternative versions of premise 2 and the conclusion, both of
which follow formulations of mine quoted by Greco, make a difference to the
force of the argument for a conclusion that the belief in question is *justified*. The
consequents of 2B and 3B are presumably designed to be read as alternative
ways of attributing justification to the belief. But the consequents of 2A and 3A
are in terms of what Greco calls "objective probability." For that version he
points out that an additional premise is needed to the effect that beliefs that are
grounded in such a way as to be objectively likely to be true are thereby justified. This reflects the position of both Greco and my earlier self that what justifies a belief must be "truth-conducive," such as to render the belief objectively
likely to be true. And, assuming that truth-conducivity constraint on justification, the version involving 2B and 3B also requires an additional premise connecting having an adequate truth-conducive ground with being justified, though,
so to say, in the opposite direction. In both versions the crucial point is the claim
that when a perceptual belief is formed on the sort of basis specified in premise
1, it will thereby be formed on a ground that is truth-conducive and that therefore is sufficient to make the belief prima facie justified.

Greco's main criticism of these arguments is that sense-data and adverbial
accounts of perception could mount parallel arguments with the same force. For
example, "a sense-data theorist or an adverbial theorist could just as well wed
their accounts of perceptual consciousness to reliabilism" and would get the
same result. That is, Greco thinks that these other accounts of perceptual consciousness could claim that basing a perceptual belief on perceptual consciousness as construed by their accounts gives that belief a truth-conducively adequate ground that renders the belief prima facie justified. Greco puts his

conclusion from this point by saying, "TA has no advantage here, epistemically speaking" and "TA has no advantage over its rivals." I will shortly make an objection to his claim that the other theories can do just as well at this as TA. But even if that claim were acceptable, it only refutes my claim (2); it does nothing to refute (1). It obviously does not show that TA cannot also do the job. It does not show that TA fails to enable us to understand that, and how, perceptual experience provides justification for beliefs about the perceived object. Greco himself holds that more than one account of perception can do the job. Then what warrants him from excluding TA from the club? The fact that there are other members certainly can't.

At one point in the course of presenting the "they can do it too" criticism, Greco puts what he takes this to show against (1) by saying, "But then TA is not doing any epistemic work here." But this is, if anything, more obviously unwarranted than saying, "Therefore TA can't do the job after all." The point is the same. The fact that someone else can do a job equally well doesn't show that I didn't or can't do it. What would we think of a building inspector saying to a carpenter, "Other carpenters could do just as well at this; therefore you didn't do the job (you didn't do any carpentry work)." We would certainly be at a loss for words.

Since the "they can do it too" criticism does not show that TA doesn't enable us to understand that and how perceptual experience is a source of justification for beliefs based on it, it has no force against the claim of mine against which Greco takes it to be directed (1). If it has any force it is against (2), the claim that TA does better than the competition. Greco has failed to distinguish properly the two claims, perhaps because he was not clearly aware of their difference.

Now let's consider whether the other accounts of perceptual experience he mentions could do as good a job of providing the explanation in question as TA. Of course they could claim to. But with what warrant? Talk is cheap. I am reminded of the bit in Shakespeare's Henry IV, part I, in which the wild Welshman, Glendower, boasting of his magical powers, says: "I can call spirits from the vasty deep," to which Hotspur replies: "Why, so can I, or so can any man; But will they come when you do call for them?" I am accustomed to use this passage to illustrate the difference between illocutionary and perlocutionary speech acts. But it also has relevance to the present point.

Despite Greco's flat statement that the other accounts of perceptual experience can "do the same," the further course of his discussion makes it plain that he recognizes, as I do, that it is necessary to address the question of which account of perceptual experience provides the strongest basis for taking perceptual experience to render a perceptual belief based on that experience likely to be true. His quotations of what I have to say about this issue are taken from the very short and not fully developed bit at the end of BTA. Indeed, I have not yet published, or even worked out, a thoroughgoing treatment of the issue, though pieces of such a treatment appear in various publications, as I will point out.

From the essay just mentioned, Greco takes two reasons I give for the superiority of TA in this regard: (A) Since according to TA but not its competitors the perceived object is, so to say, one of the constituents of the experience. By virtue of the fact that its appearing so-and-so to S is what the experience consists in, TA can appeal to the intuitively very plausible principle that whatever appears so-and-so is thereby likely, in the absence of sufficient contrary considerations, to be so-and-so. (B) The competitors, lacking any comparable access to such a principle, are forced to attempt to argue that being aware of a certain sense-datum or being "appeared to" in a certain way renders a perceptual belief based on that prima facie likely to be true. And these arguments are unsuccessful. Greco criticizes only the first of these claims, presumably because the second one is given only the sketchiest kind of support in BTA.

On (A), he says that "the appearance that Alston's principle is 'natural and plausible' is an illusion." His reason involves an ambiguity between comparative and phenomenal senses of 'appear.' Greco notes my point that these are not kinds of appearing but kinds of *concepts* of appearing, and that both kinds of concepts can be used to pick out cases of the same appearing (look, feel, smell, etc.), which is denoted more directly, though less publicly, by the phenomenal concept. Once we grasp this, we see that Greco's objections fail to have the force he supposes them to have. He argues that in the comparative sense it is trivially and unhelpfully true that X's looking in one of the ways that computers normally look prima facie justifies the belief that X is a computer and makes it prima facie objectively likely that X is a computer. At least, he says, this is the case on normal assumptions about the "distribution of perceptual properties." But given that the comparative sense is just a way of picking out a phenomenal way of looking (or a family thereof), there is nothing at all trivial about the conclusion of the argument. Greco's point about the non-comparative (phenomenal) concept is that whether the conclusion is true depends on the laws of nature governing how external objects appear. That is quite correct. But I never meant to suggest that the conclusions of the arguments Greco is considering are logically necessary. I meant them to hold as things are in the actual world, and to hold with the degree of precision that it is reasonable to expect in such matters. I will have more to say about this at the end of my response.

As for (B)—the lack of success sense-datum theories and adverbial theories have in carrying through an argument for perceptual beliefs' being rendered probable by being based on perceptual experience as they construe it—that is a long story, one that I couldn't possibly go into in this response, especially since it would not be a response to any of Greco's criticisms. I will just refer the reader to two works of mine: "Perceptual Knowledge" in *The Blackwell Guide to Epistemology*, 1999 (which, despite the title, is mostly concerned with the justification of perceptual beliefs), in section v of which I document the difficulties sense-datum and adverbial theorists have in showing that perceptual experience renders perceptual beliefs likely to be true; and RSP, especially Chapter 4, in which I give extended criticisms of attempts to give a successful non-circular argument for the reliability of perceptual beliefs. Though that criticism is not specifically addressed to sense-datum and adverbial theories, its relevance to the present issue should be obvious.

IV

Section (b) does not completely disappoint natural expectations, as section (a) did. But there is still no argument against the necessity or the sufficiency of (b), as originally stated, for the justification of perceptual beliefs. Most of the section is devoted to arguing that we can have one part of (b), the reliability of the practice, without the other part, its social establishment. Since I have never supposed that the social establishment of a practice is required for its reliability, this argumentation leaves me untouched. Greco does quote me as saying that idiosyncratic practices don't have the same claim to a prima facie credibility as socially established ones, but credibility is not equivalent to reliability, as he himself insists. Moreover I did assert that our basic and most salient doxastic practices are in fact socially established. And in my latest version of the doxastic practice approach in PG, Chapter 4, I list a number of other features of doxastic practices, including mutual involvement, pre-reflective genesis, involvement in wider spheres of practice, and others. But I did not claim and do not believe that any of these are required for a practice to be reliable. I do take social establishment to be some indication of reliability, though not an absolutely conclusive one.

I find the end of section (b) rather puzzling. In the final paragraph Greco says, "It is Alston's grounds reliabilism that is fundamental in his epistemology of perception, rather than his theory of appearing or his social practices approach." Then he repeats (a) and (b) in their original concise formulation and denies that either of them "explains what makes it the case that perceptual beliefs are justified." But how can he deny this of (a) and (b) on any understanding of it on which he can claim that it is true of (c), the contrast for the sake of which he makes these claims? I can't make any sense at all of this on his original concise version of these "features," the version he repeats here. How could any of them in the concise version "explain what makes it the case that perceptual beliefs are justified"? To take (c), which is being presented here as the fair-haired boy, how could X's appearing P to S being a reliable indication that X is P, *all by itself*, give an adequate explanation of what makes it the case that the perceptual belief that X is P is justified? We also (at least) need something connecting the grounds being a reliable indication that X is P with the perceptual belief that X is P being justified, just the sort of connection the need for which Greco pointed out in section (a). And what's sauce for the goose is sauce for the gander. So though neither (a), even in my enriched form, nor (b) as stated are enough by themselves to explain why perceptual beliefs based on X's appearing P to S are justified, the same holds for (c), and the desired contrast is lost.

V

This brings us to section (c). Here Greco's criticism is directed not to (c) as he stated it earlier, but to a beefed-up version that involves my view in "An Internalist Externalism" (IE) that justification requires that the belief be based on grounds that are "fairly directly accessible." Against this view in application to perceptual beliefs, Greco argues that some or all justified perceptual beliefs may owe an essential part or all of what renders them justified to "non-conscious information uptake," and hence that where this is an essential part, directly accessible grounds are not (logically) sufficient for their being justified, and where it is the whole of what confers justification, directly accessible grounds are not (logically) necessary.

I accept this as an objection to the internalist part of my position on epistemic justification in IE, or would if I were still concerned with epistemic justification, and assuming that I meant the requirement as logically necessary. (As for the last assumption, I must plead guilty to not being completely determinate about the modality intended.) I agree that it is possible and even actual in this world that cognitive subjects, including human beings, form reliable beliefs from perception without undergoing conscious experience. In addition to phenomena like "blindsight" that he mentions, there are plausible theories of perceptual processing that posit much extraction of information prior to any formation of conscious perceptual experience.

Note, moreover, that the argument against the necessity of accessible grounds for the justification of perceptual beliefs carries out a bit of Greco's announced program that was lacking in section (a). For if accessible grounds are not required for the justification of perceptual beliefs, then X's appearing P to S is thereby not necessary for a justified perceptual belief. And this is a successful argument against the necessity of one of Greco's "features."

VI

The upshot of all this is that I do not find much in Greco's paper to cause me a great deal of worry about my epistemology of perception. But I have learned a lot by mulling over his discussion and making such attempts as you see here to respond to it.

7

Disagreement in Philosophy

Alvin I. Goldman

Bill Alston hired me to my first job in philosophy and rapidly became my most valued colleague and philosophical conversationalist during my early years at the University of Michigan. Our initial philosophical interactions were in philosophy of mind, but we soon made independent plunges into epistemology and influenced one another in a variety of ways. That interanimation of epistemological ideas has continued fruitfully over several decades, and I have always found Bill's careful delineation of the epistemological terrain unusually revealing. Leading-edge philosophy often consists in unraveling subtle confusions hidden in the literature, demonstrating the hitherto unappreciated significance of crucial concepts, and tracking relationships among rival theories. Alston's leadership in epistemology has often been in these molds. He has exposed potentially lethal "level confusions" in epistemology ("Level Confusions in Epistemology"), plumbed the significance of epistemic circularity (*The Reliability of Sense Perception*), and charted relationships among diverse epistemic theories ("Concepts of Epistemic Justification") and types of epistemic worth (*Beyond "Justification": Dimensions of Epistemic Evaluation*). He provides the kind of shoulders on which young epistemologists should stand to attain a suitably synoptic and discriminating view of the epistemological landscape.

Turning to Alston's most recent work, what do I say to his current crusade for doing epistemology without justification? Wouldn't his proposal effect a truly revolutionary change in the epistemological landscape? Does the landscape need such a scorched-earth policy? Have debates in the theory of justification produced so unsightly a pattern of growth that only radical pruning will restore beauty, grace, and order to the scene?

What exactly are Alston's reasons for proposing to excise justification from epistemology's agenda? The reasons are put forward in three works: "Epistemic Desiderata," "Doing Epistemology without Justification," and *Beyond "Justification": Dimensions of Epistemic Evaluation*.[1] I shall refer to them, respectively, as ED, DEWJ, and DEE. Perhaps the pithiest statement of his rationale is given in DEWJ, where he summarizes his argument as follows:

> [U]pon considering various controverted candidates for necessary conditions
> for the epistemic justification of beliefs, I concluded that the best diagnosis of
> the situation is that there has been persistent failure to identify any one objec-
> tive epistemic status concerning which the various accounts of epistemic justi-
> fication are differing. (DEWJ, 1–2)

Similar statements occur in DEE. Alston asks, for example, "[W]hy should we
suppose that there is any objective property of beliefs picked out by 'justified'?"
(DEE, 8). To the contrary, he contends: "There is no such reality as epistemic
justification to perform [the] function [of validating epistemic credentials]. . . . A
belief's being justified has no more objective reality than ether or ghosts"
(DEWJ, 9). In further support of his doubts that there is a unique objective property about which different justification theorists or contestants have been disagreeing, he complains that nobody has managed to provide a "theoretically
neutral way of identifying th[e] alleged property about which our contestants are
disagreeing" (DEE, 9–10).

Alston's argument proceeds from the observation that there is great diversity of theoretical opinion about what it is for a belief to be justified. "[W]e are
confronted with a wildly chaotic picture of an enormous plurality of incompatible views as to what it is for a belief to be justified. . . . One could be pardoned
for taking this alone as a sufficient reason for abandoning the search for the true
account of epistemic justification" (DEE, 8). He acknowledges, however, that
there are many cases of long-continued disagreement in which there is a unique
correct answer to the question. Despite this acknowledgement, he treats the fact
of persistent disagreement as an important datum. Why do philosophers who
think long and deeply about epistemology take such different positions on justification? One possibility, he says, is that it's just a very tough problem. A second possibility is that there is no unique property of beliefs picked out by 'justified.' The second explanation is the one Alston finds compelling. It is more
reasonable to conclude, he says, that epistemological theorists "are chasing a
phantom" (DEE, 8).

A key step in coming to this conclusion is Alston's observation that nobody
has identified the putative quarry in a neutral way, a way that does not rely on
one of the competing theories. This failure is supposed to buttress his rationale
for the non-existence of the quarry, and his plan to drop the subject entirely. In
reply, it should first be pointed out that epistemologists do provide partial specifications of the quarry that are pretty neutral. They often give approximate
synonyms of 'justified' such as 'warranted' and 'rational'; and they explain the
type of justification in question by characterizing it as intellectual or evidential
rather than moral or prudential. Is it reasonable to demand more than this? And
does failure to provide more in the way of theory-neutral description support

Alston's conclusion of the nonexistence of the quarry? In other areas of philosophy, it commonly proves difficult to give theory-neutral characterizations of the central topics of the domain. In the philosophy of color, for example, it is very tricky to say, in a theory-neutral way, what it takes for an object to be red. In meta-ethics it proves hard to give a theory-neutral specification of the notion of morality. For example, is a moral consideration necessarily a reason—perhaps even an overriding reason—for action? Such a question cannot be answered without taking a position on the theory-laden controversy between ethical externalism and internalism. Is the absence of theory-neutral characterizations a ground for concluding that there are no colors and no moral considerations?

Alston's proposed cure for the problem on the topic of justification is simply to abandon the subject. Is this the best cure? Is that how to end disagreement in epistemology? If this is right, then a similar cure may well be required in other parts of philosophy, where there are also persisting disagreements. In the theory of consciousness there is a welter of conflicting theories and no obvious way to resolve them. In metaphysics there are innumerable rival accounts of identity, identity over time, and objecthood, and it is hard to see how to choose decisively among them. If we follow Alston's recipe for ending disagreement in epistemology, won't we jettison so many other topics near and dear to philosophers' hearts? Some might regard this as throwing the baby out with the bathwater. Now, Alston's approach to ending conflict—simply drop the subject—has its appeal in certain contexts. When confronting interminable family squabbles, perhaps it is sound advice to take the troublesome subject off the (verbal) table. But although this has its practical virtues, it is not intellectually very satisfying. Philosophy is preeminently an intellectual subject, so we would like to know, at a minimum, how it happens that there are so many rival views, each with considerable surface plausibility. The subject should only be dropped, if it should be dropped at all, once we have a decent theoretical handle on why the disputes are so nagging and persistent. This paper will consider some proposals for shedding light on this question. No single and unified diagnosis will be presented, but several different sources of fundamental disagreement will be examined. Because I view this as a problem for many areas of philosophy, not just epistemology, I will not restrict my attention, as Alston does, to epistemology.

Alston calls justification a "phantom," with "no more objective reality than ether or ghosts." What kind of objective reality does he mean to be denying? What sort of objective reality are epistemologists committed to, or should they be committed to, when theorizing about justification? Alston typically expresses his nihilism or eliminativism about justification by denying that there is a (unique) *property* expressed by the term 'justified.' What sense of "property" does he have in mind? In a well-known paper Putnam (1970) distinguished two notions of "property," one referring to predicates or expressions—where identity of property is a matter of synonymy—and one referring to physical magnitudes like temperature. I take it to be obvious that Alston does not mean to suggest that justification would have to be a physical magnitude like temperature in or-

der for epistemologists to be warranted in pursuing it as a quarry. Nobody, not
even the staunchest realist in meta-epistemology, thinks that justification is a
physical magnitude. A close cousin of this view, however, is the view that justification is a natural kind or a natural phenomenon. Hilary Kornblith takes this
view of knowledge, and his view of justification seems to lean in a similar direction.[2] But across all of philosophy, normative status is a highly controversial
matter, and it would be surely too restrictive to say that epistemologists should
have no truck with the normative status of justification unless it qualifies as a
natural kind or natural phenomenon. That would be an excessively narrow meta-
epistemology, and it isn't clear that Alston means to subscribe to it.

An alternative interpretation is to think of properties in Putnam's other
sense, or some related sense. If we follow the letter of what Putnam says, 'justification' might pick out a property simply by being a predicate with a determinate meaning. In roughly the same ballpark, 'justification' might pick out a
property by expressing a *concept* with a determinate content. The latter interpretation seems particularly appropriate to a large epistemological literature, in
which writers say they are trying to analyze epistemic "concepts" like knowledge and justification. One might think that Alston would be happy to regard
justification as a suitable target as long as there is a determinate sense or concept
of justification, even if justification doesn't qualify as a property in the stronger
sense of a natural phenomenon or natural kind. However, I doubt that Alston
would be mollified by this prospect. He would undoubtedly insist that the problem for justification theory is that there is no reason to think that different theorists have agreed on any unique *meaning, sense,* or *concept* of justification.
That's just another way of phrasing the problem, he would say. Indeed, in ED
this is one way he formulates it: "Is there a unique *concept* of epistemic justification?" (ED, 532, emphasis added). And he thinks the answer is negative.

I am pretty well persuaded by Alston that there is no unique sense of 'justification' that epistemologists are arguing over. Actually, I myself argued for two
senses of 'justified' in an earlier paper ("Strong and Weak Justification"),
though I haven't consistently pursued this. But I disagree with Alston that this is
a reason to abandon inquiry about justification. I think we should approach the
topic as a puzzle. There does not seem to be much difficulty in communicating
with other epistemologists about the rudiments, at least, of epistemic justification. One can also find uses of the term 'justified,' or closely related expressions, in books and newspapers for the general public, where it is presumed that
the phrases are understood.[3] How is it possible, then, that the term should lack a
determinate, generic sense that is conveyed in these communications? Perhaps
the term as ordinarily used is ambiguous, or polysemous. If so, how do we manage to achieve (apparent) mutual understanding in ordinary conversation? And
how many senses does it have? Three? Seven? Seventeen? If polysemy is the
right story, how does a hearer manage to select among the multiple senses when

encountering the term in conversation, including a philosophical conversation? These are problems of applied linguistics, especially the branch of linguistics called lexical semantics. While I do not think that lexical semanticists have a consensus theory to offer that bears on this question, their discipline is one from which illumination would be profitably sought. The problem about 'justified' is not unique, and we can get a better grip on it by seeing where it fits within the larger domain of semantics. In short, although Alston may be right that 'justified' and 'justified belief' do not have unique and perfectly determinate meanings (at least not determinate enough for philosophical purposes), understanding why and how that can be so is important to epistemology. Epistemologists should not abandon the subject, but should study it in a wider setting.

There are several possible diagnoses of Alston's problem. First, perhaps some theorists of justification—maybe all of them—put forward erroneous theories. Each such theorist claims that 'justified' in its epistemic sense means such-and-so, but such-and-so does not correspond to any established sense of 'justified' (not even established in the epistemological community). Different theorists make different mistakes; hence the disagreement. This diagnosis, of course, fits one possible explanation. Alston mentions, namely, that the nature or meaning of 'justified' is simply a very tough problem. A second possible diagnosis is that 'justified' (at least in its epistemic sense) is simply ambiguous, or polysemous. Some epistemologists correctly latch onto one of these multiple senses and others latch onto others; hence the theoretical disagreement. A third diagnosis would be a combination of the first two.

Focusing on the second diagnosis, we have to ask whether the source of semantic ambiguity is located specifically in the lexical unit 'justified' or located a bit more broadly. What epistemologists analyze is not 'justified' in its most generic sense, but 'epistemically justified,' where 'epistemic' is a technical term (the meaning of which could itself be subjected to Alston's worries).[4] Or, perhaps, they analyze not the simple lexical item 'justified' but the phrase 'justified belief.' Adding these further lexical items ('epistemic' or 'belief') places extra constraints on what the meaning might be. Nonetheless, the second diagnosis is still potentially available—that 'justified belief' has more than one reading or semantic interpretation.

For the moment, let's pretend we are dealing with a single lexical unit, 'justified.' Is that word polysemous? How would lexical semantics approach the matter, based on general theory? Following James Pustejovsky (who in turn follows Weinreich),[5] we should first distinguish two types of polysemy: contrastive polysemy and complementary polysemy. Contrastive polysemy involves the essentially arbitrary association of multiple senses with a single word. In contrastive polysemy, a word carries two distinct and unrelated meanings (i.e., homonymy). Examples include 'bank,' which can mean either the shore of a river or a financial institution, and 'line,' which can mean, among other things, a message ('drop me a line') or a narrow elongated mark ('the fence is along the property line'). The second type of polysemy, complementary polysemy, involves overlapping, dependent, or shared meanings. For example, the word 'window' has one sense in which it refers to an aperture and another sense in which it refers to a physical object used to frame such an aperture. This ambiguity is illustrated by the difference between 'John crawled through the window' (aperture) and 'The window is rotting' (physical object that frames the aperture). Although these are different senses, they are obviously interdependent. Another example is 'lamb,' which has one sense referring to a certain type of animal ('The lamb is running in the field') and another sense referring to meat from that kind of animal ('John ate lamb for dinner').

An initial question for the second diagnosis of the 'justification' debates is whether the multiple senses that should be postulated for 'justified' instantiate contrastive or complementary polysemy. The answer, presumably, is complementary polysemy. The senses hypothesized by different theorists—assuming these hypotheses are accurate—are presumably related.[6] Here, then, we already have a response to Alston. We shouldn't abandon the topic of justification simply because there is polysemy. We should try to reveal exactly *how* the various senses are related. That seems like a worthwhile epistemological enterprise, on the assumption that justification is prima facie an important epistemological topic.

Very quickly, however, matters concerning general semantic theory become complicated. There is one possible tack in lexical semantics that would assign numerous different meanings to a lot of words. For example, 'fast' has several separate senses, associated with 'move quickly,' 'accomplish some act quickly,' or 'do something that takes little time.'[7] When examined under the semanticist's microscope, many words seem to have more senses than one might suspect. How are those senses represented in the mind, that is, in the mental lexicon? And how do compositional devices operate on such senses, along with other lexical units in a sentence or larger discourse, to yield interpretations for these larger linguistic units?

Pustejovsky formulates (and rejects) a very simple model of how word meaning is represented in the mind, called a "Sense Enumeration Lexicon" (SEL). A SEL has multiple listings of words, each annotated with a separate meaning or lexical sense. To assign a correct semantic interpretation to any string in the language, the mind has to exploit clues from the linguistic and nonlinguistic context to select from among these senses and compose an appropriate interpretation for the string. Pustejovsky then argues that the simple model of a SEL is inadequate for the semantic description of language. Matters are more complicated. One piece of the argument is the creative use of words. Words assume new senses in novel contexts. Consider the sentence 'The Autobahn is the fastest motorway in Germany.' The adjective 'fast' here seems to express a new sense, that is, the ability of vehicles (on the motorway) to sustain high speed. Should this be a separate lexical sense for 'fast'? Probably not. But, then, how is this interpretation arrived at in the semantics? Another problem Pustejovsky cites is the permeability of word senses. A verb like 'bake' requires discrimination with respect to change-of-state versus creation readings. 'John baked the potato' refers to the potato's change-of-state, whereas 'John baked a cake' refers to the creation of a cake (which did not exist prior to its baking). Clearly, there is a lot of overlap between the semantic contents of the two readings. Should one represent the matter in terms of two different senses? That seems unnatural.

I won't venture any further into Pustejovsky's discussion. Matters are obviously complex. One important moral for our purposes, however, is that problems of ambiguity or polysemy pervade language, so the situation of 'justification' is far from unusual. It doesn't mean there is no coherence or unity to the meaning of 'justification.' There is just a lot of theoretical work to be done in analyzing such matters, both in the general case and in the specific case of 'justification.' What we shouldn't do is throw up our hands in despair and discard the term entirely, as Alston proposes. If we follow this course whenever there is ambiguity, there will be little left to work with.

Perhaps I am neglecting a line of argument Alston could deploy that would also draw on work by linguists. Like Pustejovsky, Deirdre Wilson[8] calls attention to the creative aspect of understanding. She emphasizes the theme that meanings are often modified in use, and what a speaker communicates with a word often differs from the concept encoded in the mental lexicon (in virtue of the word's 'literal' meaning). A word can be used to convey a more specific sense than is standard—"lexical narrowing"—and a word can be used to convey a wider sense than is standard—"lexical broadening." To illustrate narrowing, consider 'All doctors drink.' Here 'drink' does not convey 'imbibe liquid.' It probably doesn't even mean 'imbibe alcohol,' but, rather, 'imbibe alcohol in large quantities.' Broadening is illustrated by cases of approximation, in which '1,000 dollars' is not restricted in meaning to 'exactly 1,000 dollars,' but encompasses a wider range of dollar values. Another example is a category extension, in which a word is used to represent a different category of thing than it standardly refers to. For instance, 'Ironing is the new yoga' conveys something like 'ironing is the new fad,' where 'yoga' takes on a considerably different meaning than its literal one. Alston could seize on such examples and suggest that something of this sort has happened to 'justification' in epistemology, and perhaps to other terms in other branches of philosophy. Philosophers use words creatively, and different philosophers make different creative moves. The upshot is different extensions (in Wilson's sense) of the term 'justified.' These extensions get semi-established within the discipline, or subdiscipline, and then one has multiple senses of the term, each with some currency in the field. Isn't this just the sort of chaotic picture Alston describes, now explained with the help of semantics (and pragmatics), but not thereby resolved?

I don't mean to disregard this possibility. But the proper response, I urge, is not to hide one's face from the phenomenon by ceasing to discourse about 'justification,' but by tracing out exactly how this process occurs and what the morals are for work on epistemic justification. What is the root meaning (or meanings) of 'justified,' how is it affected by being a modifier of 'belief' (and itself being modified by 'epistemic'), and how have various creative extensions possibly changed what is conveyed by the term?

Let me now turn to a different tradition in semantics that might shed light on the situation in epistemology. I have in mind the tradition of frame semantics, associated with such linguists as Fillmore, Lakoff, and Fauconnier.[9] As Fillmore explains it (also see Coulson 2001), the meaning of many words relies on speakers' experience with the scenarios and social institutions they presuppose. The word 'Tuesday' cannot be defined without providing background information about the organization of the week. The full significance of the terms 'week' and 'weekend' presupposes the practice of the five-day work week. Thus, Fillmore emphasizes how the meanings of words grow out of motivating experiences or social practices. The meaning of 'bachelor,' classically defined as an unmarried man, depends on background information grounded in social practice. It is doubtful that the pope, Tarzan, or a gay man in a long-term relationship would count as a bachelor. When the common assumptions about the normal course of a man's life in Western society fail to apply, as in the case of the pope, we hesitate to apply the term 'bachelor.'

In keeping with this tradition, one might try to illuminate the meaning of 'justified' and other epistemic terms by appealing to the commonsense norms for belief-evaluation that exist in social life. This sort of approach is prominently exemplified by Wittgenstein (1969), but also by epistemologists with different substantive theories. For example, I have appealed to it in defending a two-tiered version of reliabilism.[10] According to this approach, our norms for justification attribution pinpoint belief-forming processes or methods that are regarded as reliable by the community. Thus, according to this theory, the concept of justification is rooted in reliability assessments. Reliability considerations might not be encoded in a definition of 'justified,' or 'justified belief,' but they might lie behind social practices that fix the norms of justification attribution. Other accounts of justification might have different stories to tell about existing epistemic norms, and more than one such story could have at least part of the truth. Viewed in this light, what appear as competing theories might not be mutually exclusive.

Let me turn now to other philosophical subject-matters where problems analogous to the ones Alston poses could inspire similar nihilist crusades. I'll first turn to consciousness, where a number of philosophers of consciousness claim that the term 'conscious' is multiply ambiguous. Here is William Lycan on the subject:

> From time to time philosophers have acknowledged and even articulated a multiplicity of meanings, especially of the term "consciousness", but the fact of the

multiplicity has never properly been taken to heart. Both psychologists and some philosophers still use the word univocally and without explication, as if it had one clear meaning and we all knew what it meant; many sharply distinct phenomena are still being lumped together under that heading.[11]

Lycan provides eight different senses.[12] The eight senses are: (1) organism consciousness, (2) control consciousness, (3) consciousness of, (4) state/event consciousness, (5) reportability, (6) introspective consciousness, (7) subjective consciousness, and (8) self-consciousness. Many other philosophers of mind also invoke distinct senses of "consciousness." Block (1995) distinguishes phenomenal consciousness, access consciousness, monitoring consciousness, reflective consciousness, and self-consciousness. Rosenthal (1997) distinguishes state consciousness, creature consciousness, transitive consciousness, and introspective consciousness. Armstrong (1981) distinguishes minimal consciousness, perceptual consciousness, and introspective consciousness. Tye (1995) distinguishes higher-order consciousness, discriminatory consciousness, responsive consciousness, and phenomenal consciousness.

If Alston were working in philosophy of mind, he might advocate the same move there as he advocates in epistemology. He would first point out that we are confronted with a wildly chaotic set of theories of consciousness. Next he would point out that there is no reason to suppose that the different theories have a unique, common subject-matter. They are really addressed to different things. Finally, he would conclude that there is no reason to think that 'conscious' or 'consciousness' picks out a unique property of the mind. Theorists are just chasing a phantom, with no more reality than ether or ghosts. Hence, philosophy of mind should abandon the project of saying what consciousness is, or what 'consciousness' means. Just do philosophy of mind without consciousness.

Michael Antony has replied to this ambiguity charge by taking a page from lexical semantics.[13] Antony invokes an idea from the lexical semanticist D. A. Cruse, who seeks to minimize the multiplication of senses. Like other semanticists, Cruse focuses on the effect of linguistic context to explain what might otherwise seem to require a multiplication of senses. Particularly relevant here is a phenomenon Cruse calls modulation.[14] Different linguistic contexts in which a lexical item appears can emphasize certain semantic traits of the unit and obscure or suppress others. One type of modulation involves highlighting or backgrounding. A *part* of an object or process, for example, may be thrown into relief by the context. For instance, 'The car needs servicing' and 'The car needs washing' highlight different parts of the car. What is highlighted or backgrounded is usually an attribute, or range of attributes, of the entity referred to. Although 'car' in each case refers to the whole car, 'The car needs servicing' highlights the car's engine, whereas 'The car needs washing' highlights its body. Similarly, 'We can't afford that car' highlights the car's price, whereas 'Our car couldn't keep up with his' highlights its performance. Cruse allows that there is a sense in which a lexical unit may be said to have a different meaning in distinct contexts, but presumably it has all those different meanings in those contexts because of its antecedent possession of core semantic traits independent of context. The various contexts simply serve to bring out, or call attention to, those core traits. Furthermore, Cruse contrasts a word's susceptibility to modulation with the status of being ambiguous, or polysemous. 'Car' is not ambiguous in the way that 'bank' is ambiguous; it does not have multiple senses.

Going beyond Antony's discussion but staying in its spirit, we might try to apply this theme to the term 'consciousness.' 'Phenomenal consciousness' is perhaps the core meaning of consciousness; it is roughly synonymous with 'awareness.' 'Creature consciousness' refers to a creature's having one or more states of phenomenal consciousness. 'Access consciousness' refers to functional properties associated with a phenomenally conscious state. When a state is phenomenally conscious, it will also have the functional property of being "poised" to participate in other mental or cognitive activities; for example, reasoning, control of action, and control of speech. 'Reportability' is not a separate type of consciousness but a property associated with, or made possible by, phenomenal consciousness, viz., being available for report. 'Introspective' or 'higher-order' consciousness is not a new type of consciousness but another property that arises from, or is associated with, phenomenal consciousness, namely the property of being open or prone to being introspected by a higher-order state. (The higher-order thought view contends that consciousness requires a state to be actually introspected rather than merely potentially introspectible; that is not endorsed here.) On this approach, 'consciousness' does not refer to multiple phenomena and does not even have multiple meanings (senses). It has one meaning and one type of referent, although different aspects or attributes of that type of referent can be invoked in different uses.[15]

Finally, let me turn to a third area of philosophy where controversy might set the stage for an Alstonian crusade. Here I shall comment on such a crusade not from the perspective of linguistics, but from a different set of considerations. The philosophical arena in question is a region of metaphysics, specifically, the topics of identity and persistence. As in the case of justification, the nature of identity—including identity over time—is a subject about which there are innumerable conflicting theories. There are even disagreements about some of the "data"; for example, whether a lump of bronze is identical to a statue made of that same bronze or merely constitutes that statue. An Alston-inspired metaphysician might claim that there is just too much chaotic disagreement here. The recommended conclusion is that there is no unique property (or even concept) of identity that different metaphysicians are arguing over. Their imagined target has no more objective reality than ether or ghosts; it's just a phantom. So metaphysicians should stop debating issues of identity and turn to other topics. Should we accept this recommendation?

Let us review some of the questions about identity that elicit sharply clashing answers. One question is whether identity is absolute or relative. Standard quantificational theory assumes that identity is an absolute relation, which need not be relativized in any way. X is either identical to Y or non-identical to it. According to Geach and others, however, identity is really a relative notion or relation. One can only ask whether X = Y relative to some specified sortal (Geach, 1980). Another controversial question in the metaphysics of identity concerns identity over time. It is generally agreed that objects persist over time, but should persistence be cashed out in terms of "endurance" or "perdurance"? An enduring object is "wholly present" at all times at which it exists. This theory is sometimes called "three-dimensionalism." The perdurance theory is that persistence consists of an object being "stretched out" in time. Its successive temporal parts together compose the whole object, though no single temporal slice is the (entire) object. When you touch a person (no matter how much of him you touch, three-dimensionally speaking) you only touch one *part* of him; for not all the person is *then* to be touched. This view is called "four-dimensionalism," and it has sub-species consisting of the "worm" theory and the "stage" theory (Sider, 2001). The controversy in metaphysics between three-dimensionalism and four-dimensionalism is as rampant as the epistemological controversy between internalism and externalism. In the midst of the debate is another fundamental question: Is persistence over time a question of identity or rather of a different relation, *genidentity*? What, exactly, is the connection between identity and genidentity?

Should metaphysics divest itself of the identity topic, on the grounds that theorists are really talking about different subject-matters, or because there is no "objective" subject-matter to talk about? Such an Alstonian proposal would strike me as wrongheaded. But my own reflections on this case run in a rather different direction than in the previous cases.

Here I am sympathetic to the idea that, in one sense of "objective," there may be no objective matter over which metaphysicians are disagreeing. I would side with Alan Sidelle on this matter. Sidelle surveys a multiplicity of competing views about material objects and identity over time, showing how each has a certain coherence and plausibility while suffering from identifiable defects or weaknesses. How should we choose among these metaphysical "packages"? More significantly, is there reason to think that exactly one package is *right*? Sidelle answers the latter question in the negative.

> I will argue that there is no fact of the matter about which package is true—each is metaphysically as good as the others, and the world is incapable of discriminating among them.[16]

> I don't see what in the world can *make* one true; or, equivalently, while the theories plainly *differ*, I don't see how *that with respect to which they differ* can be understood as a factual matter.[17]

One way to resist this conclusion, and thereby resist Alston-inspired nihilism in this region of metaphysics, is to resist Sidelle's assumption that correctness is a matter of correspondence with special metaphysical facts. Maybe what makes one of the packages in question "correct" is its maximization of coherence and utility. This would make room for a kind of objectivity that would deflect an Alston-style maneuver. I wouldn't myself endorse this response, but it may appeal to others.

Another way to rescue metaphysical subject-matter from Alstonian deletion is to say that what metaphysicians are arguing about—or what they should be arguing about—is the nature of our commonsense *concepts*, or *conceptions, of* identity and objecthood. By "concepts" or "conceptions" I have in mind states that are mental in character. The contents of those concepts or conceptions deserve elucidation and analysis even if there is nothing in the extra-mental world that makes them right or wrong. Under this approach, questions of metaphysics become psychological questions; for example, "What principles do our cognitive systems use to 'connect' or 'unify' objects, either at a time or over time?"[18] Construed as psychological questions, they presumably have factual answers that are, in principle, right or wrong. Some people might prefer to reformulate these questions as questions about language: What is meant by the *words* 'identity' and 'object'? But developmental psychology makes it quite clear that very young, pre-linguistic children have conceptions of objecthood that antedate their learning of language.[19] So a non-linguistic formulation is actually to be preferred. This is not the occasion on which to explore the empirical research that supports this contention. The important point is that this interpretation preserves an objective subject-matter about which competing theories can be correct or incorrect. Obviously, this proposal requires a more sustained presentation and defense than the present occasion permits.[20]

In conclusion, we see that the conditions are ripe in many areas of philosophy to raise the kinds of worries Alston raises in epistemology. Although these worries are legitimate, Alston has not persuaded me of the appropriateness of his eliminative program. Nonetheless, there is plenty of room for debate about how, precisely, one should respond to his proposal, or to "copycat" proposals that could arise elsewhere in philosophy. Intriguing questions are posed about the sources of disagreement in philosophy and what to make of such disagreement. Some initial forays have been undertaken here, but I hope that others will also see the problems as both interesting and pressing.

References

Alston, William P. *Beyond "Justification": Dimensions of Epistemic Evaluation* (DEE). Ithaca, NY: Cornell University Press, 2005.
———. "Doing Epistemology without Justification" (DEWJ). *Philosophical Topics* 29 (2001): 1–18.

————. "Epistemic Desiderata" (ED). *Philosophy and Phenomenological Research* 53, no. 3 (September 1993): 527–551.

————. *The Reliability of Sense Perception* (RSP). Ithaca, NY: Cornell University Press, 1993.

————. "Concepts of Epistemic Justification." *The Monist* 68, no. 1 (January 1985): 57–89.

————. "Level Confusions in Epistemology." *Midwest Studies in Philosophy* 5 (1980): 135–150.

Antony, M. V. "Is 'Consciousness' Ambiguous?" *Journal of Consciousness Studies* 8, no. 2 (2001): 19–44.

Armstrong, D. M. "What Is Consciousness?" Pp. 55–67 in D. M. Armstrong, *The Nature of Mind*. Ithaca, NY: Cornell University Press, 1981.

Block, N. "On a Confusion about a Function of Consciousness." *Behavioral and Brain Sciences* 18 (1995): 227–247.

Carey, S. and F. Xu. "Infants' Knowledge of Objects." *Cognition* 80, no. 1–2 (June 2001): 179–213.

Coulter, S. *Semantic Leaps: Frame-Shifting and Conceptual Blending in Meaning Construction*. Cambridge: Cambridge University Press, 2001.

Cruse, D. A. *Lexical Semantics*. Cambridge: Cambridge University Press, 1986.

Fauconnier, G. *Mental Spaces: Aspects of Meaning Construction in Natural Language*. Cambridge: Cambridge University Press, 1994.

Fillmore, C. J. "Frame Semantics." Pp. 111–137 in *Linguistics in the Morning Calm*, edited by Linguistic Society of Korea. Seoul: Hanshin, 1982.

Geach, P. T. *Reference and Generality*. Ithaca, NY: Cornell University Press, 1980.

Goldman, Alvin I. "A Priori Warrant and Naturalistic Epistemology." Pp. 24–50 in Alvin I. Goldman, *Pathways to Knowledge*. New York: Oxford University Press, 2002.

————. *Philosophical Applications of Cognitive Science*. Boulder, CO: Westview Press, 1993.

————. "Epistemic Folkways and Scientific Epistemology." Pp. 155–175 in Alvin I. Goldman, *Liaisons: Philosophy Meets the Cognitive and Social Sciences*. Cambridge, MA: MIT Press, 1992.

————. "Metaphysics, Mind, and Mental Science." Pp. 35–48 in Alvin I. Goldman, *Liaisons: Philosophy Meets the Cognitive and Social Sciences*. Cambridge, MA: MIT Press, 1992.

————. "Strong and Weak Justification." Pp. 51–69 in *Philosophical Perspectives 2: Epistemology*, edited by James E. Tomberlin. Atascadero, CA: Ridgeview, 1988.

Kornblith, H. *Knowledge and Its Place in Nature*. New York: Oxford University Press, 2002.

Lakoff, G. *Women, Fire, and Dangerous Things: What Categories Reveal about the Mind*. Chicago, IL: University of Chicago Press, 1987.

Lycan, W. *Consciousness and Experience*. Cambridge, MA: The MIT Press, 1996.

Pustejovsky, J. *The Generative Lexicon*. Cambridge, MA: The MIT Press, 1995.

Putnam, H. "On Properties." Pp. 235–254 in *Essays in Honor of Carl G. Hempel*, edited by N. Rescher et al. Dordrecht: D. Reidel Pub. Co., 1969.

Rosenthal, D. "A Theory of Consciousness." Pp. 729–754 in *The Nature of Consciousness*, edited by N. Block, O. Flanagan, and G. Guzeldere. Cambridge, MA: The MIT Press, 1997.

Sidelle, A. "Is There a True Metaphysics of Material Objects?" *Philosophical Issues*, 12 (2002): 118–145.

Sider, T. *Four-Dimensionalism: An Ontology of Persistence and Time*. New York: Oxford University Press, 2001.

Soja, N., S. Carey and E. Spelke. "Ontological Categories Guide Young Children's Inductions of Word Meaning." *Cognition* 38, no. 2 (February 1991): 179–211.

Tye, M. "The Burning House." Pp. 81–90 in *Conscious Experience*, edited by T. Metzinger. Exeter: Imprint Academic, 1995.

Weinreich, U. "*Webster's Third:* A Critique of its Semantics." *International Journal of American Linguistics* 30 (1964): 405–409.

Wilson, D. "Ad Hoc Concepts, Word Meaning and Communication." Paper presented at the European Society of Philosophy and Psychology, Turin, Italy, 2003.

Wittgenstein, L. *On Certainty*. New York: Harper and Row, 1969.

Notes

1. William P. Alston, "Epistemic Desiderata" (ED), *Philosophy and Phenomenological Research* 53, no. 3 (September 1993): 527–551. William P. Alston, "Doing Epistemology without Justification" (DEWJ), *Philosophical Topics* 29: 1–18. William P. Alston, *Beyond "Justification": Dimensions of Epistemic Evaluation* (DEE) (Ithaca, NY: Cornell University Press, 2005). All page references to DEE are to manuscript pages. Page numbers in the published version, which is forthcoming, may differ.

2. See Hilary Kornblith, *Knowledge and Its Place in Nature* (New York: Oxford University Press, 2002).

3. For example, the *New York Times* of August 12, 2003, contains a headline, "U.S. Says Shot Fired at Hotel Was Justified." Presumably, the term 'justified' was assumed to be one that the general reader would understand. Admittedly, the headline predicates 'justified' of an action, which suggests that the term is not used in its epistemic sense. But the text of the article reads: "Troops were justified in firing at what they had reason to believe was an enemy position." The phrase "had reason to believe" is itself an epistemic expression. So the writer and editorial staff presumably thought that this epistemic expression had a recognizable and clear sense associated with it.

4. This points to a concern I have about the positive program of Alston's DEE. That program seems to be predicated on the determinacy and univocality of the term 'epistemic,' which Alston uses to identify the desiderata with which epistemology should

concern itself. But does the term 'epistemic' have the needed semantic properties that 'justified' lacks? I doubt it, but I won't pursue the matter further.

5. J. Pustejovsky, *The Generative Lexicon* (Cambridge, MA: The MIT Press, 1996); U. Weinreich, *"Webster's Third*: A Critique of Semantics," *International Journal of American Linguistics* 30 (1964): 405–409.

6. If they are not accurate, then we must move to the first or third diagnosis. If I read Alston correctly, however, the prospect of error in epistemological theorizing is not a source of concern. If he were persuaded that epistemological disagreement is explained by mere error, he would abandon his crusade for dropping the justification topic. Thus, in the text, I give scant attention to the error scenario, although personally I think it accounts for a lot of the observed disagreement.

7. Pustejovsky, *The Generative Lexicon*, 44–45.

8. Diedre Wilson, "Ad Hoc Concepts, Word Meaning and Communication," presented at the European Society of Philosophy and Psychology, Turin, Italy, 2003.

9. See C. J. Fillmore, "Frame Semantics," in *Linguistics in the Morning Calm*, ed. Linguistic Society of Korea (Seoul: Hanshin, 1982), 111–137; G. Lakoff, *Women, Fire, and Dangerous Things* (Chicago, IL: University of Chicago Press, 1987); and G. Fauconnier, *Mental Spaces: Aspects of Meaning Construction in Natural Language* (Cambridge: Cambridge University Press, 1994).

10. See my "Epistemic Folkways and Scientific Epistemology," in Goldman, *Liaisons* (Cambridge, MA: MIT Press, 1992), 155–175; and "A Priori Warrant and Naturalistic Epistemology," in Goldman, *Pathways to Knowledge* (New York: Oxford University Press, 2002), 24–50.

11. William Lycan, *Consciousness and Experience* (Cambridge, MA: The MIT Press, 1996), 2.

12. Actually, Lycan says eight different "uses." But since the term "meanings" occurs in the passage just quoted in the text, I infer that he doesn't intend to place much weight on the meaning/sense/use distinction.

13. M. V. Antony, "Is 'Consciousness' Ambiguous?" *Journal of Consciousness Studies* 8, no. 2 (2001): 19–44.

14. D. A. Cruse, *Lexical Semantics* (Cambridge: Cambridge University Press, 1986), 52.

15. The suggestion entertained here is that the lexical unit 'consciousness' has only one sense. The semantic contents of the various nominal expressions 'phenomenal consciousness,' 'access consciousness,' etc. will all be different, of course, just as 'surface of the car' and 'engine of the car' have different contents.

16. Alan Sidelle, "Is There a True Metaphysics of Material Objects?" *Philosophical Issues* 12 (2002): 118.

17. Sidelle, "Is There a True Metaphysics of Material Objects?" 134. His emphasis.

18. I don't intend this as a full account of metaphysics, but this is not a suitable occasion to explore the matter in depth.

19. See Soja, Carey, and Spelke, 1991; and Carey and Xu, 2001.

20. For earlier work suggesting views along these lines, see Goldman, "Metaphysics, Mind, and Mental Science" and *Philosophical Applications of Cognitive Science*, Chapter 4. Additional work on these themes is presently underway.

8

Response to Goldman

William P. Alston

Thanks to Al Goldman for the more than kind words. On my side I can say that I have found association with Al over the years to be richly rewarding both personally and in terms of philosophical stimulation and enlightenment. Especially in epistemology, there is no one from whom I have learned more, as the many references to him in the forthcoming *Beyond "Justification": Dimensions of Epistemic Evaluation* (DEE) will testify.

Goldman's paper is rich in interesting and useful discussions of the concept(s) of epistemic justification and of philosophical disagreements. I will have a few things to say about them in the latter part of this response. He presents these discussions as parts of a response to my views on doing philosophy without attention to the justification of beliefs. And that presentation, I am sorry to say, suffers from some misconstruals of those views. I will get into this by first giving a brief presentation of my anti-justificationist position.

As Goldman points out, I begin with the wide diversity of incompatible views as to what it is for a belief to be justified and as to further conditions for that status. And, as he also recognizes, I do not take that diversity itself to be a sufficient reason for abandoning the quest for a correct account of epistemic justification. The argument for the latter proceeds through asking about the best explanation of that diversity, which I claim to be that 'justified' as used by epistemologists in application to belief fails to pick out a unique objective status of beliefs about which the various competing accounts of epistemic justification are disagreeing. And the key argument for that claim is that no one has succeeded in locating any such target in a neutral way, that is, without relying on one of the competing theories to do so. This is the way the argument goes in the two writings, "Epistemic Desiderata" (ED) and DEE, in which it is presented, though much more clearly in the latter.

I will take this opportunity to say that I regret having launched my argument in the way summarized above. It's not that I have abandoned any of the parts of it, but that it gives a misleading impression of what is crucial for the argument.

By presenting the argument in the way I did, it looks as if what is crucial is what is the best explanation of the diversity. And I still think that my favored explanation is the best one. But I now also realize, and I thank Goldman for helping me to see (though I assume that was not his intention) that even if my chosen explanation were not the best one, I would still take the absence of any neutral way of locating the common target of different theories of justification to be a sufficient ground for denying that 'justified' picks out a unique epistemically crucial desideratum for beliefs. Suppose, to take a possibility that Goldman suggests, that the best explanation is that even though there is a common target for theories of justification, most such theorists are mistaken about it. Even so, I would still take the absence of a satisfactory way of zeroing in on that common target to support the conclusion of the argument on its own without any mention of what explains the diversity. And this would highlight most sharply what is really crucial for the argument.

Goldman takes issue with this crucial claim. He first points out neutral "partial specifications," and there are a number including the ones he cites, but their partiality prevents them from uniquely applying to epistemic justification. He asks whether "it is reasonable to demand more than this." I will not contest the view that a uniquely referring description is required, but here is what I take to be a non-negotiable condition for A and B to be disagreeing about what is required for a belief to be justified. That condition is that A and B are both making statements about the same object (property or status of belief) and for that it is necessary that they both have the same object in mind—that what they assert is intended to bear on the same target. Otherwise they are not disagreeing. Goldman thinks that the only way I recognize to satisfy this condition is by giving a theory-neutral (unique) description. And in the writings where the argument is presented, ED and DEE, I do begin the search for a satisfaction of the condition by considering a few candidates for such a description, all of which I reject. But that is not the end of the matter. In both writings, I point out that there are other ways of mentally zeroing in on a target other than by giving a uniquely applicable description. The one I present and discuss is a reliance on shared paradigms. This works very well with, for example, natural kind terms like 'dog,' where most people are unable to give identifying descriptions but have learned to do pretty well at recognizing clear cases in common with other members of their society. But I point out that it doesn't work so well with 'justified' as applied to beliefs. Though there are widely shared examples of justified and unjustified beliefs, it is also the case that among philosophers different theories of epistemic justification intrude themselves to a considerable extent in the choice of paradigms and also in extrapolating from agreed on cases to others. Hence this rescue for the justificationist does not pan out either. (For more details see ED, 535–538). Near the end of this response, I will suggest that Goldman's other cases of persistent disagreement in philosophy do better by way of relying on a mastery of commonly shared clear cases to individuate the target of the disagreement.

Now I turn to misconstruals of my position. The first indication that something is amiss comes from Goldman's supposition that the problem to which my proposal to abandon the practice of looking for the right account of the justification of belief (call this "Alston's proposal") is addressed is "how to end disagreement in epistemology." (He also speaks of Alston's "recipe for ending disagreement in epistemology.") But to this I enter a plea of innocent. I have never either had or expressed any such idea. It's true that I have stressed the point that adopting my proposal enables us to avoid disputes about what it takes for a belief to be justified. But ending all disagreement in epistemology? What an idea! I confidently expect epistemologists to be disagreeing as long as the discipline is pursued. There will be plenty of scope for disagreement in my "Epistemic Desiderata" approach. There is the question of which desiderata are most important or fundamental, which are the ones by relation to which others owe their title, not to mention how to construe such desiderata as a belief's being based on an adequate ground, and a belief's being formed by a generally reliable belief-forming process. It would be a major miracle if epistemologists stopped arguing about those and other matters just because they had quit supposing that 'justified' picks out a unique and centrally important epistemic desideratum.

I find no support in my writings for the above construal. But I can't say the same for the next misinterpretation. "He [Alston] would undoubtedly insist that the problem for justification theory is that there is no reason to think that different theorists have agreed on any unique *meaning, sense* or *concept* of justification. . . . But I disagree with Alston that this is a reason to abandon inquiry about justification." The main support for attributing to me at least the first of these claims is the one Goldman cites, viz., a misguided section heading in ED that reads "Is There a Unique Concept of Epistemic Justification?" Taken out of context, this can suggest that I take this to be another way of formulating the question of whether there is an objective status of beliefs picked out by 'justified.' Unfortunately, I was also insufficiently consistent in distinguishing these two questions in other places in ED, a lapse corrected in DEE. But even in the former, and more unambiguously in the latter, the main emphasis is on the latter question. There is a serious issue as to how a plurality of concepts expressed by 'justified' in epistemic contexts (alternatively a multiplicity of senses of 'justified' in those contexts) is related to the denial that 'justified' in such contexts picks out a unique centrally important status of beliefs. It may well seem that the former guarantees the latter, at least for the uniqueness part. And that is so provided there are differences among the concepts (senses) that are not simply getting at different aspects of the same target. And there surely are such differences. Consider, for example, the difference between such alleged concepts of epistemic justification as *conducting one's cognitive activities responsibly* and *acquiring a belief by a reliable process.*

But the matter is not this simple. For even if there is a variety of concepts (senses) expressed by 'justified' over the whole range of epistemologists who use the term, it may still be that it is possible, and even actual, for epistemologists (or some of them) to use some more generic device to locate a common subject matter about which divergent theories of epistemic justification can be disagreeing. And that is the reason (though not, I fear, articulated as such) that I did not put the stress in my argument on a wide diversity of concepts (senses) expressed by 'justified,' but rather on whether it is possible to locate a common target for competing theorists of justification to be disagreeing about. The application of all this to Goldman's very interesting and valuable survey of different semantic approaches to polysemy is that it is only tangentially related to the Alston proposal. Goldman thinks otherwise because he thinks that he is contradicting me by saying, "We shouldn't abandon the topic of justification simply because there is polysemy," whereas I would never dream of giving that as a reason for the abandonment. But I also want to recognize that the exploration, for example, of ways in which different senses of 'justified' are related is eminently worthwhile. A last word on this topic is that at the end of section iv of Chapter 1 of DEE there is a discussion of ways in which my position is similar to, but also different from, positions according to which 'justified' expresses different concepts in epistemic contexts.

As his title indicates, Goldman was centrally concerned in his paper with disagreement in philosophy. In the latter part of the paper he begins an exploration of philosophical areas other than epistemic justification in which we find a wide diversity of competing views, and "where problems analogous to the ones Alston poses could inspire similar nihilist crusades." It is certainly of interest to see where a position like mine would or would not be warranted and why. The examples Goldman chooses are consciousness and identity. In general, I find his treatment of these convincing. I would add that in both cases we have something lacking in the epistemic justification case, viz., a well-established ordinary language term for which there is a enormous run of uncontroversially clear cases, thereby inhibiting any supposition that a common target for divergent theories has not been located. In the case of consciousness, Lycan's claim of a radical ambiguity can be handled in Goldman's way by separating out a fundamental sense in terms of which all the others can be explicated and that serves to indicate the common target of most so-called "theories of consciousness." Just to add to the list, consider truth. Here too there is a wide diversity of incompatible accounts, but there is an anchor that provides clear indication of a common target, viz., a schema like 'It is true that p if and only if p' or its Tarskian neighbor, 'X is true iff p,' where instances of the latter result from replacing 'p' with a declarative sentence and 'X' with an expression referring to that sentence. The difference between these "anchors" has to do with whether one concentrates on sentences or propositions as the primary truth-value-bearers, rather than differences in what would be taken as clear cases of truth. Again consider causality.

Here too there is a plethora of incompatible accounts, but there is a very well-established ordinary language term with virtually no disagreement as to clear cases of its application. In contrast to these cases, 'justified' in epistemic contexts is mostly a philosophers' term that lacks the support from a well-established term of ordinary language. Moreover, differences between theories of epistemic justification seem to have a powerful effect on what clear cases are recognized.

I will make just one further comment on Goldman's paper. After saying "Alston typically expresses his nihilism or eliminativism about justification by denying that there is a (unique) property expressed by the term 'justified'", he continues, "What sense of 'property' does he have in mind?" His discussion of this reminds me of Berkeley's comment on his materialist opponents that they raise a dust and then complain that they cannot see. He offers me a choice between two notions of "property" he takes from Putnam, one referring to predicates and one referring to physical magnitudes. I certainly don't think that epistemic justification could be a physical magnitude, nor is it a predicate of which I am denying the objective existence. Nor was I using 'property' in a sense, if there is such a sense, in which synonymy of predicates is the criterion for two predicates expressing the same property. Let's say that what I deny is that 'justified' in epistemic contexts picks out some evaluative status of beliefs, or if you prefer, an objective state of a belief's being justified. And depending on your preferences about 'property,' you may or may not be willing to speak of evaluative properties. I have no problem with that myself.

Part II: Philosophy of Religion

9

Is Alston's Response to Religious Diversity an Overstated Case?

Philip L. Quinn

The beginning of the twenty-first century produced striking evidence that problems of religious diversity have come to occupy a prominent spot on the agenda of philosophy of religion. Within a period of three years, leading publishers produced four philosophical books with the phrase "religious diversity" in their titles. *The Philosophical Challenge of Religious Diversity*, a collection of previously published papers meant for classroom use and edited by Philip L. Quinn and Kevin Meeker, came from Oxford University Press in 2000. In 2001, Oxford also published *Religious Ambiguity and Religious Diversity*, a substantial monograph by Robert McKim. In the same year, Blackwell Publishers launched a textbook series, Exploring the Philosophy of Religion, with *Problems of Religious Diversity* by Paul J. Griffiths. And in 2002 a competitor, Ashgate Publishing Company, started its rival textbook series, Ashgate Philosophy of Religion Series, with David Basinger's *Religious Diversity: A Philosophical Assessment*.[1] It is noteworthy that three of these books aim to provide philosophy instructors with resources for their teaching. Apparently publishers and those who advise them are persuaded that student demand for coverage of religious diversity in philosophy of religion courses offers a promising marketing opportunity. They must also suppose that professional philosophers can, as a result of their work on problems of religious diversity, supply teaching resources that will help to meet the demand.

In addition to their partially shared titles, these books have something else in common. Each of them acknowledges the importance of William P. Alston's contributions to philosophical discussion of religious diversity by paying special attention to his views on this topic. The volume edited by Quinn and Meeker reprints a paper by Alston in which he summarizes those views, and it also contains three other papers that subject them to critical scrutiny. The final chapter of McKim's monograph, which bears the title "Alston on Religious Experience," is devoted to critical examination of Alston's defense of his own epistemology of religious experience against difficulties for it to which religious diversity gives rise. Griffiths and Basinger also focus on Alston's claims about the epistemological significance of religious diversity. In his chapter on religious diversity and epistemic confidence, Griffiths has included a section aptly called "The Epistemic Significance of Religious Diversity: A Christian View in Conversation with William Alston." And in his chapter on diversity and justified belief, Basinger begins a survey of the positions of several philosophers who have written on religious diversity with a section whose title is simply "William Alston." The Alstonian views to which these philosophers are all responding are set forth most fully in the penultimate chapter of his magisterial *Perceiving God: The Epistemology of Religious Experience* (PG). That chapter, entitled "The Problem of Religious Diversity," opens with a candid admission by Alston that he has "saved the most difficult problem for my position—religious diversity—for a separate chapter."[2] The ingenious solution to the problem Alston proposes in that chapter is subjected to critical evaluation in each of the four recent books on religious diversity I have mentioned.

It would be nice to be in a position to discuss in this essay the responses to Alston's views in all of these books. However, constraints on its length do not permit me to do so. I shall instead focus exclusively on the response in the last chapter of McKim's book. My choice of a target for discussion is prompted by three reasons. First, because his book is a scholarly monograph, McKim seems to me to engage with Alston in a more sophisticated way than is possible for Griffiths or Basinger within the limits of a textbook format. Second, having appeared in print more recently than the views of the critics whose papers are reprinted in the Quinn and Meeker anthology, McKim's thoughts have the allure of novelty. And third, even when I disagree with him, McKim seems to me to be both a painstaking reader and an interesting critic of Alston. Taken together, these reasons lead me to believe that an essay dealing with McKim's response to Alston in some detail is more likely to prove philosophically instructive than anything I might produce covering different ground.

The essay has three parts. In the first, I come to grips with and try to resolve an exegetical puzzle McKim extracts from Alston's account of the epistemology of religious experience. The second and third parts defend Alston's account against McKim's contention, from which I derive the essay's title, "that he overstates his case and that more modest conclusions are in order" (McKim, 245). My defense involves a critical examination of the arguments McKim constructs to support his contention. Though I believe that these arguments raise issues worth discussing, I aim to show that they fall short of establishing McKim's main thesis.

I. Strong and Weak Readings of Alston's Project

The notion of a doxastic practice is central to Alston's general epistemology. He thinks of a doxastic practice as a way of forming beliefs and evaluating them epistemically in terms of a background system of beliefs that furnish potential overriders. For example, sense perceptual practice (SP) is a basic secular practice whose outputs are perceptual beliefs about the physical environment and whose inputs are sensory experiences. In the religious sphere, there is, according to Alston, something akin to sense perception. Mystical perception is the particular sort of religious experience in which a presentation or appearance to the subject of something the subject identifies as the Ultimate occurs. When the notion of a doxastic practice is applied to mystical perception, the result is a kind or sort of mystical perceptual practice (MP) whose outputs are beliefs about how the Ultimate is manifesting itself to the subject and whose inputs are mystical perceptions. But while there is just one SP that is shared by all of humankind, there are, in Alston's view, different MPs in different religious traditions. He considers it important to acknowledge a plurality of MPs because of the substantial diversity in the overrider systems of background beliefs to be found in the world's major religious traditions. One such practice is Christian mystical practice (CMP), in which the Ultimate is taken to be a personal deity. Others are Hindu mystical practice (HMP), Buddhist mystical practice (BMP), and so forth.

A crucial question for any doxastic practice is whether it confers prima facie justification on the beliefs that are its outputs. This is not an easy question for Alston to answer because he operates with an externalist conception of justification according to which justification requires that a belief have an adequate ground and an adequate ground must be sufficiently indicative of truth. So a doxastic practice must be sufficiently reliable if it is to confer prima facie justification on the beliefs that issue from it. Unfortunately, however, when Alston surveys direct arguments for the reliability of SP, he concludes that they all suffer from epistemic circularity or are otherwise flawed. He therefore finds himself forced to fall back to a pragmatic argument for the rationality of engaging in SP. When that argument is generalized, its conclusion is that it is prima facie practically rational to engage in socially established doxastic practices. This prima facie rational acceptability of a doxastic practice can, of course, be overridden by factors that are sufficiently indicative of unreliability such as massive internal inconsistency of the practice's outputs or external inconsistency of its outputs with those of other socially established practices. Encapsulated in a simple formula, Alston's view is that "*a firmly established doxastic practice is rationally engaged in unless the total output of all our firmly established doxastic practices sufficiently indicates its unreliability*" (PG, 175, his emphasis). He also believes that the prima facie practical rationality of engaging in a practice will be enhanced if it enjoys significant self-support. And he holds that SP and other basic doxastic practices satisfy all these conditions. They are firmly enough established to qualify as prima facie rationally acceptable; they are not plagued by massive and persistent internal or external inconsistencies; and they enjoy significant self-support. Thus it is practically rational without qualification to engage in SP and other familiar basic doxastic practices.

But what, if anything, does this have to do with the issue of whether SP is reliable? Alston admits that the practical rationality of engaging in SP does not entail its reliability. Indeed, he grants that "the practical rationality of SP does not even provide nondeductive but sufficient grounds for supposing it to be reliable" (PG, 178). Nevertheless, he believes that in showing it to be practically rational to engage in SP, he has thereby shown it to be rational to suppose that SP is reliable. This belief is supported by the following considerations:

> To engage in a certain doxastic practice and to accept the beliefs one thereby generates is to commit oneself to those beliefs being true (at least for the most part), and hence to commit oneself to the practice's being reliable. It is irrational to engage in SP, to form beliefs in the ways constitutive of that practice, and refrain from acknowledging them as true, and hence the practice as reliable, if the question arises. (PG, 179)

Such considerations do not, of course, show that SP is reliable. Nor do they show that it is epistemically rational to suppose that SP is reliable in the sense that showing this supposition to be epistemically rational would involve showing that it is at least probably true that SP is reliable. Because McKim quotes it in order to base a criticism of Alston on it, I quote in full the passage in which Alston spells out the connection between the practical rationality of taking SP to be reliable and the issue of whether the beliefs that issue from SP are prima facie justified in a truth-conducive sense:

> The lower epistemic status we have settled for attaches to the *higher-level* claim that SP is reliable, not [to] the particular perceptual beliefs that issue from that practice. As for the latter, what we are claiming is still the full-blooded (prima facie) justification . . . that involves likelihood of truth. To be sure, the fact remains that the higher-level claim that they enjoy that status has not itself been shown to enjoy such a status (one entailing likelihood of truth), and we have despaired of being able to show that it does. At the higher level we have settled for showing that it is (practically) *rational* to take SP to confer justification in the full-blooded sense. But it would be a level confusion to suppose that this implies that perceptual beliefs themselves are not justified in the stronger sense. Once more, according to our account of justification, the justification of perceptual beliefs requires that it is *true* that SP is reliable, not that we are truth-conducively justified in believing this. Moreover, though I do not claim to have shown that SP is reliable, and that its products are prima facie justified in my strong sense, I do claim to have shown that it is *reasonable* to take SP to be reliable, and hence reasonable to suppose that its products are prima facie justified in that strong sense. (PG, 181–182, his emphasis)

In short, Alston claims no more than that he has shown it to be practically rational to take SP to be reliable, and hence practically rational to take the beliefs that are its products to be prima facie justified in a truth-conducive sense. He does not claim that he has shown that SP is reliable, or that he has shown that the beliefs issuing from it are prima facie justified in a truth-conducive sense. He does not even claim that he has shown it to be epistemically rational in a truth-conducive sense to take SP to be reliable, or that he has shown it to be epistemically rational in a truth-conducive sense to take the beliefs that are its products to be prima facie justified in that strong sense.

Alston models his discussion of CMP on his treatment of SP and its kin. He first notes that CMP is a socially established doxastic practice. It is therefore prima facie practically rational to engage in CMP. He then proceeds to examine various considerations that might serve to override this prima facie practical rationality. He argues that the products of CMP are not massively and persistently inconsistent with the deliverances of more basic socially established secular practices such as SP. Hence an external inconsistency of this sort does not disqualify CMP from rational acceptance. He also argues that the products of CMP do not display massive and persistent internal inconsistency. At this stage of the argument it is important for Alston to be able to focus on the mystical practice of a single religious tradition. For if he were faced with the task of evaluating a generic MP, he would confront severe difficulties in trying to argue against the charge of internal inconsistency. Even if the outputs of such a generic practice were not themselves massively inconsistent, it seems obvious that its system of background beliefs would be. However, Alston's ability to focus narrowly on CMP instead of on a generic MP does not get him a free lunch. He avoids a threat of internal inconsistency only to find himself faced with another sort of problem of external inconsistency. Both the outputs of CMP and especially its overrider system of background beliefs at least appear to be massively inconsistent with their equally well-established counterparts in the mystical practices of other religious traditions such as HMP or BMP. Does this disqualify CMP and its rivals such as HMP or BMP from being rationally engaged in? The problem religious diversity poses for Alston's position can be put in terms of an argument for a positive answer to this question. All the competing mystical practices are equally socially well-established; none is superior to its rivals on grounds of deeper social entrenchment. So each of the competing mystical practices is confronted with a plurality of uneliminated alternatives. In such a situation, it seems too tempting to draw the following conclusions:

> Thus, in the absence of some sufficient independent reason, no one is justified in supposing her own practice to be superior in epistemic status to those with which it is in competition. And hence, in this situation no one is being rational in proceeding to employ that practice to form beliefs and to regard beliefs so formed as ipso facto justified (PG, 270).

Unless the inference to these conclusions can be blocked, religious diversity does disqualify CMP as well as rivals such as HMP and BMP from being rationally engaged in.

Alston's response to this problem is to build a case for the practical rationality of continuing to engage in CMP, if one is a practitioner of it, even if one is aware of religious diversity. An argument from analogy is at the heart of this case. Alston asks us to imagine a counterfactual situation in which there is a plurality of sense perceptual practices approximately as diverse as forms of mystical practice actually are. One of them is our Aristotelian practice of experiencing the physical environments as, and believing it to be, composed of more or less discrete objects scattered about in space. The rival practices involve experiencing the physical environment as, and believing it to be, constituted as it is portrayed in the theories of Descartes and Whitehead. We are to imagine that each of these sense perceptual practices is socially established. Moreover, each serves its practitioners well in their dealings with the environment and has associated with it a developed physical science. Now imagine that in this situation I am as firmly wedded to the Aristotelian practice as I am in fact, even though I can find no neutral or independent grounds on which to argue that it yields more accurate beliefs than the Cartesian and Whiteheadian alternatives. It seems clear to Alston that "in the absence of an external reason for supposing that one of the competing practices is more accurate than my own, the only rational course for me is to sit tight with the practice of which I am a master and which serves me so well in guiding my activity in the world" (PG, 274). But our imaginary situation is analogous in the relevant respects to the actual situation of the practitioner of CMP. Hence, by parity of reasoning, the only practically rational thing for a practitioner of CMP to do is to stick with it and, more generally, to continue to accept and operate in accordance with the system of Christian belief. And since it is practically rational for the practitioner of CMP to continue to engage in the practice of CMP, it will by Alston's lights also be practically rational for the practitioner of CMP to take CMP to be reliable, and it will be practically rational for the practitioner of CMP to suppose that the beliefs issuing from CMP are prima facie justified in a truth-conducive sense.

As Alston is quick to add, "It goes without saying, I hope, that the conclusions I have been drawing concerning the epistemic situation of practitioners of CMP hold, *pari passu*, for practitioners of other internally validated forms of MP" (PG, 274–275). So it will be practically rational for the practitioners of HMP and BMP to continue to engage in the practice of HMP and BMP, respectively. It will be practically rational for them to take their respective practices to be reliable and to suppose that the beliefs their respective practices yield are prima facie justified in a truth-conducive sense.

The account I have just given of Alston's position corresponds fairly well to what McKim thinks of as a weak reading of Alston's project. According to McKim, the weak reading is supported by "PR-passages," which are so-called on account of their emphasis on what it is practically rational to believe about justification, and he takes it that "the PR-passages express Alston's considered view, which is that at most we can make a practical case both for the reliability of a practice and for the outputs of a practice being justified" (McKim, 242). I agree that this is indeed Alston's considered view. However, McKim also claims that other passages in Alston's text at least suggest, even if they do not demand, a stronger reading of the project. These "J-passages" are so-called because they "suggest that Alston believes himself to show that people *are justified* in holding various beliefs about God on the basis of mystical experience" (McKim, 242, his emphasis).

In order to see whether J-passages do in fact suggest McKim's stronger reading, let us look at one of the half-dozen examples he actually cites. Speaking of Alston, McKim asserts this: "And he says that 'a Christian is epistemically justified (at least prima facie) on the basis of mystical perception in holding certain Christian beliefs about God' (PG, 278)" (McKim, 242). Interestingly, the words McKim quotes from Alston actually constitute only a part of a longer sentence. It reads as follows:

> It should be clear from the above that even though I hold that a Christian is epistemically justified (at least prima facie) on the basis of mystical perception in holding certain Christian beliefs about God, I do *not* take this to imply that the proper procedure for the Christian, or the member of any religious community, is to shut herself up within the boundaries of her own community and ignore the rest of the world. (PG, 278, his emphasis)

In this passage, Alston says he *holds* that a Christian is prima facie justified in holding certain beliefs about God on the basis of mystical perception. He does not say or imply that he has *shown* that a Christian is prima facie justified in holding those beliefs on that basis. And, as I have explained, he carefully avoids claiming that he has shown any such thing. What he claims that he has shown is only that it is practically rational for a Christian to suppose that she is prima facie justified in holding those beliefs on that basis. Hence charity in interpretation seems to demand that we not read into the passage under consideration any suggestion that Alston believes himself to have shown that a Christian is justified in holding various beliefs about God on the basis of mystical experience. In short, we should not read this passage as a J-passage.

It therefore seems clear to me that we should let the PR-passages in Alston's text control our reading of what might otherwise appear to be J-passages. But if we do this, McKim protests, it "would make for coherence, although in that case the J-passages are misleading" (McKim, 242). In developing this line of thought, McKim quotes the long passage from Alston I quoted six paragraphs back. His commentary on it begins with the following claim:

> If, as Alston says at the end of this passage, his aim is to show that it is reasonable to suppose that SP is reliable and (hence) reasonable to suppose that the

outputs of SP are prima facie justified in the strong sense that requires SP to be
reliable, it seems misleading to say that the lower epistemic status in question—which arises from our inability to go beyond showing that it is practically
rational to continue with the practice—attaches only to the higher-level claim
that SP is reliable and not to the outputs of SP. (McKim, 243)

I think McKim has failed to grasp Alston's point here. According to Alston, the
lower epistemic status, being reasonable, attaches to the higher-level claims that
SP is reliable and that its outputs are prima facie justified in a truth-conducive
sense. Alston claims that he has shown this to be the case. He also holds, but
does not claim to have shown, that the higher epistemic status of being prima
facie justified in a truth-conducive sense attaches to the lower-level outputs of
SP. But he does not say that the lower status attaches only to the higher-level
claim, and he does not say that it does not attach to the lower-level outputs of
SP. I can see no reason to think that Alston is or would want to be committed to
either of these claims. Thus I can see no reason to attribute to Alston the view
that McKim regards as misleading or even to suggest that he might be committed to it.

It thus seems to me that McKim's attempt to find grounds in Alston's text
for his stronger reading of its project is misguided. The principle of charity argues against the tenability of such a reading. In addition, it entices McKim to
suggest that Alston makes, or is committed to, misleading claims that we have
no reason to attribute to him.

II. Reduced Justification: The First Overstatement Objection

In the fifth section of his chapter on Alston, which is entitled "Reduced Justification," McKim sets forth the first of his arguments for the thesis that Alston's
case is overstated. McKim's discussion in this section focuses on Alston's views
about the prima facie justification of beliefs that are the outputs of perceptual
doxastic practices. The discussion's opening move attributes to Alston a view
about the degree of prima facie justification conferred by perceptual practices on
their outputs. McKim says: "Alston thinks that beliefs that are the outputs of
functioning, socially established, perceptual doxastic practices, each of which
has distinctive inputs and outputs, associated overrider systems, and so forth,
receive *the same degree of* prima facie justification" (McKim, 246–247, my
emphasis). The attribution of this thought to Alston may initially seem puzzling,
since, as we have seen, he does not typically speak of degrees of prima facie
justification. In a parenthetical remark, McKim refers to a passage he takes to
indicate that Alston is sympathetic to the idea of degrees of prima facie justification. In that passage, Alston, having granted that the reliability of practices
comes in degrees, goes on to say this: "Perhaps we should distinguish degrees of

justification in correlation with degrees of reliability, but I won't get into that" (PG, 105). To be sure, in the sentence I have just quoted Alston speaks explicitly of justification, not prima facie justification. However, since Alston himself correlates prima facie justification with reliability when he infers from the practical rationality of supposing a doxastic practice to be reliable to the practical rationality of supposing its outputs to be prima facie justified, McKim is certainly reasonable in thinking that the quoted sentence at least suggests that Alston is sympathetic to the idea of degrees of prima facie justification. But a question remains unanswered. Even if we imagine Alston working with the idea of degrees of prima facie justification, why should we suppose, as McKim does, that Alston would think that reliable practices confer the same degree of prima facie justification on their outputs? I shall come back to this question.

In any event, quite apart from the issue of what Alston thinks or would think about this issue, it is clear that McKim endorses the idea that prima facie justification admits of degrees. He also holds that a single perceptual practice confers different degrees of prima facie justification on its outputs in different situations. He argues for the latter claim by contrasting two cases that involve SP. In the first case, you and I are hiking in the Canadian Rockies. You think there is a bear yonder, though what you take to be a bear is far away and hard to see. I think that it is not a bear; I suspect it is a tree stump that from a distance resembles a bear. In the second case, I look out the window and form the belief that a person in a red coat is walking past. The day is bright, and the person passes within a few feet of my window and is in full view for quite a while. According to McKim, "If there is prima facie justification in both cases in virtue of how things appear, and in virtue of the generally reliable character of SP, it differs with respect to what it is natural to think of as the *degree* of prima facie justification" (McKim, 247, his emphasis). On his view, you do not have the same degree of prima facie justification in the first case for believing that there is a bear yonder as I have in the second case for believing that a person in a red coat is walking past.[3] McKim supposes that this is so after I have given my opinion in the first case, but it seems reasonable to him to think that it was so even before I told you what I think in that case. This analysis of the two cases strikes me as eminently sensible. I do not wish to dispute any of it. But I cannot see any reason to suppose that Alston would dissent from any of it if he were working with a conception of prima facie justification according to which it comes in degrees. So I see no grounds for thinking that Alston would deny McKim's thesis that a single perceptual practice confers different degrees of prima facie justification on its outputs in different situations. If we are to locate a genuine disagreement between them, we must, I think, seek it elsewhere.

I think such a disagreement emerges when we look at what McKim takes to be consequences of conceiving of prima facie justification as an epistemic status that admits of degrees. As he sees it, there are four possible cases worth mentioning:

> There seem to be cases in which a belief has what we might think of as first-class prima facie justification and cases in which it just barely meets the necessary conditions for prima facie justification. . . . Then, too, there are cases in which a belief just barely falls short of meeting the necessary conditions for prima facie justification, and cases in which it falls far short of doing so (McKim, 247).

I take it we are to understand the necessary conditions referred to in this simple taxonomy of possibilities as necessary conditions that are jointly sufficient for prima facie justification. If this is correct, the taxonomy distinguishes the following four types of cases: cases in which a belief does much better than barely satisfying a sufficient condition for prima facie justification, cases in which a belief just barely satisfies a sufficient condition for prima facie justification, cases in which a belief just barely falls short of satisfying any sufficient condition for prima facie justification, and cases in which a belief falls far short of satisfying any sufficient condition for prima facie justification. McKim wants us to pay special attention to cases of the last two types. About them, he has this to say:

> In the latter two types of cases, the fact that some belief is among the outputs of a practice in which it is practically rational to engage may merely provide *some reason* for people who follow the doxastic practice in question, and who have the relevant experience, to believe the relevant proposition. That is, the fact that a belief is the output of a generally reliable doxastic practice may merely provide some reason to accept it, and may not suffice to provide full-blown prima facie justification. (McKim, 247, his emphasis)

Let us grant to McKim for the sake of argument the possibility that a belief issuing from a generally reliable doxastic practice should fall short, either just barely or by a long way, of having prima facie justification. Is it reasonable to suppose that any beliefs that are products of the socially established doxastic practices discussed by Alston do fall short of having full-blown prima facie justification?

McKim's response to this question is made clear in his discussion of another case that involves SP. It is a case in which disagreement is salient. Though McKim does not mention this fact, it is thus analogous to the competition between diverse MPs in some respects. The obvious disanalogy is that it is an intrapractice case rather than an interpractice case. We are now to imagine that three of us are lost in a desert. With our naked eyes, we see a speck on the distant horizon. Prompted by curiosity, we set up our telescope, focus it on the speck, and look at it through the telescope. When you look through the telescope, it seems to you that there is a tent with some bedouin beside it in the distance. When our companion looks, it seems to her that there is an oasis on the horizon. And when I look, it seems to me that there is a man riding on a camel in the distance. According to McKim, "It is clear that whatever prima facie justification may arise for my belief that I see a man riding on a camel from my seeming to myself to do so, it is a greatly diminished degree of justification" (McKim, 248).[4] In other words, my belief is at best a case of the second type in McKim's taxonomy; at best my belief just barely satisfies a sufficient condition for being prima facie justified.

McKim rightly points out that many factors may bear on our epistemic assessment of the case. For example, the likelihood of there actually being a camel in the distance depends in part on whether we are in a desert in California or in Saudi Arabia. Or we might have heard from a reliable source that there is a group of bedouin in the neighborhood who amuse themselves by creating illusions of camels and oases in order to fool naïve tourists. Nevertheless, according to McKim, we may conclude that "at the very least, under the circumstances, my belief that it is a man on a camel will either have a very low level of prima facie justification *or fail even to have that much going for it*" (McKim, 249, my emphasis). In short, my belief will not fall into the first category in McKim's taxonomy; it will not have first-class prima facie justification. At best it will fall into the second category and just barely satisfy a sufficient condition for prima facie justification. And it may do worse than that, for it may fall into the third or fourth categories and thereby fall short, either just barely or by a long way, of satisfying any sufficient condition for prima facie justification.

We are now in a position to state what I take to be a genuine disagreement between McKim and Alston. As we have seen, Alston makes inferences from the practical rationality of supposing a doxastic practice to be reliable to the practical rationality of supposing its outputs to be prima facie justified. It is thus natural enough to read him as being committed to the view that the reliability of a doxastic practice suffices to insure that all its outputs are prima facie justified. Given this reading, McKim's charge that Alston overstates his case will, with respect to this issue, amount to this. McKim thinks that Alston has not ruled out the possibility that some of the outputs of even those doxastic practices that are reliable fall short, either just barely or by a long way, of being prima facie justified. So McKim will deny something which, according to this reading, Alston is committed to affirming, namely, the legitimacy of inference from the practical rationality of supposing a doxastic practice to be reliable to the practical rationality of supposing all its outputs to be prima facie justified.

We may now return to the question I earlier left unanswered. Why should we suppose, as McKim does, that Alston would think that reliable practices confer the same degree of prima facie justification on all their outputs if he were to work with the idea of degrees of prima facie justification? The answer is that McKim is mistaken about Alston's commitments on this topic. According to the reading of Alston now under consideration, he is committed to thinking that all of the outputs of reliable practices fall into the first two categories of McKim's taxonomy and thereby are prima facie justified. And he is committed to thinking that none of the outputs of reliable practices fall into the last two categories of that taxonomy and thereby fall short of being prima facie justified. But he is not committed to thinking that all the outputs of reliable practices fall into just one of the first two categories, that they all enjoy what McKim describes as first-class prima facie justification or that they all just barely qualify as prima facie justified. So Alston's view contains no obstacle to holding that some of the outputs of reliable practices fall into the taxonomy's first category while others, because they possess a lesser degree of prima facie justification, fall into its second category. Indeed, it is open to Alston to hold that the outputs of reliable practices are distributed over all the fine-grained degrees of prima facie justification that McKim correctly insists can be distinguished within his first two categories.

Having clarified what is involved in this version of McKim's overstatement objection, I now turn to the issue of how Alston might reply to McKim. I suppose that he could consistently offer a concessive response. That is, he might say that were he to go into the issue of degrees of prima facie justification and develop his own account of the matter, he would concede that some of the outputs of even practices that are reliable do not have enough going for them to qualify as prima facie justified. However, I propose to explore another option that it seems to me Alston could consistently and plausibly choose. In this option, he hangs tough and insists that all the outputs of reliable doxastic practices are prima facie justified, even though they do not all have the same degree of prima facie justification. In offering this response to McKim on behalf of Alston, I assume, as I believe Alston would, that some degree of idealization is permissible in discussing this topic. Thus, for example, I suppose that I may ignore outputs of a perceptual practice that are "wild" in the sense that they are not based on experience in the way specified by the functions from experiential inputs to doxastic outputs that are constitutive of the practice. I will not worry about the odd case in which someone forms the belief that there is a snowy alp over there, when she has the visual experience of there seeming to be a green tree in front of her, solely as the result of a wayward causal process. And I shall also idealize by assuming that doxastic practices are more or less homogeneous with respect to their reliability. Though I realize that there is a serious issue for reliabilist theories in epistemology about how to individuate processes, methods, or practices in order to assess their reliability, I shall ignore McKim's suggestion that in the cases which concern us "what we seem to have is an array of subpractices that differ greatly in their reliability, or a single practice whose different applications vary widely in their reliability" (McKim, 249). The conclusions of my subsequent arguments in this part of the essay may therefore be thought of as conditionalized upon such idealizing assumptions.

In order to spell out the hang-tough response I believe to be available to Alston, I must begin with a sketch of his views on prima facie justification. As he defines it, "to be prima facie justified in believing that p by virtue of the satisfaction of conditions, C, is to be so situated that one will be unqualifiedly justi-

fied in that belief provided there are no sufficient 'overriders', that is, no sufficient considerations to the contrary" (PG, 72). The considerations Alston calls
"overriders" are equivalent to those called "defeaters" by some other philosophers. There are two kinds of overriders. Those that are reasons for believing
that not-p are rebutters; those that are reasons for supposing that C fails to provide adequate justification in a particular case are underminers. Alston says repeatedly that justification is a matter of degree, but he often speaks of justification without any indication of its degree. In a terminological note, he explains
that "although justification is a degree concept, when I speak of justification tout
court that is to be understood as a degree of justification sufficient for rational
acceptance" (PG, 81). He then goes on to indicate the consequences of this way
of understanding things for purely immediate perceptual justification. He claims
that "in suggesting that a belief may be prima facie justified solely by experience, I am suggesting that this mode of justification can suffice for rational acceptance, in the absence of sufficient overriders" (PG, 81). I think these remarks
provide the basis for a plausible response to McKim's first overstatement objection.

It seems to me to be open to Alston to insist that any belief which satisfies
the condition of being an output of a reliable doxastic practice is prima facie
justified simply in virtue of satisfying that condition. Beliefs that issue from
reliable doxastic practices may have degrees of prima facie justification ranging
from a minimum to a maximum if we wish to distinguish degrees within prima
facie justification. However, all such beliefs have a degree of justification that
will suffice for rational acceptance in the absence of sufficient overriders or considerations to the contrary.

These claims do not conflict with intuitions worth preserving about the
cases that figure in McKim's discussion. This is mainly because of the operation
of overriders. Consider first the case of our hike in the Canadian Rockies. On the
view now being considered, your belief that there is a bear yonder is prima facie
justified in virtue of being an output of SP, which is a reliable doxastic practice.
This implies that it will have a degree of justification sufficient for rational acceptance, in the absence of sufficient overriders. But overriders are not absent.
For one thing, as McKim himself emphasizes, what you take to be a bear is far
away and hard to see. This is an underminer because it is a reason for supposing
that being an output of SP fails to provide adequate justification for your belief
in this case. For another, later on I tell you that I think it is not a bear. My testimony is a rebutter because it is a reason for believing that there is not a bear
yonder. Are these overriders sufficient to make it the case that your belief has a
degree of justification not sufficient for rational acceptance? Maybe they are not
sufficient. Perhaps, despite their presence, your belief that there is a bear yonder
still has a degree of justification just barely sufficient for rational acceptance.
Maybe they are sufficient. Perhaps, given their presence, your belief that there is
a bear yonder only has a degree of justification that falls short, either just barely
or by a long way, of being sufficient for rational acceptance. No matter how this

turns out, however, the result will be consistent with and will cast no doubt on the claim that your belief is prima facie justified simply in virtue of being an output of SP.

Consider next the desert case. On the view under consideration, my belief that there is a man riding on a camel in the distance is prima facie justified in virtue of being an output of SP. It will have a degree of justification sufficient for rational acceptance, in the absence of overriders. But overriders are not absent. The disagreements with my belief testified to by my two companions are rebutters. Are these overriders sufficient to make it the case that my belief has a degree of justification insufficient for rational acceptance? Maybe they are not. Perhaps, despite their presence, my belief still has a degree of justification just barely sufficient for rational acceptance. Maybe they are. Perhaps, given their presence, my belief only has a degree of justification that falls short, either just barely or by a long way, of being sufficient for rational acceptance. But again, no matter how this turns out, the result will be consistent with and will cast no doubt on the claim that my belief is prima facie justified simply in virtue of being an output of SP.

The upshot is that Alston can consistently hang tough and insist on ruling out the possibility that some of the outputs of reliable doxastic practices fall short of being prima facie justified, while at the same time giving a plausible account of the cases on which McKim bases his first overstatement objection. So these cases by themselves are not sufficient to establish that Alston overstates his case about prima facie justification. The burden is on McKim to provide additional argument if he wants to make good on the first overstatement objection despite the availability to Alston of the hang-tough response.

This McKim tries to do in a single, long sentence. It reads as follows:

> If we think of the prima facie justification that is conferred by our doxastic practices as a matter of degree, and if, for instance, the amount of ambiguity or uncertainty in what is perceived is one of the considerations that is relevant to whether or not, and to what extent, the belief in question is justified, then there must be some degree of ambiguity or uncertainty (etc.) below [sic] which there is no prima facie justification at all. (McKim, 249–250)

The consequent of the conditional stated by this sentence seems to get things backwards. It is natural to suppose that the degree of prima facie justification would be inversely proportional to the degree of ambiguity or uncertainty: the greater the degree of ambiguity or uncertainty, the less the degree of prima facie justification. Hence, in the interest of reading charitably, we should suppose that McKim wanted his conditional to have the consequent that there must be some degree of ambiguity or uncertainty (etc.) *above* which there is no prima facie justification at all. What are we to make of the argument expressed by the conditional revised in this way?

Its premises are the clauses in the conditional's antecedent. So let us suppose that the prima facie justification conferred by our doxastic practices comes in degrees. And let us also suppose that the amount of ambiguity or uncertainty is relevant to the extent of prima facie justification in the precise sense that degree of prima facie justification is a monotonically decreasing function of degree of ambiguity or uncertainty. Even given these assumptions, however, it can turn out that there is no degree of ambiguity or uncertainty above which there is no prima facie justification at all.[5] Thus, even when these assumptions are granted, it is not the case that there must be some degree of ambiguity or uncertainty above which there is no prima facie justification at all. Hence, though the argument's premises are true, its conclusion is false. Therefore the argument is invalid.

My conclusion is that McKim has not shown that Alston overstates his case about prima facie justification. The first overstatement objection fails.

III. Reduced Rationality: The Second Overstatement Objection

In the sixth section of his chapter on Alston, which bears the title "Reduced Rationality," McKim transfers his attention from the justification of beliefs that are the outputs of doxastic practices to the practical rationality of engaging in doxastic practices. He begins with a statement of a principle, called "DAM" because of its emphasis on disagreement, ambiguity, and malfunction, that he takes to summarize the lessons to be learned from the previous section. It claims this: "Beliefs with respect to which (a) there is disagreement, that are (b) about matters that are ambiguous and hence difficult to interpret, and that are (c) generated by a doxastic practice that we have reason to suspect may be at its limit or out of its depth or malfunctioning (such as when we are in the desert and the sun has been baking down on our heads) are less justified on that account" (McKim, 250). He next states a reformulation of DAM that aims to make it suitable for application to the practical rationality of engaging in doxastic practices and hence supposing them to be reliable. It asserts this:

> The practical rationality of judging to be reliable any doxastic practice that issues to a very considerable extent in beliefs that satisfy conditions (a) and (b) above, and that (d) we have reason to suspect may be at its limit or out of its depth or malfunctioning (such as when we are in the desert and the sun has been baking down on our heads) is considerably reduced. (McKim, 251)

McKim then goes on to propose that we ought to think of the conditions of disagreement, ambiguity, and malfunction specified in the reformulation of DAM "as together constituting an underminer for a practice, or perhaps as what I shall call a 'restrainer,' which is a weaker version of an underminer" (McKim, 251). I shall come back to the issue of whether the distinction between underminers and restrainers adumbrated in this remark is valuable. First, however, let me comment on some of the more general features of McKim's proposal.

Up to a point, it seems to be a suggestion Alston could accept as a friendly amendment. As we have seen, Alston holds that engagement in a doxastic practice and thus judging it to be reliable is prima facie practically rational provided the practice is socially established. This prima facie rationality can be overridden by internal and external inconsistencies. In the case of an MP, external inconsistency might involve either conflict with the outputs of a more basic and firmly established secular practice such as SP or conflict with a competing MP that is equally well-established. Since internal and external inconsistency come in degrees, Alston would seem to be in a position to allow that there are correlated degrees of practical rationality if he were to choose to go into that issue. And practical rationality tout court could then be understood as a degree of practical rationality sufficient for rational engagement in a doxastic practice and commitment to the supposition of its reliability. The idea that the factors of disagreement, ambiguity, and malfunction specified in the reformulation of DAM constitute conjunctively an undermining overrider for practical rationality, whose presence reduces its degree, fits comfortably into this way of thinking about practical rationality. On Alston's view of overriders, however, the presence of an overrider does not necessarily reduce the degree of practical rationality to such an extent that it falls short of sufficiency for rational engagement. As we have seen, Alston is careful to say that it is *sufficient* overriders whose presence has that effect. For example, a little internal inconsistency is not sufficient to reduce the practical rationality of engaging in a practice to such an extent that it is disqualified for rational engagement. It takes massive and persistent internal inconsistency to yield this result, for, as Alston observes, even the best-regulated of our socially established doxastic practices occasionally issue in inconsistent outputs. So if we go along with McKim in supposing that the three factors mentioned in reformulated DAM together compose an underminer for practical rationality whose presence reduces it, we need to keep in mind that the presence of this underminer, though it reduces the degree of practical rationality, may not reduce it to such an extent as to disqualify a practice from rational engagement.

In my view, McKim's failure to grasp this point leads him to misinterpret Alston, and this misinterpretation then leads him to suggest a solution to a problem for Alston's view that does not exist. After stating his proposal that the factors mentioned in reformulated DAM are best thought of as an underminer for the prima facie practical rationality of engagement in a practice, McKim quotes two remarks by Alston about how underminers function in the case of justification and proceeds to offer an interpretation of them. According to Alston, an underminer of prima facie justification for a belief provides "sufficient reasons to think that in this instance the ground of the belief does not wield its usual justificatory force" (PG, 79). Note that Alston does not say in this passage, and what he says does not entail, that the reasons provided by an underminer are sufficient for thinking that in this instance the belief's ground has no justificatory force at all. And Alston does not even say, nor does what he says even entail, that the reasons provided by an underminer are sufficient for thinking that in this instance the belief's ground has so little justificatory force that the belief's degree of justification is too low for rational acceptance. Speaking of perceptual justification, Alston also says of undermining that "this would involve reasons for supposing the situation of perception to be abnormal in some way that would prevent the perceptual experience from functioning as a reliable sign of what is believed" (PG, 191). But note now that Alston does not say, nor does what he says entail, that undermining involves *sufficient* reasons for supposing the situation's abnormality prevents the experience from functioning as a reliable sign of the state of affairs that is believed to obtain.

Relying mainly on the second of the two quoted passages and switching from underminers of the prima facie justification of beliefs to underminers of the prima facie practical rationality of engaging in practices, McKim goes on to assert the following exegetical conclusion:

> And I take it to be clear from this last quoted remark from Alston, therefore, that an underminer has the result that justification, which otherwise would have been provided, is not provided. That is, an underminer does not exactly have the effect that a practice does not have its usual justificatory force: rather its effect is that the practice lacks all justificatory force. (McKim, 251)

McKim is mistaken here. An underminer of the prima facie practical rationality of engaging in a practice has the effect of reducing the degree of practical rationality of engagement. In that sense, its exact effect is indeed that the practice does not have the degree of practical rationality it would have were the underminer not present. The effect may or may not be reduction to such an extent that the degree of practical rationality is not sufficient for rational engagement in the practice or even to such an extent that the degree of practical rationality is zero. Underminers, though they do reduce the degree of justification for beliefs or degree of practical rationality of engagement for practices below what they would otherwise be, do not necessarily result in reduction to such an extent that degree of justification falls short of sufficiency for rational acceptance or degree of practical rationality falls short of sufficiency for rational engagement. A fortiori, the reduction resulting from the presence of underminers is not necessarily or in all cases maximal in the sense that what remains is justification or practical rationality of degree zero.

Having misinterpreted Alston in this way, McKim, to his credit, sees that underminers thus understood do not allow for a possibility we ought to recognize. Switching his attention back to justification for beliefs, he says this: "There is, in any case, another possibility here, namely, that one or more factors might reduce *somewhat* the prima facie justification provided for the outputs of a practice" (McKim, 251, his emphasis). Such factors will be what McKim thinks of as restrainers provided the reduction is not so drastic as to render the degree of justification insufficient for rational acceptance or, even worse, drive it to zero, in which case we would, I take it, have what McKim thinks of as underminers. Presumably the situation with respect to the practical rationality of engaging in a practice is similar. Factors that reduce the degree of practical rationality somewhat but not to such an extent that it is insufficient for rational engagement will be, by McKim's lights, restrainers. Factors that reduce the degree of practical rationality to zero will be, according to McKim, underminers.

If we are not captives of McKim's misreading of Alston, however, it is easy to see that Alston's way of thinking about overriders already allows for the possibility McKim rightly holds that we ought to recognize. There are overriders that are not sufficient in the sense that, though they reduce practical rationality somewhat, they do not lower its degree to such an extent that it falls short of sufficiency for rational engagement. These overriders play the role McKim marks out for his restrainers. But there are also overriders that are sufficient in the sense that they do reduce the degree of practical rationality to such an extent that it falls short of sufficiency for rational engagement. In the limit case for overriders that are underminers, we get a reduction of degree of practical rationality to zero or utter nullification of practical rationality, which corresponds to what McKim understands as the effect of the operation of underminers.

That Alston thinks of overriders in the way I am claiming is confirmed by his response to the problem of religious diversity. Practitioners of CMP who are aware of religious diversity have an overrider to the prima facie practical rationality of engaging in CMP that it derives from social establishment because of the external inconsistency of its outputs and background beliefs with those of equally well-established rival MPs such as HMP and BMP. But since CMP is internally validated by significant self-support, this overrider is not sufficient to reduce the degree of practical rationality of engaging in CMP to such an extent that it falls short of sufficiency for rational engagement. Hence it is practically rational for the practitioner of CMP to continue to engage in it. Yet this overrider would be sufficient to reduce the degree of practical rationality of engaging in CMP to such an extent that it falls short of sufficiency for rational engagement, were CMP not to enjoy significant self-support. So overriders can reduce the degree of practical rationality to such an extent that it falls short of sufficiency for rational engagement or perhaps even nullify it completely.

McKim holds that reformulated DAM applies to all doxastic practices. He supposes that "it is best thought of as a commonsense background belief we bring to whatever doxastic practice we engage in" (McKim, 252). This may or may not be so. Even if it is the case, however, this does not by itself yield a conflict with Alston's position. Reformulated DAM claims only that the factors it specifies reduce practical rationality considerably; it does not claim or entail that they ever reduce it to such an extent that a practice falls short of having a degree of practical rationality sufficient for rational engagement. Hence the applicability of reformulated DAM to all doxastic practices is entirely consistent with Alston's conclusion that SP and various internally validated MPs do have degrees of practical rationality sufficient for rational engagement. Thus far, therefore, we have not discovered a disagreement between McKim and Alston. Neither have we found in McKim's text an argument for the conclusion that Alston's case about practical rationality is overstated.

What appears to be a disagreement emerges only in the final paragraph of McKim's section on reduced rationality. Focusing on MPs, McKim asks himself how we ought to engage in them under the conditions specified in reformulated DAM. His answer is worth quoting in full:

> One relevant consideration is whether there is any alternative to "business as usual": that is, to continuing with doxastic practices upon which one has relied provided that they are internally validated. And in the religious case there are such options. One such option is to continue to accept the outputs of an MP (or other doxastic practice that is established within a religious tradition) that is internally validated and to continue to take it seriously as a source of beliefs, but to do all this in the tentative mode. There are alternatives to either "sitting tight" with your practice or abandoning it: one can sit loosely with it, or at any rate one can do so in the case of religiously based MPs. It is not practically rational to carry on with business as usual under the DAM conditions. (McKim, 252)

As we have seen, Alston argues that, despite the problem of religious diversity, the only practically rational thing for a practitioner of a socially established and internally validated MP such as CMP, HMP, or BMP to do is to sit tight with it. McKim seems to disagree. He claims that under the DAM conditions, which such MPs satisfy, it is not practically rational to carry on with business as usual, and he seems to think this is tantamount to it not being practically rational to sit tight. The alternative to sitting tight to which he attributes practically rationality is sitting loose. So the overstatement objection in this case apparently comes to this. Alston's conclusion that it is practically rational to sit tight is too strong. Given the DAM conditions, only the more modest conclusion that it is practically rational to sit loose is in order.

In my opinion, the disagreement here is merely apparent. For Alston, sitting tight with a practice means continuing to engage in it. The alternative is ceasing to engage in it, either by switching to a rival practice or by abandoning it without replacing it with a competitor. But for McKim, sitting loose with a practice consists in continuing to engage in it but doing so in a tentative manner or mode. Hence sitting loose is actually a way of sitting tight; McKim's claim that sitting loose is an alternative to sitting tight is mistaken. Sitting loose with a practice entails sitting tight with it, odd though that may sound. A practitioner sits loose while sitting tight, not instead of sitting tight. Hence McKim's claim that it is practically rational for a practitioner of a socially established and internally validated MP to sit loose with it entails Alston's claim that it is practically rational for such a practitioner to sit tight with it, and so McKim's claim is not more modest than Alston's. Moreover, since Alston's argument entails nothing about which particular ways of sitting tight, if any, are not practically rational, he is not committed to denying McKim's thesis that sitting loose is practically rational. McKim has therefore not shown Alston's case involving the practical rationality of engaging in an MP to be overstated by means of this argument.

Yet there may be a genuine disagreement between Alston and McKim in the neighborhood of this issue. It begins to emerge when we reflect on remarks Alston makes about the need for faith in a section of his chapter on religious diversity in which he discusses its genuine epistemic consequences. Alston says this:

> Since it is an essential part of the religious package that we hold beliefs that go beyond what is conclusively established by such objective indications as are available to us (or alternatively, holds [sic] beliefs more firmly than the available objective evidence warrants), it should be the reverse of surprising that religious diversity should render us less than fully epistemically justified in the beliefs of a particular religion. This is an additional reason for denying that the appropriate response to the lowering of the degree of epistemic justification that is consequent on religious diversity is the abandonment of beliefs that would otherwise be held with confidence. (PG, 277)

Though Alston is in this passage speaking of the epistemic justification of beliefs, not the practical rationality of practices, I suggest that it is in the spirit of his thought to extrapolate from these remarks to a view about the practical rationality of engaging in practices that may plausibly be attributed to him. Various factors, including religious diversity and perhaps McKim's DAM conditions, reduce the degree of practical rationality of engaging in socially established and internally validated MPs such as CMP, HMP, and BMP to such an extent that, though it remains sufficient for rational engagement, it is less than sufficient to warrant fully confident engagement. Nevertheless, because faith is part of the religious package, practitioners of such MPs ought, all things considered, to engage in them with full confidence.

If my extrapolation should prove acceptable to Alston, there will indeed be a disagreement between him and McKim. They both think that it is practically rational for practitioners of socially established and internally validated MPs to continue to engage in them, even when they are aware of such factors as religious diversity and the presence of the DAM conditions. But McKim believes that the mode of engagement should be no stronger than tentative, while Alston holds that it should be the stronger mode of fully confident engagement. Or, at least, Alston holds this in the case of MPs such as CMP for which faith is part of the religious package. Even if Alston and McKim do disagree in this way, however, it remains the case that McKim has not shown that Alston has presented an overstated case in his treatment of the practical rationality of engaging in MPs. For McKim does not even discuss Alston's views on faith, and a fortiori he does not show that they are in any way flawed. So the second overstatement objection fails too.

Alston's attempt to solve his problem of religious diversity has, of course, attracted criticism from philosophers other than McKim and the authors of the other two books mentioned in the introduction to this essay. I have elsewhere argued that sitting tight with an MP, though it is a rational alternative, is not the only rational alternative for a practitioner.[6] William Wainwright has argued that the existence of conflicting MPs seems to provide those who are not practitioners of any of them with strong reasons for remaining uncommitted.[7] Indeed, McKim makes a similar point in the final section of his chapter on Alston, though he does not refer there to Wainwright's earlier essay. I have not tried to evaluate any of that criticism in this essay. I have focused narrowly on the task of scrutinizing the two versions of the overstatement objection found in the sections on reduced justification and reduced rationality in McKim's chapter on Alston. My conclusion is that McKim has failed to show that Alston's case is overstated.

Notes

1. Philip L. Quinn and Kevin Meeker, eds., *The Philosophical Challenge of Religious Diversity* (New York: Oxford University Press, 2000); Robert McKim, *Religious Ambiguity and Religious Diversity* (New York: Oxford University Press, 2001); Paul J. Griffiths, *Problems of Religious Diversity* (Malden, MA: Blackwell Publishers, 2001); and David Basinger, *Religious Diversity: A Philosophical Assessment* (Burlington, VT: Ashgate Publishing, 2002). I make page references to McKim's book parenthetically in the body of my text.

2. William P. Alston, *Perceiving God: The Epistemology of Religious Experience* (PG) (Ithaca, NY: Cornell University Press, 1991), 255. Hereafter I make page references to Alston's book parenthetically in the body of my text.

3. In presenting the two cases in the body of my text I have silently corrected an infelicity in McKim's presentation in the book. In the first case McKim attributes to you the belief that you see a bear, and in the second case he attributes to me the belief that I see a person in a red coat. But the beliefs that issue from SP are usually not beliefs about ourselves. Hence in my presentation I attribute to you in the first case the belief that there is a bear yonder and to myself in the second case the belief that a person in a red coat is walking past. Nothing important in my argument turns on this small alteration.

4. In this case too, the output of SP would ordinarily be the belief that there is a man riding on a camel in the distance, not, as McKim puts it, the belief that I see a man riding on a camel. But, again, nothing important turns on this point.

5. Perhaps an example will serve to drive this point home. Let n represent degree of ambiguity or uncertainty, where n ranges over the nonnegative integers 0, 1, 2, 3, . . . Let

$f(n)$ represent degree of prima facie justification. Suppose that

$$f(n) = 3 - \sum_{m=0}^{n} \frac{1}{2}m.$$

When n = 0, $f(n)$ = 3 − 1 = 2.
When n = 1, $f(n)$ = 3 − (1 + ½) = 1 ½.
When n = 2, $f(n)$ = 3 − (1 + ½ + ¼) = 1 ¼
When n = 3, $f(n)$ = 3 − (1 + ½ + ¼ + ⅛) = 1 ⅛

As n goes to infinity, $f(n)$ approaches 1 asymptotically. Though $f(n)$ is a monotonically decreasing function of n, there is no value of n, no matter how large, such that $f(n)$ = 0. Hence, though degree of prima facie justification is a monotonically decreasing function of degree of ambiguity or uncertainty, there is no degree of ambiguity or uncertainty, no matter how great, such that the degree of prima facie justification is zero and there is no prima facie justification at all.

6. Philip L. Quinn, "Toward Thinner Theologies: Hick and Alston on Religious Diversity," *International Journal for Philosophy of Religion* 38, (1995): 145–164. This paper is reprinted in the Quinn and Meeker collection cited in note 1.

7. William J. Wainwright, "Religious Language, Religious Experience and Religious Pluralism," in *The Rationality of Belief and the Plurality of Faith: Essays in Honor of William P. Alston*, ed. Thomas D. Senor (Ithaca, NY: Cornell University Press, 1995), 170–88. This essay is reprinted in part, under the title "Religious Experience and Religious Pluralism," in the Quinn and Meeker collection cited in note 1.

10

Response to Quinn

William P. Alston

First let me say how much I appreciate Phil Quinn's meticulous, near unerringly accurate, and insightful reading of what I have written on religious diversity. He not only has what I have written exactly straight. He has even divined correctly what I would have said had I committed myself on various points on which I had not committed myself. And of course I greatly appreciate his consummate job of defending me against criticisms by Robert McKim, no small achievement since McKim's criticisms do pose a considerable challenge. My only quibble is that Quinn does not leave me much to do in a response. I could display my virtuosity by taking up the cudgel in support of McKim and in criticism of Quinn's defense of my position against McKim's criticism of it, but the reader will undoubtedly be gratified that I have resisted any temptation to complicate matters to that extent. Besides I am completely satisfied with what Quinn has done on this score, with one small exception to be specified below.

But being a philosopher, I feel that I need to write something. And so I will make two comments on Quinn's paper of very different sizes.

The minor comment concerns Quinn's bringing in my reference to faith at the end of his paper. He takes it that I think that faith will bridge whatever gap there is between the evidence (including possible overriders) for and against religious belief and holding it with full confidence. He even writes, speaking of my view, "because faith is part of the religious package, practitioners of such MP's [such as CMP] ought, all things considered, to engage in them with full confidence." I plead innocent of any such view. I recognize, of course, that some religious believers hold their beliefs with full confidence, but I think it a great overstatement to suppose that anything worthy of the title 'faith' will always lead to this, much less that it "ought to." There is room in the religious life for faith, plus whatever epistemic support there is for religious belief, along with various degrees of doubt and lack of full confidence, both concurrently and sequentially. Quinn may have been misled on this point by a misreading of the end of the quotation from me that he gives just before discussing this matter. He may have supposed that "beliefs that would otherwise be held with confidence" implies that with faith they are held with confidence, whereas what I intended, and what I believe to be clear from the larger context of the quotation, is that they would be held with confidence if it were not for such overriders as religious diversity.

The larger comment on Quinn's paper concerns what I take to be the best way to think of prima facie (PF) justification. The issue I will address arises equally for other statuses where we use a PF qualification—obligations, reliability, guilt or innocence, or whatever—but since the three parties to the discussion in Quinn's paper are speaking of PF justification, I will focus the following discussion on that. A PF status looks forward, as we might way, to the possibility of that status's being "overridden" by contrary factors sufficient to do so. Quinn makes this sufficiently explicit. The issue I have in mind is this. Suppose belief B is PF justified, but there are sufficient overriders to prevent B from being justified, *all things considered* (ATC). The question is as to whether B *remains* PF justified after it is clear that it is not justified ATC. The reference to its being clear points to another complication in this topic that is rarely if ever made explicit; namely, that the PF justification–justification ATC distinction is relative to an individual subject or group of subjects. If we are thinking of the objective facts of the matter, then if there are sufficient overriders, then B was never justified ATC. It doesn't *become* unjustified ATC only when it "becomes clear" that there are sufficient overriders. For that matter, if we are thinking of the objective epistemic facts of the matter, then there is no point in introducing the notion of PF justification at all. Either the belief is justified ATC or not, and that is the end of the matter. So this whole conceptual framework only holds with respect to the perspective of a given individual or group, a perspective that can change as more relevant facts are discovered, and perhaps lost.

Taking account of this, the crucial thing about PF justification is that it is an initial status, one that holds at an early stage of considering the epistemic status of a belief by some particular individual or group. It is natural to think of issuing from a reliable doxastic practice as conferring PF justification, and sensory malfunction in a particular case as an overrider, rather than vice versa, because it is generally clear on reflection what doxastic practice gave rise to the belief, but not clear on reflection whether there was sensory malfunction.

Now for the bearing of all this on the issue as to whether being PF justified is a permanent status of a belief that enjoys it or one that is lost when sufficient overriders are discovered. The above points make it clear, I believe, that the PF status is not a permanent one. Since PF justification is an early status, if the subject or group in question goes on to explore the possibility of overriders and sufficient overriders are discovered, then B is unjustified ATC, in which case the possibility of its being prima facie justified has been left behind. Or, if no sufficient overriders have been discovered, the verdict is that B is justified ATC so far as one can tell at that point, though the possibility remains that sufficient overriders will be unearthed, thereby showing that B was unjustified ATC all along. And, again, the preliminary status of being PF justified has ceased to be of any relevance. An alternative reading for this second eventuality is that we could take it that B is still PF justified, with the judgment of being justified ATC being more strongly supported than in the initial stage. The difference between these two readings is parallel to the difference between the glass being half full and half empty.

I am not sure what either Quinn or McKim think about the issue I have been discussing. Like practically everyone else in the literature on this topic, they do not raise the issue. The issue between them is whether, as Quinn correctly points out, my view that any output of a sufficiently reliable doxastic practice is thereby PF justified is correct, or whether McKim is correct in holding that some such outputs lack enough for even PF justification. I am not sure just how the above suggestions about how to think about the PF justification–justification ATC distinction bear on that issue. I am inclined to think that if we recognize the temporary (early stage) character of PF justification, and hence the relatively modest claim made in ascribing PF justification to a belief, there will be less tendency to suppose, as McKim does, that when a belief is an exception to the general reliability of the doxastic practice in question (something that is discoverable by further investigation) this counts against its even being PF justified. And so I am inclined to think that when we realize the right way to think about this conceptual network, Quinn's position on this disagreement with McKim will be strengthened.

11

Born of the Virgin Mary

George I. Mavrodes

Mary, wife of Joseph the carpenter, came late to the well that day, with her first-born son toddling along beside her. Most of the Nazareth women had already come and gone with their water pots full for the evening meal. But there were two stragglers left. One of the women leaned over to pat Jesus on the head. Then she turned to Mary, smiling, and said, "He looks more like his father every day, doesn't he?" The other woman chimed in, saying, "It's his eyes. He has Joseph's eyes." Mary answered very quietly, "Yes, he looks like his father." And she smiled uncertainly. For Mary had noticed the resemblance years earlier, before the Nazareth women had ever seen Jesus, and she was puzzled by it.

That little vignette may, of course, be entirely fictional. But in this paper I intend to explore the possibility that there is some grain of truth in it, after all.

It is not unusual for little boys to look something like their fathers. And often people pick out particular features in which the resemblance is especially prominent. They may comment on the shape of the nose, the set of the jaw, or, as in this story, something about the eyes. And for a long time people have accounted for such resemblances in terms of what we might call "folk genetics." "It runs in the family," they might say. Or, "He gets it from his father." And so on. So the story I told above seems natural enough.

From very early times, however, there have been Christians who have believed that there was something very unusual, very special, about the birth of Jesus. This belief is expressed in one of the ancient creeds in the statement that Jesus "was conceived by the Holy Spirit, born of the Virgin Mary."[1] And this claim goes back to the Gospel of Luke which describes an angel visiting a young woman named Mary, a woman who is described as "a virgin betrothed to a man whose name was Joseph." And the angel has some news for Mary. "And behold,

you will conceive in your womb and bear a son, and you shall call his name Jesus." Mary expresses some puzzlement over this news, asking, "How can this
be, since I have no husband?" The angel replies, "The Holy Spirit will come
upon you, and the power of the most high will overshadow you; therefore the
child to be born will be called holy, the Son of God."[2]

The Gospel of Matthew also mentions this special feature of the birth of Jesus. "Now the birth of Jesus Christ took place in this way. When his mother
Mary had been betrothed to Joseph, before they came together she was found to
be with child of the Holy Spirit."[3]

These two Gospel accounts constitute the biblical roots of the doctrine of
the virgin birth. But, of course, the virgin birth is not the only thing that Christians have believed about Jesus. Another ancient creed, speaking of Jesus, says
that:

> This selfsame one is perfect both in deity and also in human-ness; this selfsame
> one is also actually God and actually man, with a rational soul and a body. He
> is of the same reality as God as far as his deity is concerned and of the same re-
> ality as we are ourselves as far as his human-ness is concerned; thus like us in
> all respects, sin only excepted.[4]

This combination, of course, raises very difficult problems. These problems
belong to the doctrine of the divine incarnation, the eternal son of God taking on
a human nature. For better or worse, I do not intend to explore those problems
here. But I do intend to proceed on the assumption expressed in the claim that
Jesus is truly human. He may have been the son of God (I believe that he was),
but he was not a god just dressed up as a man. He really was a man, he really
was human. And, of course, he was a particular, individual, man. He was of a
particular height, probably shorter than some men and taller than others. He
weighed a certain amount, his eyes were one color and not another, and so on.

I'm inclined to believe that both of these claims about Jesus, the virgin birth
and the full humanity, are true. But I will not argue that case here. I will simply
take both of these as assumptions. This paper is really an exploration of possibilities, of how one might relate these two claims to each other, especially in
connection with a modern understanding of human genetics. And in discussing
this particular case, I will make some use of William Alston's much more general discussion of the possible modes of divine action in the natural world.

In that general discussion Alston says, "I am taking seriously and realistically the idea of God as a personal agent, an agent who performs actions in the
light of knowledge and in order to realize the divine purposes." He says that he
takes this to imply that when we attribute to God one or another action, "We are,
on my construal, making truth claims, the truth conditions of which involve God
actually engaging in the appropriate sort of activity." And, he adds, "There are
facts of the matter about God's purposes, plans, activities, and so on; and what

we say about God is true or false depending on their relations to those facts."⁵ I share that intention of construing the claims about the virgin birth seriously and realistically, and I intend to carry on this discussion in that way.

The virgin birth would seem to fall into a class of actions that Alston calls "divine interventions." He distinguishes this class of divine actions from the act of creating the world in the first place and the continuous conservation of the universe in existence. Divine interventions are constituted by God's "bringing about particular states of affairs at particular times and places. That is, I am assuming with the tradition that there are occasions on which God brings it about that some particular outcome is different from what it would have been had only natural, created factors been operative."⁶

Those observations naturally bring to mind the idea of a miracle. And, of course, believers in the virgin birth have usually thought of it as a miracle. David Hume, in what is probably the single most influential discussion of miracles in Western philosophical literature, defined a miracle as follows: "A miracle may be accurately defined, a transgression of a law of nature by a particular volition of the deity, or by the interposition of some invisible agent."⁷ Almost all the subsequent discussion of the Humean concept of a miracle has focused on the relation of the miracle to a law of nature. It is worth noting, however, that Hume himself introduced a second element into his definition, stipulating that a miracle is performed by a special agent, either the deity or "some invisible agent."

Alston holds that "divine action at particular times and places is quite consistent with physical laws of a deterministic form." He argues that the laws of nature which we are justified in accepting are qualified (perhaps implicitly) by the proviso that the law will hold "in the absence of any relevant factors other than those specified in the law."⁸ But such laws would specify only the actions of natural agents, natural forces, natural conditions, and so on. Such laws of nature would not say anything about what God, a supernatural agent, might do or would do. They would not imply that God could not, or does not, intervene anywhere in the world. Consequently, a divine intervention would not constitute a violation of that law. And so Alston prefers to specify the idea of a divine intervention without reference to any violation of a law of nature.⁹

It would seem, however, that there may be alternative ways of thinking about a particular putative miracle. Some of these ways will strongly suggest the idea of a violation, while others will not. Hume mentions "the raising of a feather, when the wind wants ever so little of a force requisite for that purpose" as an example of a miracle. The effect involved in this miracle seems clear enough. It is the fact of the feather blowing about in the wind instead of falling to the ground. But we can think of this miracle as being accomplished in either of (at least) two ways. Both of these involve a divine action, but they seem to involve different divine actions. Thinking in one way we might suppose that the "ordinary" weight of the feather is one gram, and that the wind exerts an upward force of one-half gram. In the ordinary course of events the feather would sink to the ground. But if God were to apply an additional upward force of more than half a gram, then the feather could be expected to rise in the air. And it would be hard to see what law of nature would be violated in that case. After all, if I were to exert an additional gram of upward force to the feather it would rise, and I don't suppose that anyone would take that to be a miracle or a violation of a law of nature.

However, there is another way to think about the feather case. The ordinary weight of the feather is simply the gravitational force between the feather and the earth. In the Newtonian formulation of the law of gravity, that force is inversely proportional to the square of the distance between the bodies, in this case the distance between the feather and the center of the earth. Here we have a law of nature that specifies the mode of interaction of two natural entities, the earth and the feather. So we might think of a divine intervention that does not apply any additional force to the feather, but instead alters the natural mode of gravitational interaction in this particular case. Perhaps the divine intervention consists of making the gravitational force inversely proportional to twice the square of the distance. In that case the effective weight of the feather would be only one-half gram. And so the force of the wind would be sufficient to keep it in the air.

This second case has the flavor of a divine tampering with a law of nature in order to produce a special effect at a particular time and place. But if we think about the miracle as being generated in that way, then it might well seem natural to think that the law of gravity had been violated in this particular case.

Well, what about the virgin birth? Just what does the doctrine of the virgin birth claim? At the very least it claims that at the time of Jesus's birth his mother, Mary, was a virgin. That is, she had never had sexual intercourse; she and Joseph had not "come together."

It is now, in the twenty-first century, quite possible for a virgin woman to give birth to a child, and this need not involve any miraculous intervention. Probably this sort of thing has actually happened a few times in the past twenty or thirty years, perhaps even many times. What it requires now, as an occurrence within the scope of natural agents and powers, is a sequence of moderately high-tech procedures. These include the "capture" of a mature unfertilized ovum, in vitro fertilization with donor sperm, and the successful implantation of the resulting embryo in the uterus. Each of these procedures has now been done many times in fertility clinics. If the combination is performed for a virgin woman, then the result will be a virgin birth. None of these procedures seems to require a violation of a law of nature. Consequently, it would seem that a virgin birth is not per se a Humean miracle. And if there are any natural events at all, events that do not require any special divine intervention, then a virgin birth under these circumstances would seem to be a natural event.

Of course, these high-tech procedures were not available in first-century Palestine. So the virgin birth of Jesus, if it happened at all, did not happen in that way. The biblical accounts, and later formulations of the doctrine, attribute the onset of the pregnancy to the action of a divine agent, the Holy Spirit. "And the power of the most high will overshadow you." So the virgin birth would seem to be a good candidate for exemplifying Alston's idea of a divine intervention which does not violate any law of nature. It would be, as he says, one of those "occasions on which God brings it about that some particular outcome is different from what it would have been had only natural, created factors been operative." If only natural agents had been involved in the first century, then either Mary would have had sexual intercourse, and so would not have been a virgin when her first child was born, or she would not have had sexual intercourse, and so she would not have become pregnant. But a divine action resulted in her pregnancy without intercourse.

I suggested above that there are at least two ways of thinking of Hume's feather example. How might we think about the divine action involved in the virgin birth? Alston suggests that for God to bring about a certain state of affairs is for God to will that state of affairs, "whereupon, since anything God wills necessarily comes about, the willed state of affairs eventuates."[10] That may be so, but the state of affairs that consists of Mary's pregnancy and the birth of Jesus includes several particular elements. We can think about that state of affairs as a single large complex, but we can also think about particular elements which it may (or may not) have included.

Luke begins a genealogical table with the words, "Jesus being the son (as was supposed) of Joseph."[11] The parenthetical qualification suggests that in some sense Jesus was not the son of Joseph. In what sense? There certainly seem to be some senses in which Joseph was indeed the father of Jesus, regardless of what the biological facts were. Joseph was Jesus's legal father, he was Jesus's social father, he was probably the nurturing father who cared for Jesus when he was a baby, and so on. In fact, even before Jesus was born Joseph was performing a fatherly role in caring for Mary and supporting her during her pregnancy. These are, it seems to me, genuine senses of fatherhood, real ways of being a father. But of course there might be some other sense in which Joseph was not the father of Jesus. At one time I was inclined to say that Joseph was not Jesus's *genetic* father. But now I think that this may not be quite the right way to put it.

As my second assumption about Jesus I am taking it for granted that Jesus was completely human. And I intend to take that assumption as robustly as possible. Jesus, I suppose, had the normal human complement of muscles, bones, internal organs, nerves, and so on. And here I will assume that he was also completely human genetically. That is, Jesus had the full human genome, twenty-three pairs of chromosomes (including a Y chromosome for masculinity). The great bulk of that genetic information would, of course, be shared with the rest of the human race. That is, it would consist of the genetic information which makes one a member of the human species. And much (though not all) of that information would also be shared with other mammalian species, other classes of animals, and so on down the line. But, as I said before, Jesus was a particular human being, not just humanity in general. So he would have had some genes which were shared with perhaps some other human beings, but not with every human being. He would have had the genetic information for some particular color of eyes, some particular shape of nose, and so on.

At this point it may be useful to clarify what may be a troublesome ambiguity. Terms like "gene" and "chromosome" have at least two senses. In one sense a gene is a physical object. It is a tiny piece of protein that is linked to other such pieces to form a chromosome. Every ordinary somatic human cell contains twenty-three pairs of such chromosomes. In this sense, you have your genes and I have mine. My genes are in my body, and your genes are in a different place, your body. In fact, every cell in my body has its own complement of genes, its own set of those tiny bits of protein.

There is another sense, however, in which the gene is not the piece of protein but is rather the pattern in that bit of matter, a pattern which can be thought of as an instruction according to which the body does something or other. In this sense, all of the somatic cells in my body have the same genes. And, of course, in this sense I have many of the same genes that you have. All the babies who have Tay-Sachs disease have the same gene that tragically disrupts their physiology. And I may have the same genes for eye color that you have.

We are all familiar with this sort of distinction in other contexts. If I buy a copy of the newspaper, and you buy a copy of that "same" newspaper, then I take home one physical object, one piece of paper, and you take home another. But you and I will be taking home the same body of information (or misinformation). In the following discussion, I will usually use "gene" and "chromosome" in the sense of the information involved. Where I mean the physical object, I will try to indicate that sense specifically.

Now, to return to the virgin birth. Jesus, I am supposing, had a fully human set of genes, a human genome. The doctrine of the virgin birth generates at least two questions about this genome. One is the question of how that genome was generated. And the other question is about just what was in that genome. Both of these questions can be easily answered with respect to one-half of Jesus's genome, or at least so I will assume here. Just as in any ordinary pregnancy, one-half of Jesus's genetic inheritance was contributed by his mother Mary. She provided, in the ovum, twenty-three physical chromosomes, one from each pair. And each of these chromosomes encoded a body of genetic information. So far as I can see, the doctrine of the virgin birth gives us no reason to doubt that Jesus's birth includes this natural element.

Human reproductive cells, ova and sperm, contain twenty-three chromosomes. An ordinary human somatic cell, however, does not contain only twenty-three chromosomes. It contains twenty-three *pairs* of chromosomes. Mary contributed twenty-three chromosomes in the ovum. What about the other half of the genetic information, the other twenty-three chromosomes which would complete each pair? In an ordinary pregnancy these additional chromosomes would be contributed by the father, by way of a sperm introduced by sexual intercourse. But, according to the doctrine, Mary had not had sexual intercourse. She was a virgin. So, a divine intervention. But just what intervention? What could it have consisted of?

One can perhaps think of several different interventions that might suffice here. I will consider only one, an intervention of creation. The story about Jesus's birth belongs in the context of a religion that holds that God created the entire physical universe. Within that context it seems plausible to suppose that God, if he wished, could create a very small additional amount of matter, twenty-three chromosomes, in the right place and time.[12] And these twenty-three newly created chromosomes would, of course, encode a particular body of genetic information. This would, I think, make a good fit with Alston's notion of a divine intervention that was not a violation of a law of nature. For the purpose of this paper, then, this can stand as the answer to the question of how the other half (the "fatherly" half) of Jesus's genome was generated.

There remains, however, the question of what was in that genome. These genes were divinely created, but they were not divine genes. Probably there are no divine genes. That is, genes may be a feature of only the created world. In any case, if Jesus was fully human, then his entire genome (just like the rest of his body) must have been appropriate for a human being. Perhaps the proteins that went into those twenty-three chromosomes that filled out the full diploid number in that first cell were newly created. Possibly even the atoms in those chromosomes were newly created. But even so, the genetic information which was encoded in those newly created proteins was old, much of it very old. Almost all of it would have been genetic information shared throughout the human race, and much of that (though not all) would be information also shared with chimpanzees, with goats, and so on.[13]

Jesus's genome of course, like that of other people, would have had some features which were not shared with the whole human race. But much of that information would have been shared with some smaller group. I suppose that Jesus must have looked more or less like a Palestinian Jewish man of the first century. After all, if he had looked more like a Norwegian, or a Nigerian, then surely some of the stories about him would have reported such an anomalous fact.

It seems, then, that Jesus's genome must have had a very high degree of commonality with the genomes of many other men who had a purely natural birth. He must have shared that large genetic component which is common to the whole human species. Otherwise, he would not have been "perfect in human-ness, actually man, like us in all respects" as the fathers of Chalcedon said. He must also have shared that somewhat more special genetic component which was common to Palestinian men and not to Norwegians and Nigerians. And finally he would have had, like other men, some "particularizing" genetic component which gave him some of the particular characteristics by which his friends could recognize him on the street.

Half of that genome, as I said before, was contributed by Mary, his mother. In a purely natural first-century pregnancy the other half would be contributed by a man, the father, by way of sexual intercourse. The virgin birth rules that out in the case of Jesus. Nevertheless, the "fatherly" component in Jesus genome, though it was created by a special divine intervention, must have been very much like the component that could have been contributed by an ordinary human sperm. And, so far as I can see, it could have been an *exact* match for the genetic information in a particular sperm produced by some actual man.[14] That is, nothing in the doctrine of the virgin birth rules out that possibility. If the perfect human-ness of Jesus is taken in a robust way, then there has to be an enormous degree of convergence of his genome with one that could have been produced by a natural impregnation. If the virgin birth can survive that massive convergence, then it is hard to see why it cannot equally well survive an exact convergence with what might have been provided by some actual man.

So, suppose there was that kind of exact convergence, an exact match with a sperm which could have been produced by an actual man. Who might that man be? The vignette with which I began, of course, is meant to suggest that Jesus really did resemble Joseph, and that this resemblance was not coincidental. Of course, that is a speculative suggestion. But if Jesus did not resemble Joseph, then he may have resembled someone else, and not coincidentally. For the "fatherly" component in his genome may have been an exact match for a sperm which that other man could have produced.

Joseph, however, may strike some of us as a particularly "salient" candidate for such a match. That is, there may be something especially fitting in the divinely produced genetic component in Jesus's genome being a match for a component in Joseph's genome. And anyone who wishes to take that seriously as a speculation can do so without rejecting the idea of the virgin birth.

Notes

1. The Apostle's Creed, The Niceno-Constantinopolitan Creed, and the Creed of Chalcedon, in *Creeds of the Churches*, ed. John H. Leith (Richmond VA: John Knox Press, 1973), 24, 33, 36.

2. Luke 1:26–35. The biblical quotations in this chapter are taken from *The Holy Bible*, Revised Standard Version (New York: Meridian Books, 1962).

3. Matthew 1:18.

4. The Creed of Chalcedon, in *Creeds of the Churches*, 35, 36.

5. All three quotes are from William P. Alston, "Divine Action, Human Freedom,

and the Laws of Nature" (DA), in *Quantum Cosmology and the Laws of Nature*, ed. Robert J. Russell et al. (Vatican City State: Vatican Observatory Publications, 1993), 185, 186.

6. DA, 185, 186.

7. David Hume, *An Enquiry Concerning Human Understanding* (1777), Section X (Of Miracles).

8. DA, 190.

9. DA, 189–191.

10. DA, 187.

11. Luke 3:23.

12. Strictly speaking, God need not create an entirely new quantity of matter. He might take existing matter, existing atoms, and use them in making (physical) genes and chromosomes with the desired pattern (i.e., the desired genetic information).

13. We humans share a large amount of physiology with other animals, we make many of the same proteins, enzymes, etc., and so we have in our genomes many of the same instructions that the other animals have.

14. Any man, of course, produces sperm with many different combinations of the particularizing elements by which a chromosome may differ from its paired partner.

12

Response to Mavrodes

William P. Alston

This is a typical Mavrodes production. He takes a well-worn topic and with his customary ingenuity and imaginativeness comes up with new and even surprising twists that no one had thought of before, but wished they had. The prime example of that in this paper is the inference from "Jesus was fully human (as well as fully divine)" to "Jesus had some particular genome." From that we go to: "If Jesus's conception was as Luke's gospel has it, then God must have decided on a particular genome." And from that he goes to the suggestion that the genome could well have been just what it would have been had Joseph been the biological father. Why didn't I think of that?

But despite the distinctively Mavrodean virtues of the paper, it lacks one important desideratum. The author doesn't argue with me. Hence I can't respond to it as I do to the other papers in this volume by defending my views and arguments that are criticized and following out other issues that are raised by that interaction. George does cite and make use of my way of construing "divine interventions" in the world, though he rightly points out that this is not the only way of thinking of the matter; there is also "Hume's way," which takes such interventions to involve a violation of a law of nature. And that is the closest he comes to any criticism of a position of mine! However, he does give me a couple of openings for complaining about what he says. The first and more important of these is that he misrepresents my reasons for holding that a "divine intervention" need not violate any laws of nature, as is customarily supposed by Hume and innumerable others.

To lead up to this I need first to explain 'divine intervention.' As Mavrodes points out, my conception of this is God's bringing about some outcome in the universe that is different from what it would have been if only natural factors had been operative. It is also important that if a natural law is construed as a simple universally generalized proposition, then a violation of such a law is logically impossible. To use my example from the essay Mavrodes is discussing, a law of hydrostatics could be formulated as:

> A body will sink in still water of sufficient depth if the density of that
> body is greater than that of the water.

But if that is a simple generalization, a human body not sinking on the surface of
a still lake would not be a violation of the law, but a counterexample that shows
it not to be a universally true generalization. However most (though hardly all!)
philosophers take laws of nature to have more teeth than that by carrying a mo-
dal force, the exact nature of which is both obscure and highly controversial.
Thus the above law would be better formulated in terms of "must sink" in place
of "will sink"; its not sinking, as we say, would be "nomologically" impossible
(rather than logically impossible). In this richer way of construing laws of nature, it is conceivable that God would violate a law of nature in doing something. Mavrodes gives a nice example with the feather case. It has been suggested to me by one of the editors of this volume, Heather Battaly, that this
would be better characterized as a replacement of the previous law by another
than as a violation. But I think that this depends on how we fill out the case further. If God alters the mode of gravitational interaction for all cases, even if only
temporarily, that would be better described as a (perhaps temporary) change of
law. But if God makes this alteration only for this particular case and leaves
gravitation as it was for everything else, it would be best described as a violation. And so the Humean construal of divine interventions is conceivable.

Now back to Mavrodes's misconstrual of my reasons for supposing that a
divine intervention without violation of a natural law is possible. He takes that
reason to be that the laws we are justified in accepting:

> would specify only the actions of natural agents, natural forces, natural condi-
> tions, and so on. Such laws of nature would not say anything about what God, a
> supernatural agent, might do or would do. They would not imply that God
> could not, or would not, intervene anywhere in the world. Consequently, a di-
> vine intervention would not constitute a violation of that law.

But that is *not* what I give as a reason in this essay or anywhere else. This is
Mavrodes's contribution to the discussion. And it is just as well that I didn't
give this as my reason. Of course, what is asserted in this reason—that laws of
nature say nothing about what God could or would do—is quite correct. But it
doesn't imply that divine intervention without law violation is possible. So long
as a law asserts unqualifiedly that certain natural conditions must yield a certain
result, then it isn't possible for God to bring about a different result in the presence of those conditions without violating it.

The reason I give, here and elsewhere, for saying that this is possible is that
the laws we have reasons to accept, even laws of a deterministic form, do not
make such unqualified statements. Go back to the law of hydrostatics that specifies as a sufficient condition of a body sinking in still water (of sufficient depth)

that the body is of a density greater than the water. Immediately after the statement quoted by Mavrodes—that such laws are qualified by the proviso that the law will hold "in the absence of any relevant factors other than those specified in the law"—I proceed as follows:

> The laws we have reason to accept lay down sufficient conditions only within a "closed system", i.e., a system closed to influences other than those specified in the law. None of our laws take account of all possible influences. . . . A man standing upright on the surface of a lake will sink, *unless* he is being supported by a device dangling from a helicopter, or *unless* he is being drawn by a motor boat, or *unless* a sufficiently strong magnetic attraction is keeping him afloat, or. . . . Since the laws we have reason to accept make provision for interference by outside forces unanticipated by the law, it can hardly be claimed that such a law will be violated if a divine force intervenes. No doubt that is not the sort of outside force scientists normally envisage, but that is neither here nor there. If we were to make the rider read "in the absence of outside forces of the sort we are prepared to recognize as such", our confidence in all our law formulations would be greatly weakened. We have no basis for supposing that science identifies all the factors that can influence natural phenomena. ("Divine Action, Human Freedom, and the Laws of Nature" [DA], 190)

Thus natural laws even of a deterministic form, properly understood, do not rule out God's bringing about an outcome other than what would have eventuated if only natural causal factors were involved. Hence God's doing so need not be construed as a violation of the law.

Given that Mavrodes might give the impression that he thinks that my "no violation" position and the more common "violation" position are equally acceptable alternatives, I will say a word in support of the superiority of my way of construing divine interventions over its "Humean" rival. The superiority is of two sorts. (1) My view of deterministic natural laws adheres closely to the way they actually function—as accounts of what will necessarily eventuate in the absence of "outside" factors; that is, the absence of any causal influences other than those specified (or presupposed) in the law. (2) It represents particular divine actions in the world as a special case of the sort of thing we always get when outside influences (including those of a physical sort) produce something other than what would happen if the system were closed to outside influences. Hence this construal of special divine actions in the world renders it less abhorrent to theists who are strongly impressed with the "scientific view of the universe." Divine intervention is just a special case, albeit a *very* special case, of the sort of thing exemplified by the above examples of what might keep a man afloat on the surface of a deep lake, in spite of the law of hydrostatics just cited.

Still searching for things to complain about in Mavrodes's paper, I will just mention a point that may counter the impression that he takes the two ways of thinking of divine interventions to be equally acceptable. When it comes to his central concern in the paper, the virgin birth of Jesus Christ, he restricts himself to thinking of it as a divine intervention as I construe that, and he makes no attempt to spell out how it might involve a violation of a law of nature. But it is not difficult to see in a sketchy way how this might go. Taking his alternate treatments of the feather case as a model, instead of thinking of the action of the Holy Spirit as an "outside" influence not within the "closed system" of the laws of human reproduction, we could think of God as temporarily setting aside the relevant laws (construed as unqualifiedly deterministic laws) just for this case while leaving them operative for all other cases. I don't see anything about the virgin birth case that would prevent us from thinking of it in both the no-violation and the violation ways. Of course, I still plump for the superiority of my no-violation construal. But both are conceivable.

Apart from these minor cavils, I confine myself to the appreciative remarks of my first paragraph.

13
More Suggestions for Divine Command Theorists

Linda Zagzebski

I. Introduction

In "Some Suggestions for Divine Command Theorists" (SDC),[1] William Alston argues that DC (divine command) theory can be made invulnerable to familiar objections. While not endorsing the theory, he clearly is sympathetic with it, and since there has been increasing attention to Divine Command theory in recent years,[2] I think this is a good time to look at Alston's recommendations.

The version of the theory Alston finds most promising is the one proposed by Robert M. Adams in 1979: Moral obligation is constituted by divine commands in roughly the way water is constituted by H_2O.[3] Adams includes the claim that the *property* of being a moral obligation is the same as the property of being commanded by a loving God. I find property identity problematic, but since I doubt that Alston's suggestions require that part of Adams's proposal, I will not assume it in my discussion. The key idea from Adams is this:

(DC) It is metaphysically necessary that an act X is a moral obligation for a human being if and only if X is commanded by God.

(DC) makes the connection between divine commands and obligation stronger than mere extensional equivalence, which is theoretically uninteresting, but not as strong as identity of meaning, which is plainly false. Alston argues that (DC) can embrace both horns of the Euthyphro dilemma, suitably interpreted, without problematic implications.

Alston considers "S ought to do X" an alternative formulation of "S has an obligation to do X." So the version of DC theory he is considering maintains that it is metaphysically necessary that a human being ought to do an act X if and only if X is commanded by God.

As Alston presents the Euthyphro dilemma for DC theory it is this:

> Dilemma 1: Ought we to do X because God commands X, or does God command X because we ought to do X?

There is a related dilemma that is important for Alston's proposal:

> Dilemma 2: Is moral goodness what it is because of God's commands, or are God's commands what they are because of moral goodness?

Alston's answer is to separate value and obligation, embracing the first horn of Dilemma 1 and the second horn of Dilemma 2. Obligation/oughtness is what it is because of God's commands, but God's commands are what they are because of moral goodness, so the commands are not arbitrary. Since divine commands constitute human obligation, not divine goodness, DC theory does not prevent the attribution of goodness to God. And since God is identical with perfect goodness, all of morality ultimately depends upon God.

I will argue that the move Alston proposes to blunt the force of the second horn of the second dilemma is exactly right and it is independent of DC theory. The move he proposes to blunt the first horn of the first dilemma fails to fully answer one of the traditional objections. To answer that objection, obligation must be based on something deeper in the divine psyche than the making of commands. If all commands are determined by the divine nature, then commands are not the metaphysical basis of moral obligation. If commands play an essential role in obligation, there must be something in between the divine nature and divine commands in virtue of which God makes the commands he makes, but which also explains why the commands are not superfluous. I will argue that this is the personhood of God. This variation permits an interesting version of DC theory that can escape the traditional objections. It also makes DC theory optional.

II. Does God Have Obligations?

Alston says that separating value and obligation in the way needed to permit the DC theorist to embrace the first horn of Dilemma 1 and the second horn of Dilemma 2 requires that obligation and other properties in the ought family do not apply to God himself, and he devotes quite a lot of attention to arguing that the lack of any possibility of God's doing other than the best prevents the application of these terms (SDC, 308). I recommend that the DC theorist not insist that God has no obligations. In the first place, Alston's proposal does not require it. All that it requires is that the area of human obligation is "fenced off" from other areas of morality. The latter would include the good, but it could also include divine obligation. The DC theorist might want to opt for this approach because she might think that God makes promises and he would be violating an obligation or doing what he ought not to do were he to break his promises, a point made by Eleonore Stump (SDC, 315). Alston replies that if it is not true that God ought to keep his promises because ought does not apply to God, God does not literally make promises at all (SDC, 315–316). But I can see why DC theorists might not want to take either the route of denying that God makes promises or the route of saying that God makes promises but is not obligated to keep them. At least they might want to leave it open that God has obligations for the purposes of answering the traditional objections to their theory.

Alston recognizes the possibility of separating divine and human obligation so that only the latter is constituted by divine commands, but he says that he has no idea what divine obligation would be like if it is separated from human obligation in the way needed for DC theory to work (SDC, 306). But there is reason to think that even if it is metaphysically necessary that an act is an obligation for a human being if and only if it is commanded by God, what we mean by "obligation" in humans has an analogue for God. To see this, we will have to look more carefully at the analogy Adams and Alston use between "obligation" and natural kind terms like "water."

When Kripke and Putnam proposed the theory of direct reference in the 1970's, they were concerned to argue that "water" does not refer through any descriptive meaning; it refers directly.[4] "Water" is defined, roughly, as "stuff like that," where there is a demonstrative reference to a sample of water. What it takes to be stuff like that is subject to empirical investigation. We investigate water samples and discover that they have the chemical constitution H_2O. Arguably, the inference that being H_2O is essential to water, that necessarily something is water if and only if it is H_2O, is validated by the conjunction of the a priori assumption that whatever the chemical structure of water is, that is its nature, and empirical investigation.[5] The DC theorist could use this approach to argue that thesis (DC) is validated by the conjunction of the a priori principle that the metaphysical source of an obligation for a being of a certain kind is necessary to it and the theological thesis that obligations for human beings have their source in divine commands. The conclusion would be that necessarily X is an obligation for a human being if and only if X is commanded by God. That is an important similarity between "obligation" and "water" that can be used by DC theorists if they wish.

But there is also an important dissimilarity. Unlike "water," "obligation" does have a descriptive meaning. "Obligation" certainly is not defined as "whatever acts are like those," where we make direct reference to obligation paradigms—keeping promises, not telling lies, and so on. What we mean by "the obligatory" is arguable, but I suggest that the obligatory and the good but non-obligatory are *conceptually* distinct. What we mean by "obligation," I believe, is essentially this: There is no other option compatible with moral goodness. The "force" of obligation lies in the perception of the lack of alternatives compatible with goodness. That is why an obligation is whatever is correctly expressed as a "must."

If this is what we mean by "obligation," there are no doubt acts of even a being who is perfectly good that admit of no good alternative, and hence, are obligatory. Loving others can easily be something that admits of no alternative compatible with God's nature, and if so, God would experience it that way. God would experience loving others as a demand of his nature, not as a mere preference or desire, much less as something about which he could choose. If so, God ought to love others. Alston says the closest we get to a moral law that God ought to love others is the conjunction of the evaluative statement that it is good for God to love others, along with the statement that God necessarily does so (SDC, 313). But I do not find this convincing. If obligation applies to acts which are such that they admit of no alternative consistent with moral goodness, God would have obligations as long as God perceives certain acts as admitting of no alternative consistent with his nature. But this is compatible with the proposal that the metaphysical source of divine obligation and the metaphysical source of human obligation are distinct. The metaphysical source of the property of an act of a human being which makes it the case that there is no alternative act compatible with goodness is that it is commanded by God. The metaphysical source of the property of an act of God which makes it the case that there is no alternative act compatible with goodness is that any alternative is incompatible with God's nature.[6] So it is metaphysically necessary that an act X is an obligation for a human if and only if X is commanded by God. It is metaphysically necessary that an act X is an obligation for God if and only if the failure to do X is incompatible with God's nature. The force of an obligation for God is internal; the force of an obligation for humans is external, although there is often a derivative internal force as well. It is consistent with this difference that what "obligation" means for God is the same as what it means for human beings.

So the DC theorist can maintain that God has obligations without jeopardizing the approach Alston proposes. However, if the DC theorist wishes to argue that God has no obligations, I recommend that he not use Alston's main argument for this conclusion, the argument that properties in the ought family do not apply to an essentially perfect being. The trouble with that argument is that it can and has been used to show that other moral properties do not apply to God, in particular, moral praiseworthiness, and I assume the DC theorist wishes to maintain that God is morally praiseworthy. Here is the problem. Under the assumption that a perfectly good being is incapable of doing wrong or anything but good, such a being does not appear to be free in any morally significant sense. We think that persons are praiseworthy only if they do good when they could have done evil, and they are blameworthy only if they do evil when they could have done good. Beings who cannot help doing good are admirable in a different, non-moral way. Their inability to do evil is like physical beauty or strength. It is a wonderful thing, but it is not the sort of thing for which they are responsible. We admire them, but praise is not something they *deserve*.[7]

I am not claiming that this argument is sound, only that it is parallel to the argument proposed by Alston. So the problem with ruling out obligation for a being with a perfectly good will is that it rules out too much. Not only is it unacceptable on its face to rule out divine praiseworthiness, it jeopardizes Alston's strategy of separating value properties and properties in the ought family. Perhaps DC theorists can manage to argue that essential goodness rules out oughtness but not morally significant freedom and praiseworthiness, but I think better strategies are available, as we shall see.

In arguing that moral obligation does not apply to a perfectly good being, Alston borrows Kant's argument for the same conclusion. If Kant's argument works, there is the problem just noted that it seems to rule out too much, but I'm not sure Alston can use it to show God has no obligations if "obligation" means what I have suggested above. Kant says that obligation has no application to a being with a perfectly good (holy) will (*Groundwork*, 86), but Kant does not deny that there are actions that are objectively necessary for a perfectly good being. In fact, he asserts the contrary in the passage Alston quotes (*Groundwork*, 39). There Kant says, "A perfectly good will, therefore, would be equally subject to objective laws (of the good)." So there are actions for a being with a holy will that fall under an objective moral law. Kant denies that these acts are obligations because the latter applies only to beings for whom the moral law is subjectively contingent. Alston says that Kant thinks of the objective laws of the good that apply to a being with a holy will as like supererogation, not obligations (SDC, 312), but I do not think that is what Kant means. They are the same kind of objective laws that *would* be laws of obligation were the being to which they apply capable of willing otherwise. They can include laws like: Keep promises, Do not tell lies, and so on. These laws admit of no alternative compatible with God's goodness. They are not like counsels of supererogation.

Suppose, then, that the DC theorist wants to deny that God has obligations. What argument should he use? Alston gives at least one of them himself, the argument that the governing and regulative function of obligation is intrinsic to it (a move that does not require essential goodness). Another option is to use Adams's argument (1999) that obligation arises only within a social context in which what is obligatory is something demanded by another person in a relationship we value. When we violate the obligation we alienate ourselves from that person, who is on that account appropriately angry, and we are thereby guilty and blamed by others. The DC theorist could then argue that God does not fill the appropriate role in the social context of obligation. Or perhaps obligation only arises when there is a threat to the self, as has been argued by Christine Korsgaard[8] and in a different way by Bernard Williams,[9] but God can suffer no such threat.

There are no doubt other arguments as well. Some probably require a modification of my proposal on the meaning of "obligation" above, but the DC theorist may wish to do that. My point is not to insist that "obligation" means what I have proposed, but to argue that the view that God has obligations or that there are acts God ought to do is optional for the DC theorist. I have argued that the theorist might be motivated to maintain God has obligations, that God can have obligations without jeopardizing the approach Alston recommends, and I have suggested a way of thinking about obligation that would apply to God as well as to humans. If instead the DC theorist denies that God has obligations, the reason for thinking so should be something other than the fact that God cannot do anything less than the best.

III. The Two Traditional Objections

Let us now turn to the Euthyphro problem. Alston's strategy, as I've said, is to embrace the first horn of Dilemma 1 and the second horn of Dilemma 2. The first horn of Dilemma 1 is that we ought to do X because God commands X. That is the central claim of DC theory, but it faces two classic objections.

First, it allegedly leaves us without an adequate way to construe God's own goodness. That is because oughtness might be construed in a way broad enough to make it look like the first horn of Dilemma 1 implies the first horn of Dilemma 2. In other words, DC theory might appear to be committed to making all moral goodness as well as oughtness posterior to God's commands. But this is fairly easy to answer, and Alston's strategy is the way to do it. The first horn of Dilemma 1 surely does not commit us to the first horn of Dilemma 2. We fence in the area of morality constituted by divine commands so that the divine nature and goodness fall outside that area. Moral oughtness/obligation for human beings is constituted by divine commands, not moral goodness. God's goodness is untouched by DC theory.

The second classic objection to embracing the first horn of Dilemma 1 is that it seems to make morality arbitrary. If God is not constrained by morality from commanding what he commands, God could command anything, including cruelty, which would thereby be morally obligatory. This objection has two related parts: (1) It looks like God commands without a reason. But if God commands without a reason it looks like (2) God could have commanded something like cruelty, in which case cruelty could have been an obligation. Both (1) and (2) are problematic.

Now it seems to me that the arbitrariness objection is also fairly easy to answer if the objection is that God could have commanded anything at all, including cruelty, punishing the innocent, and so on. All God needs is a reason or a ground for his commands sufficient to preclude these latter commands. But presumably God's commands are not unhinged from his nature, and the divine nature prevents God from commanding certain things, such as those things that are, as a matter of fact, morally horrific. I am not denying that there have been divine command theorists who thought that God *could* command cruelty, that God's sovereignty requires the capacity of his will to do anything, but there is also a long tradition to the contrary, and Alston's advice to take the latter route seems to me to be right.[10]

So if the objection is only that God could have commanded absolutely anything, including the morally evil, the objection can be easily answered. But there is quite a distance between complete arbitrariness on the one hand, and necessity on the other. The first part of the objection above is harder to answer than the second. A theory might not make obligation completely arbitrary even when it entails that obligation could be other than it is. But many philosophers think that morality is necessary—it couldn't be otherwise. And even those who do not insist that morality is necessary can object that a command needs a sufficient reason. But if the divine nature is compatible with alternative commands, arbitrariness creeps in. Why command X rather than Y if both X and Y are compatible with the divine nature? So even if God has reasons that rule out certain commands such as cruelty, God lacks a sufficient reason for the particular commands he makes.

This forces us to face the more serious question of whether divine commands are under-determined by the divine goodness. This, I think, is the weakest aspect of DC theory and it needs to be faced squarely. Bill says, "So far from being arbitrary, God's commands to us are an expression of his perfect goodness" (SDC, 317). But even if a command is an expression of perfect goodness, if the former is not entailed by the latter, the command seems to lack a sufficient reason. If there is no morally sufficient reason for this command rather than some other command that is equally expressive of God's goodness, there is no full explanation for the fact that God commands the one rather than the other. Bill says that a moral reason could be something like the fact that an act would be repaying a kindness or it is a morally good thing to do (SDC, 318). But either a command adds something to goodness or it does not. If it does not, the command is not the metaphysical source of obligation; goodness is. If an obligation does add a moral feature to an act that it does not already have in virtue of having evaluative properties, we still lack a reason for the fact that God commands one thing rather than another that is equally compatible with his good nature. The arbitrariness objection has not been fully answered.

Adams has a response to this. He says that obligation arises in a social context between actual persons who love each other, as in a marriage. When A makes a demand on B, B has an obligation to satisfy the demand. If the demand is not met, the relationship is harmed, B should feel guilty, A is appropriately angry, and C can appropriately blame B. The relationship between A and B gives A the right to make demands on the other. There need be no reason for the demand deducible from the nature of the parties to the relationship, although demands are, of course, constrained by the goodness of each party. Now I certainly do not deny that if someone with whom I have a loving relationship requests that I do X, that I have a reason to do X. What I do not see is that it takes a command/demand to give me a reason to do what such a person wants or prefers, even when that person is God. A request will do as well. A request is not as strong as a command, and this probably means that even though I have a reason to comply, the reason does not constitute an obligation. But the lines are not clear-cut since all of the following can be true of a request by God that I do X: If I do not do X my relationship with God is harmed; I justifiably feel guilty; God blames me for not caring about him enough to do what he asks. I have a reason to do X, even a sufficient reason. And I would propose that the word "ought" is flexible enough that we can say I ought to do X. All of this can be the case even though it is going too far to say I am obliged to do X. Our inheritance from Kant makes obligation in modern philosophy a very strong notion. Obligation has a special force that admits of no alternative. Moral philosophers like to draw a sharp line between those acts that are our obligations and those that are not, and much of modern ethics has been devoted to making that line both sharp and clear. This creates a problem for the DC theorist because the distinctions among a demand, a request, an avowed preference, and an implicit wish are blurry; the distinction between on obligation and a non-obligation is not.

Or maybe it is. That is an option I think the DC theorist should take seriously. Suppose there is a range of God's psychological attitudes towards potential human acts. Some acts are such that God cannot abide our doing the contrary. Others are strong requests; still others are weaker requests or just expressed preferences. The weaker the attitude, the less the problem of arbitrariness arises. A command or demand needs a reason, and the issue of what that reason is has been a long-standing objection to DC theory. But a preference does not need a reason. Nobody worries that a preference is arbitrary.[11]

But the DC theorist may find that this approach moves too far away from DC theory. Suppose instead that she wants to accept the conventional modern approach to obligation. There is a sharp and clear line between what we are obliged to do and what we are not obliged to do. If the only resource available to the DC theorist to avoid the arbitrariness problem is the divine nature, she will have to say our obligations are those acts that admit of no alternative compatible with the divine nature. Obligations are entailed by goodness, which is to say, they are entailed by the nature of God. God makes these obligations explicit by issuing commands, but the commands are not the source of the obligation; God's nature is the source. This approach has the advantage of explaining why we can figure out many of our obligations without consulting God's commands. Our own goodness is an imitation of divine goodness, and while imperfect, it often allows us an awareness of what is incompatible with goodness.

The problem with this approach is that it also moves away from DC theory, only it moves in the other direction. Instead of weakening commands to requests, thereby weakening obligation with it, it makes obligation rest on the divine nature, thereby leading to the conclusion that divine commands serve no metaphysical function. All they do is to make the divine nature explicit. So it is a divine nature theory of obligation, not a divine command theory. But one consideration that may alleviate this worry is that the theory does satisfy the form of DC theory with which we began: It is metaphysically necessary that an act X is an obligation for a human being if and only if God commands X. Further, the theorist can add a divine preference theory of moral reasons for action to a divine nature theory of obligation. God issues commands that are entailed by his goodness, but he also has preferences that are not entailed by his goodness, and the latter also give us moral reasons to act in a certain way. It is hard to avoid the conclusion that the combined theory still fails to give divine commands a special metaphysical role in grounding obligation.

To keep DC theory from collapsing into either a divine nature theory or a divine preference theory or some combination of the two, the DC theorist should insist that X is an obligation and Y is not because God commands X rather than Y even though both X and Y are equally compatible with his nature. But then he should admit that reference to the divine nature will not answer the arbitrariness objection. To answer it, I think he will need to move in a very interesting direction, one I have explored in my own theory, and one that is detachable from DC theory. This direction is proposed by Bill Alston in the paper I am discussing. He uses it to blunt the second horn of Dilemma 2.

IV. Exemplarism: God as Exemplary Nature; Christ as Exemplary Person

The second horn of the second dilemma is this: God commands an act (say, that we love one another) because of moral goodness. I have argued that this horn is insufficient to answer the first objection to the first horn, that as long as God's moral goodness does not give him a sufficient reason to command what he commands, there is still a problem in explaining where God's commands come from. There is a gap between divine nature and divine commands that needs to be filled. Instead, if God's goodness does give him a sufficient reason to command what he commands, actual divine commands do not serve the metaphysical purpose of grounding obligation, although they may serve an epistemic purpose—to inform us of the divine nature. I want now to turn to Alston's defense of the second horn because the position he proposes is not only good advice for DC theorists, it is good advice for Christian theists. It can be used to avoid the problems I have discussed in the first horn, and it permits a number of variations in theories of obligation, of which DC theory is one option.

Alston points out that a Christian theist might find this horn of the dilemma objectionable if it is interpreted in a way that presupposes a Platonic conception of goodness according to which goodness is an external standard against which all good beings are measured. This might appear to weaken God's sovereignty, making God's goodness derivative from a goodness outside of himself. Another objection not mentioned by Alston is that the Platonic conception does not require an actual deity. An imaginary deity would do as well. Like an Ideal Observer (IO), as long as there is some essence of perfect goodness distinct from its exemplification in a real being, there need be no real being to serve the purpose of grounding morality. The hypothetical commands of a hypothetical perfectly good deity could be the ground of obligation in the same way the hypothetical responses of a hypothetical Ideal Observer are the ground of the application of moral properties in the IO theory.[12]

Alston's response is that God himself is the supreme standard of goodness, like the standard meter stick used to be the standard for being one meter.[13]

> What makes this table a meter in length is not its conformity to a Platonic essence but its conformity to a certain existing individual. Similarly . . . what makes an act of love a good thing is not its conformity to some general principle but its conformity to, or approximation to, God, who is both the ultimate source of the existence of things and the supreme standard by reference to which they are to be assessed. (SDC, 320)

I think this is exactly right. It brings us back to the distinction between terms that refer through general descriptions that comprise the meaning of the term, like "triangle" (Alston calls these "Platonic predicates"), and terms that refer via direct reference to either an exemplar, as is the case with "meter," or a typical instance of the class of objects to which the term applies, as is the case with natural kind terms like "water," "dog," and "gold." Alston proposes that "good" is in the latter category. It refers directly. As mentioned above, the theory of direct reference maintains that "water" is "whatever is the same kind of liquid as that," "dog" is "whatever is the same species of animal as that," and so on. But almost any dog or sample of water is good enough to be the standard against which other animals or liquids are measured because membership in a natural kind does not admit of degree. At least, we normally do not say that some portion of water is more water than some other portion, or one dog is more a dog than another.[14] Alston proposes, then, that the way "meter" refers is a closer analogy with "good" since the standard meter stick is a unique stick similarity to which is (was) the criterion for the correct application of the term "meter."[15]

The analogy between God and the standard meter stick is not perfect, as Alston mentions (SDC, note 15), because the particular stick chosen to serve as the standard is arbitrary, whereas it is the reverse of arbitrary that God is the standard of goodness. The difference arises from the fact that Alston's claim is metaphysical as well as semantical. God is both the ultimate standard and the source of good. The standard meter stick is certainly not the source of other meter sticks even if it is the standard. So the analogy between "good" and terms that refer directly like "meter" and "water" is semantical. The semantical point is illuminating, and it is one I have explored elsewhere. I call a theory of this kind "exemplarism" and have argued that it has theoretical and practical advantages for ethics, as well as many interesting consequences.[16] Here I would like to explore the way the theory can be used to aid the divine command theorist.

Let us begin with the semantics. One of the main reasons Kripke and Putnam proposed that natural kind terms are defined via direct reference to instances of the kind was that they believed that often we do not know the nature of the thing we are defining, and yet we know how to construct a definition that links up with its nature. Many of us do not know the nature of gold, and for millennia nobody did, but that did not prevent people from defining "gold" in a way that fixed the reference of the term and continued to do so after its nature was discovered. The theory of direct reference explains why the referent of the word "gold" remained invariant after it was discovered that what makes gold what it is is that it is the element with atomic number 79. Even after that discovery it was not necessary that individual speakers know the nature of gold in order to successfully refer to gold. All that is required is that they be related by a chain of communication to actual instances of gold. It is not even necessary that every speaker be able to reliably identify gold themselves as long as some speakers in the community can do so and the other speakers rely on the judgment of the experts.

Very few people have ever seen the standard meter stick, and even those who have do not use it in any explicit way in their use of the term "meter." They learned what "meter" refers to by the experience of ordinary meter sticks whose length approximates the length of the standard meter stick. When they say something is one meter in length, they mean that it is the same length as a meter stick. They may not be aware that the length of the many ordinary meter sticks is not identical. What permits them to refer successfully to "one meter" when using many meter sticks of differing lengths is the relationship between the meter sticks of their experience and a standard of whose existence they may not even be aware. Similarly, people learn what "good" means by the experience of good persons whose goodness in degree and kind approximates a standard of goodness of whose existence they may not be aware. Something is more or less one meter to the degree that it approximates the length of the standard meter stick. Something is more or less good to the degree that it approximates the goodness of God, the perfectly good being. Ordinary meter sticks are a close enough approximation to the standard meter stick for most purposes. Ordinary human exemplars are an infinite distance from God, but sufficient to give us the idea of what good is for most of the purposes of practical life. Ordinary drinking water is close enough to pure H_2O for us to successfully refer to water when pointing to a glass of drinking water.

An advantage of this kind of theory is that a host of issues, metaphysical and scientific, need not be settled in advance of fixing the reference of the terms used. And one of its most interesting consequences is that it means that necessary truths can be revealed partly by empirical investigation. When we say that water is whatever is the same liquid as the stuff in this glass, we are implicitly leaving open the question of what properties of the stuff in this glass are essential to its being water. For the same reason, when we say that a good person is a person like that, and we directly refer to Socrates or St. Francis of Assisi or Jesus Christ, we are implicitly leaving open the question of what properties of Socrates, Francis, or Jesus are essential to their goodness. It is unlikely that a priori principles will be sufficient to answer that question and that is why we need narratives. Narratives will reveal the connection between their motives and other psychological states and their resultant acts. Careful observation of the exemplar can show us what the relevant properties are. And like the discovery that water is H_2O, it is possible to find out what is essential to the good person *qua* good.

Now if God is the supreme exemplar of goodness, there is an analogue to the empirical investigation of water. That is Revelation. Through Revelation we find out the traits of God's character, God's motives in acting, and some of God's acts. What the DC theorist should do, I suggest, is to begin with exemplarism and let the issues about what makes God good and how God wants us to think about how we ought to act and the other moral properties of those acts be settled by investigation of the exemplar's revelation of himself. We find out that God gives commands in the Hebrew Scriptures. The Christian also believes that how God wants us to interpret those commands and how God wants us to think of the rest of morality is revealed in the New Testament.

Let us now return to the gap left over from the first horn of the Euthyphro dilemma. Recall that the problem is that there is no direct line from God's nature to God's commands. If there were, commands would be superfluous. I said that the DC theorist should say that the divine nature does not uniquely determine all of the divine commands, and this means that the divine nature does not uniquely determine all our obligations. If an obligation is something which is such that there is no alternative compatible with goodness, in those cases where God commands X but both X and an alternative command Y are equally compatible with his goodness, it is not incompatible with the goodness of God to fail to command X, which means that it is not incompatible with the goodness of God that we are not obliged to do X, and so it is not incompatible with goodness that we are not obliged to do X. Nonetheless, the following is true: Given that God commands X, it is not compatible with goodness that we fail to do X. It follows that some obligations might not have been obligations. Some acts that are compatible with God's nature are nonetheless incompatible with goodness, given the way God has acted. So at least part of morality is not necessary; it could have been otherwise. The DC theorist should insist upon that.

The conclusion is that there must be something good about God that is not entailed by the divine nature in virtue of which God commands one thing rather than another equally compatible with the divine nature. This must mean that the divine nature, which is perfect goodness, does not exhaust the ways in which God is good. That might seem impossible, but the exemplarist approach shows us a way to discover what that is.

Let us look again at what it means to say that God is the exemplar of goodness. Do we mean the exemplar is the unique instantiation of the divine nature, or do we mean the exemplar is God himself, a personal being? I presume it is the latter. God is not simply the unique and only possible instantiation of the divine nature. God is a person(s) and has what we call, for lack of a better word, personality. The metaphysics of persons is one of the most difficult problems in philosophy, of course, and I am not going to try to deepen our understanding of persons in this paper. But I want to make one metaphysical point and one ethical point about persons that I believe can be useful to the DC theorist.

The metaphysical point is negative. A person is not reducible to the instantiation of a nature, even if that nature is an individual essence. That follows from the doctrine of the Trinity according to which the Father, Son, and Holy Spirit have the same individual essence, divinity, but are three distinct persons. I also suspect that their nature does not entail that *these* persons are the instantiation of the divine natures. Who those persons are and the acts they perform could not be deduced, even in principle, from an exhaustive description of the divine nature. A person is a who, not a what, and can only be known by acquaintance, whether direct or indirect.

The ethical point is this. A person is good in a way that is different from the goodness of qualities/natures. The personhood of a person is revealed in their unique psychology which includes distinctive emotions and perceptions, some of which motivate acts. When the person is a divine person, some of those acts are acts of requesting/demanding acts of certain kinds from us.

The gap between the divine nature and the divine commands is filled by God's personality. General divine motives such as love are part of the divine nature, but many specific motives in specific circumstances are part of God's personality. I propose that the DC theorist should say that motives and the acts they cause which are such that alternative motives/acts are compatible with the divine nature arise from the personality of God. This move permits them to be neither necessary nor arbitrary. Are they entailed by the divine personality? No. Personality is not the sort of thing that entails things. To think so is to confuse it with a nature. Then how can personalities include constituents that are not arbitrary? That is a question I cannot answer. I believe it leads into the mystery of the uniqueness of persons and the unresolved problem of free will. Persons clearly are not random collections of psychic states. They are rational beings whose goodness is partly constituted by their difference from everything else in the universe, including every other person.

Since there are three persons with the divine nature, there is the issue of which person or persons of the Trinity act in situations related to human beings, but I will leave that question aside since I don't think it need be addressed for the purposes of the DC theorist. The traditional position has been that the Father, Son, and Holy Spirit act together, but whether they do or not, their acts express personality, either that of one or of more than one person. Motives and acts that are grounded in personhood are good because of the goodness of the divine persons. This is a distinct goodness from that of the divine nature. The distinctiveness of the divine persons out of which the divine acts arise, including commands, explains why God's commands are good without being necessary. They are partially constitutive of the divine goodness, the standard against which all other good persons are measured.

The exemplarist approach I have been describing shows the importance of Revelation for moral theology. I would not deny that we can figure out many moral truths a priori because we were created by God whose goodness is reflected in ourselves. But we can never know God as a person by natural theology or any a priori means. I suggest, then, that the issue of where the divine commands fit into the personality of God should be left to an investigation of Scripture and the tradition of interpreting Scripture. What I think we find is that the Incarnation shifts the ethical direction from that of the Old Testament. If Christ is the Word made flesh, the perfect revelation of the Father, it follows that God is most perfectly revealed, not in a set of commandments or any written or spoken words, but in a person. Jesus says he does not come to destroy the law, but to fulfill it (Matt. 5:17), and through him we have access to the Father and come to share in the divine nature (see Eph. 1:9). We do that by imitation. "In a word, as God's dear children, try to be like him, and live in love as Christ loved you" (Eph. 5:1). The whole law is summed up in love (Rom. 13:8–10). In the New Testament our motive for loving and forgiving is not that we are to follow God's commands, but that God himself loves and forgives. We see that there is no limit on the forgiveness of injuries because it corresponds to God's forgiveness of us (Matt. 18:21ff). The motive for imitation is that what we are imitating is a love which we have already received. "We love because He first loved us" (I John 4:18).

My point is not that the Ten Commandments disappear in the New Testament, but that the Gospels and Epistles present a different perspective on commands and obligation than we see in the Hebrew Scriptures. I suggest that if the DC theorist is Christian, it is important to put special emphasis on Christology in the way the ethical theory is developed. Alston mentions the connection between exemplarism (what he calls particularism) and the imitation of Christ (SDC, 323). I think that the connection is even closer than he suggests. "Good" is defined via reference to a paradigm of good, and the ultimate paradigm is God. To find out what good is, we look at what God is. To find out what God is like, not just in his nature, but in his personhood, we look at revelation. What we find out when we look at revelation is that God is most perfectly revealed in Jesus Christ. For human beings the imitation of God is the imitation of Christ. To follow the commands of God is the same thing as to imitate Christ. The doctrines of the Trinity and the Incarnation make DC theory work. But what makes the theory work is something that makes commands themselves much less important than thesis (DC) implies.

In summary, I think that exemplarism has numerous advantages:

- It explains why it takes a real being to be the standard of morality, not just a Platonic essence.
- It explains the importance of looking at revelation as a way of finding out what God is like, what God's motives are, what God wants from us. If God commands, we find that out also.
- It explains the transition from Old Testament to New Testament ethics. The perfect revelation of the Father is not a set of commands, but a person.
- It explains the importance of the imitation of Christ in Christian ethics. It gives a prominent place in the theory to the Christian doctrines of the Trinity and the Incarnation.
- It fills in the gap between the divine nature and the divine commands that is the heart of the objection from arbitrariness.

I have one final suggestion for DC theorists. Rather than spend a lot of time defending the theory against objections, I think the DC theorist should go on the attack. The Euthyphro dilemma is not unique to Divine Command theory. Many other theories of obligation face a parallel problem and some avoid it only by not offering a theory of the metaphysical source of obligation at all. So when the Social Contract theorist proposes that an act is an obligation if and only if it follows from principles that persons in a situation described by the theory would agree to, one can reasonably ask whether something is an obligation because people agree to it or whether they agree to it because it is an obligation. The dilemma does not reveal a mistake in the theory, but it does show where the theory is missing something. My own view is that divine commands are not the bottom-level metaphysical source of obligation, but Christians should be grateful to DC theorists for showing us where to look.

Notes

1. William P. Alston, "Some Suggestions for Divine Command Theorists" (SDC), in *Christian Theism and the Problems of Philosophy*, ed. Michael Beaty (Notre Dame, IN: University of Notre Dame Press, 1990), 303–326; and in William P. Alston, *Divine Nature and Human Language: Essays in Philosophical Theology* (Ithaca, NY: Cornell University Press, 1989), 253–273. Page references are to the Beaty volume.

2. One of the sources of the renewed interest in Divine Command theory is Robert M. Adams's book, *Finite and Infinite Goods* (New York: Oxford University Press, 1999), which was published after Alston's paper was written. But some of Adams's ideas on DC theory appear in his earlier papers, including the paper to which Alston refers (see note 3 below).

3. Robert M. Adams, "Divine Command Metaethics Modified Again," *Journal of*

Religious Ethics 7, no. 1 (1979): 66–79; reprinted as chapter 9 of Adams, *The Virtue of Faith and Other Essays in Philosophical Theology* (New York: Oxford University Press, 1987).

4. The theory originated with Saul Kripke's *Naming and Necessity* (Oxford: Blackwell, 1980), and Hilary Putnam's paper "The Meaning of 'Meaning,'" in Putnam, *Mind, Language, and Reality, Philosophical Papers* vol. 2 (Cambridge: Cambridge University Press, 1975), 215–271.

5. I recall that this proposal appears in an unpublished paper by Keith Donnellan, "Natural Kinds, Rigid Designators, and Individuals," written in the mid-1970's. Note that the inference, "Water is H_2O," is a posteriori as long as empirical investigation is necessary to reach the conclusion. The fact that the inference also uses an a priori principle does not prevent the conclusion from being a posteriori.

6. There is a sense in which the ultimate metaphysical source of both human and divine obligation is the divine nature, but I will argue below that if commands play an essential role in human obligation the DC theorist must not maintain that divine commands are entailed by the divine nature. The nature of God is not the source of human obligation in the same sense in which it is the source of divine obligation.

7. For a good contemporary formulation of this problem see William L. Rowe, "The Problem of Divine Perfection and Freedom," in *Reasoned Faith*, ed. Eleonore Stump (Ithaca, NY: Cornell University Press, 1993), 223–233; and Rowe's "Divine Freedom" in *The Stanford Encyclopedia of Philosophy*, ed. Edward N. Zalta, Summer 2003, <http://plato.stanford.edu/archives/sum2003/entries/divine-freedom> (July 29, 2004).

8. Christine Korsgaard, *The Sources of Normativity* (Cambridge: Cambridge University Press, 1996), 102.

9. Bernard Williams, *Shame and Necessity* (Berkeley and Los Angeles: University of California Press, 1993). See, for example, 75–76.

10. Ockham, for example, maintained that God could change his commands and make something like stealing morally right. Bob Adams argues that God could command such things as cruelty, but if so, morality would fall apart. An obligation is a command of a loving God. See Robert Adams, "A Modified Divine Command Theory of Ethical Wrongness," in Adams, *The Virtue of Faith and Other Essays in Philosophical Theology*, 97–122.

11. For a Divine Preference theory, see Thomas Carson, *Value and the Good Life* (Notre Dame, IN: University of Notre Dame Press, 2000).

12. Curiously, some moral philosophers might actually prefer a theory based on a nonactual perfect being, which may explain the popularity of the IO theory and Social Contract theories where the seat of authority is not in any actual being. I assume that theists have a different point of view on this matter. Charles Taliaferro, for example, supports a version of the IO theory in which the IO is God. See his *Contemporary Philosophy of Religion* (Oxford: Blackwell, 1998).

13. Unfortunately, "meter" is no longer defined as the distance between two etchings on a metal bar in Paris. It is now set as the distance that light from a helium-neon laser travels in 1/299,792,458 second. Even more precise ways of fixing the reference have been proposed.

14. But even in the case of water we think that the purity of samples of water vary since some are closer to pure H_2O than others. A sample of pure H_2O would be a better water paradigm than ordinary drinking water.

15. Kripke discusses the function of the standard meter stick in the way "meter" refers in *Naming and Necessity*.

16. Linda Zagzebski, "The Incarnation and Virtue Ethics," in *The Incarnation*, ed. Daniel Kendall and Gerald O'Collins (Oxford: Oxford University Press, 2000); and Linda Zagzebski, *Divine Motivation Theory* (Cambridge University Press, 2004).

14

Response to Zagzebski

William P. Alston

Zabzebski's paper is a paradigm of cooperative philosophical work. She takes my fragmentary "Some Suggestions for Divine Command Theorists," modifies it in various ways where she finds it defective or unacceptable, develops and extends it in the light of her own work in the area, and winds up with further suggestions for divine command (DC) theorists. I have learned, and am learning, from her efforts, and I am happy for a chance to continue the cooperative project in this response.

Despite the impression that might be given by the above paragraph, since this is philosophy the accolades contained therein by no means imply that I agree with everything she says, though they do imply that I find it all thoughtful, insightful, and well worth taking seriously. And as will appear, I even agree with some of it! Her paper is rich in content, and I would like to comment on all of her suggestions. But in order to keep this response from being as long as the paper, I will restrict myself to what I consider the main line of argument—her criticisms of my version of DC theory, and her suggestions for a different version. As a bit of Ariadne's thread through the Labyrinth, I offer the following big picture as a prelude.

As Linda points out, I do not endorse DC theory. My concern in my paper was limited to showing a way in which it could be developed so as to avoid being impaled on the horns of two Euthyphro-like dilemmas. Those dilemmas are formulated by Linda as follows.

(I) Ought we to do X because God commands us to do X, or does God command us to do X because we ought to do X?

(II) Is moral goodness what it is because of God's commands, or are God's commands what they are because of moral goodness?

The objection is that whichever horn is chosen in each dilemma the DC theorist is in big trouble. My strategy was to show how to construe DC theory so that the first horn of (I) and the second horn of (II) are acceptable. In gross outline terms, Linda's strategy is to accept my reaction to the second horn of (II) with further developments of her own, but to criticize the adequacy of my way of showing the first horn of (I) to be acceptable and to reject a key move in that way and my arguments for it. What follows is my reaction to all that.

One objection to the first horn of (I) is that it leaves us without any way of construing God's obligations. We can hardly suppose that God is obliged to love his creatures because he commands himself to do so! Here I suggest cutting the Gordian knot by denying that God has obligations. The basic reason for this is that an agent, A, is obliged to do X only where there is the possibility of a failure to do X. That is connected with the fundamental feature of obligations that they *bind* us, *constrain* us to act in ways we otherwise might not act. Hence principles of obligation, duty, and the like have the function of governing, regulating our behavior. But since God is perfectly good, there is no possibility of his doing anything contrary to what such (objectively true) principles would dictate. Hence being bound or constrained has no application to his case. Since God has no obligations, the first horn does not require divine obligations to be generated in the same way as ours. (Linda splits this argument up into several pieces, thereby diminishing its force.)

In response Linda holds (1) there are reasons to think of God as obliged to, for example, do what he has promised to do, and (2) my proposals do not require the absence of divine obligations. I agree that DC theory on my construal has to do something about divine promises, for example, reconstruing them as expressions of firm intentions. But as for (2) I would need some other way of meeting the objection under consideration. Linda substitutes a different conception of obligation, according to which one is obliged to do X provided there is no option to doing X that is compatible with moral goodness. That would certainly wreck my argument for denying divine obligations, but I am not at all inclined to abandon my conception of obligation set out above. It conforms to the etymology of 'oblige,' from Latin 'obligare' to *bind together*. But I don't want to rest my case on that. Indeed, the crucial issue is not over how to use terms like 'obligation.' However that is decided, the crucial point is that there is a concept that is captured by my account of obligation, a concept that is of crucial importance in human morality. And what is expressed by that concept binds and constrains us in a way that we cannot think of as applying to God. Using 'obligation' for that concept, we have to say that God does not have obligations in the same sense as humans. Of course, both God and we can have obligations in Linda's sense. But I take it that DC theory thinks of obligation more in my sense, and if that is the case, avoiding the objection in question does require denying divine obligations. Moreover, despite Linda's assurance that DC theory could make use of her construal of obligation, I can't see how commands, divine or otherwise, could be constitutive of obligation as she construes it. How could God's commanding me to do X be constitutive of *doing X not having any alternative compatible with moral goodness*? It either is or it isn't, and issuing a command to do X would seem to have nothing to do with it. But on my construal of obligation, it is easy to see how commands of a proper authority can bind or constrain me to do X.

The other classic objection to the first horn of (I) is that it makes morality arbitrary. If whatever God commands is obligatory, then if God were to command us to inflict pain, where we can do so, just for the pleasure of seeing the victim suffer, then that would be our moral obligation; and that won't do. Here my strategy was to use my espousal of the second horn of (II), avoiding objections to that by holding that it doesn't make God dependent on something other than himself. For God is himself the supreme standard of goodness, the view that Linda calls "exemplarism." That standard is an individual being, God, rather than some Platonic essence or other impersonal item. Hence God is not dependent on something other than himself but merely acts in accordance with his essence. And getting back to the objection to the first horn of (I), this doesn't make morality arbitrary, just because God's commands are in accordance with himself, the supreme standard of moral and other goodness. Here Linda is in hearty agreement. But she makes an acute comment on my way of doing it. She points out that if divine commands were *determined* by the divine nature (which it looks as if I was supposing), then we would have a Divine Nature theory rather than a DC theory. If divine commands are to constitute the metaphysical source of moral obligation, they have to be more loosely related to the divine nature than that. There must be something "between" the divine perfection and divine commands. At first she flirts with the idea that the "between" could be divine preferences, which are themselves not determined by the divine nature, though they are constrained by it. In her development of this, she says both that no one worries about preferences being arbitrary and also that they can be moral reasons for commanding one thing rather than another when both commands are compatible with divine goodness; I don't see how these are compatible. But in any event she abandons this "divine preferences" solution on the grounds that it does not give DC's the role of the metaphysical ground of obligation. Her substitute candidate is the divine *personality* (or personalities in the doctrine of the Trinity). She arrives at this conception in developing the exemplarism that she shares with me. She argues convincingly that personality is something irreducibly particular (personal), something that goes beyond one's nature or essence, even an individual essence. And she holds that many divine motives in particular circumstances are part of God's personality rather than his nature (though still constrained by the latter). And it is these motives that give rise to commands as well as to other divine acts. Since these motives are an aspect of the divine perfect goodness, the commands to which they give rise are not at all arbitrary.

In my paper that Linda is discussing, I did not go into the features that a viable DC theory would have, other than what I took to be needed to answer the

Euthyphro-like objections. I will take this opportunity to say a few words about further aspects of the divine nature–DC–human moral obligation relationship, beyond Linda's point that the divine nature does not determine a choice between two alternative divine acts, both of which are in equal accordance with the goodness of the divine nature. Once we reflect on the matter, we realize that the phenomenon of supererogation shows that God does not command us to do everything it is morally good for us to do. Of course, this depends on what God has commanded us to do, and how do we determine that? In considering that question, remember that a command has no function unless it is communicated to the addressee. How does God communicate his commands to us? Linda makes the eminently sensible suggestion that he does so through Biblical revelation. I would add that we should consider the possibility that God sometimes issues commands to individuals (other than the Biblical writers and their subjects), though this has to be handled with care, given that many of us are all too prone to mistake our preferences for DC's. Proceeding in that way I would suggest that even on the most liberal, halfway plausible account of what God has commanded us to do, it turns out to be a small selection of the acts within our power that it would be morally good for us to do. This reinforces the point that the divine nature does not determine DC's.

Another point is that DC theory has to modify its pretensions to the extent of recognizing that A's being commanded by God to do X is not *necessary* for A's being morally obliged to do X. Again, on reflection and on any halfway plausible account of what God has commanded, it seems obvious that we all have many moral obligations that are not so engendered. We have moral obligations that arise from our social positions, employment, family connections, and so on, that are neither specifically required by God nor fall under general divine commands. Much more could be said on this score, but I must return to Linda's paper.

Here is a quick summary of the version of DC theory that emerges from Linda's suggestions. Given her conception of obligation, God and humans can have obligations in the same sense of the term but with different metaphysical sources, assuming that DC's are still playing a role (more on this last point in a moment). The divine nature puts constraints on what God commands but by no means determines it. Its influence on what is commanded goes through the divine personality, which is an irreducibly individual aspect of God's goodness distinguishable from the divine nature.

Has Linda carried out the program to rescue DC theory she announced early in her paper? "If commands play an essential role in obligation, there must be something in between the divine nature and divine commands in virtue of which God makes the commands he makes, but which also explains why the commands are not superfluous." Her claim, as we have seen, is that what does this job is the divine personality. I enthusiastically applaud her development of that last notion, but I can't accept her claim that it makes possible a viable DC theory. The most glaring defect in her version of DC theory is that, as I pointed out earlier, her construal of obligation, though it permits God and humans to have obligations in the same sense, leaves us without any intelligible way in which DC's could engender human obligations. Moreover, I can't see that her divine nature + divine personality account of what gives rise to DC's escapes her objection to a straight divine nature determination of DC's. To be sure, she holds (or seems to suppose) that the operation of God's personality leaves God free to choose between alternatives in a way that determination by the divine nature doesn't. But the fact remains that the view looks like a Divine Nature + Divine Personality Theory of moral obligation rather than a Divine Command Theory of moral obligation. Even if DC's are the proximate source of human moral obligation, they seem to be acting as a "conduit" for the influence of those divine sources rather than playing a generative role on their own.

Indeed, Linda displays a good deal of ambivalence over whether she has succeeded in making DC theory respectable. Just after the announcement of the program quoted above she writes: "This variation [that involves the personhood of God] permits an interesting version of DC theory that can escape the traditional objections. *It also makes DC theory optional.*" (My emphasis.) And near the end she says, "But what makes the theory work is something that makes commands themselves much less important than thesis DC implies." Another statement that I take to be an expression of ambivalence, though she undoubtedly does not consider it as such, is connected with her development of the idea that "God is most perfectly revealed in Jesus Christ." She goes on to say, "To follow the commands of God is the same thing as to imitate Christ." Either that is palpably false, or she understands 'commands of God' differently from DC theorists. And so I find myself unclear as to just how much Linda is claiming that her exemplarist approach gives us a genuine and viable DC theory of human moral obligation.

Finally I would like to express appreciation for all the insights and the enjoyment I have received from my interaction with Linda over the years. We go back quite a way, most pertinently for the present context to a conference in the mid-1980's at which Linda commented on an ancestor of the paper she is discussing in her essay for this volume. (That doesn't imply that after all these years she is doing the same thing! For she has learned and developed quite a lot in those years, and I hope that I have as well.) This interaction continued in a variety of settings. Much more recently I was privileged to read and comment on a number of chapters of a draft of her forthcoming *Divine Motivation Theory*. We continued that discussion at a conference connected with her inauguration as the Kingfisher Professor of Philosophy at the University of Oklahoma. I have to thank Linda for providing a paper that is admirably suited to continue this fruitful philosophical interaction.

15

Alston on Aquinas on Theological Predication

Nicholas Wolterstorff

I

In the 1980's, William Alston published a number of important papers in which he argued that it is possible to affirm something true of God by speaking literally.[1] The topic was not one that just happened to pique his curiosity. What drew his attention to the topic, and made it important, was the fact that, as he put it in the earliest of the articles, "the impossibility of literal talk about God has become almost an article of faith for theology in this century."[2]

I share Alston's reason for regarding the issue as important. But I have a more specific interest as well. In my *Divine Discourse* I claimed that it is philosophically tenable to hold that it is literally true of God that God speaks— commands, asserts, asks, promises, and the like. What I had in mind by "speaking" was the performance of illocutionary acts.[3] Though I myself see nothing impossible in God's performing locutionary acts, nonetheless the traditional claim or assumption that God cannot literally speak very much depended on not having available J. L. Austin's distinction between locutionary and illocutionary acts; the traditional argument, that since God has no body, God cannot literally speak, does not work if it is illocutionary acts that one has in mind. What I did not do is mount a more general argument to the effect that one can predicate of God what is true of God by speaking literally. Thus I have a vested interest in the cogency of Alston's argumentation.

Alston did not content himself with easy victory in these articles. He did not content himself with observing that even the most hardened opponents of literal speech about God must concede that one can affirm something true of God by the literal use of such negative or disjunctive predicates as "is not a toucan" or "is either a toucan or not a toucan." Nor did he content himself with observing that what have come to be called "Cambridge predicates" must be true of God— for example, "is said by many theologians to be insusceptible of having predicates true of him when they are used literally." It was what he called "intrinsic" predicates that Alston had his eye on—predicates that, as he put it, "tell us something" about the nature or operations of the subject.

Apart from observing that some of those who insist, in their theory, that such speech is impossible, nonetheless take its possibility for granted in their practice, Alston's argument in these articles came in two parts. He offered an account of metaphor, according to which a condition of saying something true about some entity by way of speaking metaphorically about it is that it be possible to say something true about that entity by speaking literally about it; and he argued that there is good reason to think there is sufficient similarity between God's actions and states of self, and our actions and states of self, for certain predicates to be literally true of both. I judge both parts of Alston's argument to be conclusive.[4]

In spite of the cogency of his argumentation, however, Alston's articles appear to have had little influence on those whom he was addressing, namely, the theological community. Why is that? Well, for one thing, most theologians don't pay much attention to what contemporary analytic philosophers are saying, even if the latter are speaking directly to theological issues and to claims made by theologians. But I think there is another reason as well. Alston addresses the conclusion of the theologians, namely, that literal speech about God is impossible, but not the lines of thought that led them to this conclusion. He explicitly announces that he will not be doing the latter.[5] It seems evident to me that, in general, human beings who find themselves in situations of this sort will often stick with what they have believed all along—believed for what were supposedly good reasons—and either ignore arguments against their view or live with cognitive dissonance.

In the course of his articles, Alston identifies three major lines of thought that have led theologians to the conclusion he is contesting. Some regard the conclusion as an implication of their view that God is not *a* being but the *ground* of all beings; some regard it as an implication of their view that God is an ontologically simple being; and some regard it as an implication of their view that God is transcendent, "wholly other." I myself regard this latter claim as coming in two forms; or more precisely, I regard the language of transcendence and otherness as regularly used to express two quite different claims. Some theologians regard Scripture as teaching that God is transcendent, and hold that it is an implication of this Scriptural teaching that none of our predicates is true of God when used literally; others hold the philosophical thesis that God, being outside of time, transcends the bounds of literal use of concepts. Behind the first, the second, and the fourth of these lines of thought there is a philosophical figure who is generally regarded as having given to that line of thought its classic formulation—Plotinus, Aquinas, and Kant, respectively.

One way to supplement Alston's argumentation, thus making it more likely that his goal will be achieved of disabusing theologians of the view that nothing true can be said of God when using intrinsic predicates literally, would be to contest the claims that God lacks individuality, that God is simple, and that God is outside of time. Another way to go would be to concede these claims for the purpose of the argument and then go on to argue that it does not follow that nothing true can be said of God when speaking literally. No doubt it would be especially effective in persuading theologians of this last point if one could show that not even their great patron philosophers—Plotinus, Aquinas, and Kant—held that nothing true can be said of God when using intrinsic predicates literally.

This seems to me in fact to be the case. Plotinus, though he certainly denied that *The Supreme,* as he sometimes called it, is an entity, nonetheless did not hold that nothing true can be said of it when using intrinsic predicates literally. He did hold this thesis, so far as I can tell, for one-term predicates; but most definitely he did not hold it for multi-term predicates. For example, he held it to be true of The Supreme that it was the ultimate ground of everything other than itself, ultimately accounting for the existence and character of all else. So too Aquinas explicitly says that when one predicates of God the intrinsic predicates "good" and "powerful" and speaks literally, one affirms of God what is true of God. And Kant held that when one abstracts from our ordinary concept of causation its temporal component, retaining just the idea of a ground, then one has a concept that is literally true of God. In short, it turns out that our contemporary theologians, in denying the possibility of literally true intrinsic predications concerning God, are departing from the thought of their great patron figures from the philosophical tradition. And more generally: There are very few important figures from the philosophical and theological traditions whom they can summon in support of their position—pseudo-Dionysius perhaps, though even that is debatable.

In what follows I propose to elaborate and defend the claim I have just made concerning Aquinas. Full support, of the sort I have just indicated, of Alston's program would require a defense of my claim concerning each of the three classic figures; but that's impossible in a single article. My reason for settling on Aquinas is that, in 1993, Alston published a full article in which he offers his interpretation of Aquinas on predications concerning God: "Aquinas on Theological Predication: A Look Backward and a Look Forward" (ATP).[6] I will be engaging that article.

Before I turn to what Alston says in this article, let me quote a passage from an earlier article in which he helpfully distinguishes "various ways in which creaturely terms can be used in speaking of God." He distinguishes six such ways:

1. Straight univocity. Ordinary terms are used in the same ordinary senses of God and human beings.
2. Modified univocity. Meanings can be defined or otherwise established such

that terms can be used with those meanings of both God and human beings.

3.   Special literal meanings. Terms can be given, or otherwise take on, special technical senses in which they apply to God.

4.   Analogy. Terms for creatures can be given analogical extensions so as to be applicable to God.

5.   Metaphor. Terms that apply literally to creatures can be metaphorically applied to God.

6.   Symbol. Ditto for "symbol," in one or another meaning of that term.[7]

Immediately after presenting this six-fold typology, Alston says that "the most radical partisans of otherness, from Dionysius through Aquinas to Tillich, plump for something in the (4) to (6) range and explicitly reject (1). The possibility of (3) has been almost wholly ignored, and (2) has not fared much better." Alston agrees that it is Aquinas's view that we can speak truly of God using terms in their literal sense; his argument is that Aquinas sees himself as having to pay the price, for that position, of denying "straight univocity." My argument will be that Aquinas affirms both straight univocity and the possibility of saying of God what is literally true of him—while also affirming analogy.

II

Let us get Alston's interpretation before us. A great many commentators give the impression of doing their best to put out of mind Aquinas's answer to his question in Article 3 of Question 13, Part I of *Summa Theologiae*. Alston does not. The question is "whether any term (*nomen*) can be said (*dicatur*) literally (*proprie*) of God?"[8] Employing the distinction between saying a term literally of some thing and saying it metaphorically of it, Aquinas answers that "not all terms are said metaphorically of God; but some are said literally" (*sed contra*). These are those terms that signify "the perfections that flow from [God] and are to be found in creatures, yet which exist in [God] in an eminent way" (*responsio*). Aquinas cites "being," "good," and "living" as examples; these terms, he says, "can be said literally of God" (*ad* 1).

There is no reason in the text to suppose that Aquinas is not using "literal" ("*proprie*") strictly and in its literal sense. And given that it is "*metaphorice*" that he contrasts with "*proprie*," our term "literal" is surely the correct translation. In short, it was clearly Aquinas's view that, when using the terms literally, we can affirm of God what is true of God by predicating of God such perfection terms as "exists," "good," and "living." Here is Alston's summary of Aquinas's thought on the matter:

In article 3 [Aquinas] argues that some terms can be used literally [*proprie*] of God, namely, those that do not include in their meaning the imperfect mode in which a perfection is realized in creatures, for example, such terms as 'being', good', and 'living'. Let's call these "pure perfection terms". By contrast, those terms that do include a creaturely mode in their meaning, for example, 'rock' and 'lion', can be said of God only metaphorically. (ATP, 147)

In the same *responsio* (I, 13, 3) Aquinas clarifies his claim by means of the distinction between that which is signified by a term, its *res significata*, and the term's mode of signification, its *modus significandi*. It is only "so far as that which is signified is concerned" that some terms "are applied literally (*proprie*) to God." Indeed, such terms are applied "more properly [to God] than to creatures, and are said primarily (*per prius*) of God." With respect to mode of signification, however, there are no terms that can be "literally (*proprie*) said of God; for they [all] have a mode of signification that is relevant to creatures" (*responsio*).

Aquinas assumes familiarity with the distinction between *res significata* and *modus significandi*; he does not explain it. What's meant by the *res significata* of a predicate term is clear enough—or given that many predicate terms have a number of distinct meanings, what's clear enough is what is meant by the *res significata* of a predicate term with a certain meaning. It's the property "signified" by the term with that meaning—that is, the property that one would attribute to something if, speaking literally, one predicated of it the predicate with that meaning. When it is pure perfection terms that we are using, the *res significata* is the perfection designated (signified): goodness, life, existence, and so forth.

What Aquinas has in mind by the *modus significandi* of a term is less clear—though still clear enough for our purposes here. We get the essential information in his remark that "our intellect apprehends these perfections in the mode that they are present in creatures, and thus they are signified by our terms." Take any case of apprehending some predicable entity, any case of having it in mind. Aquinas distinguishes between, on the one hand, the entity apprehended, and, on the other hand, one's way of apprehending it. One's way of apprehending it is determined by the mode in which that predicable is present in creatures—by which Aquinas surely means, creatures with which one is familiar. Thus when I am thinking of *power,* one can distinguish between that which I am apprehending, namely, power, and my way of apprehending it, this latter being shaped by the powerful things—the things possessing power—with which I am familiar from my experience. Of course, not only do *I* apprehend the abstract predicable, power; you do so as well, along with almost all other human beings out of infancy. Hence we can speak not just of my way of apprehending power and your way of apprehending power; we can speak of our way.

Aquinas's thought is that the distinction between the object of our apprehension of some predicable and our way of apprehending it is carried over into, or preserved within, the corresponding predicate term. A predicate term will not only signify a certain predicable; it will also express—"express" is probably the best word here—our way of apprehending that predicable, this latter, to say it once again, being shaped by the instantiations of that predicable familiar to us from our experience. And whatever else may be true of such experiences of ours, this will be true: They will have been experiences of creatures.

The highly schematic character of Aquinas's remark about the *modus significandi* of a term leaves room for the idea to be fleshed out in a number of different ways. Let me quote a passage from one of those earlier articles of Alston in which he draws a distinction that he describes as "reminiscent" of Aquinas's distinction between "the property signified by a term and the mode of signifying." The general point, he says:

> [I]s that the common possession of abstract features is compatible with as great a difference as you like in the way in which these features are realized. A meeting and a train of thought can both be "orderly" even though what it is for the one to be orderly is enormously different from what it is for the other to be orderly. . . . This general point suggests the possibility that the radical otherness of God might manifest itself in the *way* in which common abstract features are realized in the divine being, rather than in the absence of common features. What it is for God to *make something* is radically different from what it is for a human being to make something; but that does not rule out an abstract feature in common, e.g., that *by the exercise of agency something comes into existence* . . . . Many theistic thinkers have moved too quickly from radical otherness to the impossibility of any univocity, neglecting this possibility that the otherness may come from the way in which common features are realized.[9]

In the essay we are engaging, "Aquinas on Theological Predication," Alston suggests a somewhat different way of articulating Aquinas's thought (ATP, 161–162) on *modus significandi*. For our purposes here, however, there is no point in selecting any one way. What is important is just Aquinas's contention that aspects of the mode in which some "perfection" is manifested in our creaturely experience become ingredients in our way of apprehending that perfection, and thereby also ingredients in the mode of signification of a term which signifies that perfection. Thus it is that he says, when distinguishing between terms that can be said literally of God and those that can only be said metaphorically: "Those terms that are said literally of God do not include bodily conditions in that which is signified but only in their mode of signification, whereas those that are said (*dicuntur*) metaphorically of God include bodily conditions in the very thing signified" (I, 13, 3, *ad* 3). Speaking more elaborately, he says this:

> There are some names which signify these perfections flowing from God to creatures in such a way that the imperfect way in which creatures receive the divine perfection is part of the very signification of the name itself, as *stone* signifies a material being; and names of this kind can be applied to (*attribui*) God only in a metaphorical sense. Other names, however, signify these perfections absolutely, without any such mode of participation being part of their signification, as the words *being, good, living,* and the like and such names can be literally said of (*dicuntur*) God. (I, 13, 3, *ad* 1)[10]

Using Aquinas's conceptuality, I can now formulate my own thesis about the attribution of speech to God as follows: Though the predicate "performs illocutionary acts" includes corporeal conditions in its mode of signification, it does not include corporeal conditions in the action signified. To say of God that he speaks (i.e., performs illocutionary acts) is thus quite unlike saying of God that he is a rock—and also quite unlike saying of a forest that it speaks.

Two articles later, in this same question on "The Names of God," Aquinas poses the question "whether terms are said univocally or equivocally of God and creatures" (I, 13, 5). It is of critical importance to see that this question has not already been answered in what Aquinas has said about the literality of speech about God. When considering whether a term has been used literally or metaphorically, one takes a single instance of its use and poses the question concerning that instance. By contrast, one cannot take a single instance of the use of a term and ask whether the term, in that instance, is being used univocally or equivocally. That makes no sense. It is only with reference to two or more uses of a term that one can raise the issue of univocity or equivocation. The issue is whether the term, in these two or more uses, is being used to designate the same property or different properties. If the same, then it is being used univocally; if not, then it is being used equivocally.

So consider two instances of the use of a single term. One might be using it literally in each instance while nonetheless using it equivocally as between the two; that would be the case if the term had two established senses, and in one instance one was using it literally in one of those senses and in the other instance one was using it literally in the other of those two established senses. Or suppose one is using it metaphorically in the two instances; one might nonetheless be using it to say the same thing, in which case one would be using it univocally; alternatively, one might be using it to say different things, in which case one would be using it equivocally as between the two instances. Or yet again, one might be using the term literally in one instance and metaphorically in the other, in which case, as between the two, one would be using it equivocally. And so forth. Alston sees all of this clearly in his discussion.

So back to Aquinas's question, whether terms are said univocally or equivocally of God and creatures. Aquinas's answer is that "it is impossible to predicate (*praedicare*) anything univocally of God and creatures." The predication will always be equivocal. And this is always Aquinas's answer to this question. As Alston says, "Aquinas always takes the first order of business [when dealing with this issue] to be to show that terms are not, and cannot be, used univocally of God and creatures" (ATP, 148).

Alston goes on to make a point that will be of critical importance for my subsequent discussion. "All Aquinas's reasons for this, at least all those that make explicit the differences between God and creatures that prevent univocity, stem from one basic divine attribute—simplicity" (ATP, 148). This is correct; Aquinas never fails to make clear, when discussing this issue, that the doctrine of divine simplicity is what forces him to deny univocity. Alston remarks that "twentieth-century philosophers, in arguing against univocity, are more likely to cite divine immateriality or atemporality, and theologians are more likely to make unspecific appeals to 'otherness' or to God's not counting as 'a being'." For Aquinas, on the other hand, "it is simplicity that makes all the difference" (ATP, 148).

Here is one passage in which Aquinas makes the point, from the *sed contra* of I, 13, 5 of the *Summa Theologiae*: "That which is predicated (*praedicatur*) of several things according to the same term, but not according to the same *ratio*, is predicated of them equivocally. But no term applies (*convenit*) to God with that *ratio* according to which it is said (*dicitur*) of a creature." Using "is wise" as an example, Aquinas then offers his reason for this claim: "For wisdom in creatures is a quality, though not in God."

Everyone reading this essay will know that Aquinas did not content himself with saying that when we predicate the same term of God and of creatures, and we speak truly in both cases, our terms are always "said equivocally of God and creatures." The equivocation is not *mere* equivocation. Though different things are being said, there's a relation between the things said, making the predications *analogous*. Equivocal, yes; but the equivocation of analogy.

Cajetan, in *The Analogy of Names* (1498), distinguished three types of analogy—inequality, attribution, and proportionality—and argued that Aquinas, in his teaching concerning predications of God, had in mind the analogy of proportionality (i.e., of relationality). Cajetan's interpretation became canonical among followers of Aquinas, especially among neo-Thomists of the twentieth century. Alston argues that there is no indication whatsoever in the Thomistic texts that Aquinas had the analogy of proportionality in mind; everything indicates that he was thinking in terms of the analogy of attribution. Alston's argument seems to me decisive. For my purposes here, however, it makes no difference one way or the other. What is important is just Aquinas's consistent teaching that, given God's ontological simplicity and our ontological complexity, terms are never said univocally of God and creatures but at best analogically.

III

Alston perceives with greater clarity than any other interpreter I know of that Aquinas now appears to have a serious problem on his hands. Pure perfection terms are literally true of God. The *res significata* of those pure perfection terms is just those perfections themselves, not any particular mode of participation in the perfection. Hence such terms can be applied literally to God, even though our creaturely mode of participation in those perfections is different from God's mode of participation. Yet as between God and creatures, these perfection terms, like all others, are predicated at best analogically, never univocally.

But if in the two instances, predication of creatures and predication of God, the same perfection is designated by the predicate term, and if both God and we have that perfection (albeit in a different mode), and if the term applies literally to God, how could the term not apply literally to us as well as to God? But if it does, then the predication is univocal as between us and God. Let me quote Alston:

> It appears that the doctrine of an analogical meaning of theological terms has been frozen out; there is no place for it. Instead of analogically related crea-turely and divine senses [of the terms we predicate], what we have are crea-turely senses all up and down the line, together with the recognition that one aspect of each such sense [i.e., its *modus significandi*] is ineluctably inappro-priate for application to the divine. . . . On Aquinas's own showing there is no room for an analogy of meaning for creaturely and divine applications of terms. (ATP, 165)

IV

Alston remarks that "at one point in [his] decades-long reflection on this topic, [he] thought that this was the last word" (ATP, 165). He now thinks he has a solution to the problem. His solution is to back away from interpreting Aquinas as holding that God and we participate in the same perfection; the difference in our modes of participation makes for a difference in the perfections (forms). In Alston's words, "both difference of form and difference of mode of being of the form are derived from the same basic divine-creature difference: the simplicity of God. There can be no exact reproduction of form just because creatures have in a divided way what is found in God in an absolutely simple way, without any real distinction between the perfections" (ATP, 167). Hence in predicating a pure perfection term of God and of creatures, we are not predicating the same *res significata* after all.

Alston cites two passages in favor of this interpretation, one from *Summa Theologiae* (STh) and one from *Summa contra Gentiles*. Let me say something about the latter passage a bit later, and consider the former here. Here is the pas-sage, in the rather more literal translation of the Dominicans than in the Black-friars' translation that Alston uses:

> God prepossesses in Himself all the perfections of creatures, being Himself simply and universally perfect. Hence every creature represents Him, and is like Him so far as it possesses some perfection; yet it represents Him not as something of the same species or genus, but as the excelling principle of whose form the effects fall short, although they derive some kind of likeness thereto. (STh I, 13, 2, *responsio*)

Though the passage is compatible with Alston's interpretation, it strikes me as not supporting it. Read all by itself, it can be interpreted as saying that the perfections of creatures are not identical with the perfections of God but only similar to them; they "fall short" of God's perfections. But let us not forget that over and over in these articles of Question 13, Aquinas cites as the relevant difference between us and God that God participates in perfections as a simple being whereas we participate in perfections as complex beings. So when Aquinas speaks of "the effects [falling] short," what effect does he have in mind—the perfection itself that is to be found in us, or our mode of participation in the shared perfection? The passage all by itself seems to me ambiguous on the matter (in Latin, that is). But if so, it cannot be used as evidence for Alston's point.[11]

Apart from the fact that neither this passage nor, as we shall see shortly, the other that Alston cites, support his interpretation, there are a number of textual and systematic reasons for not embracing his solution. Recall that in the very next article after the one from which Alston has just quoted, Aquinas, employing his distinction between the *res significata* of terms and their *modus significandi*, says that, as regards the former, perfection terms apply literally (*proprie*) to God. So if Alston's present view were correct, then, given that predication is analogous as between God and us, and given Aquinas's clear statement that perfection terms are literally true of God, it would follow that perfection terms are only metaphorically true of us. I think there are at least three good reasons for not interpreting Aquinas as holding this.

First, Aquinas nowhere *says* that perfection terms apply only metaphorically to us, not literally. Admittedly it is also true, so far as I know, that he nowhere says that they do apply to us literally. But if you and I were writing, we wouldn't bother to make a point of that; it would seem too obvious. Only if we held that no such terms apply to us literally would we even raise the issue of whether they apply to us literally or metaphorically. So too for Aquinas. The only question in the region he thinks worth discussing is whether any terms apply to God literally.

Second, this interpretation conflicts with the way Aquinas employs the distinction between the *res significata* and the *modus significandi* of terms. We quoted him as saying, in I, 13, 3, *ad* 1, that certain terms signify "perfections absolutely, without any [creaturely] mode of participation being part of their signification." Given the looming presence of the doctrine of divine simplicity in these articles, he surely means to include, under the category, "creaturely mode of participation," the fact that creatures participate in perfections as complex beings rather than simple. Aquinas's teaching is that the *res significata* of pure perfection terms is stripped entirely clean of all creaturely modes of signification, including the fact that we participate in perfections as complex beings.

And third, an implication of this interpretation is a very non-Thomistic doctrine concerning the learning of language. Aquinas's constant doctrine is that we learn the meaning of our terms from their application to creatures; having learned their meanings, we then extrapolate to using them in discourse about God. So if Alston's interpretation were correct, we would first learn the metaphorical use of "good," "exists," "is alive," etc., since it is in their metaphorical use that they are true of creatures; and we would then extrapolate from that to using the term literally in speaking of God. Now it may be that you and I do sometimes first learn a metaphorical use of a term and then later learn its literal use—though, so far as I can see, before learning the literal use we would not realize that we had all along been using it metaphorically (unless someone explicitly told us that.) But this will be the case when the term in both its metaphorical and its literal use applies to creatures. I fail to see how we human beings could first learn a metaphorical use of these perfection terms and then, by extrapolation, get a hang on how to use them in speaking literally about God.

In addition to reasons for not interpreting Aquinas as holding that perfection terms apply only metaphorically to us, I think there are also reasons for doubting the ontology that Alston now attributes to Aquinas; namely, that perfections are not the same in God and in us, the difference in mode of participation causing a lack of identity in the object of participation. Here too I have three difficulties, the first, once again, being Aquinas's silence on the matter. Or not to prejudge the case against Alston, his *relative* silence—his allusiveness. If this were Aquinas's position, one would expect him to call attention to it. At best he alludes to it in the passages Alston cites.

But second, the proposed ontology remains obscure, to say the least. How are we to understand this purported phenomenon, that a difference in one's mode of participation in a perfection makes a difference in the perfection in which one participates? Presumably not every difference in mode of participation makes such a difference. What makes for the difference between the cases in which it does make a difference and those in which it does not? And why exactly does it make a difference, in the cases in which it does?

And third, one has to weigh up against those two rather allusive passages that Alston cites in favor of his new interpretation, all those other passages that Alston himself cites when leading up to his statement of the problem that Aquinas has apparently created for himself. These latter passages seem to me much more clear in their affirmation that the perfection is identical, than are the passages Alston now cites, in their affirmation that the perfections are not identical. Here is one of those clearer passages. I will quote it in the translation that Alston was using, that of the Blackfriars:

> All the perfections of all things are in God. . . . This may be seen from two considerations. First, because whatever perfection exists in an effect must be found in the producing cause: either in the same formality . . . or in a more eminent degree. . . . Since therefore God is the first producing cause of things, the perfections of all things must pre-exist in God in a more eminent way. . . . Second . . . God is being itself, of itself subsistent. Consequently, He must contain within Himself the whole perfection of being. . . . Now all the perfections of all things pertain to the perfection of being: for things are perfect precisely so far

as they have being after some fashion. It follows therefore that the perfection of
no thing is wanting to God. (STh I, 4, 2, *responsio*)

"All the perfections of all things are in God." This seems to me as clear a statement as one could want of the view that the perfections in God and in us are the
same.

V

If the problem that Alston so acutely identifies is not to be solved his way, how
then is it to be solved? Well, Alston assumes, along with all other interpreters I
am familiar with, that when Aquinas is talking about analogous predications of a
term, he means to say that the *res significata* in the one instance is analogous to,
but not identical with, the *res significata* in the other instance. That is to say,
Alston and the other commentators assume that the property predicated in the
one case is not identical with the property predicated in the other case. In
Alston's own words, Aquinas's view is that pure perfection terms "are predicated of God in a sense not exactly the same as that in which they are predicated
of creatures but in a sense that is related to the latter" (ATP, 160). I suggest that
we give up that assumption. That is not what Aquinas had in mind when he says
that predications as between God and creatures are at best analogous. He is not
saying that the terms predicated have a different sense. They have a different
mode of signification, undeniably; but the thing designated (signified) is exactly
the same.

Suppose that you and I held Aquinas's ontology. What would we say on
this matter of predication? Given our conviction that God and we participate in
the same perfections, we would say that in assertively uttering "God is alive,"
"God is good," "God is powerful," and the like, the predicate terms "alive,"
"good," and "powerful" have exactly the same sense that they do when we assertively utter, about some human being, "he is alive," "he is good," "he is powerful." The predicate terms designate (signify) the same perfection in both cases.
In assertively uttering "God is alive" and assertively uttering "Joe is alive," we
are predicating the same "form" of two different things. But given our other
conviction, that God "participates" in perfections as a simple being whereas Joe
participates in them as a complex being, we would say that we are claiming a
different relationship to hold in the two cases—though not entirely different,
since in both cases we can describe the subject as "participating in" what is designated by the predicate term. It's our *predicating* of the predicate term to God
that is analogous to our predicating it of Joe; the analogy is to be located, not in
the sense (meaning) of the predicate term itself but in the copula. This, I submit,
is what we would say if we held Aquinas's ontology.

And this is what Aquinas says. Consider, once again, his comment in the *sed contra* of I, 13, 5: "That which is predicated of several things according to the same term, but not according to the same *ratio,* is predicated of them equivocally. But no term applies *(convenit)* to God with that *ratio* according to which it is said *(dicitur)* of a creature." The clue to Aquinas's doctrine of analogical predication lies in taking with full seriousness the reason he proceeds to give for this claim. The reason is that "wisdom in creatures is a quality, though not in God."

In Question 3 of Part I of the *Summa Theologiae,* Aquinas had argued for the doctrine of divine simplicity; in God there is no distinction between God and God's essence, between God and God's attributes, between one of God's attributes and another, and so forth. It follows that in predicating "is wise" of God we are claiming a different relation to hold between wisdom and God from that which we claim to hold between wisdom and some human being when we predicate "is wise" of that human being. The "is" in "God is wise" necessarily has a different force, a different *ratio,* from the "is" in "Socrates is wise"—assuming that we are using our words in such a way that in each case what we say is true. But the force *(ratio)* of the copula in the two cases is not completely different and unconnected; the copula is not being used *purely* equivocally. Its force *(ratio)* when used to speak of creatures is *analogical* to its force *(ratio)* when used to speak of God; in both cases one is claiming some mode of participation in the perfection by the entity referred to.

In short, Aquinas's doctrine of analogy pertains to the predicating, not to what's predicated, to the copula, not to the predicate term. When we say "is wise" of God, the predicate term "wise" is being used literally, as it is when we say "is wise" of some human being; but the copula when used to speak of creatures has a sense that is only analogical to its sense when used to speak of God. Aquinas uses the literal/metaphorical contrast when speaking of predicate terms; he uses the univocal/analogical contrast when speaking of the copula.

It might be replied that this amounts to a radical over-interpretation of Aquinas's brief remark in the *sed contra* of the Fifth Article. But that it was in fact Aquinas's thought, that analogy pertains to the predicating and not to the term predicated, to the copula and not to the predicate term, becomes incontestably clear in the *responsio* of the article. Let me quote some of what he says:

> Univocal predication is impossible between God and creatures. The reason for this is that every effect which is not an adequate result of the power of the efficient cause receives the similitude of the agent not in its full degree, but in a measure that falls short, so that what is divided and multiplied in the effects resides in the agent simply, and in the same manner; as for example the sun by the exercise of its one power produces manifold and various forms in all inferior things. In the same way, . . . all perfections existing in creatures divided and multiplied, pre-exist in God unitedly. Thus when some term pertaining to a perfection is said of a creature, it signifies that particular perfection in distinction from others. For example, when the term "wise" is said of a human being, we signify a perfection distinct from the essence of the person, from his pow-

ers, his existence, and from all the other things about him. But when we say this term of God, we do not intend to signify something distinct from his essence, or power, or existence. . . . Hence it is clear that this term "wise" is not said of God and of a human being according to the same *ratio*. The same point holds for other terms. Accordingly, no term is predicated univocally of God and creatures. But also not purely (*pure*) equivocally, as some have said. . . . Therefore it must be said that terms are said of God and of creatures according to analogy, that is, proportion.

This is Aquinas's argument for holding that our predication of perfection-terms of God is not univocal with our predication of perfection-terms of creatures. His argument for holding that it is nonetheless not *purely* equivocal, but analogical, goes as follows:

Whatever is said of God and creatures is said, according to the relation of a creature to God as its principle and cause, wherein all perfections of things pre-exist excellently. Now this mode of community of idea is a mean between pure equivocation and simple univocation. For in analogies the idea is not, as it is in univocals, one and the same, yet it is not totally diverse as in equivocals; but a term which is thus used in a multiple sense signifies various proportions to some one thing; thus *healthy* applied to urine signifies the sign of animal health, and applied to medicine signifies the cause of the same health. (I, q. 13, art. 5, *responsio*)

VI

That this is Aquinas's thought is concealed from us by our English translations. Consider once again the sentence that I quoted from the *sed contra* of STh I, 13, 5: "That which is predicated of several things according to the same term, but not according to the same *ratio*, is predicated of them equivocally. But no term applies (*convenit*) to God with that *ratio* according to which it is said (*dicitur*) of a creature." The Blackfriars' translation (done by Herbert McCabe, O.P.) renders the second sentence (clause) as follows: "but no word when used of God means the same as when it is used of a creature." This is interpretation, not translation. Aquinas does not say that no word *means the same* when used of God as when used of a creature. The Latin is this: "*Sed nullum nomen convenit Deo secundum illam rationem, secundum quam dicitur de creatura.*" Literally, "But no name applies to God according to the same *ratio* according to which it is said of a creature." Aquinas does not say that the term does not mean the same in the two cases; he says that no term *is said of* God and of creatures according to the same *ratio*.

The Dominican translation renders the sentence (clause) this way: "But no name belongs to God in the same sense that it belongs to creatures." It could be argued, I suppose, that this rendering leaves it ambiguous as to whether it is the *name* that has a different sense in the two cases or whether it is the *belonging to* that is different; and this would be a virtue of the translation, since Aquinas's own mode of expression leaves the issue open. But given that we much more naturally speak of different senses of names (words, terms) than of different senses of belonging to, I judge that the English reader will almost inevitably misinterpret what Aquinas is saying.

Again, consider the passage from the *responsio* of STh I, 13, 5, which I translated this way: "Hence it is clear that this term 'wise' is not said of (*dicitur*) God and of a human being according to the same *ratio*. The same point holds for other terms." McCabe, in the Blackfriars' translation, renders the passage as follows: "Hence it is clear that the word 'wise' is not used in the same sense of God and man, and the same is true of all other words." But Aquinas does not say that the word is not used in the same sense. He says that the term is not *said of* (*dicitur*) God and creatures according to the same *ratio*.

Consider a third passage, part of the *sed contra* of the same question. McCabe translates it this way: "'Wisdom', for example, means a quality when it is used of creatures, but not when it is applied to God. So then it must have a different meaning, for we have here a difference in the genus which is part of the definition." I have already quoted part of the paragraph in my own translation. Let me now quote the whole passage in a literal translation:

> That which is predicated (*praedicatur*) of several things according to the same term, but not according to the same *ratio*, is predicated of them equivocally. But no term applies (*convenit*) to God according to that *ratio* according to which it is said of (*dicitur*) a creature; for wisdom in creatures is a quality, though not in God. Now a different genus changes [the] *ratio*, since it is part of the definition; and the point is the same in [i.e., for] others. Therefore that which is said (*dicitur*) of God and of creatures is said equivocally.

Aquinas does not say that the term "wise" has a different meaning when applied to God and to creatures.

VII

I mentioned earlier that Alston cited two passages in support of his claim that Aquinas thinks the perfections in which creatures participate are not identical with those in which God participates—similar to and derived from, but not identical with. Life, existence, goodness, power, and the like, are not the same in us as in God. Let me now quote the second passage he cites in support of his interpretation. It comes from *Summa contra Gentiles* I, 32, 2–3. The first part of the passage, from section 2, runs as follows:

> An effect that does not receive a form specifically the same as that through which the agent acts cannot receive according to a univocal predication the

> name arising from that form. . . . Now, the forms of the things God has made do
> not measure up to a specific likeness of the divine power: for the things that
> God has made receive in a divided and particular way that which in Him is
> found in a simple and universal way. It is evident, then, that nothing can be said
> univocally of God and other things.

Notice that the way forms in things are said not to "measure up to" forms in God
is just that God receives forms in a simple way and we receive forms in a divided way. It's for that reason that nothing can be said univocally of God and us.
The saying-of, the predicating-of, is what is not univocal; the terms predicated
designate the same perfection in both cases.

The passage from section 3 makes the same point:

> If, furthermore, an effect should measure up to the species of its cause, it will
> not receive the univocal predication of the name unless it receives the same
> form according to the same mode of being. For the form of the house that is in
> the art of the maker is not univocally the same being in the two locations. Now,
> even though the rest of things were to receive a form that is absolutely the same
> as it is in God, yet they do not receive it according to the same mode of being.
> For as is clear from what we have said, there is nothing in God that is not the
> divine being itself, which is not the case with other things. Nothing, therefore,
> can be predicated of God and other things univocally.

The same pure perfection terms apply literally to both God and creatures with
respect to their *res significata*. It's the *act of predicating* that is not univocal—or
if you prefer, the force of the copula. Of course, if one dissents from Aquinas's
doctrine of divine simplicity, as Alston and I both do, then Aquinas's reason for
holding that the predicating of terms of God is only analogical to the predicating
of terms of creatures falls away.

Those contemporary theologians who hold that no terms apply literally to
God have no support for their contention in Aquinas, nor do those slightly more
guarded ones who hold that predicate terms that apply to God never have the
same sense as those that apply to creatures.

VIII

In conclusion, let me return to my vested interest in these matters. I hold that
God speaks—that is, discourses, performs illocutionary acts; and as I indicated
earlier, I have argued, in *Divine Discourse*, that it is philosophically tenable to
hold that this is literally true of God. If, when speaking literally, one predicates
of God that he discourses, one says what is true of God.[12]

In the course of arguing, in the Third Article of Question 13 of Part I of his
Summa Theologiae, that certain terms which apply literally to creatures also
apply literally to God—with respect to their *res significata*, not their *modus sig-*

nificandi—Aquinas remarked that perfections which flow from God to creatures exist in what he calls "a more eminent" way in God than in creatures. Take the perfection *wisdom*. What he means is that though the *res significata* of the term "wise," namely, wisdom, is to be found in both God and creatures, the way in which God is wise is eminent compared to the way in which we are wise, indeed, pre-eminent. The difference that is ontologically most fundamental is that, whereas for us wisdom is one among other attributes, God's wisdom is identical with God. Another difference, though less fundamental ontologically, is that whereas we are always limited in what we know, God is unlimited in knowledge, in wisdom. *Being one among other attributes* and *being limited with respect to what's known* do not, however, belong to the things signified by our term "wise," only to its mode of signification.

May it be that similar things are to be said about speech, that is, discourse—the performance of illocutionary acts? Is discourse a perfection that exists eminently in God but only non-eminently, limitedly, in us? And does *being limited in discourse*, though not belonging to the *res significata* of our term "speaks," nonetheless belong to its *modus significandi*, so that though the term applies literally to both God and creatures with respect to what it signifies, it applies to creatures alone with respect to the way it signifies? What we have seen is that, for Aquinas, this question is different from the question as to whether predicating the term "speaks" of creatures is only analogical to predicating the term of God, not equivocal. But since Alston and I deny that God is ontologically simple, Aquinas's reason for holding that predication of terms to God is only analogous to predication of terms to us is rendered irrelevant.

I doubt that there is an eminent/non-eminent distinction between God and us with respect to discourse. Eminence with respect to discourse would presumably consist of being capable of performing any appropriately responsible act of discourse whatsoever, and necessarily so; non-eminence would consist of lacking that capacity, or if not lacking it, at least not possessing it necessarily. Now it is clear that you and I are limited in all sorts of ways in our capacity for performing acts of discourse. There are countless truths I cannot assert because, among other considerations, I lack the conceptual repertoire for doing so, and so also for you. And there are countless declarations I cannot make because I lack the standing requisite for doing so, and so also for you; I cannot make the judicial declaration "guilty," since I am not a judge. But God is also limited in such ways. Though it is my view, contra Alston, that God can literally promise, nonetheless there are all sorts of promises I can make that God cannot make. I can promise my grandchildren to drive them to the zoo; God cannot promise that. And if there are so-called "essential indexicals," with the English personal pronoun "I" being among them—as I am inclined to think is the case—then the proposition I assert when I assertively utter, "I am running late for class," is not one that anyone else, including God, can assertively utter.

Nonetheless, it is the case that God is very different indeed from the sort of speaker that we come across in our experience—thus very different from the sort of person to whom we learn to apply the concept *speaking* and the word "speaks." The persons to whom we learn to apply that concept and that word are all embodied persons, whereas God has no body. That difference between us does not imply, so I have argued, that it cannot be said literally and truly of God that God speaks—that is, discourses. But it does imply, I freely concede, that application to God of the term "speaks" or "discourses" is for us a highly idiosyncratic application of the term.

I have no objection to using Aquinas's conceptuality at this point and saying that though *having a body* belongs to the *modus significandi* of our term "speaks," it does not belong to the *res significata* of the term. Alston's way of explaining the distinction, in his essay "Functionalism and Theological Language," seems to me here the best. Let me quote again what he says, changing the example this time from *making* to *speaking*:

> The most general idea . . . is that the common possession of abstract features is compatible with as great a difference as you like in the way in which these features are realized. . . . This general point suggests the possibility that the radical otherness of God might manifest itself in the *way* in which common abstract features are realized in the divine being, rather than in the absence of common features. What it is for God to speak is radically different from what it is for a human being to speak; but that does not rule out an abstract feature in common, viz., that of *performing an illocutionary act*. (*Divine Nature and Human Language*, 66–67)

Notes

1. I have in mind "Irreducible Metaphors in Theology," "Can We Speak Literally of God," and "Functionalism and Theological Language." These can now be found in the collection of Alston's articles, *Divine Nature and Human Language: Essays in Philosophical Theology* (DNHL) (Ithaca, NY: Cornell University Press, 1989). An important paper on a closely related topic, "Referring to God," is also to be found in the collection.

2. Quoted from William P. Alston, "Irreducible Metaphors in Theology," in DNHL, 17.

3. Nicholas Wolterstorff, *Divine Discourse* (Cambridge: Cambridge University Press, 1995).

4. At one point, Alston makes the argument more difficult for himself than it need be by affirming the thesis that all human basic actions consist in moving some part of one's body (DNHL, 55ff.). This seems to me not correct. For example, this morning I have been thinking about Alston's case for literal speech about God because I decided to do so. My thinking about the topic is a basic action; I did not perform it by performing

some other action. And my thinking about Alston's case does not consist of moving some part of my body.

5. In "Can We Speak Literally of God?" he says, "In my opinion, all these arguments are radically insufficient to support the sweeping denial that *any* intrinsic predicate can be literally true of God. But this is not the place to go into that" (DNHL, 41, his emphasis).

6. William P. Alston, "Aquinas on Theological Predication: A Look Backward and a Look Forward" (ATP), in *Reasoned Faith: Essays in Honor of Norman Kretzmann*, ed. Eleonore Stump (Ithaca, NY: Cornell University Press, 1993), 145–178.

7. William P. Alston, "Functionalism and Theological Language," in DNHL, 65.

8. Neither the Dominican nor the Blackfriars' translation of the *Summa Theologiae* is entirely satisfactory for my purposes, since both misinterpret Aquinas on the very points that I will be discussing. In general, however, I will be following the Dominican translation, on the ground that it is more literal, revising it when I deem that necessary.

9. From "Functionalism and Theological Language," in DNHL, 66–67. His emphasis. Alston adds, in a footnote, that "neither Thomas nor the Thomistic tradition has seized this opportunity to locate an area of univocal predication." What I will be arguing is that Aquinas does what Alston here says he does not do; viz., he uses the distinction between the property signified by a term and the mode of signifying to "locate an area of univocal predication."

10. Also see Aquinas, *Summa contra Gentiles* I, 30, 3: "And so with reference to the mode of signification no name is fittingly applied to God; this is done only with reference to that which the name has been imposed to signify. Such names, therefore, as Dionysius teaches, can be both affirmed and denied of God. They can be affirmed because of the meaning of the name; they can be denied because of the mode of signification."

11. Herbert McCabe, in the Blackfriars' translation that Alston is using, pretty much eliminates the ambiguity; he translates it Alston's way: "But a creature is not like to God as it is like to another member of its species or genus, but resembles him as an effect may in some way resemble a transcendent cause although failing to reproduce perfectly the form of the cause."

12. It's clear from the three articles under discussion that Alston and I are in agreement on this; he too has a vested interest in the issue of whether it is literally true that God speaks. In another article collected in DNHL, "Some Suggestions for Divine Command Theorists," Alston argues that God's speaking should not be understood as including God's promising or covenanting; in my *Divine Discourse* I give reasons for concluding that his argument on this point is not compelling.

16
Response to Wolterstorff

William P. Alston

In the subject area covered by Nick Wolterstorff's essay there is very considerable agreement between us. Most centrally we both hold that it is possible to make true statements about God by using predicate terms literally, and we agree that Aquinas thought this as well. In Aquinas exegesis, which occupies a prominent place in Nick's essay, we both emphasize the importance of the doctrine of divine simplicity in Aquinas's reasons for denying univocal predication of terms to God and creatures. But we come to the parting of the ways on the question of how to understand Aquinas's denial of univocity. Since I would make this response even shorter than the editors would like it if I were to confine myself to expressing agreement, along with expressing admiration for the masterful and penetrating way in which Nick has set out the problems he is considering and has gone about supporting his solutions, I feel that I must concentrate on our disagreements concerning Thomistic exegesis and giving my reasons for preferring my position on that. But first let me say that I have no intention of claiming that I am obviously right and Nick obviously wrong where we disagree, or that I have conclusive reasons for my side of the dispute. It is notorious that there is more than one way to give defensible interpretations of a philosopher's thought, especially one as powerful, deep, and wide-ranging as Aquinas, and it is clear to me that both Nick and I have positions that can be accepted for good reasons by an accomplished exegete. But that said, it should come as no surprise that if I must make a choice it will be for my position.

In my essay "Aquinas on Theological Predication: A Look Backward and a Look Forward" I conclude that Aquinas left no room for univocal predication of any term to both God and creatures. I then proceed to argue that if Aquinas had been willing to give up the doctrine of divine simplicity, he could have recognized that the rest of his position was quite compatible with the possibility of some predicates, while used literally, being univocally attributed to God and creatures. Whereas Nick, thinking that Aquinas did in fact hold such a view, takes him to have beaten me to the punch by recognizing an area of univocity in talk about God, and without giving up divine simplicity. So the juxtaposition of our views makes for an interesting dialogue.

One interesting feature is that Nick's allegation of a kind of univocity recognized by Aquinas is based on a set of distinctions that we both find in Aquinas. These are (1) between "pure perfection terms" and those the signification of which contains something distinctive of creatures; (2) between the *res significata* (RS), the property or "perfection" that is signified by a predicate term, and the *modus significandi* (MS), the way in which the term signifies or "presents" the perfection in question; and (3) between univocal, equivocal, and analogical (U-E-A) uses of terms in two or more applications. Before going any further, let me make explicit that E holds whenever two terms are not used in exactly the same sense. So in this strict sense of E, A is a special case of E. For if two uses of a term are analogically related, their senses in these uses are not exactly the same but only analogous. Since it is common to use 'E' in the sense of *merely, wholly equivocal*, this is liable to cause confusion. In the following I will sometimes speak of uses as "E-A" to indicate this special, analogical brand of equivocity.

I don't see any way of dealing with the issues between Nick and myself except by citing crucial texts in Aquinas and considering how they are best read. Before getting into that, I want to point out a serious difficulty that confronts any attempt to make a judgment on the issue. This concerns how to relate semantic terms in Aquinas's medieval Latin and the terms in which we discuss the issue today in English and other modern European languages. We tend to think of univocity as holding between two uses of a term when it is used in the same sense or with the same meaning. But it is not clear on the face of it which of Aquinas's terms have the best claim to be translated as 'sense' or 'meaning,' if any of them do. Otherwise put, it is not obvious on the face of it what, according to Aquinas, the *vox* is that we have only one of when a term is used on two or more occasions *univoce*, one-*vox*-ly. We have to approach the issue indirectly by taking everything Aquinas says using 'univoce,' 'ratio,' and the other semantic terms and making a judgment as to what translation best reflects this whole panoply of passages.

To get more specific about the issues between Nick and myself, there are two main areas of disagreement between us as to Aquinas's position on univocity. According to Nick, Aquinas took the very perfections that can be truly asserted of God to be also truly assertable of humans. Since these perfections constitute the RS of pure perfection terms, these terms, so far as their RS is concerned, can be univocally predicated of God and us. Whereas I take Aquinas to hold that even pure perfection terms pick out somewhat different (though analogically related) properties when applied to God and to us.

The other disagreement is more tortuous and will require some unpacking. It has to do with where we locate the E-A in Aquinas's account. We both recognize that even with pure perfection terms there is some E-A to be inserted into the picture. A simple way of doing so would be to exploit the RS-MS distinction by taking Aquinas to hold that even if, as Nick supposes, pure perfection terms can be univocally said of God and us with respect to their RS, they cannot with respect to their MS. My position is that Aquinas took this, as well as differences in the exact properties signified, to be a source of E-A predication of predicates to God and man. But Nick shies away from locating the source of E-A in the MS of predicates, and though surprising this is understandable. If such equivocity as Aquinas might recognize between saying 'God is wise' and saying 'Socrates is wise' comes from the MS of 'wise,' then it follows that 'wise' is not wholly univocal in these two applications. For unless the MS of 'wise' is one component in its total meaning, how could a difference in its MS in the two uses be a source of equivocity? If being used equivocally in two applications doesn't amount to being used with (at least a partly) different meaning, then we have lost touch with the standard sense of terms like 'equivocal' and 'univocal.' And so if Nick were to take this alternative he would be left with the position that 'wise' is only partly univocal in those two applications, univocal only so far as the RS part of its meaning is concerned, and the position he wants is that (Aquinas thinks that) it is wholly univocal in those applications.

So Nick, instead of locating the E-A in the MS aspect of the meaning of predicates, says things like this: "It's our *predicating* of the predicate term to God that is analogous to our predicating it of Joe; the analogy is to be located, not in the sense (meaning) of the predicate term itself but in the copula." And:

> [I]n predicating 'is wise' of God we are claiming a different relation to hold between wisdom and God from that which we claim to hold between wisdom and some human being when we predicate 'is wise' of that human being. The 'is' in 'God is wise' necessarily has a different force, a different *ratio,* from the 'is' in 'Socrates is wise'—assuming that we are using our words in such a way that in each case what we say is true.

The negative part of what Nick is claiming here is clear—the E-A is not to be located in any aspect of the meaning of the predicate term. But as for his positive alternative, it may look as if he makes three different suggestions as to the source of the E-A:

1. In predicating the term of its subject.
2. In the copula of the predication (specifically its "force").
3. In the relation between the perfection predicated and its subject.

But 1 and 3 are the wrong sorts of items to be possible subjects of U, E, or A. These are semantic terms that apply only to linguistic items or the intentional mental states they express or signify. Only what is capable of being used with a certain meaning can be used univocally or equivocally with some other item of that same sort. A relation between a property and its possessor or an act of predication doesn't fit that bill. I take it that 2 is Nick's serious suggestion as to what is used in an E-A way in attributions of pure perfections to God and us. 1 and 3 are aspects of the analogical forces he supposes that Aquinas supposes the copula carries in these uses.

Thus there are two main disagreements between Nick and myself about Aquinas's views. (I) I hold that Aquinas took the perfections attributed to God and us by a pure perfection term to be not exactly the same but only analogically related, while Nick holds that Aquinas took them to be exactly the same, and hence the term to be used univocally in the two attributions. (II) I hold that Aquinas thought that E-A enters into the picture both from the RS and the MS of a predicate term, while Nick holds that Aquinas took its source to be the analogically related forces of the copula.

Before surveying relevant texts I will point out some serious difficulties with Nick's position on (II), difficulties that would appear to short-circuit that position prior to an examination of particular Thomistic texts. First, so far as I know, Aquinas never commits himself to the supposition. As we will see, the texts that Nick cites in support are better taken to support his position on (I) or the view he rejects that the E-A comes from the MS aspect of the predicate terms. That being the case we would need some reason for thinking this is a plausible position before even considering whether there is sufficient reason for attributing it to Aquinas. The other difficulties indicate it is very implausible. Second, what has happened to the MS side of the RS-MS contrast? Nick makes no use whatsoever of the MS of predicate terms, taking what in my view Aquinas attributes to that and charging it to the forces of the copula. And, indeed, he was wise to speak of 'force' here. Since a copula doesn't signify anything, there is no place for a *mode* of signifying. It certainly doesn't refer to anything. Try using it as the subject of a declarative sentence. Nor does it signify some property in the way Aquinas takes a predicate to do. It doesn't fit any better into a predicate position in a sentence. And so we would need some reason to credit the difference in the mode in which wisdom is said to be realized in 'God is wise' and 'Socrates is wise' to different forces of 'is.' And to do so seems very implausible. 'Is' is simply binding subject and predicate into a predicative attribution. Any difference in what is being claimed (other than the subject) would seem to be due to differences in the two occurrences of 'wise.' Third, the whole discussion in ST, I, 13 is in terms of "names" (*nomina*), and there is no indication whatsoever that Aquinas takes the copula to be a name, a very implausible supposition in any event. And so I consider Nick's position on (II) to have been disqualified before leaving the starting gate.

In examining Thomistic texts, I will first cite passages that I take to be most crucial in supporting my position and respond to Nick's view of those passages. After this I will examine some of what Nick cites as his main supports.

The passages in which Aquinas lays out most trenchantly his position that no predicates can be used univocally of God and us and his supports for that are in the *Summa contra Gentiles* (SCG). The translation from SCG is by Anton Pegis, printed under the title *On the Truth of the Catholic Faith* (Doubleday, 1955). Here is the first one:

> An effect that does not receive a form specifically the same as that through which the agent acts cannot receive according to a univocal predication the name arising from that form. . . . Now, the forms of the things God has made do not measure up to a specific likeness of the divine power: for the things that God has made receive in a divided and particular way that which in Him is found in a simple and universal way. It is evident, then, that nothing can be said univocally of God and other things. (SCG I, 32, 2)

Here Aquinas denies that any terms can be used univocally of God and creatures with respect to the RS. For the *res* signified by a predicate is the property signified by that term, as Nick insists. Aquinas uses the Aristotelian way of referring to a property, viz., 'form.' And he makes it as explicit as possible that even with respect to that aspect of the meaning of a term, no term can be used univocally of God and creatures. In case the reader has missed that point he goes on in the next section to say that even if this were not the case, the difference in the MS would prevent univocal predication.

> If, furthermore, an effect should measure up to the species of its cause, it will not receive the univocal predication of the name unless it receives the same form according to the same mode of being. For the form of the house that is in the art of the maker is not univocally the same being in the two locations. Now, even though the rest of things were to receive a form that is absolutely the same as it is in God, yet they do not receive it according to the same mode of being. For as is clear from what we have said, there is nothing in God that is not the divine being itself, which is not the case with other things. Nothing, therefore, can be predicated of God and other things univocally. (SCG, I, 32, 3)

Several things are to be noted about this pair of passages. First, they represent a "double whammy" against univocal predication of God and creatures. This is prevented both by a difference in the RS aspect and by a difference in the MS aspect. Second, it is significant that the former is presented first, and the latter comes in as an addition, as a fallback just in case Aquinas was mistaken about the former (something he has no inclination to admit). Thus the primary emphasis is on the RS aspect. Third, the MS aspect is represented not by that term itself, but in a way that is congenial to Nick's understanding of the MS, viz., as the kind of "being" the form has in one or another subject.

Nick says of the first passage:

> Notice that the way forms in things are said not to "measure up to" forms in God is just that God receives forms in a simple way and we receive forms in a divided way. It's for that reason that nothing can be said univocally of God and

us. The saying-of, the predicating-of, is what is not univocal; the terms predicated designate the same perfection in both cases.

I have already pointed out that "the saying of" or the "predicating of" is not the
sort of item that is characterizable as being used univocally or in contrary ways.
But a deeper objection is that although Nick is on target as to the reason Aquinas
gives for his conclusion, that does not alter the fact that the conclusion is that the
forms differ for God and creatures; that is, the RS differs for the predicates used
of God and creatures. The reason could support the claim that the MS interferes
with univocity, as it does in the second passage. But the conclusion in the first
passage is that the *form* of a divine perfection is not the same as the *form* closest
to that in God, whatever the reason given for that conclusion.

Of the second passage Nick says that it "makes the same point," that is, the
point we have just seen him suppose that the first passage makes. But the two
passages clearly make quite different points, the first that the RS of the predicate
interferes with univocity and the second that its MS interferes with it.

Nick then goes on to what is the only serious lapse in an otherwise excellent
paper. He says that if, as I claim Aquinas holds, the RS in a creaturely attribution is only analogous to the RS in a divine attribution, then since Aquinas is
clear that pure perfection terms can be literally (*proprie*) predicated of God, the
creaturely attribution would have to be metaphorical. He then proceeds to give
very cogent arguments against the view that when one says, for example, that
Socrates is wise one is speaking metaphorically. The reasoning leading to the
claim that I am committed to this absurd view is based on more than one confusion. First, even if the terms are only analogically related rather than univocal, it
doesn't follow that they can't both be used literally in their respective predications. Second, metaphorical use is not the only alternative to literal use. There
are, for example, other figures of speech, such as irony. Aquinas restricted himself to metaphor as a contrast to literality because he took it to be the most salient alternative to literality with respect to talk about God. Third, in any event,
since it is as obvious as anything can be in this area that when I predicate a pure
perfection term like 'wise' to a creature like Socrates I am not speaking metaphorically, if the view in question did follow from my position, then the better
part of wisdom would be to give up the view that I can speak literally when
predicating wisdom of God.

Continuing the incomplete survey of passages that support my take on
Aquinas on univocity, the obvious place to look further in ST is article 5 of
Question 13, "Whether What is Said of God and of Creatures is Univocally
Predicated of Them." Here if anywhere we would naturally expect to find Aqui-
nas's definitive word on the topic. But, as we shall see, this definitive word still
needs to be interpreted, and, unsurprisingly, Nick and I do not see eye to eye on
the interpretation. Consider the beginning of the *sed contra*. I will first give the
Dominicans' translation with 'ratio' left untranslated for the nonce, along with

minor changes to accommodate that.

> Whatever is predicated of various things under the same name but not accord-
> ing to the same *ratio*, is predicated equivocally. But no name belongs to God
> according to the same *ratio* according to which it is said of creatures; for in-
> stance, wisdom in creatures is a quality, but not in God.

Nick in his discussion of this passage upbraids the Blackfriars for translating the
second sentence, "But no word when used of God means the same as when it is
used of a creature." He says that this is interpretation, not translation. This obviously hangs on how we understand 'ratio.' Nick objects to understanding 'according to the same *ratio*' as 'having the same meaning.' But fortunately there is
a passage in the preceding article in which Aquinas spells out how he understands 'ratio.' It occurs in the *responsio* of that article. I first give the Latin. "*Ratio enim quam significat nomen est conceptio intellectus de re significata per
nomen.*" Literally translated, "For *ratio*, which the name signifies, is the conception the intellect has of the thing signified by the name." Aquinas is obviously
thinking of a double signification by a name—a mental conception and the thing
(*res*) conceived; the latter signification of something external is by means of the
more internal signification of a mental concept. As Aquinas puts it at the end of
the ad 1 of this article, "the term only signifies the thing through the medium of
the intellectual conception." Thus the Blackfriars were not so far off in their
translation of the second sentence. It is, one might say, defective only in being
under-interpreted, not bringing in Aquinas's view as to what it takes for a name
to mean (signify) a thing.

Nick in his treatment makes no use of the clue given in the *Responsio* of article 4 as to how Aquinas understands 'ratio.' Instead he construes 'according to
the same ratio' as 'the copula having the same force.' So when Aquinas says
that we do not have univocal predication in 'God is wise' and 'Socrates is wise,'
Nick locates the equivocity in 'is' rather than in 'wise.' I can't see that he has
any textual support for this. He is presumably influenced by his taking the reason for equivocity, in this case "because wisdom is a quality of Socrates and not
of God," to tell us what kind of equivocity it is a reason for, rather than attending to what Aquinas says it is a reason for; though even if that were allowed, it
would hardly count as a reason for his reading. By reading on in the *sed contra*
we find Aquinas saying "now a different genus changes an essence, since the
genus is part of the definition." The genus in question for Socrates's wisdom is
the genus of quality and for God (if one could call it a genus) the absolutely
simple divine being. And the invocation of the Aristotelian notion of specifying
(defining) the essence of a species by giving the genus and the differentia that
distinguishes that species from others in the same genus tells us that since Socrates's wisdom and God's wisdom do not share the same genus they can't be identical. That is not to say that we don't also have a lack of identity in how the copula works in the two cases; but that is not the point Aquinas is making here. The
fact that Nick is off target is reinforced at the end of the first paragraph of the

Responsio, in the Dominicans' translation. "Hence no name is predicated univocally of God and of creatures." Nick comments on this as follows:

> In short, Aquinas's doctrine of analogy pertains to the predicating, not to what's predicated, to the copula, not to the predicate term. When we say "is wise" of God, the predicate term "wise" is being used literally [sic], as it is when we say "is wise" of some human being; but the copula when used to speak of creatures has a sense that is only analogical to its sense when used to speak of God. Aquinas uses the literal/metaphorical contrast when speaking of predicate terms; he uses the univocal/analogical contrast when speaking of the copula.

But if anything is obvious, it is that the copula is not a *name* as Aquinas uses the term 'name,' and that Aquinas frequently uses the U-A contrast when speaking of predicate terms.

Now I turn to a passage Nick cites in support of his position on issue (I). Nick cites it in the Blackfriars' translation. (This is the first half of his citation.)

> All the perfections of all things are in God. . . . This may be seen from two considerations. First, because whatever perfection exists in an effect must be found in the producing cause: either in the same formality . . . or in a more eminent degree. . . . Since therefore God is the first producing cause of things, the perfections of all things must pre-exist in God in a more eminent way. . . . (*ST* I, 4, 2, *Responsio*)

Nick comments on this as follows. "'All the perfections of all things are in God.' This seems to me as clear a statement as one could want of the view that the perfections in God and in us are the same." In saying this he seems to ignore the bit that specifies that the perfections are in God in a more eminent degree. But perhaps he takes this to be the *way* the same perfection is in God rather than what the perfection is. But I fear this would commit him to such absurdities as that corporeality is the same perfection in God and in corporeal creatures. Nick might point out that in attributing a kind of univocity to Aquinas he is concerned only with pure perfection terms, among which is definitely not corporeality by Aquinas's lights. But the above passage makes no such restriction. And so if Nick cites it as support, I take him to be stuck with the consequence I drew from it.

Finally Nick questions whether it makes sense to suppose that a difference in the MS of a predicate could make a difference in its RS. Well, I did say something close to that in the essay Nick criticizes, and though I wouldn't put it that way now, it seems to me to be understandable. Given Nick's understanding of MS as reflecting the enormous ontological difference between the way a perfection is realized in an absolutely simple being and in an ontologically complex being, what difference could be greater? Why shouldn't it affect precisely what perfections are possible for the two cases?

Part III: Meaning and Truth

17

A Theory of Assertives

Alessandra Tanesini

In the first part of his book *Illocutionary Acts and Sentence Meaning* (IASM), William P. Alston offers a very sophisticated account of the nature of illocutionary acts.[1] This account is the foundation for the theory of the nature of sentence meaning presented in the second half of the same book. Alston claims that a distinctive advantage of his theory of sentence meaning in terms of the potential to perform an illocutionary act of a matching kind over, for example, truth-conditional accounts is that, unlike its rivals, his theory does not leave "semantic statuses dangling in the void" (IASM, 300). A use theory of sentence meaning, like Alston's, offers an explanation of what it is for a sentence to have a given meaning in terms of facts about its use by a community; supporters of truth-conditional approaches reject this explanation but offer no alternative grounds for the semantic statuses which they employ in their accounts. I agree with Alston that any account of the facts which constitute a sentence having a given meaning must take these facts to supervene upon facts about how expressions are used by speakers of the language to which those expressions belong (IASM, 285). But I believe that his own theory is at risk of failing to satisfy this requirement.

In the first section of this paper I argue that as a result of his account of the nature of illocutionary acts, Alston's theory of the nature of sentence meaning could also leave some semantic statuses dangling in the void. In particular, I claim that Alston's account of the nature of assertion which includes a restriction on the nature of the sentential vehicle is either explanatorily circular or relies on facts which are not supervenient upon use. Since sentence meaning is presented by Alston as being identical with the potential to be used to perform an illocutionary act of a specific kind, if part of what it takes for a sentence to be usable to perform an act of that kind has nothing to do with facts about use, then the meaning of that sentence also will be partly dependent on facts which are not supervenient upon use. In the second section I make a proposal about how to remedy this shortcoming. My proposal relies on the idea that any satisfactory

239

account of assertives must also explain the connection between these types of illocutionary act and attributions of truth.

I

There are many different kinds of illocutionary acts: for example, asserting that some apples are green, warning Mary that the floor is slippery, promising to write a paper, expressing one's disgust at something. Alston initially identifies illocutionary acts as what is reported in *oratio obliqua* reports. In other words, illocutionary acts are those acts which are reported by reports of what somebody said (in a suitably broad sense of 'saying') (IASM, 14). For instance, whenever I state that John warned Mary that the floor was slippery, I report an illocutionary act performed by John. I report that it was a warning, and that it involved the proposition that the floor is slippery; both aspects of the report are part of what the speaker said in the broad sense of the word.

To specify which illocutionary act was performed by a speaker on a given occasion is, given Alston's initial characterization of these acts, to specify what the speaker said (in a suitably inflated sense of the word). It is therefore hardly surprising, as Alston himself acknowledges (IASM, 160), that sentence meaning turns out to be the potential to perform a given type of illocutionary act. It is not surprising because the illocutionary acts are classified into types on the basis of what is said by the speaker who performs a given act.[2]

After his initial pre-theoretical specification of illocutionary acts, Alston provides an account of their nature. In his view, the normative stance of the speaker toward his or her utterance is what makes that utterance a performance of an illocutionary act of a given type (IASM, 71). This idea that normative attitudes play a crucial role in an account of what endows an act with the significance of being a performance of an illocutionary act is, I believe, on the right track. The restriction to the attitudes of the performer alone is, as I show below, more problematic.

Alston fleshes out the idea of having a normative stance toward one's utterance in terms of taking responsibility for the satisfaction of some conditions. More specifically, Alston holds that what makes an utterance of a sentence by a speaker a performance of an illocutionary act of a given type is that the speaker takes responsibility for the obtaining of some conditions which are necessary for correct utterance.[3]

An example should help to clarify Alston's position. Consider the sentence 'You are not going to buy cigarettes today.' This sentence can be used by a person to order another not to buy cigarettes on the day of utterance, or it can be used to make a prediction that the other person is not going to buy cigarettes on the day of utterance. Thus, the same sentence with the same meaning can be used to make very different illocutionary acts. Alston's account is intended to specify the facts in virtue of which one utterance of this sentence counts as an order, and another counts as a prediction. In his opinion, these are normative facts about the commitments undertaken by the speaker in making the utterance.

For example, if I utter 'you are not going to buy cigarettes today,' and my utterance is to count as an order, I am thereby committed to it being possible for you not to buy cigarettes today. I am also committed to the obtaining of those conditions which are necessary if I am to have the authority to give you orders on these matters. Or, in Alston's preferred terminology, I am taking responsibility for being wrong if it is not possible for you not to buy cigarettes today, if I do not have the authority to make the order, and so forth. However, if my utterance of 'you are not going to buy cigarettes today' is to count as a prediction, I am thereby committed to the truth of the proposition that you are not going to buy cigarettes today, but I am not committed to having any authority to place you under any obligations. That is to say, I am taking responsibility for being incorrect if you are going to buy cigarettes today, but I am not taking any responsibility for having any kind of authority over what you do.

Alston also reformulates the notion of taking responsibility in terms of subjecting one's utterance to a rule which determines when the utterance of a sentence (with a given meaning) is permissible (IASM, 60). So, what makes a speaker's utterance of a sentence a performance of an illocutionary act of a given type is the speaker's subjecting his or her utterance to a rule. This rule governs the sentence employed in the utterance, and constitutes the utterance as a performance of an illocutionary act of a given type. Because these rules are constitutive of illocutionary act types, they are called illocutionary rules.

Illocutionary acts are thus ultimately described by Alston as rule-subjection acts. They are acts which consist in subjecting other lower-level acts to a rule (IASM, 63). The lower-level act is the act of uttering a sentence or a surrogate for a sentence (IASM, 26). This is normally called a sentential act. The illocutionary act is the act that consists in subjecting one's act of uttering a given sentence to an illocutionary rule.

Assertions, as Alston notices, present a problem for this account of the nature of illocutionary act types. It might be tempting to think that an utterance of a sentence counts as an assertion if and only if what the speaker takes responsibility for coincides with what is asserted. Thus, one might say that an utterance of 'some apples are green' counts as an assertion that some apples are green if and only if the speaker takes responsibility for being wrong if it is not the case that some apples are green. The account, however, cannot be correct because it entails that every illocutionary act is among other things also an asserting of the conjunction of all the conditions of correct utterance for whose satisfaction the speaker takes responsibility. For example, an act of promising to you that I will do something would also be an act of asserting that I place myself under an obligation to do that thing, and that I intend to do it, and that you have an interest in me doing it, that it is possible for me to do it, and so forth. But this cannot be right; I am not asserting all of these things, when I make my promise to you.

There are, in Alston's opinion, two other problems that must be solved by an account of assertives. First, it must offer a criterion to distinguish between expressing a psychological attitude such as admiration, and stating that one has such an attitude. Second, it must also allow us to distinguish between what is asserted and what is presupposed by the assertion. That is, it must explain why in asserting that the chair in the corner is broken, I am not asserting but merely presupposing that there is a chair in the corner (IASM, 115).

Alston solves these three problems by providing an account of assertive illocutionary acts that imposes a condition on them that is not related to the normative stance adopted by the speaker. This condition is a restriction on the kind of sentential vehicle that can be used to make an assertion. In uttering a sentence, a speaker makes an assertion if and only if the speaker takes responsibility for the correctness of what is asserted and the sentence used explicitly presents the proposition which is being asserted or is elliptical for a sentence which explicitly presents it (IASM, 129–130). Alston does not give a precise characterization of what it takes for a sentence to present a proposition explicitly, but he hints that it has something to do with some kind of correspondence between the semantic constituents of the sentence and the elements of the proposition (IASM, 119).

There are reasons for being unhappy with this solution. As Alston writes elsewhere, a proposition just is the content of an assertion. Further, we have no independent way of identifying propositions such that it would be a discovery to find out that it is propositions that play that role.[4] Thus, our grasp of the concept of a proposition depends on our grasp of the concept of what is stated by means of an assertion. Alston's account of assertion would thus prove to be viciously circular if it were intended as an analysis of assertion, since the notion of assertion would appear in the analysis of that very notion.

Alston, however, is not in the business of analysis. Instead, he wants to give us an illuminating account of the nature of assertive illocutionary acts. Nevertheless, the closeness between the concepts of proposition and assertion generates problems even for his account of the nature of the facts that constitute assertive illocutionary acts. It might seem that such problems could be avoided by taking propositions to have a mode of existence that is independent of their role as the content of assertions. If Alston adopted this view, his account would not be vacuous because he would identify the facts which constitute types of assertive illocutionary acts with normative facts about what the speaker takes responsibility for, and the fact that the sentence used bears in the context of the utterance a special relation to a given entity (an abstract object or a state of affairs or a function).

This option is not really open to Alston because he does not want to leave "semantic statuses dangling in the void" (IASM, 300). There would be no dangling in Alston's position if all the facts, which for him constitute a sentence having a given meaning, are supervenient upon facts about use. But the fact that a sentence bears in a given context of utterance a special relation to an independently existing entity is not a fact about use. Yet this fact would be part of what it takes for the sentence to have the meaning it has, since sentence meaning is identical with the potential to perform an illocutionary act of the matching kind, and whether a sentence is suitable to perform an assertion would on this account depend on whether it is related in the right way to an independently existing proposition. Thus, were Alston to take this option, he would, like his opponents, leave semantic statuses ungrounded.

Consequently, Alston must hold that propositions, if they exist at all, only exist as aspects of illocutionary acts. Their nature would be exhausted by their specification as being whatever is stated in assertions, for example.[5] This approach also generates problems for Alston's account of the nature of the facts that constitute assertive illocutionary acts. In order to see why, we must make a distinction between two kinds of dependency: semantic and ontological. This is a distinction which Alston also makes in a different context when he explains the relation between sentence and sub-sentential or word meaning.[6] On the one hand, the concept of the meaning of a word is (semantically) dependent upon the concept of the meaning of a sentence because it is the concept of the contribution the word makes to the meanings of the sentences in which it occurs. On the other hand, the fact that a given sentence has a certain meaning is (ontologically) dependent on facts about the meanings of the constituent words.

Propositions, when conceived as something whose nature is exhausted by their being an aspect of illocutionary acts, are ontologically dependent on the acts whose aspects they are. Since they have no independent mode of existence we cannot think of them as ontologically prior to the acts of which they are aspects. The relation between an illocutionary act and the proposition which is an aspect of it is closer to the relation between a dress and its creases, than to the relation between a house and the bricks it is made of. Further, as I mentioned above, Alston acknowledges that the concept of a proposition is semantically dependent on the concept of an illocutionary act. The semantic dependence of the notion of proposition on the notion of illocutionary act does not cause problems for Alston's account of the nature of illocutionary acts. One might still discover something significant about the facts that constitute illocutionary acts even though one needs to rely on the concept of an illocutionary act to identify those facts.

But the ontological dependence of facts about propositions on facts about illocutionary acts of which they are aspects is fatal for Alston's account. We cannot specify the facts that constitute an utterance being a performance of an illocutionary act of a given type in terms of facts that depend on those very facts. More generally, an account which aims to explain what constitutes facts of a given kind cannot rely on facts whose constitution is in turn dependent on the facts which are to be explained. For example, one can explain what makes glass fragile by reference to facts about the microphysical constitution of glass. Conversely, to say that it gives rise to the fragility of glass is no explanation of what makes the micro-physical structure of glass what it is.

To summarize the argument so far, Alston's inclusion in his account of assertive illocutionary acts of a restriction on the sentential vehicle lands him with a dilemma. Either propositions don't have a mode of existence which is independent of their being an aspect of these acts, and consequently cannot be invoked in an explanatory account of the nature of those acts; or they have some kind of independence and can be used to provide such an account, but the resulting account will not identify the facts which constitute the meanings of the sentences employed in the performance of illocutionary acts as facts which are supervenient upon what speakers do. Alston, for different reasons, cannot embrace either of these two alternatives.

II

In what follows, I present an alternative to Alston's account of what distinguishes assertives from other illocutionary acts. My alternative relies on the idea that the conditions for whose satisfaction the speaker takes responsibility when performing an assertive act do not necessarily vary depending on the speaker. The specifications of those conditions for assertions and other assertives make no indexical reference to the speaker, whereas such a reference is always present in the specifications of the relevant conditions for all other types of illocutionary acts.

Consequently, whenever two speakers undertake the same commitments, if their utterance is a performance of an assertive, they have performed two illocutionary acts of the same kind. For instance, if I utter the sentence 'lemons are sour,' I have asserted that lemons are sour only if I take the responsibility for being incorrect if it is not the case that lemons are sour. If anybody else makes an utterance of a sentence (the same or a different one), that person has performed an act of the same type as the act performed by me (i.e., has asserted that lemons are sour) only if that person also takes responsibility for being incorrect if it is not the case that lemons are sour.

The same considerations apply to assertions made employing sentences involving singular reference. If I claim that I (Alessandra Tanesini) am short by uttering the sentence 'I am short,' I commit myself to being incorrect if a given fact does not obtain: namely, the fact that I (that is, Alessandra Tanesini) am short. Whenever speakers make utterances and thereby commit themselves to being wrong if that same fact does not obtain, those speakers also (provided they have made no further commitments) have asserted that I am short, although they will have used different sentences.

Assertions are only one kind of assertives. This category also includes, for example, denials, objections, replies, explanations, and agreements. Alston takes all of these as special modes of assertion (IASM, 126). He accounts for them in terms of additional conditions which must actually be satisfied, and for whose satisfaction the speaker also normally takes responsibility. Thus, for instance, for an utterance of 'lemons are sour' to count as a reply that lemons are sour, it must first count as an assertion that lemons are sour. Secondly, the utterance must take place in a context in which a question about the taste of lemons has been raised, and also, perhaps, the speaker must take responsibility for being mistaken if no question about the taste of lemons has been raised. Any speaker who takes responsibility for the satisfaction of these same conditions will count as replying that lemons are sour provided that the additional conditions that must actually be satisfied are satisfied in this case also.

This phenomenon is unique to assertive types of illocutionary acts. In all other cases two speakers who perform an act of the same type, perhaps even by using the same sentence, will have taken responsibility for different facts. Whenever the act performed is not an assertive, the specifications of the conditions for whose obtaining a speaker must take responsibility involve an indexical reference to the speaker. Consequently, what the speaker must take responsibility for changes from speaker to speaker.

Apart from assertives, Alston distinguishes four other categories of illocutionary act types: exercitives, commissives, directives, and expressives. An utterance counts as the performance of an exercitive whenever by means of it the speaker purports to produce a conventional effect. Thus, the utterance of 'you are hired' purporting to bring it about that the person is hired or of 'the meeting is adjourned' purporting to adjourn the meeting are typical examples of exercitives.[7] In Alston's account, the speaker's utterance of a sentence is a performance of an exercitive only if the speaker takes responsibility for being incorrect if it is not the case that he or she has the authority to bring about the intended conventional effect (IASM, 93). Each speaker in performing an exercitive will take responsibility for the obtaining of a different normative fact; namely, that he or she has the right kind of authority. If a speaker undertakes a commitment that all the conditions for which the performer of an exercitive takes responsibility are satisfied, the second speaker does not also perform an exercitive with his or her utterance; instead, she asserts that the original exercitive act is in order.

Similar points can be made for the remaining three categories. Commissives are types of illocutionary acts by means of which the speaker purports to place himself or herself under an obligation. Promising is the central example. One of the conditions for which the speaker takes responsibility in performing an act of this kind is that he or she places himself or herself under an obligation (IASM, 97). In this case also, another speaker who takes responsibility for being wrong if this condition is not satisfied has not thereby placed himself or herself under an obligation, and thus has not promised anything.

Ordering is the most common example of a directive. One of the conditions for which the speaker takes responsibility in performing an act of this kind is that he or she places the audience under an obligation (IASM, 107). In this case also, no order is performed if another person takes responsibility for being wrong if these conditions are not satisfied.

Finally, expressives are all those acts by means of which a speaker expresses an attitude such as disgust, contempt, or admiration. When performing such an act the speaker takes responsibility for having the attitude in question (IASM, 109). If another speaker takes responsibility for the original speaker's having the attitude in question, he or she does not thereby express the same attitude.

It is, however, possible for one and the same speaker by means of one utterance to perform an illocutionary act which is an instance of more than one type belonging to different categories. Thus, for example, my utterance of 'I admire John' could count both as an expression of my admiration for John and an assertion that I admire him. What this example shows is that, although any account of the nature of illocutionary acts must be such that it can distinguish between the expression of an attitude and the statement that one has that attitude, it must not preclude the possibility that one and the same utterance can count as a performance of an act which is an example of both kinds.

This example does not present a difficulty for my account, since in my view what makes an utterance of 'I admire John' an expression of my admiration for John is that I take responsibility for being wrong if it is not the case that I (Alessandra Tanesini) admire John. In my own case, the condition for whose satisfaction I take responsibility in expressing my admiration for John coincides with the condition for whose satisfaction any speaker must take responsibility if their utterance is to count as the performance of an assertion that Alessandra Tanesini admires John. That is why in this case one and the same utterance of mine can perform both jobs.

My account of the distinguishing feature of assertion also deals with two of the three issues that Alston identifies as stumbling blocks in the development of an account of assertions. The first problem concerns the distinction between asserting and other acts. If asserting is simply a matter of taking responsibility for being wrong if some facts do not obtain, then every illocutionary act is, besides being a promise or an order, also an assertion. More precisely, it is an assertion of the conjunction of all the conditions for whose obtaining one takes responsibility. The second problem concerns the distinction between expressing a psychological attitude and stating that one has that attitude; this problem is closely related to the first. Both problems are handled by the account. In both instances, the difference between asserting and doing something else can be explained in terms of what somebody else would be doing if they took responsibility for the obtaining of the same conditions. In turn, this difference is explained by the fact that only with regard to assertives, the specifications of these conditions make no indexical reference to the speaker.

My account does not address the third problem which, for Alston, must be solved by a theory of assertion since it has nothing to say about the distinction between what is stated and what is merely presupposed in an act of assertion. But I do not think this fact is fatal for my account. First, as others have pointed out, Alston's account does not solve this problem either. The same proposition is explicitly presented by the sentences 'Mary got sick too' and 'Not only Mary got sick,' although while the second is standardly used to state that others beside Mary got sick, this is something which is only implied by the first.[8] Second, the distinction between what is stated with an utterance and what is merely implied or presupposed is often used to distinguish what was literally said, in the sense of what words were used, from what was said in a broader sense. And it is the broader sense with which we are concerned here.

On reflection, it should not be surprising that the difference between assertives and other types of illocutionary acts rests on the idea that the commitments one undertakes in performing acts of the first kind do not vary depending on the speaker. By means of assertion we represent things as being in such and such a way, and what is required to do this should not be relative to the speaker. Instead, it makes sense to think that, for instance, in order to count as promising the same thing, different speakers must undertake different commitments.

The connection between truth and assertives is also closely related to these matters. It is possible to reply to an assertion by stating that its content is or is not true precisely because the function of asserting is to represent things as being in a certain way; and one of the functions of truth-talk is to offer the means to undertake for oneself the same commitments one attributes to another speaker.

Truth-talk is not applicable to any other type of illocutionary act. These acts can be felicitous if the conditions for correct utterance are satisfied, but it would make no sense for the audience to concur with the speaker by claiming that his or her order, for instance, is true. Similarly, it would not make sense to express one's view that a non-assertive illocutionary act is infelicitous, by saying that it is not true. It would seem that any account of assertive illocutionary acts should make contact with this feature. Alston's theory offers no explanation for this fact.

His intuitive justification for the account in terms of presentation focuses on an entirely different aspect. He points out that a difference between, for instance, asserting that I am able to close the door and promising to close the door is that, although in both cases I am taking responsibility for being incorrect if I am not able to close the door, it is only with the assertion that I come out and explicitly put into words what I am taking responsibility for (IASM, 117). Yet it does not seem intuitively right to say that what distinguishes assertions from other acts is that by means of the first we say what we only presuppose in acts of a different kind. If I warn people that the floor is slippery by putting up a sign with the inscription 'Warning! Slippery floor,' my utterance is as explicit as can be. Nevertheless, it is not an assertion.

My account, instead, offers an explanation of why it is appropriate to respond with an utterance of 'that is (not) true' to the performance of an assertive, but the utterance would not be appropriate in any other case. Standardly, an utterance of the expression 'that is true' is used to express agreement; such an agreement indicates that one subscribes to the original assertion. Further, the utterance can be used as a time saving way of making the same assertion oneself, since 'that's true' can be seen as a sentence surrogate for 'it is true that S,' where S stands for a sentence which could be used by the speaker to make the original assertion. One and the same utterance of 'that's true' counts as an assertion, as well as an agreement that the conditions for which the original assertor has taken responsibility are satisfied, because these latter conditions are the same as those conditions whose satisfaction is a necessary condition for the permissibility of the assertion.

In other words, by saying 'that is true,' a speaker both attributes a commitment to another speaker with whom she concurs and undertakes that same commitment for herself. The speaker can do both things at once because the conditions for which she takes responsibility are the same in both cases.

All non-assertive illocutionary types are such that the conditions whose satisfaction one takes responsibility for in performing an act are different from the condition that one takes to be satisfied when one agrees that the performance of an act was in order. Thus, unsurprisingly, it is never appropriate to say of an order or a promise that it is true, since agreeing that somebody else's promise is in order is not one way of making the same promise oneself. The fact that my account has something to say about the connection between acts of asserting and attributions of truth is, I believe, what makes it superior to Alston's.

Notes

1. William P. Alston, *Illocutionary Acts and Sentence Meaning* (IASM) (Ithaca, NY: Cornell University Press, 2000).

2. See IASM, 33.

3. See IASM, 57.

4. William P. Alston, *A Realist Conception of Truth* (RCT) (Ithaca, NY: Cornell University Press, 1996), 15.

5. See RCT, 19.

6. See IASM, 159.

7. Alston argues that full-blooded exercitives such as the performance of hiring someone by saying 'You are hired' are not illocutionary acts. He points out that a report of such an exercitive cannot be plausibly characterized as a report of what somebody said; it is more than that. However, the thinner notion of purporting to do something can be used to specify genuine illocutionary acts. Thus, purporting to hire somebody by saying 'you are hired' is the performance of an illocutionary act (IASM, 89–92).

8. See Stephen Barker, "Review of William P. Alston's *Illocutionary Acts and Sentence Meaning*," *Mind* 111 (2002), 637–638.

18

Response to Tanesini

William P. Alston

Tanesini provides an interesting and promising alternative to my way of constru-ing assertive illocutionary acts. I want to think more about it. My present im-pression is that it is largely successful, though as I will bring out later, I cannot accept all her claims for its advantages. But before getting to that I will examine her criticism of my view, about which I am less enthusiastic.

Her main objection to my account of assertions has to do with the way she thinks it infects my account of sentence meaning. According to my standards, and hers, "An expression's having a certain meaning consists in its being usable to play a certain role in communication" (The Use Principle, *Illocutionary Acts and Sentence Meaning* [IASM], 154). This is necessary to prevent "semantic statuses dangling in the void," a reason I give in IASM for rejecting theories of meaning that do not honor the Use Principle. And my account of assertion makes one of the necessary conditions for asserting that p that the sentence used (or what it is elliptical for) "explicitly presents the proposition that p." This con-dition, she rightly says, is not a "fact about use." But then, asserting that p is not supervenient only on facts about use. And since I hold that sentence meaning is illocutionary act potential (IAP), where the IAP of a given sentence is assertive, one of the conditions on which its meaning is dependent is something other than a fact about use. Thereby the Use Principle is violated, and a semantic status is left "dangling."

The above argumentation is directed against one horn of an alleged di-lemma. The dilemma is between taking propositions as ontologically dependent on assertive IA's and taking them as independently existent. If the former is chosen, the account is vacuous. If the latter, the Use Principle is violated.

To come to terms with this argument against the first horn, we need to be-come more explicit as to (1) what semantic statuses are involved, (2) what "facts about use" are appealed to in my account, and (3) what the Use Principle applies to. To begin with (2), the facts of use that figure in my account of sentence meaning are facts about *usability*. That is made explicit in my formulation of the

251

Use Principle quoted above. Use enters in the guise of usability. Of course, if a sentence is standardly usable to perform, for example, assertive IA's, it will normally, though not necessarily, be used to do so. But it is usability that on my account constitutes a sentence's meaning what it does. But then Tanesini's point that the IAP of a sentence usable to make assertions is supervenient in part on something other than a fact about use does not have the force she takes it to have. There is no occasion for an IAP of a sentence to be *supervenient* on facts about use. It *is* a fact about use of the only sort that enters into my account of sentence meaning in accordance with the Use Principle (which I could have more accurately called the Usability Principle).

What does this have to do with Tanesini's objection? It subverts it altogether. The Use Principle governs *semantic* facts, facts about the meaning of linguistic items. It holds that they are supervenient on facts about the use of linguistic items. But the fact that a certain utterance is an assertion is not a fact about the meaning of any linguistic items, though, of course, meaningful linguistic items will be used in the utterance. Therefore the Use Principle is not violated by one condition for an utterance counting as an assertion being something other than a fact about use. Tanesini is correct in holding that a necessary condition for the performance of an assertive IA is also a necessary condition for a sentence with an assertive IAP meaning what it does. And this does imply that one necessary condition for such a sentence's meaning what it does, on my account, is not a fact about use. But that is not a violation of the Use Principle. The semantic fact involved here is the fact that a certain sentence means what it does. And that *is* supervenient on use on my account. It is supervenient on the sentence's *usability* to perform an assertive IA. And for the same reason no semantic status is left dangling in the void. For the only semantic status in the picture is the sentence's meaning what it does, and that, as just pointed out, is supervenient on a fact about use (usability) on my account. The "non-use" condition for the sentence's meaning what it does has that status only by virtue of its being a condition for a certain kind of use. It does not function independently as a condition on meaning. There may be some other objection to my taking the kind of sentence used to be a necessary condition for an utterance counting as an assertive IA, but Tanesini has not proffered it.

It is worth noting that on my account of IA's there are other non-use conditions for IA performance that stem from features other than what is distinctive of assertives. In particular we have such conditions for all IA's, in all categories, that involve singular reference. On pp. 239–247 of IASM, there are a number of such cases. To cite one, ordering someone to clean up a certain room requires, inter alia, that there is at least one x such that x is a room.[1]

I have been concentrating on the first horn of the alleged dilemma because dealing with it enables me to make important clarifications of my views. The second horn, by contrast, depends on some mistakes that, I hope, are easily correctable. Having said that on my view, "our grasp of the concept of a proposition depends on our grasp of the concept of what is stated by means of an assertion," she goes on to say that "[c]onsequently, Alston must hold that propositions, if they exist at all, only exist as aspects of illocutionary acts. Their nature would be exhausted by their specification as being whatever is stated in assertions, for example." In support of this attribution she refers to Chapter 1 of *A Realist Conception of Truth* (RCT). But she apparently did not note that in that discussion I repeatedly speak of our concept of a proposition as most basically derivative from our understanding of them as contents of illocutionary acts (of all sorts) *and "propositional attitudes."* But she could correct this oversight and still argue that I am committed to the view that propositions are ontologically dependent on the IA's and propositional attitudes whose aspects they are. And since they have no independent mode of existence, we cannot think of them as ontologically prior to the acts and attitudes of which they are aspects. But in Chapter 1, sections iv and v, of RCT I make it quite explicit that I look to contents of IA's and propositional attitudes as a source of our *concept* of a proposition. The question of the ontological status, in particular the conditions of existence, of propositions is a further matter. I consider various views on this without making a definite decision between them, even though I confess to a predilection to an "Aristotelian" view. And I certainly do not think that propositions only exist as contents of IA's. More generally, considerations about how we get the concept of a proposition have no implications for their mode of existence. And so the denial of an "independent" (of assertions and of other IA's and propositional attitudes) existence of propositions, which is basic to the second horn, has no support in my views.

Turning to her account of assertives, it clearly does distinguish assertives from other IA's. I wish I had thought of it. Her criterion is that one and the same assertive IA (type) can be performed by another person by taking responsibility for exactly the same conditions as the first speaker, whereas this is not the case with IA's of other types. The other IA's each have at least one condition that has to do with the speaker, but assertives are not necessarily speaker-relative in this way.[2] What is behind her ingenious suggestion is the fact that the contents of assertives range over any states of affairs whatsoever, whereas part of the content of non-assertives always has to do with the speaker. And so her theory avoids any necessity of distinguishing assertives in terms of restrictions on the sentential vehicle involved. That would be an advantage if that restriction were objectionable, and I have argued above that her reasons for finding it objectionable do not hold up.

Tanesini takes it to be an advantage of her account that it "offers an explanation of why it is appropriate to respond with 'that is true' to the performance of an assertive, but the utterance of that expression would not be appropriate in any other case." Her case for this rests on the facts that 'that is true' can express agreement with what the addressee has said and can be used to make the same assertion. And these points do obviously fit in with her way of demarcating assertives. But these seem to me to be relatively superficial features of the concept of truth; they constitute the heart of the matter only on a deflationary account of truth, something Tanesini does not invoke. If one takes, as I do in RCT, the concept of truth to be given by instances of the T-schema (It is true that p if and only if p), then we need an explanation of the fact that assertives, but not other IA's, are susceptible of truth value to make contact with the T-schema. And Tanesini does not attempt this for her account of assertives. I would like to be able to show that my way of distinguishing assertives does better at this, but I must admit that I don't see any way of doing so. The only deep explanation that I can envisage of the fact that assertives are distinctive among IA's in being susceptible of truth value is a point mentioned above that is neutral between our accounts, viz., the fact that the content of assertives ranges over any states of affairs whatever.

I should also mention that near the end of her paper Tanesini seeks to show that although her account of assertives does not provide a way of distinguishing between what is asserted in an assertive utterance and what is merely presupposed or implied, no such account is needed, contrary to what I claimed. But her treatment of this issue seems to me to misconstrue the example she cites. First, she argues that "Alston's account does not solve this problem either. The same proposition is explicitly presented by the sentences 'Mary got sick too' and 'Not only Mary got sick' although while the second is standardly used to state that others beside Mary got sick, this is something which is only implied by the first." But on my account of explicitly presenting a proposition (and I am responsible for bringing that notion into the discussion), the two sentences are not equal in this respect. Indeed I would say that neither of them explicitly presents the proposition that others besides Mary got sick, for neither of them exactly matches the constituents and structure of that proposition.

Notes

1. The actual condition given is more complex, but it entails the one mentioned in the text.

2. It is unfortunate that Tanesini puts this point by saying that non-assertives are subject to conditions that "involve an indexical reference to the speaker." But an indexical reference is not required; any successful reference to the speaker, whether by an indexical expression, a proper name, a uniquely applicable definite description, or whatever would do the trick. But even if I am right about this, it doesn't really affect her account.

19

Truisms about Truth

Michael P. Lynch

I

Bertrand Russell famously remarked that the point of philosophy is to start with something so simple that it doesn't seem worth stating, and to end with something so paradoxical that no one will believe it. By this standard, the question "what is truth?" is the philosophical question par excellence—at least with regard to the first part of Russell's dictum. For if there is one thing that most philosophers agree on about truth, it is that any serious account of the subject must begin with a simple truism, one version or another of the notorious T-schema (TS):

TS: [p] is true if and only if p.[1]

To cite the paradigmatic instance, the proposition that snow is white is true if and only if snow is white.

The really divisive question, of course, is where to go from here. An increasingly popular view is that we must not only begin with the T-schema, we must end with it as well. This is minimalism, or the idea that there is nothing more to say about truth than whatever we can glean from TS.[2] Opposing it is the more traditional view that there is quite a bit more to say—that TS is just what I said, a truism that barely brushes the surface of a very deep pool.

William Alston has pointed out a third possibility.[3] When we ask, "what is truth?"—and, unlike Pilate, mean it—there are at least two questions we might have in mind. First, we might be asking about the *concept* of truth, or roughly, about the meaning of the word "true." Secondly, we might be asking about the *property* of truth itself—about what truth is, or its nature. As Alston notes, it is important to keep these questions separate, since an answer to the first needn't give you an answer to the second. In particular, Alston argues, we can be minimalists about the concept of truth while still thinking there is much more to say about the property.

Alston's general point here is a familiar one from recent philosophy: The property F-ness might have features—even essential, important features—that are not reflected in our *ordinary concept* of an F.[4] A common way of understanding this distinction sees our ordinary folk-theoretic concepts as constituted by platitudinous beliefs or truisms. In the case of our ordinary concept of water, for example, these truisms are that water is a clear liquid, that it fills the lakes and oceans, that it is drinkable by humans and so on. These truisms constitute what most folks know about water, just in virtue of having the concept "water," but clearly, they don't exhaust all the facts about water. The truisms pick out the surface features of water but stop short of the underlying molecular features responsible for those surface features. Only further investigation, past the truisms, reveals the underlying nature of water—what it takes for some liquid to be water. Similarly, Alston claims that the truisms that make up our concept of truth don't tell us about its underlying nature. Only further investigation—in this case, further a priori investigation—will tell us more about what being true consists in.

In this paper, I will argue that while the ordinary concept of truth is basically simple, it is less minimal than Alston and others apparently believe. The T-schema does lie at the root of many of our most basic intuitions about truth. But there is at least one other independent truism about truth helping to constitute our ordinary concept; namely, that truth is good. As such, any account of the *property*, should one be possible, must respect this truism as much as the T-schema.

The remaining part of this paper is organized as follows. In the next section, I discuss the extent to which TS can be understood as underwriting our belief that truth is objective. The following sections introduce the idea that truth is good, and lay out the case for this being a truism about truth that is independent of TS. I conclude with some reflections on the significance of truth's having both a normative and descriptive nature.

II

If I know anything, it is that I don't know everything and neither does anyone else. There are some things we just won't ever know, and there are other things that we think we know but don't. Grant this bit of common sense, and you are committed to truth being at least minimally objective. Just because we believe something doesn't mean it is true, and just because something is true doesn't mean we'll believe it. As we say, believing doesn't make it so. The truth of Mt. Everest being the tallest mountain has nothing to do with whether I, or anyone else, believes it or not, even on the best of evidence. What matters is whether

Mt. Everest really is the tallest mountain.

The truism that truth is at least minimally objective is often paraphrased as "true beliefs correspond to reality." And that is fine, just so long as we realize that it leaves room for disagreement about what "correspondence" and "objectivity" amount to. Thus some hold that beliefs can't be true unless they are causally responsive to mind-independent, physical objects like mountains, electrons, battleships, and barbers.[5] On these theories, truth is always objective with a capital "O," since what makes our beliefs true on such accounts is always their causal relationship to real physical objects. This is obviously a matter of high philosophical theory, however, and not a truism. You don't have to believe it in order to believe that truth is objective in the minimal sense I've been describing. Our basic belief in truth's objectivity is like my basic idea of my computer's hard drive. I know the job my hard drive does, the role it plays in my computer's architecture, even though I don't know how it gets that job done exactly. Similarly, we know the job of true beliefs, even if we don't know exactly how they get that job done. True beliefs are those that tell it like it is, that represent the world as it is and not as we may hope, fear, or wish it to be. That is,

CP: [p] is true if and only if things are as [p] says they are.

A long tradition in analytic philosophy has it that CP, so far as it goes, is already captured by TS.[6] According to Alston, for example, TS is more or less equivalent to CP; for while CP may bring out aspects of the concept not made explicit in TS, these aspects are "latent in that schema, in such a way that the concept can be conveyed by pointing out the conceptual truth of any T-statement."[7] The idea, in other words, is that CP is implicit in TS. For CP intuitively follows from

[p] says that p

together with the suitable statement version of TS.[8] Again, this does not mean that the correspondence *theory* of truth follows from TS. The point is that CP expresses a core intuition *behind* any such theory, an intuition that is implicit in TS.

TS has even more bite. As I noted above, part of the idea that truth is objective is that believing—even believing based on good evidence, or justified believing—doesn't make it so. Call this the "truth isn't justification" truism. Plausibly, TS is the conceptual root of this idea as well. As Crispin Wright has argued, it follows from TS that a belief can be true but not justified and justified but not true.[9] Here is an abbreviated form of the argument. The first step is to note that TS is provably equivalent to

(NE): It is true that [not p] iff it is not true that [p].[10]

Now take a proposition like [It rained here 15,000 years ago today]. We are neither justified in believing this proposition nor justified in believing its negation. In such cases, the relevant instance of (NE) would be invalid were we to substitute "justified" for "true." That is,

> It is justified that it did not rain here 15,000 years ago today iff it is not justified that it rained here 15,000 years ago today

is false because we may lack justification for its having rained on that date without thereby having justification that it didn't. Consequently, in endorsing the T-schema we commit ourselves to the idea that the concept of truth is distinct from the concept of justified belief.[11]

Alston has given a slightly different argument for a related, but even stronger, conclusion.[12] He argues that the T-schema is inconsistent with any epistemic conception of truth—even much more sophisticated and plausible versions. Consider, for instance, the proposal that

> (E): [p] is true iff [p] would be ideally justified (i.e. it would be justified under ideal epistemic circumstances).

As Alston points out, (E)—when taken as a conceptual analysis of truth—is prima facie incompatible with the T-schema, since according to the latter, the proposition that is said to be true (what is on the left of the "iff") *already* specifies the necessary and sufficient conditions under which it is true. The obvious reply is that the epistemic theorist can show that the T-schema is consistent with her analysis by showing that

> (E2): p iff [p] would be ideally justified

supplies a conceptual truth which can link TS and (E). But, Alston asks, what reason do we have to think that it is a *conceptual* truism that roses are red if and only if the proposition that roses are red is ideally justifiable? Even if, for the sake of argument only, we grant that "p" and "it is ideally justifiable that p" are extensionally coincident for every proposition, it hardly seems that the concepts involved would be what was responsible for the equivalence.[13]

TS, then, is the conceptual root of the idea that truth is minimally objective. From it we can derive both the correspondence and the "truth isn't justification" truisms. Accordingly, Alston takes TS to represent the core of our concept of truth; everything important about the concept is contained in our grasp of it. More precisely, "if we understand that any T-statement [instance of the T-schema] is conceptually, analytically true, true by virtue of the meanings of the terms involved, in particular the term 'true', then we thereby understand what it is for a proposition to be true."[14] Thus we grasp the concept of truth when we grasp that it is true that grass is green if and only if grass is green, that it is true that roses are red if and only if roses are red, and so on. The T-schema acts, as he says, as a recipe of sorts—a guide for spelling out, for any given statement, the necessary and sufficient conditions under which it is true. If we wish, we can even generalize it, using substitutional quantification:

TG: (p) [p] is true iff p.

And assuming that propositions are what statements state and what believers believe, we can on that basis construct similar schema for beliefs and statements. Of course, none of these schemata act as definitions of truth, even contextual definitions. Nor, Alston cautions, should we read them as claiming that the proposition on the left side of the biconditional is semantically equivalent to that on the right. As he points out, it isn't: "The proposition that roses are red is true" does not mean the same as "Roses are red." The two claims, while conceptually linked by the concept of truth, are not synonymous. Rather, just as "Roses exemplify the property of being red" expresses a concept—exemplification—not expressed by "Roses are red," so "The proposition that roses are red is true" expresses a concept not expressed by "Roses are red."[15] In short, "the minimalist concept is the one that is *displayed* by instances of the Truth Schema."[16] Alston's account of the concept of truth is therefore minimalist: "its minimality consists in its undertaking the fewest commitments compatible with identifying the concept of truth. . . . It is confined to affirming the conceptual truth of all instantiations of the T-schema, and anything equivalent to that."[17]

There are minimalists and there are minimalists. Alston's account is very minimal in the sense that, while it entails that truth is a property, the content of our concept of truth is exhausted by our affirmation of the conceptual truth of the instances of TS. In this respect, as Alston himself points out, his account is in agreement with Paul Horwich's own "minimalist" theory of truth.[18] Like Alston, Horwich thinks that there is nothing more to grasping the concept of truth than our inclination to endorse every instance of TS, and that that "underived endorsement" is "explanatorily fundamental with respect to the overall use of the truth predicate."[19] Horwich also grants that truth is a property. But for Horwich, unlike Alston or Wright, there is nothing else to say about that property. Thus, as Wright notes,

> The real distinction, then, between minimalism and deflationism [i.e. Horwich's view] in respect of the issue whether truth is a property is not that deflationism cannot consistently allow that it is but rather that minimalism allows more: precisely, that the character of the property may not be transparent from the analysis of the concept.[20]

On this score, I side wholeheartedly with Alston and Wright. *Even if* our grasp of the concept of truth is as minimal a matter as Horwich (and Alston) believe, I think there is going to be much more to say about the nature of the property.[21] Indeed, as I will argue shortly, there is another, equally important, truism about truth that makes this highly likely. And this second truism, unlike the truism that truth is objective, can't be easily derived from TS.

III

We can begin to get a grip on this second truism by reflecting on the following question: Why do we have a concept of truth? A popular answer nowadays, especially among deflationary-minded philosophers, is that we need the concept as a device for generalization.[22] Here's the point: Someone—not me!—might like to announce that everything that the President says is true. Imagine trying to say this—or even think it—without the concept of truth. After all, the statement "everything that the President says is true" is not equivalent to the incomplete statement "everything the President says." Your only option is just to repeat everything George Bush says, has said, and will say into perpetuity. But that is impossible. So luckily we have the concept of truth, and rather than repeating everything the President says with an air of approval, someone can just say: everything he says is true.

No doubt, the fact that our concept of truth serves as a handy device for generalization is important. But I confess that—much like the child who is told "their parents" after asking "where do babies come from?"—I find it less than a deep or informative answer to my original question. In fact, I have a hard time understanding why anyone would think that the *only* reason we have a concept like truth is that we need to use it as a logical device. No doubt we do use it in this way. But we have lots of ways of blindly endorsing large strings of statements: We can endorse Bush's (highly alleged) omniscience by saying, for example, everything Bush says is what God believes. The real question is why we need this particular device for generalization rather than some other.

This does not mean that the answer is either difficult or profound. One of the things humans like to do when they are together is disagree with each other: We squabble, spat, form different opinions, and construct different theories. Yet the possibility of disagreement over opinions requires there to be a difference between getting it right and getting it wrong. When I assert an opinion on some question, I assert what I believe is correct. You do the same. And when we disagree, obviously, we disagree about whose opinion is correct. So if there is no such thing as reaching one (or none, or even more than one) correct answer to a given question, then we can't really disagree in opinion. In short, we distinguish truth from falsity because we need a way of separating right answers from wrong ones. In particular, we need a way of distinguishing between beliefs for which we have some evidence, or are accepted by the community, or make us feel good, and those that actually end up being correct. It is not that we can't evaluate beliefs in all those other ways—of course we can. We can criticize a belief for not being based on good evidence, for example. But that sort of evaluation depends for its force on a more basic sort of evaluation. We think it is good to have some evidence for your beliefs *because* we think that beliefs that are based on evidence are more likely to be true. We criticize people who engage in wishful thinking *because* wishful thinking leads to believing falsehoods.

So a primary point of having a concept of truth is that we need a very basic way of appraising and evaluating our beliefs about the world. Indeed, this is built right into our language: The very word "true" has an evaluative dimension. Part of what you are doing when you say something is true is commending it. Just as "right" and "wrong" are the most basic ways to evaluate actions, so "true" and "false" are our most basic ways to evaluate beliefs.

William James said that truth "is the good in the way of belief."[23] Other philosophers sometimes say that truth is the aim of belief. This is not literally true, of course. Beliefs don't literally aim at anything. But both expressions get at the idea that truth is a normative property of belief: It is a property that is good for beliefs to have. Since propositions are the content of beliefs, and it is the content of a belief, not the act of believing, that is true, we can say that truth is the property that makes a proposition good to believe.

A "norm" is a rule. And in believing, I am guided by the norm of truth:

TN: Other things being equal, it is good that I believe a proposition when and only when it is true.

I submit that TN is as much a truism about truth as TS. Just as someone who denies non-paradoxical instances of TS hasn't grasped our ordinary concept of truth, so too for someone who denies that, other things being equal, it is good to believe what is true.

Michael Dummett stressed the importance of this point over forty years ago. Dummett compared the concept of truth with the concept of winning a game. It is part of the concept of winning a game that a player of the game plays to win, "and this part of the concept is not conveyed by a classification of the end positions into winning ones and losing ones."[24] That is, if you simply described all the formal moves of a game that constituted winning, you would have left out one very significant fact about winning: that the point of the game is to win. Similarly, simply describing the conditions under which any given belief is true doesn't tell us everything about our concept of truth. For it is part of the concept of truth that we aim at having beliefs to which that concept applies.

In evaluating my claim that TN is a central truism about truth, it is important to guard against misunderstandings. I know from bitter experience that two in particular are crucial to head off. First, that truth is a goal does not mean that we must pursue this goal directly. The pursuit of truth is in fact always indirect. As Alston himself has emphasized, belief isn't something we have direct control over.[25] We can't believe on demand. Nonetheless, we certainly do have what Alston calls *indirect* control over what we believe, and this is control enough. I can affect what I believe by putting myself in certain situations and avoiding other situations. I can avoid forming certain beliefs about my health by simply not going to the doctor, for instance. That is, I can control how I go about pursuing the truth: for example, by whether I pay careful attention to the evidence, give and ask for reasons, do adequate research, remain open-minded, and so on. So in saying that truth is the proper goal of belief, we imply that you ought (other things being equal) to adopt policies, methods, and habits of inquiry that are reliable, or likely to result in true beliefs. We ordinarily think that it is good to give and ask for reasons, good to be open-minded, good to have empirical evidence for one's scientific conclusions, because these are methods of inquiry that lead us to the truth. If we didn't value true beliefs, we wouldn't value these sorts of activities, and we value these sorts of activities precisely because we think they will, more often than not, lead us to believing truly rather than falsely.

A second common misunderstanding of TN is this. Some philosophers reject the idea that truth is normative of belief because sometimes other values should take precedence over the value of truth.[26] This is so, but it is not a reason to reject TN. A belief's being true is always prima facie good, good considered by itself, or good other things being equal. Believing truly is not always good absolutely, or all things considered. Most everything that is good is prima facie good. Keeping your promises is like this. As everyone knows, keeping your promises is not always good without qualification, in all circumstances whatsoever. If it turns out that you can't keep your promise to meet your friend for dinner if you stop to help the drowning child, you should obviously break the date. Keeping your date with your friend is good because it honors your promise, but it is not good enough to warrant ignoring the child's pleas for help.

Cognitive goods like true belief are no different. Some propositions can be true but not good to believe all things considered. The truth, as we say, can hurt. Human cloning is hotly contested not only on the grounds that it may lead to knowledge that could ultimately be harmful, but that it may lead to knowledge that some believe is intrinsically bad or not fit for humans. Similar questions are raised about research on human embryos, nuclear weaponry, genetically altered foods, and even space exploration. And we don't need to appeal to science to see the point either. Pursuing the truth at all costs can be perilous in everyday life. People often seek the truth about things of which, in some cases at least, they might be better off ignorant: spousal fidelity, the identity of one's biological as opposed to adopting parents, even, in some cases, their health. And some true propositions would not be good to believe for more mundane reasons: Some are too complicated for any human to believe, while others may be too trivial to be worth the effort. Phonebooks and encyclopedias contain lots of information; but all things considered, spending your time memorizing their contents isn't a fruitful way to fill your time. So while being true makes it good to believe something, it may be better, all things considered, not to believe it. Conversely, a false proposition may still be good to believe all things considered. It could be good, all things considered, to believe something overwhelmingly justified by the evidence and therefore thought to be true, even if turns out later to have been false. And self-deception may sometimes be good all things considered even though it means believing something that is false.

All of this just reminds us of the obvious fact that while truth is a value, it is not the only value. And as with other values, we should not expect a formula to tell us when other concerns trump truth and when truth trumps other concerns. Life is not that accommodating.

So far I've said nothing about the *way* in which we believe truth is good. This is a complicated subject, and I will not be able to do much more than scratch the surface here.[27] As I see it, we think truth is good in at least two ways. First, and most obviously, it is good to believe what is true and only what is true because not doing so gets you into big trouble. Fail to form true beliefs when crossing a busy highway, for example, and life really will turn out to be nasty, brutish, and short. We might summarize this by saying that we believe that having true beliefs is instrumentally good—true believing gets us other things we want.[28]

A bit of reflection indicates that we also value truth for more than instrumental reasons. To show this, it will suffice to show the following: Given two beliefs p and ~p with identical instrumental value, we prefer the true belief to the false belief. The best explanation for this preference is that we believe that truth is more than instrumentally good. There are a number of ways to argue for this, but the most direct is through a brief thought experiment.

Consider Russell's scenario: that unbeknownst to us, the world began yesterday (or last month, or two minutes ago). If we really lived in a Russell world, as I'll call it, almost all my beliefs about the past would be false. Yet my beliefs in a Russell world have identical causal consequences as my beliefs in the actual world.[29] This is because the present and future of both worlds unfold in exactly the same way. If I believe truly in the actual world that if I open the refrigerator I'll get a beer, then I'll get a beer if I open the refrigerator. Since events in the Russell world are just the same as in the actual world once it begins ticking along, I will also get that beer in the Russell world if I open the refrigerator, even if (in the Russell world) I believe falsely that I put it there yesterday. In short, whatever desires I satisfy in the actual world based on plans about what happened in the past I will also fulfill in the Russell world, despite those beliefs about the past simply being false. And yet, given the choice between living in the actual world and living in a Russell world, I would strongly prefer the actual world. Of course, once "inside" that world, I wouldn't see any difference between it and the real world; in both worlds, after all, events crank along in the same way. But that is beside the point. For the fact remains that thinking only about the world insofar as it is identical in instrumental value, there continues to be a difference between the two worlds that matters to me. Even when it has no effect on my other preferences, I—and presumably you as well—prefer true beliefs to false ones.[30]

IV

In the last section, I argued that:

1. It is a truism that truth is good; we believe TN.
And
2. TN is partly constitutive of our concept of truth.
To this, I now add that
3. TN can't be derived from the purely non-normative T-schema.

My argument for this claim is simple. TS, generally understood, merely says that the content of a statement or belief specifies the necessary and sufficient conditions for its truth. It says nothing about it being good to believe true propositions. If so, then from these premises, it follows that:

4. TS does not fully capture everything about our concept of truth.

Broadly speaking, one can respond to this argument in one of several ways. First, one might reject the first premise and claim that, appearances to the contrary, we really don't value the truth—we don't think it is good to have true beliefs.[31] The problem with this objection, in my own view, is that there is nothing much to be said for it and everything against. While not everyone pursues the truth as much as they should, and not every true proposition is worth believing all things considered, it seems clear that most people do think that, prima facie at least, it is better to believe the true over the false. Once the misunderstandings above are cleared up, this objection seems like pretty much a non-starter. I'll therefore leave it aside.[32]

More likely, one might try rejecting the second premise, and argue that while we do believe TN, that belief does not constitute our concept of truth. One way (not the only way, see below) of doing so is to grant that TS may not entail TN directly, but argue that it does so given the assumption of certain other obvious facts *not* involving truth. On this basis, one might claim that whatever else TN might be, it is not part of our concept of *truth*. This is the response favored by the arch-minimalist Paul Horwich.[33] It therefore merits a look.

In Horwich's view, the value of truth is simply one more case where we are using the word "true"—via its expression in the T-schema, to generalize a more complicated, open-ended, and possibly infinitely long thought. Recall that the basic value of truth, or the truth norm, can be expressed like this:

TN: Other things being equal, it is good to believe [p] if and only if [p] is true.

According to the minimalist, using the T-schema, we can then show that this is simply shorthand for our disposition to accept every instance of:

(B) Other things being equal, it is good to believe [p] if and only if p

which doesn't mention truth at all. In other words, to say that it is good to believe the truth is simply shorthand for saying we are disposed to accept an open-ended stream of little belief norms, namely:

> It is good to believe that the dog has fleas if and only if the dog has fleas, and it is good to believe that roses are red if and only if roses are red and it is good to believe that . . . and so on.

The result is that we explain the value of truth in terms that don't explicitly mention truth. We are relieved from taking TN, therefore, as constitutive of that concept.

To this point I make the following reply, with which I believe Alston would agree. Even if (and this is a big "if") the Horwichian minimalist is right that the truth norm is *equivalent* to an infinite set of particular norms, this simply doesn't imply that grasping this norm *really consists* in (our disposition to accept) the individual belief norms. After all, the fact that two claims are equivalent entails that any facts about the one hold of the other and vice versa.[34] So the mere fact that TN is equivalent to B (or its instances) hardly "explains away" any commitment we have to holding that one of the key features of truth is that it is good. If they are truly equivalent, we might as well go the other way and say that the fact that we are disposed to accept instances of (B) shows that we are *really* committed to truth being a normative property of belief. The fact that we can do without the *word* "true" is neither here nor there.

But even if we put this aside, I don't see how the argument succeeds. Go back for a moment to the infinite list of particular values that Horwich says explains the value of truth. Granted that we are disposed to endorse these norms, the real question is why. Presumably, we endorse each little norm because we think, for example, that it is good to believe that Socrates was a philosopher if and only if he was a philosopher and so on. But why do we think this? That is, what do we think makes it good to believe that Socrates was a philosopher if and only if Socrates was a philosopher, and makes it good to believe that the beer is cold if and only if the beer is cold and so on? This is not a question easily evaded. Generally speaking, if we are willing, a priori, to endorse an *infinite* list of propositions *all of which fit a particular pattern*, it is highly likely that there is a reason, and a general, principled reason, that we do so. So while it is clear that we would endorse the little belief norms, what we need is an explanation for why we do.

In order to see the force of this demand, notice the difference between this question and the analogous one in the case of the T-schema. Suppose we ask why we are inclined, a priori, to endorse every (non-paradoxical) instance of the T-schema. Here, traditional deflationists, at least, have a stock answer: the claim that it is true that p doesn't say anything significantly more than saying p.[35] This is how the deflationary thought that there isn't anything really in common among the things that are true that makes them true is often thought to get off the ground. At first, it may look as if there must be a general principled explanation, an explanation in terms of some common property shared by all and only true propositions, for why we accept every instance of the T-schema. The traditional deflationist argues, however, that the need for this explanation is illusory, since the claim that snow is white is true, is, in some sense or other, telling us nothing more than that snow is white.

Whatever its merits in the case of the T-schema, that answer seems implausible when we turn to TN.[36] We are not talking about *snow*, elliptically or otherwise, when we say that it is good to believe that snow is white! We are saying that one *ought* to have a certain *belief*. So, unlike the case of the T-schema, there is no reason to think there is a semantic equivalence between the right and left hand sides of (any instance of) TN. As such, we can't appeal to any such equivalence in explaining why we are disposed to accept every instance of that schema.

So we are left with our question: Why do we accept the infinite list of little belief norms? Answering this question is crucial, because the non-minimalist has a ready and obvious answer. The reason it is good to believe that snow is white just when snow is white, and good to believe that Socrates was a philosopher just when he was, is that it is good to have true beliefs. What makes it good to believe a proposition is that proposition's *being true*. But obviously the Horwichian minimalist can't at this point adopt this simple and obvious explanation, because in accepting it, we accept that TN specifies an independent fact about truth.[37] Hence TS does not capture all the relevant facts about truth picked out by our ordinary concept.

The problem is all the more pressing because, as I argued above, we believe that truth is more than just instrumentally good. This means that the most obvious explanation a minimalist might give—namely, that what makes it good to accept every instance of (B) is that it is practically valuable, or at least potentially practically valuable, to do so—is insufficient.[38] We value truth for more than instrumental reasons. In my view, the minimalist must therefore either deny that we are right to do so, which amounts to denying a central truism about truth—or allow that truth is perhaps not as minimal as it first appeared.[39]

There is more to say, of course. But I've been directing my fire at Horwich's account of minimalism, and I now want to turn to Alston's version. Alston, much like Horwich, certainly thinks that truth is good. Indeed, he describes what he calls *Alethic Realism* as the view that (a) the realist conception of truth is the right one and (b) that truth is important.[40] And he defends this second aspect of his view from Stich and others. But as we saw above, Alston, again like Horwich, also believes that our grasp of the concept of truth consists in simply grasping the fact that instances of the T-schema are conceptually, analytically true. If we take this to indicate, as I suggested, that Alston believes that the only important concept-constituting truism about truth is TS (or its in-stances), then whatever value or importance truth may have, that value is not part of the concept of truth.

Thus, insofar as the above argument demonstrates that you can't simply de-duce TN from TS, Alston is in the same hot water as Horwich. Yet matters are a good deal less dire in Alston's case, partly because he has more room to maneu-ver. This is because, unlike Horwich, Alston believes that truth is a substantive property.

In particular, the Alstonian minimalist can adopt a different form of the sec-ond strategy I suggested above. He can argue that it is not obviously incoherent to deny that it is good to believe what is true and only what is true. Therefore TN is not a conceptual truth. Nonetheless, it is necessarily true. It is a substan-tive, necessary fact about the property of truth that it makes propositions good to believe.

While I can't deny that this is an option, I am not convinced by it. For while it is true that it is not directly, obviously incoherent to deny that it is good to believe what is true and only what is true, this only shows that "it is good to believe that p" and "it is true that p" are not synonymous. But as Alston himself points out, two propositions can be conceptually equivalent without being syn-onymous. In any event, I might add, it certainly would be mysterious to deny that, other things being equal, it is good to believe that p iff it is true that p. For in denying it, one seemingly endorses what one believes is true, and to endorse something, presumably, involves thinking of it as good.

To settle this question we would need an account of when a belief is con-cept-constituting (a folk truism) and when it goes beyond the concept. Since I know of no such account, I will leave the matter here, pausing only to underline what I think we do know: that TN is as reasonable a candidate for truism-status as TS.[41]

V

In conclusion, the above reflections illustrate that our concept of truth is consti-tuted by at least the following two truisms, each of which picks out a particular feature of the property. First, truth, as I put it, is a property with a minimally objective character. Second, truth is a property that is good—in particular, it is a property that it is good for beliefs to have.

These two features of the property of truth indicate that our concept of truth has both a descriptive and normative aspect. As Adam Kovach has rightly pointed out, this hardly makes truth unique.[42] Rather, it makes it similar to other mixed or thick value concepts like courage or cruelty. When we say an act is courageous, we are both describing it and evaluating it. We are both commend-ing it as something to be emulated, and describing it as an action that was done despite the danger of doing it. Similarly, when we say that a belief is true, both description and evaluation are part of the package.

According to Alston, it is an entirely reasonable project to ask "how the property that is identified by [the truth] concept can be further characterized."[43] Yet as Alston notes himself, concepts put constraints on how we are to understand the properties they are concepts of.[44] This is because the truisms that constitute our concept of F-ness tell us what it is we are talking about, when talking about F-ness. Consequently, any account of the nature of F-ness must be suitably F-ish. If it isn't, that is, if the account denies that F-ness has those features picked out by the truisms, it is open to a charge of simply changing the subject.[45]

Unsurprisingly then, both the truism that truth is objective and the normative character of the concept of truth places constraints on how we can understand the nature of truth, or the truth property. First, and obviously, any theory must specify the property N that is necessary and sufficient for any belief, proposition, or whatever to be true. Doing so will in particular require showing how the property in question is compatible with the T-schema and related truisms. Second, theories of the property of truth must show how possession of property N could amount to something that deserves to be called the good in the way of belief. That is, they must explain what it is about N that makes it the case that I *ought* to pursue beliefs that have that property.

The existence of this second normative constraint makes the task of identifying the underlying property of truth even more complicated than is usually recognized. As you have no doubt noticed, the problem here is familiar from the realm of ethics. It is difficult to see how a normative property can be defined in terms that are not themselves normative—or by referring only to non-normative descriptive properties. Insofar as we take accounts of the property of truth as reductive in this sense—as trying, in short, to say that truth is nothing over and above some underlying descriptive property—then, I suggest, they are bound to fail. This is perhaps most obvious in the case of naturalist theories of the property—such as theories that maintain that the truth of a statement consists in the causal/referential relations of its parts. But it applies just as well to more traditional correspondence as well. Consider, by way of illustration, an updated version of Russell's early version of the correspondence theory as recently presented by Andrew Newman.[46] According to that view, beliefs are the primary bearers of truth and falsity, and beliefs are true when they correspond to the facts. Metaphysically, what this amounts to is as follows.

A subject's predicative belief [e.g. that A loves B] is true if and only if:
1. The particulars that the subject is thinking about and the relations that subject thinks of them actually form a fact.
2. In the case of an asymmetric relation, the order of the particulars that the subject is thinking about in the belief fact reflects the order of the same particulars in the object fact.

3. A predictive belief is not true (that is, false) by default if either of these conditions does not hold.[47]

The picture, in short, is one where the "complex" made up of the believing that a certain relationship R holds between some particular objects a and b (the "belief fact") shares a common structure or form with the complex made up of aRb (the object fact). This sameness of form or order is what the correspondence between fact and belief, and therefore a belief's being true, consists in.

There are all sorts of things one might say about this theory, but my present interest is whether the above account meets the second, normative, constraint. If we understand it as saying that the property of truth is identical to, or nothing over and above, the property of sharing a form with a fact, it does not. For "sharing a form with a fact" is not an essentially normative matter, and truth is. What is it about the purely descriptive property of sharing a form with a fact that makes a belief good to have? Of course, if one defines "fact" in terms of truth, then one can easily see why it is good to believe what shares a form with a fact—it simply is a consequence of its being good to believe what is true. But that, to refer to another of Russell's notable phrases, has all the virtues of theft over honest toil.

These brief remarks suggest that if we are going to give an account of the property of truth, it is not going to be a *reductive* account. We aren't going to be able to identify truth with some non-normative property. The best we will be able to do is to find that property upon which the truth of a proposition *supervenes*—or, to put it differently, to find that lower-level property of propositions that realizes truth.[48]

This, I submit, is nothing to be depressed about. One option, which I'll only briefly mention here, would be to see truth as Moore saw the property of being good. That is, one could hold that truth is a simple, unanalyzable, normative property that is nonetheless supervenient on some non-normative property. This is how Moore understood goodness, and, for a short time, truth as well.[49] It would amount to a simple property theory of truth itself, or primitivism about truth.[50]

Importantly, however, not all supervenient properties are alike. Some, like pain, are multiply realizable. And as far as I can see, there is nothing to bar us from understanding truth in just this way. If we do so, then truth not being *identical* with correspondence (or coherence, or superassertibility, or what have you) will be no more alarming than the fact that pain isn't identical with one particular type of physical activity in the brain. This doesn't make truth or pain mysterious; it just illustrates that realization isn't identity. And it opens up a new possibility: For if truth's normativity requires that it be understood as an irreducible but supervenient higher-level property, then perhaps, like pain, it supervenes on more than one lower-level property. In other words, truth might be realized by more than one "underlying" property of propositions.[51] In this way, the normativity of truth may open the door to a type of pluralism, an acknowledgment that, like so many other values, truth may manifest itself in more than one form.[52]

The seminal event of my intellectual life was a year-long independent study I took with Bill Alston during 1993-1994. The year before I had taken Bill's seminar on truth and realism. A run-up to what became *The Realist Conception of Truth*, it turned me completely around. Until then, I had thought I was going to write a dissertation on the philosophy of mind; but after only a few weeks of Bill's seminar, I knew I had to work with him on truth instead. Since I hadn't even finished my course work, Bill suggested that we spend the next year marching through the literature on realism and truth together, meeting every week in his office to discuss and argue over the issues. The meetings were intense. My papers were routinely subjected to withering criticism. But since Bill was working on the same topic himself—although at a much higher level of sophistication—there was an exciting shared sense that we were thinking through the issues together. And perhaps most important for me, he always maintained an open mind, and encouraged me to pursue my thoughts even when they drifted toward views that he thought mistaken.

It was during those discussions that I learned how to do philosophy. Over the course of that year, I came to see him not as my mentor, but as the philosopher's philosopher. He is adept at distinctions, but does not make them for their own sake; he writes widely but never shallowly; he waxes bold but leaves his feet on the ground; and as Mark Webb once put it to me, he often appears to "have the entire history of philosophy in his head." Bill is the sort of philosopher that other philosophers admire and wish to emulate, even when, as is the case with many of the contributors to this volume, they disagree with him.

I am honored to have Bill as a teacher, and more than that, as a friend.

Notes

1. Brackets refer to a proposition: Thus "[p]" means "the proposition that p"; I also read "it is true that p" as equivalent to "the proposition that p is true."

2. Recent defenses of minimalism, for example, include Paul Horwich, *Truth*, 2nd ed. (Oxford: Oxford University Press, 1998); "A Defense of Minimalism," in *The Nature of Truth*, ed. Michael P. Lynch (Cambridge, MA: MIT Press, 2001), 559–578; and Michael Williams, "On Some Critics of Deflationism," in *What is Truth?*, ed. Richard Schantz (Berlin: Walter de Gruyter, 2002), 146–160.

3. See William P. Alston, *A Realist Conception of Truth* (RCT) (Ithaca, NY: Cornell University Press, 1996); and "Truth: Concept and Property" (TCP) in *What is Truth?*, ed. Richard Schantz (Berlin: Walter de Gruyter, 2002), 11–26.

4. The popularity of this distinction is largely due to Putnam's and Kripke's seminal work on meaning and reference. See Hilary Putnam, "The Meaning of Meaning," in *Mind, Language and Reality: Philosophical Papers,* vol. 2 (Cambridge: Cambridge University Press, 1975), 215–271; and Saul Kripke, *Naming and Necessity* (Cambridge, MA: Harvard University Press, 1980).

5. See, for example, Michael Devitt, *Realism and Truth,* 2nd ed. (Princeton, NJ: Princeton University Press, 1997).

6. Tarski, for example, seemed to believe that the intuition expressed in formulations like CP can be captured in a more precise way by a similar schema: X is true if and only if p (where "p" is replaced by a declarative sentence, and "X" is replaced by a name of that sentence). See his "The Semantic Conception of Truth and the Foundations of Semantics," in *The Nature of Truth,* ed. Lynch, esp. 333–335. Of course, there is a significant difference between TS and Tarski's schema: TS involves propositions and is best seen therefore as a necessary equivalence; Tarski's concerns sentences and is contingent (since it is contingent whether, e.g., the English sentence "snow is white" means snow is white).

7. RCT, 54.

8. The point is also made by Crispin Wright, *Truth and Objectivity* (Cambridge, MA: Harvard University Press, 1992), 25.

9. Wright, *Truth and Objectivity,* 20–21; and his "Minimalism, Deflationism, Pragmatism and Pluralism," in *The Nature of Truth,* ed. Lynch, 751–788.

10. (NE) is derived from TS as follows: Negate both halves of TS and take "not-p" for "p." Transitivity results in TS. See Wright, "Minimalism," 756.

11. Wright's own presentation of this argument is as one step within a larger argument ("the inflationary argument") against deflationism.

12. RCT, 208–218.

13. Alston, "A Realist Conception of Truth," in *The Nature of Truth,* ed. Lynch, 63. For a detailed discussion of this argument, see my "The Elusive Nature of Truth," *Principia* 4, no. 2 (2000): 229–255. In my view, Alston's intensional argument applies equally well to the correspondence theory of truth.

14. RCT, 27.

15. TCP, 11.

16. TCP, 12. His emphasis.

17. Alston, "A Realist Conception of Truth," 49.

18. See RCT, 36; and TCP, 17.

19. Horwich, "A Defense of Minimalism," 560.

20. Wright, "Minimalism," 753.

21. In "Minimalism," Wright also denies that TS is the only important "platitude" about truth. His own view, which I find appealing, is that the concept is picked out by a cluster of platitudes, including ones having to do with truth and negation, the timelessness of truth, and so on. Interestingly, while Wright is certainly a strong proponent of the idea that truth is a norm, he does not include TN or an equivalent among his platitudes.

22. For example, Horwich, *Truth,* gives this answer. It stems from Quine; see W. V. O. Quine, "Truth," in *The Nature of Truth,* ed. Lynch, 475.

23. William James, *Pragmatism and The Meaning of Truth* (Cambridge, MA: Harvard University Press, 1975), 42.

24. Michael Dummett, "Truth," *Proceedings of the Aristotelian Society* 59 (1959): 141–162; reprinted in *The Nature of Truth*, ed. Lynch, 229–249.

25. William Alston, "Concepts of Epistemic Justification" (CEJ), in his *Epistemic Justification: Essays in the Theory of Knowledge* (Ithaca, NY: Cornell University Press, 1988), 81–114.

26. See for example Pascal Engel, "Is Truth a Norm?" in *Interpreting Davidson*, ed. P. Kotatko, P. Pagin, and G. Segal (Chicago: University of Chicago Press, 2001), 37–50. Richard Kirkham also misses this point; see his discussion of Dummett's analogy with a game in his *Theories of Truth* (Cambridge, MA: MIT Press, 1992), 102. He says, for example, that "[Dummett's analogy] is faulty: winning is not what one aims at when say, one's opponent is a small child suffering from undernourished self-esteem." Presumably, the point is that truth isn't something we always aim at in believing either. No doubt; but this is no more an argument for thinking that truth is not a goal of belief than the fact that sometimes it is best not to keep a promise is an argument against the goodness of keeping promises. For an account similar to the present one, see Adam Kovach's excellent "Truth as a Value Concept," in *Circularity, Definition and Truth*, ed. A. Chapuis and A. Gupta (New Delhi: Indian Council of Philosophical Research, 2000), 199–215. Kovach also recognizes the importance of the "prima facie" clause, but attaches it to our obligations to pursue truth and avoid falsity, not the good of truth itself.

27. For a fuller account, see Lynch, *True to Life* (Cambridge, MA: MIT Press, 2004).

28. Stephen Stich has infamously argued that having true beliefs is not any more instrumentally valuable than having true* or true** beliefs; see his *The Fragmentation of Reason* (Cambridge, MA: MIT Press, 1990). For criticisms of Stich's argument, see RCT and Alvin I. Goldman's *Knowledge in a Social World* (Oxford: Oxford University Press, 1999). Nonetheless, Stich seemingly grants that many of us believe that truth is instrumentally good, even if, according to Stich, we shouldn't.

29. Unlike, for example, my beliefs in Nozick's experience machine, or a world where I am deceived by the Cartesian demon. These situations are experientially identical to the actual situation, but not identical with regard to instrumental value unless we take it that all that I value is having certain experiences. That is, in the demon world, acting on my belief that there is a beer in the refrigerator, only gets me the experience of the beer, not a real beer. Real beer doesn't exist.

30. One might object that in the Russell world I won't be able to satisfy all my desires that are past-directed, like my desire to go to the store we went to last week. To this I reply as follows: It remains the case that most of my desires are identically satisfied in both worlds, despite the fact that my beliefs about the past are all wildly mistaken in the Russell world. It is therefore possible to momentarily bracket or isolate my past-directed desires and simply consider the two scenarios with regard to all my other desires. When I do so, I still clearly choose the actual world over the Russell world. I thank Tim Lewens for bringing this point to my attention. For a fuller discussion of this argument, see my "Minimalism and the Value of Truth," *The Philosophical Quarterly* 217 (2004).

31. This first alternative should be distinguished from an outright rejection of TN itself. One might think that TN is false but maintain that (a) we believe it and (b) it is con-

stitutive of our concept of truth. That would amount to an error theory with regard to the goodness of truth. This seems to be Stich's position in his (1990).

32. Donald Davidson has endorsed the idea that truth is not a norm, which one might take as rejecting TN. See his "Truth Rehabilitated," in *Rorty and His Critics*, ed. Robert Brandom (Oxford: Basil Blackwell, 2000), 65–73. But the matter is perhaps unclear, since Davidson's actual argument is brought to bear against the idea that truth is a goal. One might deny that truth is a goal we can aim at without denying that it is good to believe the truth. I discuss, and reject, Davidson's argument in *True to Life* (MIT, 2004).

33. Bernard Williams endorses this position as well in his *Truth and Truthfulness* (Princeton, NJ: Princeton University Press), 65–66.

34. The underlying point here was originally made in Alston's classic essay "Ontological Commitments," *Philosophical Studies* 9 (1958): 8–17. It bears repeating.

35. Horwich himself denies this claim; see his *Truth*, 2nd ed., 124. But it is unclear, given the minimalist's explanation of how our concept of truth is needed in order to generalize, that Horwich's position on this point is stable. For comments to this effect, see Anil Gupta, "A Critique of Deflationism," in *The Nature of Truth*, ed. Lynch, 527–559. For responses to this sort of objection, see Horwich, *Truth*, 124–125.

36. It is not very promising, of course, in the case of TS either. Certainly the generalization fails: "Newton's' third law is true" is not synonymous with "Newton's third law." And even "the proposition that snow is white is true" plausibly does not mean the same as "snow is white," since the former talks about a proposition and the latter about snow.

37. Furthermore, it demonstrates that there is a property that all and only true propositions have that plays an explanatory role—namely, the property that makes it good to believe such propositions. This is something Horwich must deny.

38. Horwich, *Truth*, 2nd ed.; *Meaning* (Oxford: Oxford University Press, 1998), 190–191; and "Norms of Truth and Meaning," in *What Is Truth?* ed. Richard Schantz, 133–145.

39. Horwich has argued ("Norms of Truth and Meaning," 143) that the reason we value truth more than instrumentally is that it is instrumentally valuable to attach more than instrumental (Horwich calls it "moral") value to true belief. In my view, this is, as ethicists sometimes say, "one thought too many." See my "Minimalism and the Value of Truth."

40. RCT, 1.

41. As I argue in "Minimalism and the Value of Truth" (forthcoming) the argument given above against Horwichian minimalism goes through whether or not one takes TN as a conceptual truth.

42. Kovach, "Truth as a Value Concept," 211–212.

43. TCP, 24.

44. TCP, 15.

45. Of course, with some concepts our truisms may turn out to be false. But it is unclear, at least to this author, how all of the conceptual truisms about a kind of thing or stuff—even about water—could turn out to be false, without our deciding that the kind in question no longer existed or that we had changed the subject.

46. Andrew Newman, *The Correspondence Theory of Truth* (Cambridge: Cambridge University Press, 2002).

47. Newman, *The Correspondence Theory of Truth*, 119.

48. Alston himself briefly alludes to the idea that truth might supervene on correspondence relations, RCT, 33.

49. See G. E. Moore, *Some Main Problems in Philosophy* (London: Allen and Unwin, 1953), 261.

50. For a contemporary defense of this view, see Ernest Sosa, "Epistemology and Primitive Truth," in *The Nature of Truth*, ed. Lynch, 641–662; and Donald Davidson, "The Folly of Trying to Define Truth" in the same volume, 624–640.

51. I explore the idea that truth is a multiply realizable concept in "A Functionalist Theory of Truth," in *The Nature of Truth*, ed. Lynch, 723–750; and in "Truth and Multiple Realizability," *Australasian Journal of Philosophy* 82 (2004): 384–408.

52. I thank the following people for helpful comments and discussion: William Alston, Simon Blackburn, Paul Bloomfield, Patrick Greenough, Paul Horwich, and Crispin Wright.

20

Response to Lynch

William P. Alston

I am greatly in Lynch's debt for the pinpoint accuracy of his understanding of my position on truth, and especially for the careful and imaginative way in which he makes use of that in further extending the position in his second section, an extension that I applaud and am happy to take on board. Indeed, my quarrel with his excellent essay is confined to a single point—the claim that the goodness of true belief is partly constitutive of the concept of truth. Perhaps it sounds inapt for me to speak of this disagreement as only a single point, since it is, after all, his central thesis. But, as I shall be indicating, we are not as far apart on this issue as a simple affirmation-denial contrast would suggest.

Here is a first approximation account of Lynch's claim. He formulates the proposition TN as follows:

> TN: Other things being equal, it is good that I believe a proposition when and only when it is true.

And he maintains that "TN is partly constitutive of our concept of truth."

Before giving my reasons for denying that last claim, let me make explicit where I agree with Lynch about TN. I agree that it is, in some important sense, a truism. It is something that most of us take for granted and take to be so obvious as not to require explicit endorsement. But it shares that truistic status with many obvious truths that are not even partly constitutive of any of their constitutive concepts, like 'Bread is nourishing for humans and grass is not.' If I were to deny that, I might, of course, be confused about the concepts of bread, grass, or nourishment, but it is not necessarily so. I might just be expressing an unusual, indeed bizarre, view about what does and does not nourish us. And so I take it to be the case with TN.

Again, I endorse his well-advised warnings against two misunderstandings of TN, and I even claim to be not guilty of either of them (not that he suggested the contrary). And I also heartily agree that we value truth both instrumentally and for its own sake. Finally, I agree that TN can't be derived from the T-schema (TS) alone.

But despite this veritable torrent of agreement, I still deny that TN is even partly constitutive of the concept of truth. Interestingly enough, Lynch, with his wonted scrupulosity, considers why someone might deny this. That discussion is in the context of an argument for the conclusion that TS does not fully capture our concept of truth, something the contradictory of which I argue for in my book on truth. Here is the argument:

1. It is a truism that truth is good.
2. TN is partly constitutive of our concept of truth.
3. TN can't be derived from the purely non-normative TS.
4. Therefore, TS does not fully capture our concept of truth.

Lynch, rightly enough in my judgment, does not take very seriously the possibility of denying 1 and 3, and he concentrates the discussion on attempts to deny 2. But I'm afraid his discussion doesn't help me in my denial of 2, because, as he himself points out, I can't accept most of the anti-2 moves he considers, and the only one he considers a possibility for me I am not at all inclined to make. That involves holding that TN is necessarily true even though not conceptually true. Available it may be, but I have no tendency to avail myself of the opportunity, as will become clear when I give my argument against 2. Before doing that let me acknowledge that Lynch begs off from going into everything that is needed to establish 2 conclusively, and says that at least what we do know is "that TN is as reasonable a candidate for truism-status as TS." (The context makes it clear that 'truism-status' is meant to be equivalent to, or at least to entail, that TN is partly constitutive of the concept of truth.) My reason for denying 2 will also be a reason for denying this more cautious claim.

Here is my reason. Consider someone who seriously denies TN. We may as well take Stephen Stich in *The Fragmentation of Reason*. There, on the basis of a causal theory of what he calls "reference", he envisages an indefinite plurality of ways of mapping a given expression in a natural language or in the "language of thought" onto a given item or class of items, using different causal relations for the different mappings. He then supposes that each of these mappings would yield a different TS, only one of which conforms to the way we normally understand the TS. These involve a plurality of "truth-like" terms: T*, T**, T***, etc. Finally he maintains that there is no sufficient reason for preferring one of these mappings to the others. And because of this last codicil he is denying TN or at least intends to. (For whether he succeeds in doing so, see the last section of *A Realist Conception of Truth* [RCT].) For if we can do just as well using one of these mappings as any of the others, then there is no T*, T**, etc. that is (specially) good for us to use, much less indispensable for our purposes.

I hope that Steve has since thought better of this position, but I am glad that he held it at one time, since it gives me an argument against 2. It is simply this. Though I believe there are conclusive objections to Stich's position, I cannot see that we would have anything like a conclusive reason for supposing on the basis of his advocacy of the position that he is confused about the ordinary concept of truth. It is certainly nothing like the reason we would have if he said, "I am quite sure that ice is cold, but I am not at all clear that it is true that ice is cold." So long as his everyday use of 'true' conforms to the TS, his ingenious maneuverings with 'T*', 'T**', etc. cast no doubt on his mastery of the ordinary concept of truth. Of course, if he were to hold that, for example, 'true*' is the ordinary concept of truth, even though there is no reason to prefer it to its siblings, that would be a different story; that would show that he was confused about the ordinary concept. But, as we have seen, that is not his position. Stich undoubtedly has a paradoxical and even wild philosophical view about truth, but it doesn't follow that he doesn't understand the concept. If that is the case, then even Lynch's weaker claim that TN is as good a candidate for being a conceptual truth as TS does not hold up.

I went into these Stichian complexities so as to have a real-life exhibit for my argument. But possible cases of someone's denying TN without thereby necessarily being confused about the concept of truth would be sufficient. Consider some nihilist type (may as well make him Russian) named Lobadefsky ("L" for short). L professes himself nauseated by all this idolatry of truth, going on about "The true, the good, and the beautiful," taking truth to be the highest aspiration of human endeavor, and so on. He even goes so far as to say that he doesn't care whether his beliefs are true or not; what matters is that they are interesting. We challenge him by asking him whether it's not important to have true beliefs about matters he has practical dealings with. He replies that he is willing to trust his instincts in those dealings; the truth status of his beliefs makes no difference.

It's clear that L is very confused about something, but like the chap previously mentioned who held that grass nourishes us and bread doesn't, that may or may not be a confusion about the concepts expressed by certain terms. Suppose we put this to the test with L. We subject him to a wide variety of TS-based tests, and he scores 100%. He recognizes that if ice is cold, then it is true that ice is cold, and so on. Surely the best diagnosis would be that he has a firm grip on the concept of truth but is very irrational about the role of true beliefs in human life. So once more TN fails to have as much claim to being a conceptual truth as TS.

It has been suggested to me by Lynch in correspondence that L is at least confused about the concept of belief, since it is constitutive of that concept that to believe that p is to take p to be true (assuming one has the concept of truth). I think that is right. But it still doesn't follow that L is confused about the concept of truth.

I admit that the above argument does not conclusively dispose of the view that there are two concepts of propositional truth, one of which is given just by the TS, the other of which is a "thick" evaluative concept that is given by TS and TN. That position accommodates the points I have been making against the view that the only concept of propositional truth is partly constituted by TN. For the two-concept position can handle my counterexamples to the one-concept position by saying that when a denier of TN is judged to be free of confusion about the concept of truth, it is the thinner concept picked out by TS alone that he is judged to have straight. But he is either not using the thicker concept, or if he is trying to that attempt is self-defeating. My argument leaves that as a possibility. But, I say, only as a possibility. To make good a claim that the possibility is realized, we would have to have sufficient reasons for supposing that people do actually use such a thick evaluative concept of truth, rather than using the thinner TS concept together with a firm belief that TN is true. And, without going further into the matter here, I will just say that I see no such reasons. Contrast this situation with more uncontroversial examples of thick evaluative concepts like 'integrity' and 'conscientiousness.' It seems clear that at least many of the users of such terms would take someone who denied that integrity or conscientiousness are good properties to have (at least prima facie) to have failed to use the term properly. But I see no such unequivocal evidence with respect to the alleged thick evaluative concept of truth.

As Lynch notes, I hold that the property of (propositional) truth might have constitutive features that go beyond the concept. In particular, some form of correspondence of the proposition with the fact that makes it true might be an essential part of the property. And that naturally leads to the suggestion that even if I am right that the goodness of true beliefs is not even partly constitutive of the concept of truth, it might be at least partly constitutive of the property—just as the chemical constitution of water is the property of being water though it is not even part of our ordinary concept of water. But I don't think that this suggestion will stand up under scrutiny. Where we have the kind of concept-property relation we have with water, the features of the property that are not part of the concept have that status because they *explain* the features that make up the concept. Being H_2O constitutes the property of being water just because it provides an explanation for the presence of the surface, perceivable properties that are constitutive of the concept—wetness in a certain temperature range, taste, satisfaction of thirst, and so on. Similarly having a certain genome has a claim to being *what it is* to be a golden retriever because it provides an explanation for features that go into the ordinary concept of a golden retriever—a certain characteristic build, size, facial configuration, temperament, etc.[1] But if the concept of truth is given by the TS, the goodness of true beliefs does *not* provide an explanation of the conformity of true beliefs to the TS. How could it? It is rather an additional feature of true beliefs (with the qualifications built into TN). This point is reinforced by the consideration that even though, as Lynch insists, true beliefs are valuable intrinsically as well as instrumentally, still both sorts of value are dependent on ways in which human beings are constituted. First, these values are values for the human believer; it is good for the human believer to have true beliefs. And if humans were otherwise constituted (if, for example, they had innate instincts that were sufficient to guide their behavior so as to satisfy their needs and desires by and large), then true beliefs wouldn't have the instrumental value they have for humans that they do in fact. And if humans had a radically different motivational structure, they would not find truth an intrinsically valuable feature of belief. These differences would leave the TS constitution of the concept of truth unchanged. Hence the goodness of true beliefs for human beings as they are does not explain the TS.

But even if I am right about all this and the goodness of true beliefs is not so intimately connected with truth as it would be if it were at least partly constitutive of either the concept or the property of truth, still TN can be a very important truth about the roles true beliefs play in human life as it is actually is. It remains to be seen whether some version of the importance Lynch attributes to the evaluative aspect of truth can be developed in this more modest fashion.

Notes

1. Lynch has pointed out to me in correspondence that not all cases of a property going beyond what is in the concept fit this paradigm, for in some cases (he mentions gold) the features involved in the ordinary concept are not universally true of what the concept picks out (yellowness in the gold case). This shows that I need to extend the claim in the text to include an explanation of features of the concept that are either believed to be universally present or that are usually or typically present. For that matter, there are golden retrievers that don't have the typical temperament of that breed.

Publications of William P. Alston

Books

Beyond "Justification": Dimensions of Epistemic Evaluation. Ithaca, NY: Cornell University Press, 2005.

Realism and Antirealism (editor). Ithaca, NY: Cornell University Press, 2003.

A Sensible Metaphysical Realism: The 2001 Aquinas Lecture. Milwaukee, WI: Marquette University Press, 2001.

Illocutionary Acts and Sentence Meaning. Ithaca, NY: Cornell University Press, 2000.

A Realist Conception of Truth. Ithaca, NY: Cornell University Press, 1996.

The Reliability of Sense Perception. Ithaca, NY: Cornell University Press, 1993.

Perceiving God: The Epistemology of Religious Experience. Ithaca, NY: Cornell University Press, 1991.

Divine Nature and Human Language: Essays in Philosophical Theology. Ithaca, NY: Cornell University Press, 1989.

Epistemic Justification: Essays in the Theory of Knowledge. Ithaca, NY: Cornell University Press, 1989.

The Problems of Philosophy: Introductory Readings (coedited with Richard B. Brandt). Boston: Allyn and Bacon, 1967; 2nd edition, 1974; 3rd edition, 1978.

Philosophy of Language. Englewood Cliffs, NJ: Prentice Hall, 1964.

Religious Belief and Philosophical Thought: Readings in the Philosophy of Religion (editor). New York: Harcourt, Brace, and World, 1963.

Readings in Twentieth Century Philosophy (coedited with George Nakhnikian). New York: The Free Press, 1963.

Articles

"Perception and Representation." *Philosophy and Phenomenological Research*, forthcoming, 2005.

"Mysticism and Perceptual Awareness of God." Pp. 198–219 in *The Blackwell Guide to the Philosophy of Religion*, edited by William E. Mann. Oxford: Blackwell, 2005.

"Sosa on Realism." In *Sosa and His Critics*, edited by John Greco. Oxford: Blackwell, 2004.

"Does Religious Experience Justify Religious Belief?" (Debate with Evan Fales.) Pp. 135–145 in *Contemporary Debates in Philosophy of Religion*, edited by Michael Peterson and Raymond VanArragon. Oxford: Blackwell, 2004.

"Religious Language and Verificationism." Pp. 17–34 in *The Rationality of Theism*, edited by Paul Copan and Paul K. Moser. New York: Routledge, 2003.

"Historical Criticism of the Synoptic Gospels." Pp. 151–180 in *"Behind" the Text: History and Biblical Interpretation*, edited by Craig Bartholomew, C. Stephen Evans, Mary Healy, and Murray Rae. Grand Rapids, MI: Zondervan, 2003.

"Truth: Concept and Property." Pp. 11–26 in *What Is Truth?*, edited by Richard Shantz. New York: Walter de Gruyter, 2002.

"What Metaphysical Realism Is Not." Pp. 97–115 in *Realism and Antirealism*, edited by William P. Alston. Ithaca, NY: Cornell University Press, 2002.

"Sellars and the 'Myth of the Given.'" *Philosophy and Phenomenological Research* 65, no. 1 (July 2002): 69–86.

"Plantinga, Naturalism, and Defeat." Pp. 176–203 in *Naturalism Defeated?*, edited by James K. Beilby. Ithaca, NY: Cornell University Press, 2002.

"Doing Epistemology without Justification." *Philosophical Topics* 29 (2001): 1–18.

"Literal Talk of God: Its Possibility and Function." Pp. 136–160 in *This Is My Name Forever*, edited by Alvin F. Kimel Jr. Downer's Grove, IL: InterVarsity Press, 2001.

"A Realist Conception of Truth." Pp. 41–66 in *The Nature of Truth: Classical and Contemporary Perspectives*, edited by Michael P. Lynch. Cambridge, MA: The MIT Press, 2001.

"Religious Beliefs and Values." *Faith and Philosophy* 18, no. 1 (January 2001): 36–49.

"Realism and Antirealism." Pp. 593–596 in *The Oxford Companion to Christian Thought*, edited by Adrian Hastings, Alistair Mason, and Hugh Pyper. Oxford: Oxford University Press, 2000.

"Virtue and Knowledge." *Philosophy and Phenomenological Research* 60, no. 1 (January 2000): 185–189.

"Substance and the Trinity." Pp. 179–202 in *The Trinity*, edited by Stephen T. Davis, Daniel Kendall, SJ, and Gerald O'Collins, SJ. Oxford: Oxford University Press, 1999.

"The Distinctiveness of the Epistemology of Religious Belief." Pp. 237–254 in *The Rationality of Theism*, edited by Godehard Brüntrup and Ronald K. Tacelli. Dordrecht: Kluwer Academic Publishers, 1999.

"What Is Distinctive About the Epistemology of Religious Belief?" Pp. 91–102 in *Proceedings of the Twentieth World Congress of Philosophy, Volume 4: Philosophies of Religion, Art, and Creativity*, edited by Kevin L. Stoehr. Bowling Green, OH: Philosophy Documentation Center, 1999.

"Back to the Theory of Appearing." Pp. 81–103 in *Philosophical Perspectives 13: Epistemology*, edited by James E. Tomberlin. Cambridge, MA: Blackwell Publishers, 1999.

"Perceptual Knowledge." Pp. 223–242 in *The Blackwell Guide to Epistemology*, edited by John Greco and Ernest Sosa. Malden, MA: Blackwell Publishers, 1999.

"Some Reminiscences of the Early Days of the Society of Christian Philosophers." *Faith and Philosophy* 15, no. 2 (April 1998): 141–143.

Articles in the *Routledge Encyclopedia of Philosophy*, edited by Edward Craig. London: Routledge, 1998.
>"Empiricism." 3: 298–303.
>"Internalism and Externalism in Epistemology." 4: 821–826.
>"Philosophy of Religion, History of." 8: 238–248.
>"Religious Language." 8: 255–260.
>"Religious Experience." 8: 250–255.

"God and Religious Experience." Pp. 65–69 in *Philosophy of Religion: A Guide to the Subject*, edited by Brian Davies. London: Cassell, 1998.

"Perception and Conception." Pp. 59–88 in *Pragmatism, Reason, & Norms*, edited by Kenneth R. Westphal. New York: Fordham University Press, 1998.

"Swinburne and Christian Theology." *International Journal for Philosophy of Religion* 41 (February 1997): 35–57.

"Realism and the Tasks of Epistemology." Pp. 53–94 in *Realism/Antirealism and Epistemology*, edited by Christopher B. Kulp. Lanham, MD: Rowman & Littlefield, 1997.

"Chisholm on the Epistemology of Perception." Pp. 107–125 in *The Philosophy of Roderick M. Chisholm*, edited by Lewis Edwin Hahn. Chicago: Open Court, 1997.

"Biblical Criticism and the Resurrection." Pp. 148–183 in *The Resurrection*, edited by Stephen T. Davis, Daniel Kendall, and Gerald O'Collins. Oxford: Oxford University Press, 1997.

"The Holy Spirit and the Trinity." Pp. 102–123 in *Philosophy and Theological Discourse*, edited by Stephen T. Davis. London: Macmillan, 1997.

"Belief, Acceptance, and Religious Faith." Pp. 10–27 in *Faith, Freedom, and Rationality*, edited by Jeff Jordan and Daniel Howard-Snyder. Lanham, MD: Rowman & Littlefield, 1996.

"Some (Temporarily) Final Thoughts on Evidential Arguments from Evil." Pp. 311–332 in *The Evidential Argument from Evil*, edited by Daniel Howard-Snyder. Bloomington, IN: Indiana, 1996.

"How to Think about Reliability." *Philosophical Topics* 23, no. 1 (1995): 10–29.

"Realism and the Christian Faith." *International Journal for Philosophy of Religion* 38 (December 1995): 37–60.

"Theism as Theory and the Problem of Evil." *Topoi* 14, no. 2 (September 1995): 135–148.

"Epistemic Warrant and Proper Function." *Philosophy and Phenomenological Research* 55, no. 2 (June 1995): 397–402.

"Taking the Curse Off Language Games: A Realist Account of Doxastic Practices." Pp. 16–47 in *Philosophy and the Grammar of Religious Belief*, edited by Timothy Tessin and Mario von der Ruhr. New York: St. Martin's Press, 1995.

"Truth and Sentence Meaning." Pp. 91–110 in *Man, Meaning, and Morality*, edited by R. Misra. New Delhi: Indian Council of Philosophical Research, 1995.

"Reply to Critics." (Symposium on *Perceiving God.*) *Journal of Philosophical Research* 20 (1995): 67–81.

"Divine Action: Shadow or Substance." Pp. 41–62 in *The God Who Acts: Philosophical and Theological Explorations*, edited by T. F. Tracy. University Park: Pennsylvania State University Press, 1994.

"Illocutionary Acts and Linguistic Meaning." Pp. 29–49 in *Foundations of Speech Act Theory: Philosophical and Linguistic Perspectives*, edited by Savas L. Tsohatzidis. London: Routledge, 1994.

"Précis of *Perceiving God*." (Symposium on *Perceiving God.*) *Philosophy and Phenomenological Research* 54, no. 4 (December 1994): 863–868.

"Reply to Commentators." (Symposium on *Perceiving God.*) *Philosophy and Phenomenological Research* 54, no. 4 (December 1994): 891–899.

"Swinburne on Faith and Belief." Pp. 21–37 in *Reason and the Christian Religion: Essays in Honor of Richard Swinburne*, edited by Alan G. Padgett. Oxford: Clarendon Press, 1994.

"Response to Critics." (Concerning *Perceiving God.*) *Religious Studies* 30 (1994): 171–180.

"Belief Forming Practices and the Social." Pp. 29–51 in *Socializing Epistemology: The Social Dimensions of Knowledge*, edited by Frederick F. Schmitt. Lanham, MD: Rowman & Littlefield, 1994.

"A Philosopher's Way Back to the Faith." Pp. 19–30 in *God and the Philosophers: The Reconciliation of Faith and Reason*, edited by Thomas V. Morris. New York: Oxford University Press, 1994.

"Swinburne's Argument for Dualism." (With Thomas W. Smythe.) *Faith and Philosophy* 11, no. 1 (January 1994): 127–133.

"On Knowing that We Know: The Application to Religious Knowledge." Pp. 15–39 in *Christian Perspectives on Religious Knowledge*, edited by C. S. Evans and M. Westphal. Grand Rapids, MI: William B. Eerdmans Pub. Co., 1993.

"Aquinas on Theological Predication: A Look Backward and a Look Forward." Pp. 145–178 in *Reasoned Faith: Essays in Philosophical Theology in Honor of Norman Kretzmann*, edited by Eleonore Stump. Ithaca, NY: Cornell University Press, 1993.

"John Hick: Faith and Knowledge." Pp. 24–30 in *God, Truth, and Reality: Essays in Honour of John Hick*, edited by Arvind Sharma. New York: St. Martin's Press, 1993.

"Divine Action, Human Freedom, and the Laws of Nature." Pp. 185–207 in *Quantum Cosmology and the Laws of Nature: Scientific Perspectives on Divine Action*, edited by R. J. Russell, N. Murphy, and C. J. Isham. Vatican City State: Vatican Observatory Publications, 1993.

"Epistemic Desiderata." *Philosophy and Phenomenological Research* 53, no. 3 (September 1993): 527–551.

"Reply to Pasnau." *Philosophical Studies* 72 (1993): 35–43.

"Literal and Non-Literal in Reports of Mystical Experience." Pp. 80–102 in *Mysticism and Language*, edited by Steven T. Katz. New York: Oxford University Press, 1992.

"The Place of Experience in the Grounds of Religious Belief." Pp. 87–112 in *Our Knowledge of God*, edited by Kelly James Clark. Boston: Kluwer Academic Publishers, 1992.

Articles in *A Companion to Epistemology*, edited by Jonathan Dancy and Ernest Sosa. Oxford: Basil Blackwell Ltd., 1992.
    "Foundationalism." 144–147.
    "Incorrigibility." 195.

"Indubitability." 200.
"Infallibility." 206.
"Principle of Credulity." 366–367.

"The Autonomy of Religious Experience." *International Journal for Philosophy of Religion* 31 (1992): 67–87.

"Knowledge of God." Pp. 6–49 in *Faith, Reason, and Skepticism*, edited by M. Hester. Philadelphia: Temple University Press, 1992.

"The Fulfillment of Promises as Evidence for Religious Belief." *Logos* 12 (1991): 1–26.

"The Inductive Argument from Evil and the Human Cognitive Condition." Pp. 29–67 in *Philosophical Perspectives 5: Philosophy of Religion*, edited by James E. Tomberlin. Atascadero, CA: Ridgeview, 1991.

"Higher Level Requirements for Epistemic Justification." Pp. 9–25 in *The Opened Curtain*, edited by Keith Lehrer and Ernest Sosa. Boulder, CO: Westview Press, 1991.

"Reid on Perception and Conception." Pp. 35–47 in *The Philosophy of Thomas Reid*, edited by Melvin Dalgarno and Eric Matthews. Dordrecht: Kluwer Academic Publishers, 1990.

"Some Suggestions for Divine Command Theorists." Pp. 303–326 in *Christian Theism and the Problems of Philosophy*, edited by Michael Beaty. South Bend, IN: University of Notre Dame Press, 1990. Reprinted pp. 253–273 in *Divine Nature and Human Language*. Ithaca, NY: Cornell University Press, 1989.

"How to Think About Divine Action." Pp. 51–70 in *Divine Action*, edited by B. Hebblethwaite and E. Henderson. Edinburgh: T & T Clark, 1990.

"Searle on Illocutionary Acts." Pp. 57–80 in *John Searle and His Critics*, edited by E. Lepore and R. Van Gulick. Oxford: Basil Blackwell, 1990.

"Externalist Theories of Perception." *Philosophy and Phenomenological Research* 50, Supplement (Fall 1990): 73–97.

"Goldman on Epistemic Justification." *Philosophia* 19 (October 1989): 115–131.

"Foley's Theory of Epistemic Rationality." *Philosophy and Phenomenological Research* 50, no. 1 (September 1989): 135–147.

"Reply to Daniels." *Philosophy and Phenomenological Research* 49, no. 3 (March 1989): 501–506.

"A 'Doxastic Practice' Approach to Epistemology." Pp. 1–29 in *Knowledge and Skepticism*, edited by M. Clay and K. Lehrer. Boulder, CO: Westview Press, 1989.

"The Deontological Conception of Epistemic Justification." Pp. 257–299 in *Philosophical Perspectives 2: Epistemology*, edited by James E. Tomberlin. Atascadero, CA: Ridgeview Publishing Co., 1988. Reprinted pp. 115–152 in *Epistemic Justification*. Ithaca, NY: Cornell University Press, 1989.

"Divine and Human Action." Pp. 257–280 in *Divine and Human Action*, edited by T. V. Morris. Ithaca, NY: Cornell University Press, 1988. Reprinted pp. 81–102 in *Divine Nature and Human Language*. Ithaca, NY: Cornell University Press, 1989.

"The Indwelling of the Holy Spirit." Pp. 121–150 in *Philosophy and the Christian Faith*, edited by T. V. Morris. South Bend, IN: University of Notre Dame Press, 1988. Reprinted pp. 223–252 in *Divine Nature and Human Language*. Ithaca, NY: Cornell University Press, 1989.

"The Perception of God." *Philosophical Topics* 16, no. 2 (1988): 23–52.

"Referring to God." *International Journal for Philosophy of Religion* 24 (November 1988): 113–128. Reprinted pp. 103–117 in *Divine Nature and Human Language*. Ithaca, NY: Cornell University Press, 1989.

"Religious Diversity and the Perceptual Knowledge of God." *Faith and Philosophy* 5 (October 1988): 433–448.

"Justification and Knowledge." In *Proceedings of the XVIIth World Congress of Philosophy, Volume 5*. Montreal: Editions Montmorency, 1988. Reprinted pp. 172–182 in *Epistemic Justification*. Ithaca, NY: Cornell University Press, 1989.

"An Internalist Externalism." *Synthese* 74 (March 1988): 265–283. Reprinted pp. 227–245 in *Epistemic Justification*. Ithaca, NY: Cornell University Press, 1989.

"Locke on People and Substances." (With Jonathan Bennett.) *Philosophical Review* 97 (January 1988): 25–46.

"Matching Illocutionary Act Types." Pp. 151–163 in *On Being and Saying*, edited by Judith Jarvis Thomson. Cambridge, MA: The MIT Press, 1987.

"Does God Have Beliefs?" *Religious Studies* 22 (1987): 287–306. Reprinted pp. 178–193 in *Divine Nature and Human Language*. Ithaca, NY: Cornell University Press, 1989.

"Perceiving God." *Journal of Philosophy* 83, no. 11 (November 1986): 655–665.

"Is Religious Belief Rational?" Pp. 1–15 in *The Life of Religion*, edited by S. M. Harrison and R. C. Taylor. Lanham, MD: University Press of America, 1986.

"Epistemic Circularity." *Philosophy and Phenomenological Research* 47, no. 1 (September 1986): 1–30. Reprinted pp. 319–349 in *Epistemic Justification*. Ithaca, NY: Cornell University Press, 1989.

"An Action-Plan Interpretation of Purposive Explanations of Actions." *Theory and Decision* 20 (May 1986): 275–299.

"Internalism and Externalism in Epistemology." *Philosophical Topics* 14, no. 1 (Spring 1986): 179–221. Reprinted pp. 185–226 in *Epistemic Justification*. Ithaca, NY: Cornell University Press, 1989.

"The Hypothetical-Deductive Model in Personality Psychology." *Annals of Theoretical Psychology* 4 (1986): 199–206.

"Religious Experience as a Ground of Religious Belief." Pp. 31–51 in *Religious Experience and Religious Belief*, edited by Joseph Runzo and Craig K. Ihara. Lanham, MD: University Press of America, 1986.

"Quine on Meaning." Pp. 49–72 in *The Philosophy of W. V. O. Quine*, edited by Lewis E. Hahn and Paul A. Schilpp. La Salle, IL: Open Court Pub. Co., 1986.

"God's Action in the World." Pp. 197–220 in *Evolution and Creation*, edited by Ernan McMullin. South Bend, IN: University of Notre Dame Press, 1985. Reprinted pp. 197–222 in *Divine Nature and Human Language*. Ithaca, NY: Cornell University Press, 1989.

"Thomas Reid on Epistemic Principles." *History of Philosophical Quarterly* 2, no. 4 (October 1985): 435–452.

"Functionalism and Theological Language." *American Philosophical Quarterly* 22, no. 3 (July 1985): 221–230. Reprinted pp. 64–80 in *Divine Nature and Human Language.* Ithaca, NY: Cornell University Press, 1989.

"Divine-Human Dialogue and the Nature of God." *Faith and Philosophy* 2, no. 1 (January 1985): 5–20. Reprinted pp. 144–161 in *Divine Nature and Human Language.* Ithaca, NY: Cornell University Press, 1989.

"Concepts of Epistemic Justification." *The Monist* 68, no. 1 (January 1985): 57–89. Reprinted pp. 81–114 in *Epistemic Justification.* Ithaca, NY: Cornell University Press, 1989.

"Divine Foreknowledge and Alternative Conceptions of Human Freedom." *International Journal for Philosophy of Religion* 18, no. 1 (1985): 18–32. Reprinted pp. 162–177 in *Divine Nature and Human Language.* Ithaca, NY: Cornell University Press, 1989.

"Why I Am a Christian." *Truth* 1 (1985): 97–98.

"Plantinga's Religious Epistemology." Pp. 287–309 in *Alvin Plantinga,* edited by James E. Tomberlin and Peter van Inwagen. Dordrecht: D. Reidel Pub. Co., 1985.

"Identity and Cardinality: Geach and Frege." (With Jonathan Bennett.) *Philosophical Review* 93, no. 4 (October 1984): 553–567.

"Hartshorne and Aquinas: A Via Media." Pp. 78–98 in *Existence and Actuality,* edited by J. B. Cobb Jr. and F. I. Gamwell. Chicago: University of Chicago Press, 1984. Reprinted pp. 121–143 in *Divine Nature and Human Language.* Ithaca, NY: Cornell University Press, 1989.

"Being-Itself and Talk About God." *Center Journal* 3, no. 3 (Summer 1984): 9–25.

"Psychology and Philosophy." (With Ned Block.) Pp. 195–239 in *Psychology and Its Allied Disciplines,* edited by Marc H. Bornstein. Hillsdale, NJ: Lawrence Erlbaum Associates, 1984.

"Christian Experience and Christian Belief." Pp.103–134 in *Faith and Rationality,* edited by Alvin Plantinga and Nicholas Wolterstorff. South Bend, IN: University of Notre Dame Press, 1983.

"Conceptual Analysis and Psychological Theory." Pp. 638–652 in *A Century of Psychology as Science*, edited by Sigmund Koch. New York: McGraw Hill, 1983.

"What's Wrong with Immediate Knowledge?" *Synthese* 55 (April 1983): 73–95. Reprinted pp. 57–78 in *Epistemic Justification*. Ithaca, NY: Cornell University Press, 1989.

"Comments on Fred I. Dretske, *Knowledge and the Flow of Information*." *Brain and Behavior Sciences* 6, no. 1 (March 1983): 63–64.

"The Role of Reason in the Regulation of Belief." Pp. 135–170 in *Rationality in the Calvinian Tradition*, edited by H. Hart, J. Van Der Hoeven and N. Wolterstorff. Lanham, MD: University Press of America, 1983.

"Religious Experience and Religious Belief." *Nous* 16 (1982): 3–12.

"Can We Speak Literally of God?" Pp. 146–177 in *Is God GOD*, edited by Axel Steuer and J. McClendon. Nashville, TN: Abingdon Press, 1981. Reprinted pp. 39–63 in *Divine Nature and Human Language*. Ithaca, NY: Cornell University Press, 1989.

"The Christian Language-Game." Pp. 128–162 in *The Autonomy of Religious Belief*, edited by F. J. Crosson. South Bend, IN: University of Notre Dame Press, 1981.

"Some Remarks on Chisholm's Epistemology." *Nous* 14, no. 3 (November 1980): 565–586.

"Level Confusions in Epistemology." *Midwest Studies in Philosophy* 5 (1980): 135–150. Reprinted pp. 153–171 in *Epistemic Justification*. Ithaca, NY: Cornell University Press, 1989.

"Irreducible Metaphors in Theology." Pp. 129–148 in *Experience, Reason, and God*, edited by Eugene T. Long. Washington, DC: Catholic University Press, 1980. Reprinted pp. 17–38 in *Divine Nature and Human Language*. Ithaca, NY: Cornell University Press, 1989.

"The Bridge between Semantics and Pragmatics." Pp. 123–134 in *The Signifying Animal*, edited by Irmengard Rauch and Gerald Carr. Bloomington, IN: Indiana University Press, 1980.

"Yes, Virginia, There is a Real World." *Proceedings and Addresses of the American Philosophical Association* 52, no. 6 (August 1979): 779–808.

"Meta-Ethics and Meta-Epistemology." Pp. 275–297 in *Values and Morals*, edited by Alvin I. Goldman and Jaegwon Kim. Dordrecht: D. Reidel Pub. Co., 1978.

"Self-Intervention and the Structure of Motivation." Pp. 65–102 in *The Self: Psychological and Philosophical Issues*, edited by T. Mischel. Oxford: Basil Blackwell, 1977.

"Sentence Meaning and Illocutionary Act Potential." *Philosophical Exchange* 2, no. 3 (Summer 1977): 17–35.

"Self-Warrant: A Neglected Form of Privileged Access." *American Philosophical Quarterly* 13, no. 4 (October 1976): 257–273. Reprinted pp. 286–315 in *Epistemic Justification*. Ithaca, NY: Cornell University Press, 1989.

"Has Foundationalism Been Refuted?" *Philosophical Studies* 29 (May 1976): 287–305. Reprinted pp. 39–56 in *Epistemic Justification*. Ithaca, NY: Cornell University Press, 1989.

"Two Types of Foundationalism." *Journal of Philosophy* 73, no. 7 (April 1976): 165–185. Reprinted pp. 19–38 in *Epistemic Justification*. Ithaca, NY: Cornell University Press, 1989.

"Traits, Consistency and Conceptual Alternatives for Personality Theory." *Journal for the Theory of Social Behavior* 5 (April 1975): 17–48.

"Conceptual Prolegomena to a Psychological Theory of Intentional Action." Pp. 71–101 in *Philosophy of Psychology*, edited by S. C. Brown. London: The MacMillan Press, 1974.

"Semantic Rules." Pp. 17–48 in *Semantics and Philosophy*, edited by Milton K. Munitz and Peter K. Unger. New York: New York University Press, 1974.

"Can Psychology Do without Private Data?" *Behaviorism* 1, no. 1 (Fall 1972): 71–102.

"Response to Weitz's 'The Concept of Human Action.'" *Philosophical Exchange* 1, no. 3 (Summer 1972): 239–247.

"Dispositions and Occurrences." *Canadian Journal of Philosophy* 1, no. 2 (December 1971): 125–154.

"How Does One Tell Whether a Word Has One, Several, or Many Senses?" Pp. 35–57 in *Semantics: An Interdisciplinary Reader in Philosophy, Linguistics, and Psychology*, edited by Danny D. Steinberg and Leon A. Jakobovits. Cambridge: Cambridge University Press, 1971.

"Comments on Kohlberg's 'From Is to Ought.'" Pp. 269–284 in *Cognitive Development and Epistemology*, edited by Theodore Mischel. New York: Academic Press, 1971.

"The Place of the Explanation of Particular Facts in Science." *Philosophy of Science* 38, no. 1 (1971): 13–34.

"Varieties of Privileged Access." *American Philosophical Quarterly* 8, no. 3 (July 1971): 223–241. Reprinted pp. 249–285 in *Epistemic Justification*. Ithaca, NY: Cornell University Press, 1989.

"Toward a Logical Geography of Personality: Traits and Deeper Lying Personality Characteristics." Pp. 59–92 in *Contemporary Philosophic Thought, Volume 2: Mind, Science, and History*, edited by Howard E. Kiefer and Milton K. Munitz. Albany, NY: State University of New York Press, 1970.

"Aune on Thought and Language." *Nous* 3, no. 2 (May 1969): 169–183.

"Unconscious Intellectual Dishonesty in Religion." Pp. 25–44 in *Intellectual Honesty and the Religious Commitment*, edited by A. J. Bellinzoni Jr. and T. V. Litzenberg Jr. Philadelphia: Fortress Press, 1969.

"Comments on 'Creativity in Hartshorne's World View' by Lewis E. Hahn." Pp. 15–18 in *Philosophy of Creativity I: Charles Hartshorne and Henry Nelson Wieman*, edited by William S. Minor. Carbondale, IL: Foundation for Creative Philosophy, Inc., 1969.

"Feelings." *Philosophical Review* 78, no. 1 (January 1969): 3–34.

"Moral Attitudes and Moral Judgments." *Nous* 2, no. 1 (February 1968): 1–23.

"Wants, Actions, and Causal Explanation." Pp. 301–341 in *Intentionality, Minds, and Perception*, edited by H. N. Castaneda. Detroit: Wayne State University Press, 1967.

Articles in the *Encyclopedia of Philosophy*, edited by Paul Edwards. New York: MacMillan and Free Press, 1967.
   "Emotion and Feeling." 2: 479–486.
   "Emotive Meaning." 2: 486–493.

"Language." 4: 384–386.
"Language, Philosophy of." 4: 386–390.
"Meaning." 5: 233–241.
"Motives and Motivation." 5: 399–409.
"Philosophy of Religion, Problems of." 6: 285–289.
"Pleasure." 6: 341–347.
"Psychoanalytic Theories, Logical Status of." 6: 512–516.
"Religion." 7: 140–145.
"Religion, Naturalistic Reconstructions of." 7: 145–147.
"Religion, Psychological Explanations of." 7: 148–150.
"Religious Language." 7: 168–174.
"Russell, Bertrand: Epistemology and Metaphysics." 7: 239–244.
"Sign and Symbol." 7: 437–441.
"Teleological Argument for the Existence of God." 8: 84–88.
"Tillich, Paul." 8: 124–126.
"Vagueness." 8: 218–221.

"Do Actions Have Causes?" Pp. 256–267 in *Proceedings of the Seventh Inter-American Congress of Philosophy*. Quebec: Laval University Press, 1967.

"Expressing." Pp. 15–34 in *Philosophy in America*, edited by Max Black. Ithaca, NY: Cornell University Press, 1965.

"The Elucidation of Religious Statements." Pp. 429–443 in *Process and Divinity: Philosophical Essays Presented to Charles Hartshorne*, edited by William L. Reese and Eugene Freeman. LaSalle, IL: Open Court Pub. Co., 1964.

"Psychoanalytic Theory and Theistic Belief." Pp. 63–102 in *Faith and the Philosophers*, edited by John Hick. New York: St. Martin's Press, 1964.

"On Sharing Concepts." Pp. 154–55 in *Faith and the Philosophers*, edited by John Hick. New York: St. Martin's Press, 1964.

"Linguistic Acts." *American Philosophical Quarterly* 1, no. 2 (April 1964): 1–9.

"The Quest for Meanings." *Mind* 72 (1963): 79–87.

"Meaning and Use." *Philosophical Quarterly* 13 (1963): 107–24.

"Ziff's Semantic Analysis." *Journal of Philosophy* 59 (1962): 5–20.

"Philosophical Analysis and Structural Linguistics." *Journal of Philosophy* 59 (1962): 709–720.

"Tillich's Concept of a Religious Symbol." Pp. 12–26 in *Religious Experience and Truth*, edited by Sidney Hook. New York: New York University Press, 1961.

"The Ontological Argument Revisited." *Philosophical Review* 69 (1960): 452–474.

"Ontological Commitments." *Philosophical Studies* 9 (1958): 8–17.

"Is a Sense-Datum Language Necessary?" *Philosophy of Science* 24 (1957): 41–45.

"Pragmatism and the Theory of Signs in Peirce." *Philosophy and Phenomenological Research* 17, no. 1 (1956): 79–88.

"Ineffability." *Philosophical Review* 65, no. 4 (1956): 506–522.

"Pragmatism and the Verifiability Theory of Meaning." *Philosophical Studies* 6 (1955): 65–71.

"Particulars—Bare and Qualified." *Philosophy and Phenomenological Research* 15 (1954): 253–258.

"Simple Location." *Review of Metaphysics* 8 (1954): 334–341.

"Are Positivists Metaphysicians?" *Philosophical Review* 63 (1954): 42–57.

"Internal Relatedness and Pluralism in Whitehead." *Review of Metaphysics* 5 (1952): 535–558.

"Whitehead's Denial of Simple Location." *Journal of Philosophy* 48 (1951): 713–721.

Reviews

Religious Experience, Justification, and History, by Matthew C. Bagger. *Mind* 110, no. 437 (January 2001): 153–160.

Atheism and Theism, by J. J. C. Smart and J. J. Haldane. *Philosophical Quarterly* 49 (1999): 128–130.

The Epistemology of Religious Experience, by Keith E. Yandell. *Philosophy and Phenomenological Research* 56, no. 1 (March 1996): 235–238.

Renewing Philosophy, by Hilary Putnam. *Philosophical Review* 103, no. 3 (July 1994): 533–536.

On the Existence and Nature of God, by Richard M. Gale. *Philosophical Review* 102, no. 3 (July 1993): 433–435.

Knowledge in Perspective: Selected Essays in Epistemology, by Ernest Sosa. *Mind* 102 (January 1993): 199–203.

John of the Cross and the Cognitive Value of Mysticism: An Analysis of Sanjuanist Teaching and its Philosophical Implications for Contemporary Discussions of Mystical Experience, by Steven Payne. *Review of Metaphysics* 45 (March 1992): 630–631.

Metaphor and Religious Language, by Janet Martin Soskice. *Philosophical Review* 97, no. 4 (October 1988): 595–597.

Religious Belief and the Will, by Louis Pojman. *Journal of the American Academy of Religion* (Spring 1988): 172–173.

God and Skepticism, by Terence Penelhum. *Philosophical Review* 94, no. 4 (October 1985): 599–602.

Annals of Theoretical Psychology, Volume I, edited by Joseph R. Royce and Leendert P. Mos. *Contemporary Psychology* (September 1985): 708–710.

Knowledge and the Flow of Information, by Fred I. Dretske. *Philosophical Review* 92, no. 3 (July 1983): 452–454.

The Sufficiency of Hope: The Conceptual Foundations of Religion, by J. L. Muyskens. *Review of Metaphysics* 35 (September 1982): 182–184.

Saying and Doing, by David Holdcroft. *Nous* 16, no. 3 (November 1982): 623–626.

Pleasures and Pains, by Rem B. Edwards. *Philosophical Review* 91, no. 1 (January 1982): 143–145.

Saying and Meaning: A Theme in J. L. Austin's Philosophy, by Mats Furberg. *Theoria* 40 (1975): 202–211.

Purposive Explanation in Psychology, by Margaret A. Boden. *Science* 177 (1977): 251–252.

Pleasure and Desire: The Case for Hedonism Reviewed, by J. C. B. Gosling. *Philosophical Quarterly* 22 (1972): 86–89.

Speech Acts, by John R. Searle. *Philosophical Quarterly* 20 (1970): 172–179.

Religion, Politics, and the Higher Learning, by Morton White. *Journal of Philosophy* 57 (1960): 339–340.

Christianity and Paradox, by Ronald W. Hepburn. *Philosophical Review* 69 (1960): 118–121.

Words and Images, by E. L. Mascall. *Philosophical Review* 68 (1959): 409–411.

Man Seeks the Divine, by Edwin A. Burtt. *Philosophical Review* 68 (1959): 124–127.

Religious Symbolism, edited by F. Ernest Johnson. *Journal of Philosophy* 54 (1957): 73–76.

The Burning Fountain: A Study in the Language of Symbolism, by Philip Wheelwright. *Journal of Philosophy* 54 (1956): 584–590.

Christian Faith and the Scientific Attitude, by W. A. Whitehouse. *Philosophical Review* 63 (1954): 451–453.

Introduction to the Philosophy of Religion, by Anthony Bertocci. *Philosophical Review* 62 (1953): 646–650.

Index

a priori insight, 16–18, 65, 68–70, 86, 89, 93n3

Adams, Robert M., 25, 185, 187, 189, 191, 199n2, 199n3, 200n10

alethic realism, 13–14, 266. *See also* realism about truth; truth, theories of, minimalist

Alston's response to problem of religious diversity, 11, 22–23, 146, 150, 162–63, 165

Alston's responses to Euthyphro dilemmas, 10, 24, 186, 190–91, 193–94, 204-205

analogy, 76, 77, 187, 194; and Aquinas, 9, 27, 212, 216–17, 224, 225, 230–32, 234; as located in the copula, 26, 220–22, 236; and response to problem of religious diversity, 11, 150. *See also* mystical perception, doxastic practice of, analogy with sense perception

Antony, Michael V., 129, 130, 133, 135n13

Aquinas, Thomas, viii, xiii, 8, 9, 25–27, 209–226, 227n8, 229–236, 286, 290

"Aquinas on Theological Predication", viii, xiii, 8, 32n25, 211, 213–217, 220, 227n6, 229, 286

arbitrariness objection, 10, 24–25, 186, 190–91, 193, 205. *See also* divine command theory

argument for existence of external world, 18, 74, 76, 91. *See also* best explanation, of character of sense experience

Armstrong, D. M., 129, 133

assertion, 27–28, 239, 244–48; problems for Alston's account of, 27–28, 241; and propositions, 242–44, 251–54. *See also* assertives

assertives, viii, 27–28, 239, 242, 244–45, 252–53; and truth, 12, 240, 247, 254. *See also* assertion

"Back to the Theory of Appearing", xiii, 19, 31n17, 97, 100–101, 109n2, 110n7, 112, 114, 117–18, 283

Basinger, David, 145, 146, 165n1

Battaly, Heather D., iii, vii, 1, 110n17, 182, 308

belief vs. acceptance, 55–56, 59, 284. *See also* voluntary control over belief

belief-forming practices. *See* doxastic practices

Bennett, Jonathan, 83n13, 288, 290

Berkeley, George, 76, 141

best explanation, 263; of character of sense experience, 5, 17, 71, 86, 91; of dispute over justification, 7, 21, 122, 137, 138. *See also* common-sense hypothesis

Beyond *"Justification"*, xiii, 2, 3, 7, 20, 31n22, 32n24, 121–22, 132, 134n1, 137–40, 281, 307

blindsight, 20, 106–107, 110n14, 120

Block, Ned, 129, 133, 134, 290

BonJour, Laurence, vii, 3, 5, 6, 16–18, 20, 31n7, 32n48, 33n49, 61, 82n3, 83n15, 85–92, 93n3, 111, 308

Cajetan, 216

causation, 140–41, 211

About the Contributors

William P. Alston is Professor Emeritus of Philosophy at Syracuse University, where he taught from 1980–2000. He earned his Ph.D. from the University of Chicago in 1951, and taught at the University of Michigan (1949–71), Rutgers University (1971–76), and the University of Illinois (1976–80). He is the author of nine books: *Beyond "Justification": Dimensions of Epistemic Evaluation* (Cornell, 2005); *A Sensible Metaphysical Realism* (Marquette, 2001); *Illocutionary Acts and Sentence Meaning* (Cornell, 2000); *A Realist Conception of Truth* (Cornell, 1996); *The Reliability of Sense Perception* (Cornell, 1993); *Perceiving God: The Epistemology of Religious Experience* (Cornell, 1991); *Divine Nature and Human Language: Essays in Philosophical Theology* (Cornell, 1989); *Epistemic Justification: Essays in the Theory of Knowledge* (Cornell, 1989); and *Philosophy of Language* (Prentice Hall, 1964). Best known for his work in epistemology, the philosophy of religion, the philosophy of language, and realism, he has published more than one hundred and fifty articles on topics as wide-ranging as perception, ontological commitment, linguistic acts, epistemic circularity, and the problem of evil. He is a past President of the Central Division of the American Philosophical Association, of the Society for Philosophy and Psychology, and of the Society of Christian Philosophers. He was a Fellow at the Center for Advanced Study in the Behavioral Sciences at Stanford in 1965–66, and Distinguished Visiting Professor of Philosophy at the Center for Advanced Study in Theoretical Psychology at the University of Alberta in 1975. He is a Fellow of the American Academy of Arts and Sciences, and he received Syracuse University's Chancellor's Citation for Exceptional Academic Achievement. He conducted National Endowment for the Humanities (NEH) Summer Seminars in 1978 and 1979, and directed an NEH Summer Institute on Philosophy of Religion in 1986. He is the founding editor of two journals—the *Journal of Philosophical Research* and *Faith and Philosophy*—and of *Cornell Studies in the Philosophy of Religion*. In 1987, he led a delegation of eight American philosophers in epistemology and philosophy of mind for a week of discussions with Soviet philosophers in Moscow and Leningrad. In 1991, he participated in a conference at Castel Gandolfo, Italy, on theology and physical cosmology sponsored by the Vatican Observatory. And, in 1994, he participated in a Symposium of Chinese-American Philosophy and Religious Studies at Peking University.

Heather D. Battaly is an Assistant Professor of Philosophy at California State University Fullerton, where she was named the 2004 Outstanding Teacher in the College of Humanities and Social Sciences. Her areas of specialty are epistemology, ethics, and virtue theory. Her publications include "Thin Concepts to the Rescue: Thinning the Concepts of Epistemic Justification and Intellectual Virtue" (in Fairweather and Zagzebski, *Virtue Epistemology*, Oxford, 2001.)

Laurence BonJour is a Professor of Philosophy at the University of Washington. His primary interests are epistemology, the history of modern philosophy, and metaphysics. He is the author of four books: *The Structure of Empirical Knowledge* (Harvard, 1985); *In Defense of Pure Reason* (Cambridge, 1998); *Epistemology: Classic Problems and Contemporary Responses* (Rowman & Littlefield, 2002); and *Epistemic Justification* (coauthored with Ernest Sosa, Blackwell, 2003). His most influential articles on foundationalism and coherence theory include "The Coherence Theory of Empirical Knowledge" (*Philosophical Studies*, 1976) and "Toward a Defense of Empirical Foundationalism" (in DePaul, *Resurrecting Old-Fashioned Foundationalism*, Rowman & Littlefield, 2000).

Carl Ginet is Professor Emeritus of Philosophy at Cornell University, where he taught from 1971–99. Besides numerous articles, mostly on topics in action theory and epistemology, his publications include *Knowledge, Perception, and Memory* (Kluwer, 1975) and *On Action* (Cambridge, 1990).

Alvin I. Goldman is Board of Governors Professor of Philosophy and Cognitive Science at Rutgers University. His principal research areas are epistemology, the philosophy of mind, cognitive science, metaphysics, and political and legal theory. He has authored six books, including *Epistemology and Cognition* (Harvard, 1986); *Liaisons* (MIT, 1992); *Knowledge in a Social World* (Oxford, 1999); and *Pathways to Knowledge* (Oxford, 2002). Some of his most influential articles in epistemology include "Discrimination and Perceptual Knowledge" (*Journal of Philosophy*, 1976); "What Is Justified Belief?" (in Pappas, *Justification and Knowledge*, 1979); and "Internalism Exposed" (*Journal of Philosophy*, 1999). He is currently writing a book on the simulation theory of mind-reading.

John Greco is an Associate Professor of Philosophy at Fordham University. He is the author of *Putting Skeptics in Their Place* (Cambridge, 2000), and editor of *Sosa and His Critics* (Blackwell, 2004) and *The Blackwell Guide to Epistemology* (with Ernest Sosa, 1999). His published articles are primarily on epistemology, especially reliabilism, virtue epistemology, Reid, Hume, and skepticism. The Scots Philosophical Club has recognized his work by making him a 2004 Centennial Fellow.

Michael P. Lynch is an Associate Professor of Philosophy at the University of Connecticut. He works primarily in metaphysics and epistemology, and especially on truth, but his interests range widely and include the philosophy of mind and the history of philosophy. He is the author of *Truth in Context* (MIT, 1998) and the editor of *The Nature of Truth* (MIT, 2001). His new book is *True to Life* (MIT, 2004).

George I. Mavrodes is Professor Emeritus of Philosophy at the University of Michigan, where he taught from 1962–95. His publications include *Belief in God* (Rowman & Littlefield, 1981); *Revelation in Religious Belief* (Temple, 1988); and articles on miracles, natural law, modality, religion and morality, and polytheism. His principal areas of interest are the philosophy of religion (and practical applications thereof), and metaphysics.

Philip L. Quinn (1940–2004) was John A. O'Brien Professor of Philosophy at the University of Notre Dame from 1985–2004. He specialized in the philosophy of religion and the philosophy of science. He is the author of *Divine Commands and Moral Requirements* (Oxford, 1978), and coeditor of *A Companion to Philosophy of Religion* (Blackwell, 1997) and of *The Philosophical Challenge of Religious Diversity* (Oxford, 2000).

Alessandra Tanesini is a Senior Lecturer at Cardiff University in the United Kingdom. Her interests include epistemology, the philosophy of language and mind, and feminist philosophy. She is the author of *An Introduction to Feminist Epistemologies* (Blackwell, 1999) and *Wittgenstein: A Feminist Introduction* (Polity Press, 2004).

Nicholas Wolterstorff is Noah Porter Professor Emeritus of Philosophical Theology at Yale University, where he taught from 1989–2001. He was invited to present the Wilde Lectures at Oxford University in 1993–94 and the Gifford Lectures at the University of St. Andrews in 1994–95. His chief areas of research are the philosophy of religion, aesthetics, metaphysics, and epistemology. He has published ten books, including *Works and Worlds of Art* (Oxford, 1980); *Divine Discourse* (Cambridge, 1995); *John Locke and the Ethics of Belief* (Cambridge, 1996); *Religion in the Public Square* (with Audi, Rowman & Littlefield, 1997); and *Thomas Reid and the Story of Epistemology* (Cambridge, 2001).

Linda Zagzebski is the Kingfisher College Chair of the Philosophy of Religion and Ethics and Professor of Philosophy at the University of Oklahoma. Her principal areas of interest are the philosophy of religion, virtue epistemology, and meta-ethics. Her publications include *Virtues of the Mind* (Cambridge, 1996) and *The Dilemma of Freedom and Foreknowledge* (Oxford, 1991). Her new book is *Divine Motivation Theory* (Cambridge, 2004).

Lightning Source UK Ltd.
Milton Keynes UK
UKHW011302280223
417795UK00003B/15